Ultimate Success Library

Compact Classics

ULTIMATE SUCCESS LIBRARY

Compact Classics

BOOKWISE & COMPANY

BOOKWISE™ PUBLISHING LEGACY LIBRARY

Bonded with Genuine Leather • 24 Kt. Gold Embossed

PERSONAL SUCCESS COLLECTION

EDITION I

This book reflects just sections of
"A Touch of Classics, Volume 1"

www.scarabbooks.com

Published by BookWise Publishing
65 E. Wadsworth Park Drive, Suite 110
Draper, UT 84020
www.bookwise.com

ISBN: 978-1-60645-033-8

TABLE OF CONTENTS

THE BEST OF BUSINESS AND LEADERSHIP

A Classic Collection

Classics in Personal Effectiveness

A Classic Collection

Personal Development

Expanded Living

Making It – Upgrading Yourself

Quotes and Anecdotes

Entrepreneurial Megabucks

The 100 Greatest Entrepreneurs of the Last 25 Years

by A. David Silver, John Wiley & Sons, 1985

Defining the entrepreneur as "America's new hero," Silver's book shows, by example, the process of entrepreneurship. As of 1985, the 92 men and 8 women biographically highlighted in *Entrepreneurial Megabucks* had aggregated approximately $100 billion, all on a combined $15 million of initial capital—and created or saved an estimated four million jobs.

Megabucks outlines an entrepreneurial "process" involving the birth, problems, solutions, team chemistry, and extraordinary growth of companies.

Silver selected his prototype entrepreneurs primarily on the basis of financial success. But he also weighed other factors—creativity, sustained entrepreneurship, absence of pride and arrogance, self-reliance, and charitable sensitivities. He feels that, despite the hectic schedules of many entrepreneurs, there is more to life than monetary success.

Only about one fourth of the entrepreneurial enterprises presented are in the "high tech" arena. Equally profitable and fast-growing firms dealing in leasing, manufacturing, transportation, medicine, education, publishing, advertising, real estate, entertainment, nutrition, clothing, safety, communications and information are included. Silver chronicles the rise of well-known corporations such as Atari, Shearson Lehman Brothers, McDonald's, MCI, U-Haul, Federal Express, Tandy, Sony, Wang, Apple, Honda, Intel, People Express, Pizza Hut, Mary Kay Cosmetics, NIKE, Toys 'R' Us, Lucasfilms, Turner Broadcasting, Hewlett-Packard, Charles Schwab & Co, as well as many modest, little-known companies.

Two shoe salesmen...find themselves in a rustic backward part of Africa. The first salesman wires back to his head office: "There is no prospect of sales. Natives do not wear shoes!" The other salesman wires: "No one wears shoes here. We can dominate the market. Send all possible stock."

This story by Akio Morita reveals Sony Corporation's philosophy "to create products for which no apparent demand exists, then create demand." The pocket radio, the tummy TV, the digital camera, the Walkman, and the Betamax all resulted from this philosophy.

The Entrepreneurial Process

The entrepreneur begins with an idea or insight, then becomes "transformed" into a "fanatical dreamchaser." Jack Tramiel, a stout survivor of Auschwitz, pushed Commodore Business Machines to the pinnacle of the home computer market. When he was forced to give up control of Commodore, he left, and, after a one-month vacation, resurfaced—as the owner of Atari...

At one time, Jack R. Simplot survived by buying "bum" lambs from sheep ranchers, raising them, then selling them back to the ranchers for a 1922 profit of 140 dollars. Simplot used this money to patent freeze-dried french-fried potatoes, which became a key to McDonald's success. A $20 million investment soon launched Micron Technology Corp., with $500 million in 1983 sales...

Generally beginning with nothing, entrepreneurs sacrifice their sleep, sweat, credit, time, and sometimes their families, to demonstrate that their dream can become reality. The equation of entrepreneurship is simple. "The goal of venture capital investing is the creation of wealth" or high valuation (V). This is reached by identifying a large problem (P), formulating an elegant solution to the problem (S), and matching these with a potentially successful entrepreneur and his or her team (E). Thus, a company is born. Looking at the formula **V = P x S x E,** the entrepreneur will naturally seek the highest values for P, S, and E, so that when they are multiplied together the result is a large V. Wealth is created!

A Six-Step Process:

1. *Identify the Problem (P):* First, point out the need for a solution; second, *show you have* a bona fide solution; and last, *convince others* that you have the credibility to make the solution work. The "concept of the big P" is crucial....*It is necessary to adopt a problem, index its many features and parts, and begin arranging and rearranging the parts until you identify areas that appear to be receptive to solutions.*

Texas Instruments failed to meet the demand for an inexpensive home computer; Topps' chocolate-flavored bubble gum fell flat; Xerox Corporation's hardware sales plummeted for lack of user-friendly oriented software. In these cases, the solution (or proper identification of the problem) was inadequate.

2. *Create the Solution (S):* Reformulate the problem until the most promising solution emerges. Objectively "see" the problem; try to be original; don't expect to be right the first time; make use of concrete representations (sketches, plans, etc.) to help you visualize and clarify the situation.
3. *Plan the Business:* Prepare a business plan to plot the potential users, how users will be located, and the all-important cash flow.
4. *Select the Entrepreneurial Team (E):* E is made up of the entrepreneur, the manager ("corporate achiever partner") and others, often—and ideally—each with very different backgrounds and aptitudes. The unifying goal of all involved should be to make the company successful.
5. *Test the Prototype:* Producing and test-marketing the product is the most critical stage of development. At this stage, failure, if seen as a chance to alter the plan and emerge more prepared, can be a seasoning experience. By listening to client response, you can work again with pricing, appearance of advertising, the target consumer, etc.
6. *Raise Venture Capital:* Most entrepreneurial companies started from little or no capital. The marketing need (the problem) was so defined that firms were funded by either the stock market, the customer, or by vendor financing. The text offers scores of means by which an entrepreneur can unearth necessary start-up funds.

A Sampling of "The 100 Greatest Entrepreneurs of the Last 25 Years"

Martin Alpert, *Tecmar, Inc.,* 1974

The company designs, develops and manufactures software and peripheral products to expand the capabilities of the IBM and Apple personal computers. Tecmar produces on average one new product per week, from memory synthesizers to boards that permit two operators to share one printer.

Henry Wollman Block and **Richard A. Block,** *H&R Block, Inc.,* 1955

H&R Block excels in preparing individual federal tax returns. Recognizing the growing complexity of tax forms, the Blocks offered a trustworthy and accurate service, and quickly gained a high reputation. Rapid franchising made competition difficult.

Ronald E. Cape, *Cetus Corp.*, 1971

Cetus' "big P" is its convincing contention that company research in genetic engineering is on the way to finding solutions for world hunger and fatal diseases. Investors listened. In 1981 Cetus received America's largest initial public stock offering—some $115 million. By "artfully selling the problem" Cetus has elicited support and contracts from some very large corporations.

Richard Dotts, *Pedus International, Inc.*, 1979

Pedus provides maintenance, janitorial, and security services for office buildings. The company meets the demand for high-quality, reasonably priced work by eliminating bureaucracy, increasing autonomy, providing incentives, and by keeping the already strong management of the businesses it buys into.

William A. Fickling, Jr., *Charter Medical Corp.*, 1969

Fickling began Charter Medical after coming across the statistic that a large proportion of Americans will suffer a substance-abuse or psychiatric problem at some point in their lives. He converted hospitals into treatment facilities with the intent of dealing with these disorders.

Debbi Fields, *Mrs. Fields Cookies, Inc.*, 1977

The chocolate chip cookie is a reminder of home and the simple life. At malls, theaters and restaurants Americans consumed over $200 million worth of Fields' warm, fresh-baked cookies in 1984.

Roger Horchow, *Horchow Collection*, 1973

Demographic changes have led to increased catalog shopping. Horchow's descriptive, colorful catalogs provide a convenient way to shop. Combined with other service features (catering to luxury merchandise, and initialing items to lessen returns), a new segment of consumers was created.

Claude and Donna Jeanloz, *Renovator's Supply, Inc.*, 1978

The Jeanlozes correctly gauged that a lot of people, trying to restore or renovate their older homes, were frustrated by not being able to find vintage-looking hardware. Their hardware catalogs later split into other specialty markets—children's toys, left-hander's products, etc.

Lane Nemeth, *Discovery Toys*, 1978

High-quality educational toys and books are sold directly to the consumer on a home-party basis. Discovery's "educational consultants" build and manage their businesses by sponsoring other consultants, receiving a portion of sales profits.

James W. Rouse, *Rouse Co.*, and *The Enterprise Development Co.*, 1939 and 1984

Enterprise Development is a not-for-profit company that renovates dilapidated buildings to create housing for the very poor. It also helps establish minority-owned-and-operated housing developments and shops to produce profitable and delightful urban centers.

James G. Treybig, *Tandem Computers, Inc.*, 1974

Computer systems break down. Tandem, Inc. makes fault-tolerant products that can help avoid breakdowns, or eliminate downtime by automatically shifting to another part of the system.

Charles Kemmons Wilson, *Holiday Inns of America, Inc.*, 1952

Wilson decided that "the public will like what I like," and came up with the world's largest motor-hotel chain by manipulating a formula of reasonable prices, standardized rooms and family accommodations, conveniently situated near major travel arteries. The Inn's many extras—besides swimming pools, ice machines, etc.—include on-call babysitters, clergymen, and dentists.

Megabucks' many entrepreneurial success stories may help generate interesting, original ideas in the minds of future entrepreneurs.

What They Don't Teach You at Harvard Business School

Notes From a Street-Smart Executive

by Mark H. McCormack, Bantam Books, 1984

McCormack's best-seller has become the prototype manual for teaching executives the fine points of leadership.

I. PEOPLE

Reading People

"Business situations always come down to people situations."

The more you learn about the person you are dealing with, and the sooner you learn it, the more effective you are going to be. "Reading people" comes down to opening your senses to what is going on around you, the "whole level of personal dynamics operating just beneath the surface," and converting this knowledge to your advantage.

"Insight demands...talking less and listening more. I believe you can learn almost everything you need to know—and more than other people would like you to know—simply by watching and listening..."

The seven steps to build your people-reading skills are: *listen aggressively; observe aggressively; talk less; take a second look at first impressions; take time to use what you have learned; be discreet; and be detached* (emotional involvement blurs your vision of reality).

"Aggressive observation means going after the big picture, [weighing] conscious and unconscious signals...and converting them into usable perceptions." Observing aggressively does not mean jumping to conclusions.

Learn to read egos. "If you can read ego, understand its impact on business events, then control it by either stroking it, poking at it, or minimizing its damage, you can be the beneficiary..." But remember, nothing blocks your insight more than your own ego. Observe people wherever you happen to meet them, not just in business situations. You can learn a great deal about a person at a restaurant or on a golf course.

Creating Impressions

The right impression may be created simply by treating someone the way he or she wants to be treated. This applies to your correspondence, phone conversations and face to face meetings. Be your best self.

To impart a positive impression, do exactly what you say you will do exactly when you say you will do it. And don't be a time thief.

Common sense is the most important personal asset in business. Additionally, the ability to laugh at yourself is a plus that will create positive, lasting impressions.

Everyone has, or should have, principles that govern his business conduct. However, claiming too often that "this is a matter of principle" is usually a cover-up for a bruised ego.

Taking the Edge

"Taking the edge is the gamesmanship of business. It is taking everything you know about others and everything you have allowed them to know about yourself and using this information to load the deck—to tilt a business situation slightly to your advantage. It is winning through intuition."

To "take the edge" requires preparation. Know the facts of your deal, and know them well. Be familiar with the other parties; learn as much as you can about them and their company. The next step is backward: take a *step back and size up the situation. See what opportunities exist.*

A situation that might allow either one of the negotiators an edge is considered a "crisis." When a crisis—or what other people may perceive as a crisis—arises, take time to examine what's happening. Don't respond immediately. Look, listen—"observe aggressively"—and decide on a response that will sway things your way. Should you use discreet questions, a humorous rejoinder, or an honest reply? Acting rather than reacting to the situation will pay off.

Getting Ahead

Climbing the corporate ladder is a game. In order to move up you must learn the system and discover how to use it. Your peers are your best allies; "you get along by getting along."

In business there are three hard-to-say but extremely useful phrases: (1) *"I don't know."* If you don't know a thing, say so, then find out; (2) *"I need help."* The other side of this is knowing when and how to give help; (3) *"I was wrong."* "It is not the mistake itself but how a mistake is handled that forms the lasting impression."

Likewise, your "boss" (shareholders, voters or manager) will judge you by three criteria: (1) Your *commitment,* (2) Your *attention to detail,* and (3) Your *ability to follow up* on tasks. To make a positive and lasting impression you need to excel in all three areas.

Prevent boredom and burnout—keep the edge. One way to prevent burnout is to schedule time for exercise and relaxation. Boredom occurs when your learning curve goes flat. Never quit learning about your job and the ways you can do it better.

II. SALES AND NEGOTIATION

The Problems of Selling

Most people are born salesmen; even in early childhood we all learned and used sales tactics. The difficulty comes, however, when we enter the business world. Then we learn that our sales abilities are *judged,* and doubts creep in.

The biggest problem most people have in selling is *fear*—fear of rejection and fear of failure. But you can learn to accept rejection—without having to learn to like it. And you can put fear of failure in its place as a constructive motivator; after all, if you are afraid to fail, then you probably care enough to succeed.

Timing

Too many good ideas fail because the *timing is not right.* "A good general common sense rule of timing is: Don't blurt out anything. Take a moment to consider whether the situation demands a certain strategy or whether you can use timing to your advantage." Take your sales cues from the buyer, letting him dictate some of the timing.

You can also benefit from the bad timing of others. "Just as you should renew a contract when the client is the happiest, sell one when the prospective buyer is unhappiest with your competition."

Some other important "timing" advice: weigh present value against the future; plan years ahead on your calendar; don't give deadlines; use (prudently) phone calls during non-business hours; quickly get to the point of presentations; take less of a person's time than you asked for; and, if you have a good proposal but the customer balks, return to try again later. The toughest part of good timing is patience.

Silence

"Silence is what keeps you from saying more than you need to—and makes the other person want to say more than he means to." In sales, "once you get to the point...where you have asked for a commitment, don't speak again until the other person has replied..."

Marketability

Know your product or service well, including the reasons why someone might not want to buy or use it. *Believe* in what you're selling, and let others know you believe in it. Sell with enthusiasm, but sell smart, putting the bulk of your effort and focus on the "top 20 percent" customers. Figure out ways to keep their interest and business.

Negotiating

First, find out what it is a person or company wants to buy. Second, find out who does the buying. Third, use effective strategies: sell "defensively" (allow the client to say "no" to some proposals); expose rather than sell; present one-on-one, when possible; and use your positive reputation.

III. RUNNING A BUSINESS

Building a Business

"This may be one of the better ways to start a business: What are you really *passionate* about in life, and is there any way to make a living at it?" When you are passionate about what you are doing, going to "work" is like going to play.

Some good rules for building a business are: commit early to *quality; grow slowly; hire people who can teach you what you don't know; charge for your expertise.*

Staying in Business

Don't let structure slow you down; when it comes to your business' structure, think small. Refrain from doing things the same way every time just because they have worked in the past. *Look for ways to be creative* and still maintain consistency. Without creativity and flexibility, it is too easy to get locked into a rut.

"Manage unconventionally. Don't just look for opportunities to do the unexpected.

Create them. Aggressively pursue change..." Spend the five hours now to train subordinates so you don't have to spend hundreds of hours in the future trying to retrain them. Hiring, training, managing and firing people takes consistency, planning, timing and sensitivity.

Getting Things Done

When you plan your time, don't look at a 40- or 50-hour work week. Examine all the available 168 hours. Plan time for sleep, exercise and relaxation, as well as for work.

Concoct some sort of *organizational system* where you can write down projects or ideas and then forget about them. Make them come back when they are needed.

Schedule your time. Decide what must be done for the day, week or month, and then establish a schedule and force yourself to stick to it. Honor appointments with yourself as you would appointments with others.

Rather than holding a formal meeting, meet in the hall for a few minutes, or else simply circulate a memo.

*What They Don't Teach You...*delves into many intricacies of business life. Sections on avoiding "telephone tag," conducting a meeting, making decisions, entrepreneurship, etc. may provide just the needed inside, "street-smart" tips and information that many business schools fail to explore.

MEGATRENDS

by John Naisbitt, Warner Books, 1982

"Megatrends" are world trends with such great impact that they are already transforming our lives. These trends will continue evolving whether we are aware of them or not. Naisbitt's *Megatrends* seeks to "discover the ways in which America is restructuring, to understand how the pieces fit together, and try to see what the new society looks like."

Megatrends examines the "cutting edge" of events developing all around us. It contends that, in our changing world, information is power. And in order to succeed we must be able to use the extensive information at our disposal to take advantage of the prevailing flow. "Trends are like horses: they are easier to ride in the direction they are already going."

The book reads like a road map of where to be and what to do in the 1990s and beyond. Ten themes—ten "megatrends"—are discussed in ten separate chapters. Naisbitt emphasizes that each trend is important and closely related to the other nine; that each can be examined singly, but can only be totally appreciated in association with the others.

MEGATRENDS—Ten New Directions

(1) From an Industrial Society to an Information Society

"The most reliable way to anticipate the future is to understand the present." The birth of an information society, and the death of the old industrial society, is the most important "megatrend"—one that is still not universally recognized as a reality.

In the past, those who controlled capital controlled the world, but in an information society the "world-controllers" will be those who control information. An example of this is the case of the founders of *Intel, Inc.* Starting with 2.5 million dollars in venture capital, they increased their sales to $900 million a year as of 1982. Having access to the facts is not the key; everyone receives more or less the same information. In fact, *we are drowning in information, but often starved for knowledge.* The trick is to filter out correct knowledge; to pull *useful* information from the endless sea of computerized data.

(2) From Forced Technology to High Tech/High Touch

In the past, technology has been forced upon us with little regard as to how we would interact with it. For this reason, some forms of technology have been sent back to the shop. Now, computers have become more "user friendly," and the ways in which we use any number of high-tech articles are increasingly being refined and simplified.

Whenever new technology is introduced, it must be coupled with human response. "*The more high technology around us, the more the need for human touch,*" though technology will never take the place of nor liberate us from personal discipline and responsibility.

(3) From a National Economy to a World Economy

Americans have for decades been the dominant industrial power in the world. But now, as the United States' share of goods on the world market has diminished, Asian nations and others have emerged as industrial powers. *Americans must play a new role if they are to continue to be a global economic power—a role of leadership, innovation and know-how.* We have already lost our industrial edge (it takes Japan eleven hours to build a car; American workers do it in thirty-one). Americans must lead out in exploring electronics, biotechnology, alternative energy sources, new mining techniques, robotics, etc.

As the world economy becomes more and more diverse, production sharing among nations will become the rule rather than the exception. And as countries become more dependent on each other for trade, the possibility of war over ideological differences will become more remote.

(4) From Short Term to Long Term

Rethinking our view of business success is essential to capitalize on this megatrend. We need to think more in terms of profits and planning over the long term. Management contracts have encouraged shortsightedness by rewarding short-term, quarterly profits rather than long-term, steady growth. Long-term planning requires insightful, futuristic vision without which strategic planning is worthless.

"*Change,*" becoming "*alert*" to change, "*rethinking*" and "*reconcept-ualizing*" our roles, are the watchwords for the coming decade.

(5) From Centralization to Decentralization

With the failure of large centralized structures, Americans are beginning to look elsewhere for leadership. We are rebuilding from the bottom up. The idea of decentralization is not a new one, but is an idea whose time has come.

We are becoming ever more involved only with events that directly affect us. Local elections, for example, are drawing more voters, while national elections draw fewer than they have in the past. Regionalism, states' rights and special-interest lobbies continue to grow. Ethnic pride, separatism, and neighborhood-watch programs are on the upswing, while centralized labor unions struggle to stay alive.

(6) From Institutional Help to Self-Help

Recently we have become inundated with a barrage of self-help books and groups of all sorts. Where we formerly relied on government, the medical establishment and corporations, we now rely more on ourselves.

People are adopting new and better personal habits (exercise, proper diet, reduced smoking and alcohol consumption). "Self-care" is now considered smart, not selfish. Alternatives in life-styles and education have replaced the stodgy customs of the past. If you don't like the boss, start your own company; if your child's institution is failing her, start your own school. The self-help approach is exploding. Our society is shifting from one of managers to one of entrepreneurs.

(7) From Representative Democracy to Participatory Democracy

Representative democracy calls for strong unified leadership, while participatory democracy relies less on central leadership and more upon individuals or special-interest groups. "*The new leader is a facilitator not an order giver.*"

Participatory democracy includes such notions as shareholders' rights, consumerism, and workers' rights. These groups don't control decisions, but their views are part of the process. With the increase in shared, instantaneous information, more people know what's going on and are more confident in their ability to make decisions. More and more, governments and corporations will operate with this in mind.

(8) From Hierarchies to Networking

Business hierarchies for years followed the old pyramidal top-to-bottom structure, where management's main purpose was to "keep track" of the workers. With the advent of the computer, however, "tracking" employees became much easier, leaving management free for more productive work.

"Networks" employ the horizontal system of management, where people interact and share ideas, information and resources. Hence, networks offer what bureaucracies never can deliver—precisely this direct, horizontal link with people. *In the network environment, "rewards come by empowering others, not climbing over them."*

(9) From North to South

The shift of American population—and job markets—from North to South has been well documented, but the reasons behind it have not. *The North represents the lagging industrial economy, while the Southwest and West represent the booming information economy.* The emerging "megastates" are California, Florida, and Texas. With industrial (northern) states losing thousands of workers each year during the '70s, the western states (plus Florida in the south) boomed: Nevada gained by 64% in population, Arizona, 53%; Florida, 43%; Wyoming, 42%; Utah, 38%; Idaho, 34%; Alaska, 32%; Colorado, 31%; New Mexico, 28%; and Texas 27%.

(10) From Either/Or to Multiple Option

We are becoming a multifaceted "Baskin Robbins Society," with thirty-one decisions at every turn. This is true even in television; where there were formerly three stations, there are now hundreds— "Something for everyone!"

A societal shift from the family towards the individual is taking place. Family life and decisions are increasingly complex. Single-parent households and homes with two working parents are now the rule, and it is projected that in the 1990s, only 14% of all two-parent households will be supported by one income. In an increasingly complicated world, understanding what options are available and acting on them is paramount.

To be financially successful in the decade of the '90s, most new companies must specialize in a product for a particular segment of people. Diversity—cultural, ethnic, religious—once decried as enemy to the "melting pot," is now celebrated.

Naisbitt alleges that we live in a "time of parenthesis, the time between eras." The information era is on the horizon, while the industrial age is ending. We will continue to use and value brainpower over physical power. These facts open up a wide range of realistic opportunities for those who are willing to take risks.

"But do we have the courage to abandon our traditional industries, industries that other countries can now do better?" Naisbitt asks. "Do we have the innovative ability to venture forward into the future?" The changing times ahead will be good to entrepreneurs. The timeless *Megatrends* urges you to take the initiative, accentuate the positive, and let the future trends work for you, not against you.

MEGATRENDS 2000

Ten New Directions For the 1990s

John Naisbitt and Patricia Aburdene, William Morrow and Co., 1990

John Naisbitt and Patricia Aburdene, the authors of *Megatrends 2000*, have been busy "uncovering the megatrends for a new millenium," trends that continue to apply today. They define "megatrends" as those large-scale social, economic, political, and technological influences that change the directions of our lives. The authors paint a fairly rosy picture for the people of the 90s, and predict ten new directions for the decade. These "millennial" trends are:

1. A Booming Global Economy
2. A Renaissance in the Arts
3. The Emergence of Free-Market Socialism
4. Global Lifestyles and Cultural Nationalism
5. The Privatization of the Welfare State
6. The Rise of the Pacific Rim
7. The Decade of Women in Leadership
8. The Age of Biology
9. The Religious Revival of the New Millennium
10. The Triumph of the Individual

Evidence for these ten trends was compiled by clipping newspaper articles, then analyzing their contents with a computer. Here are some predictions from Naisbitt and Aburdene based on the results:

The Global Economic Boom of the 1990s

Because of the increasing popularity of "doomsayers," *positive* economic indicators receive very little press right now, while any little in the economy receives blown-up coverage. But regardless of what gets covered, there is good economic news out there.

It is hard to talk about the U.S. economy today without considering the influence of Japan and the European countries. In fact, the economies of different countries are becoming more and more enmeshed all the time. For a multitude of reasons, a world economy will continue to emerge, as the European Common Market dissolves and the fall of the Iron Curtain opens the way for trade policies between more nations.

Free trade is mandatory for an effective global economy. Just as no one knows the trade imbalance between Denver and Dallas, in time the trade imbalance between the United States and Japan will be a non-issue. *As we turn to the next century, we will witness the linkup of North America, Europe, and Japan to form a golden triangle of free trade.*

Other factors that will influence the economic boom include:

- Advanced uses of telecommunications.
- No energy crisis to slow down or limit growth.
- Increased competition, which tends to lower taxes.
- A downsizing of economic output.
- Low inflation and interest rates.
- The emergence of an Asian consumer boom.
- The advancement of democracy and free enterprise.

Current media figures for trade and budget deficits are deceptive. The budget deficit, while large, represents a smaller percentage of income than in the past, and because no services are calculated into this deficit, its estimate is very inaccurate.

The fear of a Japanese takeover is media hype. Japan owns less than 5% of U.S. property, and U.S. investments in other countries far exceed foreign investments in the U.S.

Current global financial trends are swelling the ranks of the middle class and expanding the economic clout of minorities and women.

Renaissance in the Arts

In the final years before the millennium there will be a fundamental and revolutionary shift in leisure time and spending priorities. During the 1990s the arts will gradually replace sports as society's primary leisure activity.

This trend is already visible, as more and more people seek out the arts for a spiritual boost; and the future implications, both societal and economic, are staggering.

New and diversified art forms will emerge, and increased attendance at museums, symphonies, dance performances, etc. will open up many new jobs.

The Emergence of Free-Market Socialism

"Socialism, which at one time looked as if it might take over the world, is now faced with a challenge: Change or perish." There are several reasons for this:

- *The global economy.* Global economic interdependence will not allow a country with a closed, self-sufficient economy to survive. This has been the one driving force behind Mikhail Gorbachev's anti-socialist movement.

- *Technology.* Improved telecommunications have made a global economy possible in the first place, and further advances will only speed up the process.
- *The failure of centralization.* It is becoming clear that a command economy leads not to more efficient organization but to chaos.
- *The high cost of welfare-state socialist schemes.* "The cost of central-government supplied human services has caught up with almost all countries and overwhelmed many...." *The ratio of working people to pensioners has declined dramatically since the end of World War II—in the United States, for example, from 32 to 1 to 3 to 1. People everywhere are blowing the whistle on growing public spending. Many of us will spend the last decade of this century asking the questions, What should government do for those who cannot help themselves and how can government meet such obligations without bankrupting the treasury?*

In addition to these factors, there is a marked decline in the number of blue-collar workers and in socialist union solidarity. These are the anchors of socialist economies. At the same time, the power of the individual is increasing.

In the post-industrial global economy, "small enterprise, not central planning, is the road to real prosperity."

Global Lifestyles and Cultural Nationalism

As technological and transportation advances make it easier to get products and services from anywhere, "the world is becoming more and more cosmopolitan, and we are all influencing each other." The Moscow McDonalds is a highly visible example of this global lifestyle.

But even as our lifestyles grow more similar, there are unmistakable signs of a powerful countertrend: a backlash against uniformity, a desire to assert the uniqueness of one's culture and language, a repudiation of foreign influence.

The Privatization of the Welfare State

Between 1980 and 1988, over 40 percent of the British government sector was transformed to private enterprise, resulting in the shift of more than 600,000 former government employees into the private sector. During the same 8-year period, over 1 million former tenants of public housing became homeowners.

In the United States, governmental controls are relaxing as private enterprise expands. The U.S. Postal Service is a prime example of privatization that will become more prevalent worldwide.

The Rise of the Pacific Rim

"The cities of the Pacific Rim—Los Angeles, Sydney, and Tokyo—are taking over from the old, established cities of the Atlantic—New York, Paris, and London. The population of Asia's Pacific Rim region is twice as large as that of Europe and the United States put together. "Any way you measure it, geographically, demographically, or economically, the Pacific Rim is a powerful global presence."

The Decade of Women in Leadership

For the last two decades U.S. women have taken two thirds of the millions of new jobs created in the information era and will continue to do so well into the millennium.

Women now hold a large percentage of white-collar jobs (especially in business), and are starting up their own businesses at twice the rate of men. Realizing that they missed out on the past industrial era that began decades ago, women are positioning themselves in jobs that will blossom in the information era.

The Age of Biology

With the industrial age in the outmoded past, "we are shifting from the models and metaphors of physics to the models and metaphors of biology to help us understand today's dilemmas and opportunities."

Physics...suggests: energy-intensive, linear, macro, mechanistic, deterministic, outer directed.... Today, however, we are in the process of creating a society that is an elaborate array of information feedback systems, the very structure of the biological organism. Furthermore, we are poised on the threshold of a great era of biotechnology.

Biology as metaphor suggests: information-intensive, micro, inner-directed, adaptive, holistic.

Biology is the trend for the 1990s.

Religious Revival of the Third Millennium

The baby boomers, who rejected religion in the 1970s, are returning to church or joining churches at incredible rates, and taking their children with them. Mainline churches, however, which do well during stable times, will likely decline in popularity during this period of rapid change. Americans will increasingly value spirituality over organized religion.

Triumph of the Individual

"The great unifying theme at the conclusion of the 20th century is the triumph of the individual." It is individuals who seek religion, enjoy the arts, support political philosophies, become better educated, start new businesses, and do everything else that empowers the other nine "megatrends."

It remains to be seen whether these predictions will prove accurate. True, there will be many obstacles to overcome as we near the year 2000—defeating AIDs and the various forms of cancer, Third World development, ending poverty and hunger, environmental "healing"...But today's megatrends, according to Naisbitt and Aburdene, will serve to strengthen our world society. Global collaboration and cooperation are on the rise; together we will confront and find answers to these social ills. "Get ready," *Megatrends 2000* heartily advocates. "You possess a front-row seat to the most challenging yet most exciting decade in the history of civilization."

A Passion for Excellence

by Tom Peters and Nancy Austin, Random House, 1985

A Passion for Excellence offers stories, quotes, insights, questions and advice in an attempt to cultivate superb, personalized, "back-to-basics" leadership. Its authors recommend that you look for some "first steps" that fit in with your particular needs and style, and start with those. Here are some highlights:

PART I: COMMON SENSE

"The greatest problem American business faces is getting the boss back to work watching his customer and his product....[Bosses] are too busy...to the point that they no longer know what the customer is saying, how he is being treated..."

—*Stanley Marcus*

Baltimore Mayor William Donald Schaefer regularly wanders his neighborhoods to get a feel for his city. Wandering is priority. He sees potholes, broken streetlights, dirty parks, abandoned cars, dead trees...and also manages to have his crews do something about them.

The Big Idea: MBWA (Management By Wandering Around) is a "leadership technology" that promises happy customers and co-workers. Its principles are obvious but usually ignored. MBWA is the crucial element of leadership, and the one element emphasized throughout the book.

Key MBWA Recommendations

- Recognize where the real-life action is. In any industry, corporation, sports team, club or educational facility the real action is not behind a desk.
- Give MBWA quality, calendar time (25 – 50% of an average day).
- Establish an open-door policy all through the organization.
- Randomly hold meetings in other people's offices or out in the field. Evaluate employees, in part, by how directly and frequently they are "in touch" with others.

PART II: CUSTOMERS

"Serve the customer....The customer is the middle of the thrust of what we are trying to do...."

—*Edson P. Williams, VP Ford Motor Co.*

To eliminate the majority of hairs that stick to the average chicken wing, Frank Perdue, chairman of Perdue Farms, purchased a quarter-of-a-million dollar jet engine to blow them off—"the world's biggest blow dryer."

The Big Idea: Successful businesses put the customer first by providing slavish service, exceptional courtesy and responsive listening.

Key Recommendations for Satisfying Customers

- Offer superior service and quality.
- *Train* associates in "customer courtesy"—to apologize for delays or problems, to show an interest in people, to be friendly but businesslike, to answer the phone on the first ring, to do a little extra. Courtesy "buys" a lifetime of customer loyalty.
- Look out for *T.D.C.* (Thinly Disguised Contempt) that may be demonstrated in your people's language (sarcasm, blame...) or service ("sour" demeanor, tardiness...). Both complaints and compliments travel far. Your company's reputation is tested daily.
- *Trust* the customer. Questioning a product return or the validity of a complaint may appear as a lack of trust.
- Measure customer satisfaction by inviting frequent and honest *feedback* (phone calls, informal face-to-face polls, questionnaires). Ask simply, "How are we doing for you?" Then step back and "naively listen" to their response.
- Invite customers to visit your facilities.
- Use customer feedback as an opportunity to train, solve problems and adapt to the market. Share both good and bad news with employees.

• Emphasize *common sense,* rather than rules, when dealing with the public.
• Don't try to compete with the "30% OFF!" store down the street. In the long run, quality easily wins over low price.
• *Specialize* in a unique product or service. Be distinctive.
• Create a professional, modern, "clean" look. Fresh paint, flowers, shiny floors, comfortable, lighting and other details matter.
• If possible, provide an (800) call-in line, with a real live person answering the phone.

PART III: INNOVATION

Almost a dozen years elapsed between the "invention" of 3M's Post-It Note Pads and their commercial debut. The developer, Art Fry, saw the need when the little bits of paper he used to mark hymns in a church choir kept falling out of the books. Despite the fact office supply distributors thought it was a silly idea and market surveys were negative, once 3M secretaries started using the pads and were hooked, marketing went smoothly toward a $200 million success.

"A good plan violently executed right now is far better than a perfect plan executed next week."

—General George Patton

The Big Idea: Fostering innovative "champions" and workteams, who push their projects through to completion in a minimal amount of time, is better than setting up long-winded committees.

Key Recommendations for Fostering Innovation

• *Nurture experimentation* by celebrating "good failures," supporting persistence, eliminating "Mickey Mouse" rules, red tape, and procedures that stifle initiative, and passing on stories (corporate myths) that suggest—for the project's good, of course—occasional "rule-breaking."
• Allow people to freely "own" ideas and to develop them in small unified teams. *Loosen control* so that success or failure devolves directly upon the teams.
• Encourage teams to put together prototypes of ideas, and to place them on the market within 60 to 120 days. This is usually possible when management is supportive.
• Urge your people to *make at least ten mistakes a day.* In skiing, for example, if you don't fall down, you're not learning.
• *Be tough on inaction.* Demand concrete action, without excuses.
• Ask: "Are we having fun?..." "Now, tell me something interesting that's going on..." By encouraging free thought and risk-taking, you openly declare your trust in your employees.
• Keep funding low, deadline pressure high.
• Focus on actual progress, not on paperwork.

PART IV: PEOPLE, PEOPLE, PEOPLE

A first-line supervisor—responsible for 25 to 30 people and up to $4 million worth of capital—doesn't have the authority to buy a nine-dollar can of paint to clean up her people's workspace. Do you think she feels in charge or trusted with making decisions?

The Big Idea: Employees need to be given solid responsibility, and to know that as an interested, wandering leader, you respect and support them. People produce; techniques don't.

Key Recommendations For Working With People

• Make people feel they're part of the company. Trust them to do their jobs. Recognize your employees' "bill of rights"—the rights to be needed, involved, responsible and accountable.

• Call your people "associates" or "colleagues" rather than "workers"; make each a "director" or a "manager," with control.

• Decentralize. Place dedicated leaders at all levels.

• Eliminate managerial "perks"—private parking spaces, executive dining areas or washrooms, and special privileges.

• Find fifty little marks that demonstrate respect (cleanliness, name plates, proper facilities . . .) and fifty that show disrespect (inappropriate language; discriminatory labels, facilities or rules).

• Lavishly reward good and exceptional performance. Make meetings and celebrations fun, imaginative, and memorable.

• Develop a five-minute informal questioning routine to get to know people and their jobs. What's working; what's not? The best source of ideas is the front-line, vendor-to-customer person. Spend one Saturday a month, or a week each quarter, on the sales floor, in the factory, or on the street crew. This front-line, hands-on, in the trenches experience is invaluable.

• *Rub shoulders,* fiddle with equipment, ask questions. Practice MBWA. Make PEOPLE your insistent theme and focus.

PART V: LEADERSHIP

"Make it fun to work in your agency. When people aren't having any fun, they don't produce good advertising....Get rid of sad dogs who spread doom. What kind of paragons are the men and women who run successful advertising agencies? My observation has been that they are enthusiasts."

—David Ogilvy

A Domino's Pizza Store once faced the disaster of running out of pizza dough. What was President Don Vleek's immediate response? "Charter a plane. Get it there!"

"Love is loyalty. Love is teamwork. Love respects the dignity of the individual. Heartpower is the strength of your corporation."

—Coach Vince Lombardi, speaking to corporate executives

During his 57 years as Marriott Corporation's CEO, founder J. Willard Marriott, Sr. read every customer complaint card.

The Big Idea: Leadership is "show business"; it is symbolic and often dramatic. The new leader is no longer a cop, referee, sole decision-maker or dispassionate analyst. The new leader is more of a cheerleader, coach, nurturer of heroes, builder, facilitator and historian.

Key Leadership Recommendations

• When touring your plant, school or corporation, visit the doing, first-line people first; then your visit with the upper manager will take on more meaning.

• Create a unique corporate culture for your business.

• Love your associates and what you do.

• Listen deeply.

• Visit your competition to find out what they're doing.

• Routinely gather together to train, gripe, change policies, nudge programs along, demand suggestions, celebrate...

• Cut your meetings from 24 to 17 per week to give time for real MBWA.

A Passion for Excellence carries two primary messages:
1. *Choose a priority*—and clearly, repeatedly, religiously, urgently, attentively, passionately focus all your discussion and energy on that priority. Do something—right now.
2. *Practice MBWA.* Whether your priority is product quality, customer service, innovation, courtesy, autonomy, customer input, or safety, it must revolve around committed people; and the art of MBWA is working with people. It is not socializing, it's finding out. It's talking last, not first. MBWA takes patient effort.

Leadership Secrets of Attila the Hun

by Wess Roberts, Warner Books, 1987

Attila, King of the Huns, united Mongolia's "nomadic, multiracial and multilingual conglomeration of tribes" into a confederation with a common purpose—to plunder and pillage the eastern Roman Empire. Historically known as the "Scourge of God," Attila has been characterized as the incarnation of barbaric rule and ruthless terror. Thus, Attila is an unlikely subject on which to base a book on management. Yet the author of *Leadership Secrets,* Wess Roberts, formerly of the U.S. Army Combat Arms Training Board, has done just that. In this brief, witty, thought-provoking book, Roberts attempts to describe the essential qualities of leadership in terms of loyalty, courage, decisiveness, competitiveness, self-confidence, accountability, credibility, tenacity and stewardship—all by using a rich, story-telling style.

This book is not a unified thesis on leadership development. In fact, Roberts cautions that "there is no magical formula for [accelerating the development of] leadership abilities..." Rather, he uses the Hun chieftain as a symbolic mouthpiece to toss out—just as Attila himself might have done—various leadership principles. Themes are suggested by fictional story-lines, and followed by maxims hypothetically spoken by Attila to his chosen chieftains and Hun warriors in campfire settings. Here is a sampling of proverbs, listed under assorted headings.

Lust for Leadership: "You've Got to Want to Be in Charge"

- Above all other traits, one who desires to lead must possess an intrinsic desire to achieve substantial personal recognition and be willing to earn it in all fairness.
- You must remember that success in your office will depend largely upon your sustained willingness to work hard. Sweat rules over inspiration!
- You must not be threatened by capable contemporaries or subordinates. Be wise in selecting capable captains to achieve those things a chieftain can attain only through strong subordinates.

Peace in the Camp: "Morale and Discipline"

- Huns seek discipline in their lives. They more willingly follow chieftains who are themselves disciplined.
- Wise chieftains realize that unduly harsh and unnecessarily lax discipline will undo

the morale of their Huns.

The Fury of Internal Battles: "Cunning in the Tribes"

- Be wise and anticipate the "Brutus" of your camp....Beware of the treacherous Hun who pledges loyalty in public then spreads discontent in private. Make every effort to identify and remove these ignoble characters, be they chieftains or your best warriors.
- Be principled, not inflexible.
- Be approachable; listen to both good and bad news from your Huns...

The Tribute: "Paying and Receiving Deference"

- When deference is born of fear...it results in an unwillingness to serve and becomes manifested as passive resistance to authority and purpose...
- Real deference results in unyielding loyalty—a tribe full of spirit and willing to follow their chieftain into the mouth of hell...
- Always pay proper courtesy to your subordinate leaders. Should you fail to accord them respect, so will their subordinates.

Battle Dress and Armament: "Chieftains Are as they Appear to Their Huns"

- A chieftain should dress in fine skins and furs—not those draped by gold and silver adornments. Pompous appearance breeds hate and gives rise to contempt and laughter among the ranks.
- When on the hunt, be prepared to hunt. Take your best bow and lance, wear the clothing that will serve you well as you chase the wild beasts in the forest.

Leading the Charge: "Responsibilities of the Chieftain"

- By their own actions, not their word, do leaders establish the morale, integrity and sense of justice of their subordinate commanders. They cannot say one thing and do another.
- Leaders must attach value to high standards of performance and have no tolerance for the uncommitted.
- Chieftains must teach their Huns well that which is expected of them. Otherwise, Huns will probably do something not expected of them.

The Omen of Aquileia: "The Essentials of Decisiveness"

- Wise is the chieftain who never makes a decision when he doesn't understand the issue....
- A chieftain should allow his subordinates the privilege of making decisions appropriate to their level of responsibility. Weak is the chieftain who reserves every decision for himself out of fear that he might lose control.
- It takes less courage to criticize the decisions of others than to stand by your own.
- Self-confidence is critical to decisiveness, for without it, a chieftain loses his following in challenging situations.

Horse Holders: "The Art of Delegation"

- Chieftains should never delegate responsibilities necessitating their direct attention.
- Wise chieftains grant both authority and responsibility to those they have delegated assignments.

Booty: "Rewarding Your Huns"

- Be generous with small tokens of appreciation—they will multiply in returned loyalty and service.

- ...Security is utmost for those who risk not. Give them, therefore, assurance—not great booty—lest they learn large value is given those who just get by.

Attila and the Pope: "The Art of Negotiation"

- It is never wise to gain by battle what may be gained through bloodless negotiations.
- Honor all commitments you make during negotiations lest your enemy fail to trust your word in the future.
- Never trust negotiation to luck. Enter every session armed with knowledge of the enemy's strengths and weaknesses; knowing his secrets makes you strong. . . .

Surviving Defeat: "There is Another Day"

- ...Sometimes you will lose, regardless of how prepared you are to win.
- ...Lament, if necessary, but do not dwell too long on your bad moments lest they rise to rule your emotions forever.
- ...As a Hun breathes, all is not lost.

The Bones of Caravans Past: "Lessons Learned"

- We must never fail to analyze the past. No bleached bone of a battle-lost Hun must go unnoticed as we prepare for the future by laying aside the ill-conceived and undisciplined strategies of our past....

The book ends with a selection of "Attilaisms." Consider these:

- A king with chieftains who always agree with him, reaps the counsel of mediocrity.
- The greatness of a Hun is measured by the sacrifices he is willing to make....
- Seldom are self-centered, conceited and self-admiring chieftains great leaders, but they are great idolizers of themselves.
- Great chieftains never take themselves too seriously.
- A Hun can achieve anything for which he is willing to pay the price. Competition thins out at the top of the ranks.
- Every decision involves some risk.
- It is unfortunate when final decisions are made by chieftains headquartered miles away from the front.
- The ability to make difficult decisions separates chieftains from Huns.
- Wise chieftains never place their Huns in situations where their weaknesses will prevail over their strengths.
- Delegation is not abdication. Abdication is a sign of weakness. Delegation is a sign of strength.
- Appropriate stress is essential in developing chieftains.
- Huns should engage only in wars they can win.
- For Huns, conflict is a natural state.
- Chieftains should remember that hospitality, warmth and courtesy will captivate even the most oppressive foe.
- Critical to a Hun's success is a clear understanding of what the King wants.
- Chieftains should always aim high, going after things that will make a difference rather than seeking the safe path of mediocrity.
- There is more nobility in being a good Hun than in being a poor chieftain.
- If an incompetent chieftain is removed, seldom do we appoint his highest-ranking

subordinate to his place. For when a chieftain has failed, so likewise have his subordinate leaders.

- If you tell a Hun he is doing a good job when he isn't, he will not listen long and, worse, will not believe praise when it is justified.
- Suffer long for mediocre but loyal Huns. Suffer not for competent but disloyal Huns.
- Adequate training of Huns is essential to war and cannot be disregarded by chieftains in more peaceful times.

"Corporate Chieftains"—and others who are called on to lead—will find Roberts' Attila both helpful and highly entertaining.

The Managerial Mystique

Restoring Leadership in Business

by Abraham Zaleznik, Harper & Row, 1989

Abraham Zaleznik's meaty book is a critical assessment of what he terms the "managerial mystique"—a false sense of how leaders should lead. The text is directed at today's managers, from the President of the United States to the plant foreman of a small Midwestern company, who blame subordinates for incompetence or ignorance, thus absolving themselves from accountability; managers "who can shift their stance, who adopt the coloration of their surroundings, and who understand how to play the game of control and compliance." Zaleznik claims that shoddy work, reduced productivity, and a growing sense of distrust, disloyalty, and "leaderlessness" among followers are direct results of the managerial mystique.

Watergate, a classic example of the "mystique" at work, "left a corrosive residue of apathy and skepticism that has eaten away at all major institutions." (Time, July 15, 1974). More recently, according to the official Tower Commission report, the Iran-Contra arms sales debacle was the result of a leader using an impersonal, "hands-off" style—a style that has gradually won out over consistent, knowledgeable, responsible leadership. *Business strategy has overcome business leadership, while concern for self has displaced the urge to make a difference in the lives and well-being of other people.... We are fabricating managers not educating leaders.*

Only when managers finally become aware of the potential impact of their power, both positive and negative, and are held accountable for their decisions—forced to "bring the human character back to center stage in the drama of business"—will trust, substance, morality, *leadership,* again reign. Through a blend of psychology, historical perspective, and business theory, Zaleznik argues for a mending of the "leadership gap."

"Management" and "leadership" are not necessarily synonymous. Typically, "leaders grow through mastering painful conflict during their developmental years [Lee Iacocca, for example], while managers confront few of the experiences that generally cause people to turn inward" for goals and direction. So, as managers have taken over many leadership positions, they have not evolved into leaders.

Current managerial technique encourages managers to dedicate themselves to process, politics, structures, roles, and inferential forms of communication and to ignore ideas, people, emotions and direct talk. Procedure, protocol and politics become ends in themselves, rather than the means to creating and marketing better products and services. Managers brought with them "what they learned from the business schools, namely, principles of bargaining, emotional control, human relations skills....They left behind commitment, creativity, concern for others, and experimentation." The typical corporate executive distances himself from his organization, looking at company goals chiefly as a means to enhance self interest and requiring the same sort of "compliance without commitment" from his subordinates. He focuses on manipulative, impersonal control tactics: financial plans, budget allocations, monthly reviews.

True leaders, however, are not bound by the controls of protocol and "process"; they do not confuse means and ends. Unencumbered by "management theory," leaders focus on imaginative ideas; they take on risks; they're visionary, dramatic, trusting, hard-working and fair-minded. Their goals are entrepreneurial and active.

Analysis of the Mystique

It must be pointed out that managers possess many valuable assets. "Good" managers have "the ability to be dispassionate in the face of a problem, the skill to analyze facts, and the willingness to evaluate costs and benefits." But they also display typical weaknesses: fear of chaos, a need for distance in human relations, and separation of the thinking and feeling processes. Since managers "hate surprises" and "love to orchestrate events," they have the tendency to use inappropriate, sometimes unethical controls to force subordinates to meet expectations. Although in theory communication is democratic and decisions are autonomous at subordinate levels, "communication usually flows in one direction: from the top down....More often than not the superior is trying to channel subordinates' thoughts and perceptions..."Zaleznik cites Lyndon Johnson, who often invoked Isaiah's words "Come let us reason together," while at the same time "using, the power of position and personality to get his own way."

However, leaders ("wise, sensitive managers") understand that they don't have to manipulate every decision or personally instigate a "program" to rectify every problem that crops up. Somewhat weak on process but strong on substance, a leader often chooses to delegate to a trusted, personally-involved associate or subordinate the work of finding defects and implementing change in her organization.

This philosophy of "marrying" authority with competence, freeing up executives to solve problems at all levels, had a direct economic and organizational impact on the Cummins Engine Company. One Cummins executive reported that turning the company over to its best leaders simplified everyone's work: "Now we think in terms of work flow: how to reduce the handling of materials....We found, for example, that we were machining parts, moving them to a warehouse for storage, then bringing them back to complete the motor assembly. [Now], we've eliminated the warehousing...."

So, should a manager cease to wield control in his place of business? On the contrary, says Zaleznik. But control should be exercised openly and actively, rather than as a veiled, manipulative tool; it should be performance-enhancing and supportive. Professor Robert N. Anthony explains:

Action is a sure signal, probably the only effective signal, that management is interested in the control system. Basically, this involves praise or other reward for good performance, criticism of or removal of the causes for poor performance....

For years managers have used flattery, acquiescence, confrontation, indirect threats, and position to manipulate subordinates. But this type of corrupt use of power became a kind of corporate "poison," a venomous monster that has since turned and bitten the business community. High moral standards frequently make the difference between the successful leader and the manipulative, scarecrow-type manager.

The Cure: Leadership

In order to override the "MBA mentality" that exists in many offices, leaders will strive to strike a more genuine emotional stance. They will work to create a balance between expressionism (the human touch, vital to purpose, cohesion and growth) and stoicism (the suppression or redirection of particularly sensitive feelings).

The substance of business is business: making products and going to market....[And] the art of business leadership is imagination: The binding of leader and led in a cooperative relationship depends most on the respect the subordinate has for the leader's ability to originate ideas, suggest solutions to problems, and above all, translate visions into far-reaching goals.... Business needs talented people who apply their imagination to move an enterprise forward.

Substantive imagination includes the ability to:

- *Perceive opportunity*—"Opportunism," in its positive sense, means making the most of things; applying imagination to change situations or to create a new market; or, through delegation, formulating the elements necessary for success and then putting together the team to reach the goal. Back in the 1950s, Soichiro Honda recognized the need for a cleaner combustion engine. Though he did not invent the engine, through the use of "business imagination" he did perfect it.
- *Conceptualize*—New concepts—if not overworked before going to market—give industry its innovative drive.
- *Create*—Creativity is the rare ability to transcend imitation; to move toward a totally new concept or product.

People, working with ***information***, are the sources of imagination. A leader heightens her "financial imagination" (the faculty to make and use money) or her "marketing imagination" (the intuitive feel for consumer needs and desires) when she is close to the "pulse" of her company—in daily contact with managers and employees. Her understanding and skill are further honed when she keeps up her reading on the current literature in her field.

Along with imagination and skill, a leader exudes *personal influence*, approaching the ideal of a sort of "patriarchial amicitia" (an "extra-mile, the boss goes to bat for me, so I'll go to bat for him" mutual loyalty). Andrew Carnegie and John D. Rockefeller, for example, were early leaders who were able to inspire—not demand—the respect and loyalty of their followers. Today "there is not just one type of personality that inspires loyalty...but the absence of loyalty and camaraderie, both in government and business...indicates a fatal weakness in America's leadership."

Artful leaders are *realistic:* they communicate clearly; they govern themselves ethically; they espouse practical philosophies; and most importantly, they breed success....*People want to be successful at what they do. Show them how to be successful and they will feel indebted to you; set up roadblocks to their success and they will retaliate with hate if not revenge.*

Leaders are skilled listeners. They (1) take an active interest in the other person, (2) suspend judgment until all the facts are known, and (3) use a "third ear" to discover what the person wants to—but doesn't or can't—say.

Conclusion

Leaders must be critics rather than cheerleaders, yet their critical stance must avoid negativism. To be critical and positive is to be substantive. Therefore, leaders have to lead in the content and direction of change.

Zaleznik sums up his thoughts on true leadership by quoting from Machiavelli's *The Prince:*

Nothing makes a prince more esteemed than great enterprises and evidence of unusual abilities.... Furthermore, a prince should show that he is an admirer of talent by giving recognition to talented men, and honoring those who excel in a particular art.

Indeed, talent in dealing with followers will carry a leader far. Charismatic leadership—not managerial manipulation—inspires others to perform beyond expectations. "Leadership in business is the fusion of work and human relations," concludes Zaleznik. *Good ideas and exciting directions for an enterprise generate enthusiasm, support, and cohesion. Self-esteem follows, not from submerging oneself in the team and following process, but from facing problems, assuming responsibility, and doing good work.*

THRIVING ON CHAOS

Handbook for a Management Revolution

by Tom Peters, Alfred A. Knopf, 1987

In 1982 Tom Peters co-authored a much heralded book titled, In *Search of Excellence.* A sequel, *A Passion for Excellence,* came out in 1985. Both best sellers extolled the principles of managerial excellence and cited examples of companies that employ these principles. But *Thriving on Chaos* opens with the radical thesis, "There are no excellent companies."

Unlike Peters' previous upbeat books, *Thriving on Chaos* begins with a foreboding view of the nation's business climate. Peters, the guru of managerial excellence, now argues that even the paradigm cases of well-managed companies—from Citicorp to IBM, from Intell to Hewlett Packard—are undergoing economic trauma. Decline in the national savings rate, drops in industrial productivity, a large trade deficit, the current "merger mania," and a trend towards exporting major segments of manufacturing to low labor-cost countries, all hint toward the fact that the emerging global economy does not favor America's large-scale, standardized, mass-production systems of manufacturing.

In order to promote a "competitive resurgence," Peters offers his step-by-step prescriptions as a "handbook for a management revolution."

Peters emphasizes a leadership that "loves change," embraces quality consciousness, perceives human resources (personnel) as assets, seeks market fragmentation (differentiation through market niche-orientation), and fosters short-run specialization manufacturing. Sections 2 through 6 of the book contain various prescriptive strategies titled "Capability Building Blocks," which promote the "guiding premise" of each section. Some of these strategies are summarized herein.

Section II: Creating Total Customer Responsiveness

Guiding Premises: *Specialize/Create Niches/Differentiate*

- "Constantly create new market niches via new products and continuous transformation of every product."
- "Ensure that quality is always defined in terms of customer perception."
- "Become a service fanatic. Emphasizing service in terms of the customer.... Consider every customer to be a potential lifelong customer."
- "Strive more valiantly than ever to achieve uniqueness, as an organization, in the customer's mind."
- "Give manufacturing/operations people respect and a lead role at the firm's top decision-making table....Realize that manufacturing/ operations is the source of superior quality."

Launch a customer revolution. Respond to customer needs and wants by specializing or expanding into a niche that may never even have been noticed before. Remember that if customer responsiveness is the superordinate objective of a firm, then both awareness of customer needs and innovative response to those needs should be central concerns. As consultant Mike Kami is prone to shout: "What's so special about your company?...How are you different from your competitors?...What is your uniqueness in the marketplace?"

Section III: Pursuing Fast-Paced Innovation

Guiding Premise: *Invest in Applications-Oriented Small Starts*

- "Develop an innovation strategy which is marked by an explosive number of lightning-fast small starts that match the environment's turbulence."
- "Mount completely independent teams that attack and make obsolete our most cherished (and profitable) product lines and services—before competitors do."
- "Maintain in most small starts an application (customer) focus rather than overemphasizing giant technological leaps."
- "Make word-of-mouth marketing systematic."
- "Put NIH (Not Invented Here) behind you—and learn to copy (with unique adaptation/ enhancement) from the best." Practice "creative swiping."
- "Become a 'learning organization.' "
- "Get customers into the act, for they usually give more weight than insiders to minor innovation—and customer-oriented—advances."
- "Fail forward....Support failure by actively and publicly rewarding mistakes—failed efforts that were well thought out, executed with alacrity, quickly adjusted, and thoroughly learned from."

Implement these strategies by practicing "purposeful impatience," working to turn adversaries into partners, and setting quantitative innovation goals. Yawn at even the good performance that doesn't carry with it a timely and innovative approach. Your firm's "new look" will soon include an innate, comfortable "corporate capacity for innovation."

Section IV: "Achieving Flexibility by Empowering People"

Guiding Premises: *Involve Everyone in Everything and Use Self-Managing Teams*

- "Involve all personnel at all levels in all functions in virtually everything: for example, quality improvement programs and 100 percent self-inspection; productivity improvement programs; measuring and monitoring results."
- "Organize as much as possible around teams, to achieve enhanced focus, task orientation, innovativeness, and individual commitment. ...The modest-sized, task-oriented, semi-autonomous, mainly self-managing team should be the basic organization building block."
- "Wholesale worker involvement must become a national priority if we are to create the competitive strengths necessary just to maintain, let alone improve, our national economic well-being."
- "Invest in human capital as much as in hardware....Use training as a vehicle for instilling a strategic trust."
- "Spend time lavishly on recruiting."
- "Provide bold financial incentives for everyone....Above-average pay yields above-average work—or at least the converse is true."
- "Radically reduce layers of management.... Establish a radically increased ratio of non-supervisors to supervisors—a 'wide span of control'—at the organization's front line."
- "Get staffs out in the field, and encourage them to be "business team members" rather than narrow functional specialists."
- "De-bureaucratize:...Reduce and simplify paperwork and unnecessary procedures."
- "De-humiliate: Eliminate policies and practices ...of the organization which demean and belittle human dignity."

"...Genuinely invite wholesale participation and commitment necessary for survival." Increase flexibility by empowering, celebrating, and listening to others. Ironically, greater employee participation will ultimately give a manager greater overall "control." Retrain all employees to enhance their own skills and to make your business a smoother, more well-rounded, upbeat entity.

Section V: "Learning to Love Change: A New View of Leadership at All Levels"

Guiding Premise: *Master Paradox*

- "...Challenge conventional wisdom, especially cause and effect relations that have been considered axiomatic."
- "Rip one front-line job apart: Listen to those who hold it. Learn their frustrations. Then act to clean up the mess and encourage them...."
- "Practice visible management."
- "Ensure that the front-line people—the implementers, the executors—know that they are the organization's heroes."

"Master paradox," counsels Peters. As defined by Webster's New World Dictionary, a paradox is "a statement that seems contradictory, unbelievable or absurd but that may actually be true in fact." Managers often carry around with them a fear of change—

change is threatening; the status quo is the only safe road. But, paradoxically, if leaders attentively seek change and make testing and improvement part of the status quo by delegating, deferring problems to their front-line people, and "bashing bureaucracy" through "horizonal" management systems, they will be rewarded by greater progress and production.

Section VI: "Building Systems for a World Turned Upside Down"

Guiding Premise: *Measure What's Important*

- "Simple, visible measures of what's important should mark every square foot of every department in every operation."
- "Develop simple systems that encourage participation and understanding by everyone and that support initiative-taking on the front line."
- "Make...documents 'living' ones, subject to constant discussion...."
- "Decentralize control systems, and decentralize the accountants/systems people who oversee them."
- "Decentralize strategic planning."
- "The essential variables are these: (1) simplicity of presentation, (2) visibility of measurements, (3) everyone's involvement, (4) undistorted collection of primary information..., (5) the straightforward measurement of what's important, and (6) achievement of an overall feel of urgency and perpetual improvement."

Measuring only what's necessary will foster among employees a real respect for the organization; they will see it as a thoughtful and professional business that wants to make sense out of our frequently topsy-turvy world (an all too infrequent goal these days).

As a "true handbook to guide managers through the turbulent markets and economic climates of our times," Thriving on Chaos provocatively and systematically treats those problems that the author contends managers will have no choice but to face—or to flail away at—in the future.

The Greatest Management Principle in the World

For Anyone Who Needs to Get Things Done

by Michael LeBoeuf, Ph.D., Berkley Books, 1985

A weekend fisherman looked over the side of his boat and saw a snake with a frog in its mouth. Feeling sorry for the frog, he reached down, gently removed it from the snake's mouth and let it go free. But now he felt sorry for the hungry snake. Having no food, he took out a flask of bourbon and poured a few drops into the snake's mouth. The snake swam away happy, the frog was happy, and the fisherman was happy for having performed such good deeds. He thought all was well until a few minutes passed and he heard something knock against the side of his boat. The fisherman looked down and, with stunned disbelief, saw the snake was back—this time with two frogs!

This fable, told in LeBoeuf's first chapter of *The Greatest Management Principle (GMP)*, carries two important messages:

(1) *You get what you reward.*

(2) *We often reward inappropriate behaviors, while ignoring—or even punishing—correct ones.*

LeBoeuf insists that the single greatest management principle is this:

"THE THINGS THAT GET REWARDED, GET DONE."

Is your company, organization, or family ignoring this principle?

The author uses "magic questions" in an attempt to simplify the process by which leaders go about "rewarding" behavior, desirable or undesirable. He then proposes practical advice on how leaders can effectively reward their followers.

What's Commonly Being Rewarded?

In typical organizations, leaders reward busy-work, long hours, massive reports, paper-shuffling, risk avoidance and "good" excuses. Short-term profits—and the requisite short-term reports, that "better be encouraging, or else!"—are emphasized over long-term, steady growth, and responsible action.

Quick fixes (doing things the quick, easy, cheap way) often override solid solutions, which focus on long-range investing, planning and commitment.

What Needs To Be Rewarded?

- *Problem-solving* (solid solutions, not "problem identification" or "analysis").
- *Risk taking* (instead of risk avoiding). "...The 'sure thing' boat never gets far from shore."—Dale Carnegie
- *Innovation* (applied creativity, even if it ultimately leads to failure). "In 1976 a young engineer got bored with laying out computer chips. On three different occasions he asked if he could work on designing a personal computer but his company said no each time. So he went home, built one and named it the Apple...."
- *Decisive, confident action* (results; productivity). "If Moses had been a committee, the Israelites would still be in Egypt." —Anon.
- *Smart work* (not busywork). "If you can't do your job in an eight-hour work day, then either you have too much work assigned or you're incompetent."
- *Simplification* (eliminating unnecessary reports, paper-work, procedures, etc.). "...Good organizations and managers work hard to keep things simple and prevent goals from getting lost in the shuffle of daily activities."
- *Quiet, effective behavior.* "Who is rarely... absent?...Who doesn't constantly pester others for advice and guidance?...Who can be trusted to work just as well in the boss's absence?...Who is so quiet and unassuming that you hardly know he's there except for his good work?...Who smoothes out conflicts, fosters cooperation and builds morale?..."
- *Quality work done on time* (rather than fast, haphazard work). "...During World War II the U.S. government discovered its parachutes failed to open 5 percent of the time. Clearly, nothing less than zero defects was an acceptable level of quality...The problem was solved by requiring parachute packers and inspectors to put on one of their products occasionally and jump out of a plane..."
- *Loyalty.* "You can buy a man's time; you can buy his physical presence....But you

cannot buy enthusiasm....You cannot buy loyalty....You cannot buy the devotion of hearts, minds or souls. You must earn these." –Clarence Francis

- *Teamwork and cooperation* in reaching a common goal. "A man touring a mental institution was surprised to find only three guards watching over one hundred dangerous patients. 'Aren't you afraid they will overpower you and escape?' he asked. 'No,' replied one of the guards. 'Lunatics never unite.'"

Depending on the organization, magic questions might include: What behaviors do I want to see out of my staff (club members, salespeople, family members...)? How will I recognize hard and smart work (and other expected behaviors)? And how shall I reward those behaviors? Straightforward questions like these help a manager or leader gain a better "feel" for what behaviors he wants from his workers, and to determine possible ways of eliciting desired behaviors.

Rewards

Here are the ten best ways to reward good performance—in order of most powerful to least powerful motivator:

1. *Money* (raises, bonuses...)
2. *Recognition* (public citations, job title change, special praise...)
3. *Time off*
4. A *"piece of the action"* (ownership, stocks,...)
5. The opportunity to do certain *favorite work*
6. *Advancement* (promotions—possibly within a variety of career ladder systems)
7. *Freedom* (autonomy in the workplace)
8. *Personal growth* (opportunity for additional training, to do interesting work, learn new skills, expand a field...)
9. *Fun*—in addition to an enjoyable workplace (sports or health facilities, parties, travel...)
10. *Prizes* (dinners, vacation trips, gift certificates...)

LeBoeuf asserts that people and ideas are an organization's most important capital "assets." Therefore, the successful company must hold on to these assets and foster their growth by rewarding productivity. The key is to identify, together with each employee, specific productivity goals, and then to provide rewards commensurate with (1) the merits of the behavior, (2) the nature of the organization, and (3) the particular worker involved.

The "fundamental task" of a successful leader or manager is to make people feel excited about the activity at hand. To make this happen, it is vital to establish some sort of Goals/Reward Contract (outlined in the book) with each group member. Clear and effective contracts share four ingredients:

1. *A meaningful goal* (including its level of achievement and when it will be realized)
2. *A way—formal or informal—to keep score* (People actually want to know where they are in relation to where they should be, and, the fact is, "People do what gets measured.")
3. *Responsibility and autonomy* for achieving the goal
4. *A meaningful reward*

While visiting with workers or team members, openly communicate these concepts. Confer responsibility, require results, allow freedom, and, finally, reward success.

A "Manager's Action Plan," outlined below, makes reward-giving the natural culmination of a chain of behaviors elicited by four management actions:

(1) CHOOSE RESULTS THAT ARE:

- Specific
- Measurable
- Clear
- Challenging but attainable
- Compatible
- Written
- Mutually understood

(2) IDENTIFY THE BEHAVIOR NEEDED:

- Solid solutions
- Risk taking
- Applied creativity
- Decisive action
- Smart work
- Simplification
- Quietly effective behavior
- Quality work
- Loyalty
- Working together

(3) DECIDE ON THE PROPER REWARDS:

- Money
- Recognition
- Time off
- A piece of the action
- Favorite work
- Advancement
- Freedom
- Personal growth and development
- Fun
- Prizes

(4) USE THE POWER OF POSITIVE FEEDBACK:

- Frequently
- Specifically
- Sincerely
- Inconsistently
- On the spot
- Personally
- Proportionately

When the time comes for evaluation, the manager sits down with the worker and determines if the desired behaviors were shown. Were the desired results achieved? If not, you must both revaluate and clarify the goal, and try again, renewing the process. If the answer is yes, you dispense the promised rewards, bask in success for a few moments, and then set new goals; the cycle is set in motion once more.

GMP's many questions, charts and examples outline a process that can help you as a manager, parent, president—any kind of leader—to more operatively establish, advertise, review, reformulate, and achieve goals you wish your group members to achieve. And, most importantly, the book delineates practical, positive reward systems that can motivate your people to initiate suitable goals and to act consistently in order to attain them.

THE ONE MINUTE MANAGER

by Kenneth Blanchard, Ph.D., and Spencer Johnson, M.D., Berkley Books, 1981

The One Minute Manager's purpose is to help people "produce valuable results, and feel good about themselves...." The book's concepts are developed within a storyline featuring the adventures of a bright young man (you) as he discovers and applies management principles. As the story opens, this young man has sought out his mentor, the One Minute Manager, for an interview. He is on a modern-day quest to find and implement management skills that will make him successful both in production and with people.

"Effective managers manage themselves and the people they work with so that both the organization and the people profit from their presence," the Manager instructs. He teaches his disciple some other basic principles, then ushers him into his organization, to watch and visit with others who model the same techniques of leadership.

The OMM Idea

Does it really take just a minute to do all the things managers do? No; "One Minute Management" represents a philosophy and a group of tools that demonstrate that being a manager "is not as complicated as people would have you believe. And...managing people doesn't take as long as you think."

People who feel good about themselves, produce good results....Productivity is both quantity and quality....And frankly, the best way to achieve both of these results is through people.

A "One Minute Manager" can achieve big results from his people in very little time. You, as a manager, must learn to delegate authority and tasks. Then you must ensure that the people who accept these delegated responsibilities set goals, make decisions, and report to you on progress.

Three OMM Secrets

Secret #1—*One Minute Goal Setting:* At the beginning of a new assignment, spend some time making it clear what each person will be accountable for. Have him describe what he would like to see happen. Then, write out the selected goals on a single sheet of paper using less than 250 words—so that anyone can read them in one minute. Retain a copy of the list so that you can help him check periodically on progress and identify actions that promote his goals.

The "80–20 rule" applies to goal-setting: "80% of your really important results will come from 20% of your goals." Concentrate with each worker on those goals that include the person's primary responsibilities—maybe 3 to 6 goals in all. With specific objectives established, everyone knows right from the beginning what he is trying to accomplish and what the standard is for performance.

The successful manager uses a direct approach in dealing with employees. If there is a problem, she first asks that it be described in behavioral terms.

...I do not want to hear about only attitudes or feelings. Tell me what is happening in observable, measurable terms....Now tell me what you would like to see happening....If you

can't tell me what you'd like to see happening, you don't have a problem yet. You're just complaining.

After discussing the actual and desired situations, the manager responds:

Well, what are you going to do about it?...I just asked you questions—questions you are able to ask yourself. Now...start solving your own problems on your own time, not mine.

Secret #2—*One Minute Praisings:* Catch people "doing something right." Tell them up front that you are going to let them know how they are doing; that you'll provide them with frequent, crystal-clear feedback. This requires careful observation by you, the manager, plus frequent interviews and/or detailed progress reports with each employee. Progress reports provide fodder for frequent praisings; workers don't have to wait for an annual performance review to get a pat on the back.

Praise good performance immediately. You can see in a very short time the progress or mistakes a person is making. Tell people specifically what they did right. Speaking and responding in open, direct terms may be uncomfortable at first for some people. Encourage everyone to communicate in a close, direct, one-on-one way.

Secret #3—*The One Minute Reprimand:* *If you have been doing a job for some time and you know how to do it well, and you make a [significant] mistake, the One Minute Manager is quick to respond.*

She can do this because she has already been quick to praise your good work and has explained beforehand that she will let you know when you are performing well and when you are not.

Give necessary reprimands immediately after seeing a problem. "Gunnysacking" negative feelings and letting them out only because the sack is full, is a "leave alone—zap!" form of discipline employed by many managers. Early intervention doesn't overwhelm people; it only helps them realize that "performance review" is an ongoing process of education.

First, confirm the facts. Then, get close to the employee, look him straight in the eye, and indicate exactly what the mistake was without any hint of personal attack. Tell him how it makes you feel (embarrassed, annoyed, frustrated...), then be silent for a moment "to let [him] feel how you feel."

The purpose of a One Minute Reprimand "is to eliminate the behavior and keep the person." *...You have to care enough to be tough....I am very tough on the poor performance—but only on the performance. I am never tough on the person.*

A successful reprimand has three basic ingredients: (1) Telling the person what she did wrong; (2) Telling her how you feel about it; and (3) Reminding her that she is valuable and worthwhile.

Why not praise first and *then* reprimand? Because, says the manager, the most successful manager would be termed "Tough 'n' Nice" rather than "Nice 'n' Tough," as illustrated by an "ancient Chinese story":

> ...An emperor appointed a second in command. He called this prime minister in and, in effect, said to him, "Why don't we divide up the tasks? Why don't you do all the punishing and I'll do all the rewarding?" The prime minister said, "Fine. I'll do all the punishing and you do all the rewarding."
>
> Now this emperor soon noticed that whenever he asked someone to do something, they might do it or they might not do it. However, when the prime minister spoke, people moved. So the emperor called the prime minister back in and said, "Why don't we divide the tasks again? You have been doing all the punishing here for quite a while.

Now let me do the punishing and you do the rewarding." So the prime minister and the emperor switched roles again.

And, within a month the prime minister was emperor. The emperor had been a nice person, rewarding and being kind to everyone; then he started to punish people. People said, "What's wrong with that old codger?" and they threw him out on his ear. When they came to look for a replacement, they said, "You know who's really starting to come around now—the prime minister." So, they put him right into office.

If you are first tough on the behavior, and then supportive of the person, it works.

The second half of the reprimand begins with touching—shaking hands, a pat on the arm—to let the employee know you're on her side. Remind her of how valuable she is to the company. Leave her feeling that "the only reason he is angry with me is that he has so much respect for me." Then, exit; "When the reprimand is over, it's over."

Other Related OMM Concepts

On budgets and training: "It's ironic. Most companies spend 50% to 70% of their money on people's salaries. And yet they spend less than 1% of their budget to train their people...."

On direct communication and goal-setting: "In most of the organizations I worked in before, I often didn't know what I was supposed to be doing. No one bothered to tell me. If you asked me whether I was doing a good job, I would say either 'I don't know' or 'I think so'....My main motivation was to avoid punishment."

On motivation: "Feedback is the Breakfast of Champions. Feedback keeps us going....Feedback on results is the number one motivator of people. [Many managers] don't tell their people what they expect of them; they just leave them alone and then 'zap' them when they don't perform at the desired level."

On winners and losers: "Everyone is a potential winner. Some are disguised as losers; don't let their appearances fool you."

On creating winners: A manager has three choices: either hire winners (hard to do, and costly), hire potential winners and systematically train them to win, or pray ("I hope this person works out").

On punishment: If a dog had an "accident" and we shoved his nose in it, beat him with a newspaper, then threw him out the window, we would be focusing not on the behavior we wanted, but on what we didn't want. "After about three days the dog would poop on the floor and jump out the window.... "Rather than punish an employee, return to One Minute Goal Setting to clarify your expectations and help him see "what good performance looks like."

On One Minute Praising: "The key to training someone to do a new task is...to catch them doing something approximately right until they can eventually learn to do it exactly right." Training and goal setting, however, must be done with great amounts of respect and no trace of manipulation.

At the end of Blanchard and Johnson's book, the bright young protagonist—*you*—finally does become a One Minute Manager, "not because he thought like one, or talked like one, but because he behaved like one." He set goals, praised frequently, and used timely, informative reprimands.

He asked brief, important questions; spoke the simple truth; laughed, worked, and enjoyed. And, perhaps most important of all, he encouraged the people he worked with to do the same....

How to Talk so People Listen

The Real Key to Job Success

by Sonya Hamlin, Harper & Row, 1988

Communication is complex and dynamic; it is both a science and an art. No single prescription can bind it into a convenient, tractable bundle. However, Sonya Hamlin's book provides a few proven "handles" to the huge body of literature dealing with communication.

Hamlin's early experience as a television host, producer, lecturer and consultant provided the foundation from which she went on to work in the "real world" of trial lawyers, doctors, politicians and business-people. The ideas she presents and the strategies she offers have the solidity of being firmly grounded in scholarship, and also the flavor and nourishment of reality-testing. The purpose of *How to Talk So People Listen* is clear throughout: to help the reader get what he or she wants on the job through effective communication.

One basic approach to communication emphasizes the skills and abilities of the *sender*, the person actively "doing" the communicating. This approach places considerable weight on the communicator, who must somehow gauge the receptiveness, defenses, propensities, and background of his "audience," and then concoct just the right message in both form and content. Properly executed, the message hits its mark, and understanding or persuasion ensues.

Communication scholars have long since abandoned this approach, however. The current trend—of which Hamlin is a proponent—recognizes communication as a two-way, *interactive* process, where both sender and receiver continually influence each other and messages are cycled back and forth on non-verbal, barely perceptible levels. Most people do not process all these signals on a conscious, rational level; but they do process and respond to them on a semi-conscious, emotional level, and this subliminal processing leaves an indelible mark on the whole communications exchange.

The book first presents a brief outline of developmental psychology. Hamlin is concerned with looking at the "*whys*" behind the "*hows.*" Her words attempt to imbue the reader with a base of *psychological* and *linguistic* data to show why one communication technique works where others fail.

Many of us became detached from our feelings in early life, and the impact of this disengagement on our communication has been immense.

Example: You're a kid and you tell your mother, "I don't like Aunt Agnes." What happened? You were told: "That's terrible. She's your aunt! Don't you let me hear you say that again!"

The result of such an exchange? Guilt, the need to put on a false front, stifled relationships, doubt that others are being honest in their relations with you, etc. Because we have learned to deny or hide our feelings rather than accept and manage them, most of us carry hidden "*emotional agendas*" into communicative exchanges. The motivation underlying our words becomes an attempt to influence others and to win their "conditional acceptance"—conditional upon our doing and saying that which we think they expect of us. These "externalized motivations," established in early childhood when we first learn what is admired and rewarded—earning-power, compliancy, degrees, professional prestige—shape lifelong personal work styles and communication patterns.

Three basic "work personalities" are identified by the author, each distinguished by one of these "dominant motivators": "Achievers," "Affiliators," and "Influencers."

Achievers continually *strive* to *"win"* in the sense of reaching the next rung of the ladder. The business world has a preponderance of achievers. *Affiliators* are preoccupied with the quality of *social relations;* concerned with both their own and others' feelings. *Influencers* are largely interested in getting, holding, and *building a power base* within a given relationship. We must not only come to grips with the "hidden agenda" behind our own basic communications style, but also learn how to communicate with these three personality types when we encounter them in others.

Listening is treated by Hamlin in some depth. She poses an intriguing proposition about the visual orientation many of us have nowadays toward communication. Television has accustomed us to watching (not necessarily listening to) brief, yet complete, sequential, and intense stories that require little or no imagination. If in fact "the medium is the message," then television messages encourage passivity and breaks in attention. Just being aware of this can help a speaker (salesperson, presenter, parent, lawyer, teacher...) decide how best to get her message, demand or selling point across, using brief narratives and illustrations to support her main points, for example, and judiciously chosen "high-impact" visuals to help reinforce and explain. The overriding thesis here is that *the communicator needs to develop a thoughtful, listener-centered approach.*

A *"Fore-Thought Chart"* is offered as a tool to help clarify relationships between your goals and your listeners' goals, needs and expectations. *The chart's emphasis is on pre-planning.* It helps you analyze a situation before you say or do anything. What are your own objectives? What are those of the listener?

Fore-thought charts provide an explicit, deliberate occasion for thinking through how persuasive communication can best be achieved in a certain situation. Using empathy and observation, clearly state what your goals are and what you feel your audience will perceive as their own biggest needs. "...Hidden emotional needs are real and must be acknowledged and included in your communication strategy... even at the expense of your logical, well-thought-out plans." If you are speaking to an employee who happens to be an *Achiever,* he may respond more readily to how his behavior makes you feel personally; whereas, dealing with an *Affiliator* might require an approach that focuses on teamwork. By listening and applying forethought, you can uncover emotional needs, imagine outcomes, and be better prepared to respond intelligently to any circumstance.

The author goes on to describe preferred settings and times in which to discuss particular subjects. Inviting someone to a breakfast meeting who is a "night owl" instead of a "chirper," for instance, may not be at all wise.

Here are a few other communications skills that the book explores:

- Using vocal variety, eye contact, and body language.
- Structuring an interesting speech or presentation with smooth transitions, i.e. introduction, motivation, outline of agenda, main content, breaking the main topic into segments, presenting details, recapping key ideas, wrapping up, and conclusion.
- Designing high-impact visuals, i.e. deciding whether comparisons, facts, and data should be put in picture, graph, chart, slide, diagram, exhibit or video form.
- Selecting which areas to present vocally and which to present visually. Generally,

feelings and narrative are best offered orally; new facts or data, numbers or trends, and direct comparisons are most effective and memorable when presented using visuals.

- Eliciting listener involvement and feedback through questions, discussion, effective listening, and appropriate monitoring of responses and idea exchange.
- Answering difficult questions and providing "creative criticism" while still maintaining a positive environment.
- Developing empathy and rapport with listeners.
- Handling disinterested or hostile listeners. Often, by pointing out to a listener that he seems angry or defensive, you put the ball in his court. Then he can deal with what is bothering him without blaming you or looking for some type of outside interference. Hostility can be lessened by allowing and understanding the anger, then getting out of the personal realm of the conflict and finding something in common.
- Getting group attention.
- Handling egos and conflict.
- Cultivating an air of confidence and preparedness when delivering a speech, answering questions, etc.

In each topical discussion the same theme emerges: *Effective communicators design their messages to grab listeners' attention, maintain their interest, allow for feedback, and enable them to visualize and retain information.* Hamlin frequently returns to the three basic listening personalities or styles, and shows how each is influenced by—or influences—various communication behaviors.

She examines, for example, what the distinct response might be of an *Affiliator* subordinate when directing comments to an *Achiever* boss versus an *Influencer* boss. When questioned about performance, an *Affiliator* usually takes criticism very personally; she dislikes any hostility. But her *Achiever* boss, who is trying to attack the problem from a rational, task-oriented viewpoint, cannot understand the *Affiliator's* hostile response. "How did this happen?" he will ask, scanning all the variables of success, including himself. On the other hand, an *Influencer* boss might ask, "Why didn't you do this?" to make sure that the subordinate's foul-up was not the result of defiance or negligence. For either of these responses it is important that the *Affiliator* employee not turn defensive or be tempted to counter-punch. Rather, she should work with the *Achiever* to help identify the problem; and from the Influencer she should seek suggestions or a clarification of duties, and admit fault when deserved.

An issue of ethics lies just below the surface in *How to Talk So People Listen:* Is it manipulative to use communication in a goal-oriented way? Should you communicate to serve your own ends? Hamlin's response is straightforward. Business communication is a process of gaining and attaining; of getting what you want; of using communication techniques to those ends. This is precisely what the other person you're dealing with is doing. Of course, honesty, candor and openness remain the underlying ingredients in any communication exchange.

Hamlin asserts that understanding your listeners' fears and motivations, being a good listener yourself, speaking in a smooth and personal manner, and making communication interactive (incorporating your audience's responses) are essential parts of your formal and informal speech. They are the ways to talk so people will listen.

You Can Negotiate Anything

How To Get What You Want

by Herb Cohen, Citadel Press, 1980

All of us are participants in negotiation, the theme of Herb Cohen's book. We constantly negotiate with others to get what we want out of life, and the most successful people often have developed the best negotiating skills. Three crucial variables need to be addressed in the art of negotiation: *power, time,* and *information.*

POWER

Power is the ability to get things done, to achieve goals. Whenever you can expand the options available to you, you have greater power. Below are some of Cohen's suggestions for using various types of power. (Keep in mind that an ethical stance and comportment need to be incorporated into each of these suggestions.)

The Power of Competition

Whenever there is competition for a possession (money, time, or skills), that possession moves up in value. To make this power work for you, you can not let on that what you are seeking—a job, a bank loan, or whatever—means the world to you. For instance, if a prospective home-buyer's attitude is, "My wife and kids will leave home if we don't buy this dream house," he will be lucky not to pay more than the asking price! Presume that you can go elsewhere for your loan; you have other job offers you're considering. This instills within the other person greater eagerness to give you what you want.

The Power of Legitimacy

In our society, people are conditioned to regard with awe anything that's in print. Most will not challenge documents and forms; they carry an assumed authority.

The Power of Risk-Taking

Taking risks doesn't mean gambling all your savings. It simply means mixing courage with common sense. Intelligent risk-taking involves a knowledge of the odds as well as a willingness to walk away from a negotiation if things don't work out.

The Power of Expertise

To establish your power base as an expert, subtly allude to your background and credentials early in the confrontation. That way your statements may not even be challenged. And when you are confronted by an "expert" on the other side of a negotiation, don't be over-impressed; if you didn't have something she really wanted, she wouldn't be there.

The Power of Knowing "Needs"

"In all negotiations, two things are being bargained for: 1. The specific issues and demands, which are stated openly. 2. The real needs of the other side, which are rarely verbalized." Translation: When looking to buy a car, first gather specific data about the car itself (performance, costs, potential problems, etc.), and then find out about the various dealers you will visit. Do they have any cash-flow problems, larger than normal inventory, itemized costs? How are their salespeople compensated? After this preparation you can "adapt [your] purchasing style to satisfy the real needs of the seller."

The Power of Investment

If you come to a sore spot in negotiating an issue, go on and talk about other aspects of the issue. Then come back to the unresolved question. Chances are the other party will be willing to negotiate on that aspect because he has already invested a large amount of time and energy.

The Power of Reward and Punishment

The perception that someone else can either help or hurt you—physically, financially, or psychologically—gives him power in your relationship. "If I'm aware of your perceptions and needs, and if I know you think I have power over you, I can control your behavior."

The Power of Precedent

Precedent limits our way of thinking to our own past experience and basic assumptions. To justify what you are asking for in a negotiation, refer to similar past situations where you or others did so-and-so with favorable results.

The Power of Persistence

"Most people aren't persistent enough when negotiating." Stick to your goals and recognize that successful negotiations generally take some time.

TIME

Most people envision negotiations as having a definite beginning and ending. Actually, there is usually no rigidly fixed time frame. However, since most concessions are made just before a perceived deadline, remaining calm and focused right to the "end" can help you feel less pressured to conclude a deal "on time." This was the North Vietnamese delegation's "ace in the hole" when dealing with U.S. negotiators, who wanted dearly to end the conflict. The Vietnamese did have a deadline, but their nonchalant posture and eagerness to question even the most trivial matters, made their deadline seem almost infinitely flexible—and they were very successful.

Remember, *"deadlines" are often more flexible than they may seem.* Granted, they should not be ignored, but they should be analyzed: "What will happen if I go beyond the deadline? What will be the extent of any penalty?" For example, if you owe taxes and file late, you will be penalized. However, obtaining a loan to pay the tax on time would be unwise, since the interest on the loan would probably be greater than the penalty.

INFORMATION

Information-gathering—appraising the reality of the situation—can avert the "crisis" response that often mars our performance when we enter a negotiation unprepared. It gives you a huge advantage in a negotiation to anticipate what the other side really wants, along with her perceived limits and deadlines. Secretaries, technicians, customers or competitors—past or present—who deal with your opposition can provide invaluable information.

Approaching Negotiations

There are two primary methods of negotiating: "win at all costs" (sometimes called the "Soviet" style) and "win-win."

The "Soviet" negotiator sees every negotiation as a struggle between winning and losing—and he wants to win. Several clues can help you distinguish a negotiator using this style. Commonly, he will:

- Initially take positions that are extreme.

- Claim limited authority—so that you wind up bidding not against him, but against yourself.
- Employ emotional tactics.
- Treat you in an adversarial, competitive manner.
- Presume that any concessions you offer are a sign of weakness.
- Remain stingy in offering his own concessions.
- Ignore deadlines.

When confronted by someone using these tactics, you have several options:

(1) Walk away; don't play the game and get out of the negotiation.

(2) Try to use these same tactics yourself.

(3) Seek to switch the negotiation to a collaborative, win-win encounter.

By contrast, the person using a win-win approach tries to produce *acceptable gains for both parties.* She regards conflict as a problem to be solved, an opportunity to uncover creative, enhancing positions. And when both parties are committed to a win-win approach—a style marked by mutual "trust" and empathy—you can get down to hammering out an agreement.

"Have you not learned great lessons from those who braced themselves against you?" asked Walt Whitman. Certainly, fair competition and opposition is what growth is all about. In fact, you are likely skirting negotiation and conflict—and not getting even close to what you want—if you have no opponents.

"Opposition comes in two forms: A. Idea opponents, and B. Visceral opponents." Dealing with idea opponents requires pooling of information, experience and feelings. You must start from a perception of trust and agreement on something, and build from there. Maybe a "repackaging" of issues can be done to meet individual needs, i.e. moving an employment discussion away from salary itself and talk over other forms of compensation (company car, profit sharing...).

A visceral opponent is much more difficult to deal with, since he deals on an emotional level and "not only disagrees with your point of view, but disagrees with you as a human being." Often, he wants to save face publicly as well as preserve his private self-image. How do you deal with him when he attacks you personally by calling you a fraud, a clown, a liar? (1) Don't let yourself care too much, and (2) Never overtly judge your opponent's actions or motives. For example, a child arrives home and casually informs you that she's been offered a marijuana cigarette. Your judgmental and "caring too much" response? "You what!..." This will only turn any candid discussion sour. Your overall *bearing,* tone of *voice,* conveyed *attitude,* bartering method, and the *concern* exhibited for the other side's feelings and needs, all combine to help you succeed or fail.

The first few minutes of a negotiation are the most vital. Start off by stating your case *moderately,* nonjudgmentally, and with the attitude that you still harbor some questions about your own position. Instead of "This place looks like a pig sty..." (when shocked by your child's room), or "Your analysis of these data is all wrong..." (in a business meeting), try: "When this room is not tidy I feel frustrated and upset" and "I must be looking at the data differently than you. I feel that..."

The next step is to *harmonize* or *reconcile needs.* Needs must be brought out into the open so free interaction and sharing can take place. Conflicts regarding past experience, present information, or decision-making authority must also be resolved.

Finally, with no hint of intimidation or manipulation—for in collaborative negotiation there is no need for conniving or flimflamming—you can arrive at a *compromise solution;* a solution that meets both your needs.

Cohen examines other issues that can either make or break a negotiation. He treats how to personalize negotiation, how to be a "squeaky wheel," and the advantages and disadvantages of telephone negotiations. He is convinced that each of us has the inner strength to negotiate successfully—from everyday job and family matters to formal across-the-table corporate scale bargaining. The secret lies in detecting what the other side wants, and then showing him that you can help him obtain it, while still preserving your own goals and integrity. Power, Time and Information are the recognized keys to negotiating with authority.

Zig Ziglar's Secrets of Closing the Sale

by Zig Ziglar, Fleming H. Revell Company, 1984

Using many entertaining stories and examples, one of America's master salesmen—and most proficient persuaders—reveals his secrets and techniques for "closing" a sale.

The Psychology of Closing

"This is not a book on psychology," Ziglar begins, "but I can absolutely guarantee you that you're going to have to know some psychology (or common sense) if you're going to be a truly professional salesperson." The underlying logic of the book is contained in the author's conviction that *"you can get everything in life you want if you will just help enough other people get what they want."*

When a prospective customer says no, Ziglar points out, the odds are at least a hundred to one that you will not get him to change his mind. After all, people just hate to admit they were wrong the first time. When the prospect initially says no, you need to get him or her to reevaluate and make another decision based on *new* information. The prospect may still not change his mind, "but he will be delighted to make a new decision based on new information."

A buyer of real estate, for example, might say, "Why didn't you tell me the property was outside the city limits and I won't have to pay city taxes?"—a sure sign that he or she is reevaluating the desirability of the property, and thus reevaluating his or her decision. The wise salesperson will then follow Ziglar's advice: *"...Try for the close as soon as you have established value or aroused desire for ownership, but before you give all the information."*

Using Your Voice

According to Ziglar, voice inflection may be the single most underdeveloped skill you need to cultivate in a professional sales career. He suggests that you develop your voice by tape-recording a single sentence until you can—by mere inflection—arrive at eight distinct, separate meanings. For example:

(1) "I did not say he stole the money." That's a simple factual statement; you are denying

that you made the accusation.

(2)"**I** did not say he stole the money," implies that the accusation was made, but by someone else.

(3)"**I DID NOT** say he stole the money," is a vigorous denial that you accused him.

(4)"I did not **SAAYY** he stole the money," hints that you might have implied it, but you didn't say it.

(5)"I did not say **HE** stole the money," suggests that someone other than the accused stole the money.

(6)"I did not say he **STOLE** the money." Here you hint that the accused might have only "borrowed" the money.

(7)"I did not say he stole **THE** money," implies that he might have stolen some but not THE money. and

(8)"I did not say he stole the **MONEY**," intimates that he might have stolen something but certainly not the money.

Once the groundwork is laid, then you can begin to develop on tape an effective sales presentation. Ziglar recommends that you save the first recording. You will see, he promises, "a definite improvement in the recording—and more importantly, in the sales results."

The Heart of Your Sales Career

"Selling is essentially a transference of feeling," Ziglar says. "If I (the salesman) can make you (the prospect) feel about my product the way I feel about my product, you are going to buy my product, if there is any way in the world you can come up with the money."

However, Ziglar warns, "in order to transfer a feeling, you've got to have that feeling." Personal commitment to the product, then, is of the utmost importance: few people can persuade another person to buy a product when they don't believe in it themselves. Indeed, if possible, you should own the product yourself, and use it. If you *can* afford the product but haven't bought it, then you probably shouldn't try to sell it: your own lack of enthusiasm is likely to be apparent.

Enthusiasm for the product goes hand-in-hand with positive thinking. Although positive thinking won't make you a superman, it will help you do everything better. Ziglar writes: "I don't...believe I could take out your appendix and have you live. But this I know: if you and I were isolated on a desert island a thousand miles from everybody and you were to suffer an attack of appendicitis, I personally believe you would prefer I approach you with a winning attitude!...[I might say] 'I have an extremely sharp knife with me and some powerful medicine that will kill all the infection...Personally I believe that despite my lack of training I can get your appendix out of there, and I just flat believe you're going to make it!'" Such a positive approach, Ziglar points out, would be far more appealing than "looking you in the eye and saying, `Man, you're gonna die!'"

A positive approach is critical to increasing sales. If you feel positive about your product, your company, your supervisor, your city, and your family, and are able to talk enthusiastically about it wherever you go, then you are going to be a much more effective salesperson.

In my travels I see people in every walk of life selling every conceivable product, from ten-cent whatnots to multimillion-dollar computers. Regardless of the company, industry, or section of the country, some are doing extremely well, some are doing fairly well, and

some are going broke. The business is there for all but, everything else being equal, the salesperson with a good self-image and positive mental attitude will get more than his share of business, and the salesperson suffering from 'stinkin thinkin' will get a much smaller share.

The Sales Professional

Ziglar asks, "Do you respond or react?" *Responding,* he indicates, is "positive," while *reacting* is not. If you "respond" to a doctor's prescription, for instance, that's a good sign; if you're "reacting" to it, that's not! In sales, you want customers to *respond* to your presentation or product, not merely "react" to it.

Ziglar concedes that not everything you encounter in the world of selling—or the world in general—is going to be positive. For instance, probably 99 percent of all salespeople have been stood up for a sales appointment. The way you *handle* the rejection, however, makes all the difference between failure and success.

My brother, Judge Ziglar, who broke the national sales record at that time for the Saladmaster Corporation in 1964 by selling over $104,000 worth of cookware, had a most unique ***response*** *to broken appointments...On occasion, when he arrived at the appointed time, no one would be at home. Instead of* ***reacting*** *with dismay, despair, frustration, or anger, Judge* ***responded*** *by saying, "Oh, boy! That's a sure sale!"*

The next day at precisely the appointed hour for the day before, he would again appear at the door. When the host or hostess came to the door, Judge would immediately start with an apology. "I'm so sorry I missed you yesterday. I did everything in my power to see you, but it just wasn't possible." (He was being 100 percent honest. He had done everything in his power to see them. He had been there at the appointed time.)

Judge points out that you would be astonished at the number of grown people who would let him take the blame for their discourtesy. At that point, as he expressed it, he knew the sale was his. Here's why. If they did not have the courage to face him and say no at the appointed time, then they were not psychologically equipped to deal with a highly motivated, enthusiastic, well-trained professional salesman like him. By ***responding*** *with that attitude, it's not difficult to understand why he broke the record.*

The Nuts and Bolts of Selling

Objections, Ziglar maintains, are the keys to closing the sale. When prospects object to something, they are in effect demonstrating interest in the product.

I can state with considerable confidence that in most cases involving significant purchases, if you do not encounter objections from the prospect when you make your presentation, you do not have a prospect. When your prospect raises an objection you ought to grin internally and think to yourself, ***Oh, boy! I've got a live one today!*** *Just remember if all the benefits and values of your product were obvious to the prospect, the salesman (that's you) would not be necessary. Also remember that if everybody instantly bought your product, commission rates would drop dramatically.*

It is valuable to know that, while an objection may seem frivolous to you, it may be important to the prospect, especially if he or she raises it a second time. If the sale is to be made, it is critical for the salesperson to address these concerns with respect and honesty, and without intimidation or "high pressure."

...Some salesmen can be so persuasive and charming they can "hypnotize" their prospects into buying products, goods, or services which are not needed or are grossly overpriced. However, no salesman is so hypnotic in his presentation that he can ***keep*** *the prospect hypnotized and feeling good about the purchase until the product is delivered and paid for.*

Ziglar suggests that the best time to answer an objection is before it occurs.

If you are consistently getting the same objections after your presentation, it is a sure sign your presentation is in trouble. You need to analyze the presentation so you will be able to handle ***most*** *objections in the body of the presentation. This approach enables you to answer the objection before it occurs, which means you are selling on the offense instead of defensively reacting. This is far more positive and effective.*

Ziglar also urges salespeople to avoid taking objections to their products personally. If you can stay calm, he says, your chances of making a sale are greatly enhanced. Too many salespeople, Ziglar adds, take the attitude that a sale is a "win" for them and a "loss" for the prospect. When the salesperson forgets that he or she is there to *solve* a problem for the prospect or provide a *service,* then the presentation may as well be over.

Prospects Want to Say Yes

Ziglar believes that "prospects do not want to say no, because no is final and the prospect is just as eager to have his problem solved as you are to help him solve it." He also believes that "objections thrive on opposition but basically they die with agreement." It is vital, then, to avoid sounding like a lecturer when dealing with a prospect. If you can remember to answer objections with questions, then you will increase your chances of uncovering the prospect's motive for buying.

Summing up, Ziglar underscores the part played by emotions in a salesperson closing a sale:

...Just remember, the prospect...buys the future enjoyment of what you're selling, regardless of the product.He doesn't buy the house on the lot, he buys the shade of the trees in the yard; the warmth of the fireplace in the cold winter months; the convenience of the telephone in the bathroom. He buys the coolness of the evening on the lake, the exhilaration of the downhill skiing experience with his family, the joy of his motorboat on the lake, the luxury of the dip in the heated pool. Again, all of these are intangibles made possible by the tangible property which he's buying.

Swim with the Sharks

(Without Being Eaten Alive)

by Harvey Mackay, William Morrow and Co, 1988

Swim With the Sharks is a highly acclaimed and insightful look at what it takes to be successful in business. Harvey Mackay shares his ideas, secrets, and experiences on how to "outsell, outmanage, outmotivate, and outnegotiate your competition."

Mackay is a man known for making things happen. When the slumping Twins faced the possibility of being moved out of Minnesota, Mackay organized the campaign that kept them there, and later spearheaded the building of the Minneapolis Metrodome. At 26, Mackay bought a floundering envelope company for $200,000 and turned it into a 35-million-dollar-a-year business.

Most sales manuals emphasize selling yourself. This book does not, says Mackay, "because very often, my friend, you and I are lousy products."

Sharks is divided into 69 "lessons" and 19 "quickies." Here are samplings:

Short Course in Salesmanship

Marketing: If someone were to stand in front of a group, hold up a twenty-dollar bill, and try to sell it for one dollar, wouldn't most people be skeptical? We are programmed to think that there must be some kind of catch in such an offer. Good marketing doesn't depend on miracle deals; it aims at persuading others that they need your product.

Knowing the Customer: *"Knowing something about your customer is as important as knowing everything about your product."* The Japanese use the phrase, "Ready? Fire! Aim" to describe common American marketing practices. Americans tend to ignore the importance of proper marketing and public relations. "In order to supply something you must first create a demand." And to create demand you must understand your customers; their needs and their complaints. Develop an effective scenario: "Ready? Aim. Fire!"

Mackay's key to learning about customers is a 66-point questionnaire (the "Mackay 66") that must be filled out on each customer. Mackay was fully aware that sales people hate filling out forms. Hence, his questionnaire is short and to the point, but includes such details on customers as personal and family background, education, business background, special interests, and lifestyle. It ends with a section called "The Customer and You," designed to profile the customer's loyalties and ethical positions.

Children learn at an early age to wait until their parents are in a good mood to hit them for "whatever the market will bear." The same is true of sales. *Timing is everything.* When one of Mackay's customers has a birthday, she not only gets a card but is also taken to lunch. Mackay's salespeople make in commissions more than twice the average for their industry. He attributes this to his company's knowledge of customers.

The Salesman's Job: It's a customer's "job" to be suspicious and cynical about the product you are offering. "It's your job as a salesperson to neutralize these feelings so your product can get the fair hearing it deserves."

Soliciting Referrals: Most salespeople have heard of the 80/20 rule: Twenty percent of your customers provide eighty percent of your business. If suppliers depend on you for a substantial part of their business, then chances are they will feel a sense of loyalty towards you and your company. These suppliers can be a major source of referrals. They are the "second best place to look for business."

Hard, Smart Work: People in sales must be willing to work hard. Mackay quips: "I've known successful sales people who were drunks, gamblers, liars, and thieves... but I have never known a successful sales person who sat on his ass all day." Remember, it is the investment of your time in terms of availability and customer service that keeps accounts.

Preparing and Impressing for Success: While calling on tough prospects is never easy, some things can make it easier. First, find out all you can about your potential client. Second, be thorough. Send a letter stating your purpose for wanting to meet with him. Then phone to set up your meeting, referring to the earlier letter. Last, follow up with a note on the day of the meeting. Even if you don't immediately get the account, if you are in "second place" in the minds of several key decision makers, there will always be some "first place" people messing up—and you'll be there, ready to step in.

Mackay's "personalized" approach for contacting prospective clients begins with a conversation with the secretary:

Hello. Angela? I'm Harvey Mackay, President of Mackay Envelope Corporation. [Straight to her brain. Who is this guy? How does he know my name? Have I met him?] *I've written Mr. T.P. within the past two weeks, and now I'm calling him from Minneapolis. I would like to see Mr. T.P. for exactly three hundred seconds. I will go as far as... Sri Lanka just for the purpose of seeing him for those three hundred seconds. And if I take any longer, I'll donate five hundred dollars to T.P.'s favorite charity...which I believe is the Boy Scouts, isn't it?*

When you've done your homework, when you've looked up your prospect in *Who's Who* and done some reconnaissance with his suppliers, then you know you're right. And what an impression it makes!

Getting the Sale: How does Mackay handle the meeting he has arranged? He speaks straightforwardly:

As you may know, we're bidding on your contract. I just came here to tell you, as president of Mackay Envelope, that...if we are fortunate enough to receive your business, I'll take a personal interest in seeing to it that you will receive the service and craftsmanship you have every right to expect.

Setting Goals: If you don't have a destination you'll never get there. Set goals.

Short Course in Negotiation

• "Smile and say no until your tongue bleeds" is Mackay's most valuable negotiating advice. That saying is based on the premise that if you can say no with a smile, your deals will improve.

• One of the most forceful negotiating devices you have is walking away from the table without a deal. If the other party knows you have to settle a deal by a particular deadline, then all they have to do is set their terms and wait until the deadline arrives. Don't let them know your secrets.

• Make "heady"—not "heart-y"—decisions. "Make decisions with your heart and what you'll end up with is heart disease."

• One way to get a feel for a deal without "showing all your cards" is to "send in the clones." Hire someone—a ringer, if you will—to go in with a verbal offer to see how firm an asking price is. Such an arrangement can give you cheap information that you could get in no other way.

• "There is no such thing as a sold-out house." In negotiating for an "all booked up" hotel room, Mackay says to the reservations clerk:

...I know, and you know, somebody out of those five hundred people isn't going to show up....So all I'm asking is...that you put my name on the top of the waiting list....I'm sending the money in advance...

• You can buy or sell anything "if you can get the other side of the table to see how the deal works to their advantage." Gaining customer information and giving confident perceptions sums up good negotiating technique.

Short Course in Management

• The biggest mistake a manager can make is not knowing *when to stay out of the way.* As a former chairman of Tenneco counseled: "Knowing when to get the hell out of the way [is] the hardest part, but that's the one that will make you rich."

- The speed with which you get bad news is a reliable gauge of what kind of manager you are. "Nobody wants to be the bearer of bad tidings, because that triggers the kill-the-messenger syndrome." So, it is the manager's responsibility to *encourage bad news*, because faulty concerns left unchecked get worse.
- "Efficiency, achieved at the cost of creativity, is counterproductive." We should encourage our people to *spend time thinking*. Time spent in creative pondering is more effectively used than time spent in most other activities.
- You can spot a winner by the quality of people surrounding him or her. Winners don't need "yes men." They are big enough to let other winners act for them.
- People make mistakes. "The best way to chew someone out is to have them do it themselves." Mackay is notorious for summoning a worker to his office, letting her stew in the waiting room for a while, then inviting her in, giving her his own chair, and asking her what she would feel and what she would say about her own performance if she were in Mackay's position. The employee is usually harder on herself than Mackay would have been.
- *Knowing the competition* is almost as important as knowing the customer. A "competitor questionnaire" (much like the one for customers) might be designed. Know, analyze and compare each competing firm, then decide what it will take to beat the competition and improve your own business.
- Knowing when to take it easy is as important as knowing when to work.

Some Final *Swim With the Sharks* "Quickies"

- *Utilize the public library.* It is the best and most convenient research facility.
- *Have confidence in yourself.* "Humility is the most overrated of human emotions."
- *Write things down.* Don't waste your energy remembering information you can just as easily look up.
- *Fly first class.* That's where you'll meet valuable contacts.
- *Maintain the illusion of demand.* On one occasion, hundreds of Twins season tickets were cancelled when the team was on a losing streak. Management didn't panic. Instead they ran a blind ad: "Leaving town. Four season tickets for sale." The response was overwhelming; the cancelled tickets were all resold.
- *Keep in touch with your mentors.* They are the ones that got you to where you are.
- There is always a place in the world for the person who says, *"I'll take care of it."*

MANAGING CONFLICT

He had been hand-picked by Steven Jobs, the company's founder, to become Apple Computer's president and CEO. But soon after his arrival, John Scully began to disagree sharply with Jobs about Apple's strategic direction. Jobs tried to outflank Scully by gaining board support for firing him; but, even though Jobs was Apple's largest stockholder, the board backed Scully, who, as president, removed Jobs' operating authority. Within six months Jobs cut all ties to Apple Computer.

Conflicts like this capture the headlines. But conflicts of lesser proportions are a daily reality for every man and woman who holds a job, and particularly for managers, who are expected to resolve the conflicts.

Two Approaches to Conflict

Tradition has it that conflict is bad; it's something to be avoided. Experts during the 1940s and 50s believed that conflict arose from interpersonal problems, and that the resolution of these problems would lead to improved work performance. Most of us still cling to the idea that good managers *resolve* conflicts.

Current thinking disputes this view. Contemporary perspective holds that conflict can actually be a positive force at work if it is managed skillfully. Experts now speak in terms of *Conflict Management.* Not only is conflict seen as a natural outgrowth of human interaction, but certain types of conflict are considered desirable.

In the absence of conflicting opinions, harmonious, tranquil work groups are prone to becoming static, apathetic and unresponsive to pressures for change and innovation. They also risk the danger of becoming so self-satisfied that dissenting views—which may offer important alternative information—are shut out. The world came the closest it has ever come to nuclear war for this very reason. President John F. Kennedy and his advisors had become very insular from the onset of the Cuban Missile Crisis. They had spurned outside information, heeding only those opinions consistent with their own. Historians subsequently discovered that these top decision makers operated with some wildly inaccurate information that needlessly inflamed the situation.

A Conflict Model

Ken Thomas, an influential conflict theorist and writer, has developed a useful model to assess conflict-handling styles. It starts by recognizing that any conflict situation is held in balance by two opposing factors:

(1) *The degree to which each participant wants to satisfy his own concerns (assertiveness).*

(2) The degree to which each wants to satisfy the other's concerns (cooperativeness).

When placed at right angles on a grid, these opposing forces can be used to structure five primary conflict-handling styles. (Each managerial style is charted by plotting independent trajectories from the horizontal and vertical axes.):

1. Competition

When one party struggles to achieve his or her goals regardless of the impact on other parties involved, the conflict is handled by competition and dominance. These familiar "*Win-Lose*" conditions occur when one party prevails only at the other's expense. Organiza-tional gamesmen using Competition frequently call the formal authority system into play, seeking the support of organizational "power players" who will help them dominate their opposition. Notice that this style is high on the assertiveness scale and

Choice of Conflict-Handling Styles

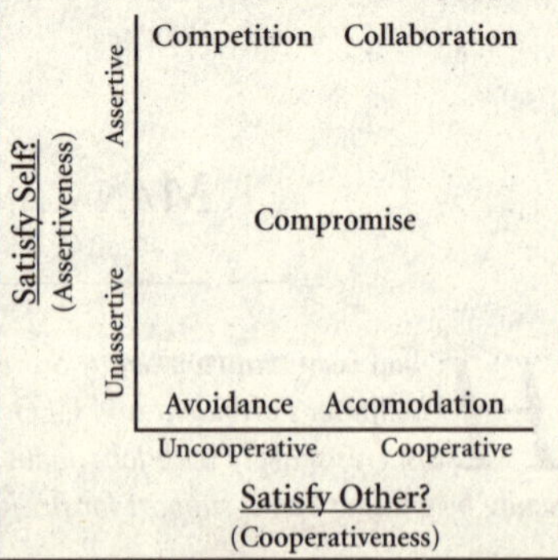

low with respect to cooperation.

2. Collaboration

When both conflicting parties work to satisfy each others' concerns, the style becomes one of Collaboration. Searching for a mutually beneficial outcome, both individuals or groups *emphasize solving the problem* by (1) sharpening the understanding of where differences lie, (2) generating as many alternatives as possible, and, only then (3) selecting a solution that fits both sets of concerns. Since the desired solution is advantageous to both parties, this is referred to as a "*Win-Win*" approach. Collaboration is a frequent tool of marriage counselors and labor mediators, who keep each side generating alternative solutions until an acceptable one is found.

3. Avoidance

By far the most frequent response, Avoidance occurs when one or both parties simply *withdraw from or suppress the conflict.* People avoid the problem either out of simple indifference to the outcome or because they feel inadequate to deal with it. If withdrawal is not possible, one or both parties may suppress the conflict, keeping it simmering just below the surface of everyday interaction, where it waits for the right (or wrong) moment to break through.

4. Accommodation

This style comes into play when one party is prepared to appease the other—to give them what they want—with little or no regard for personal concerns. This is generally done in the spirit of *self-sacrifice*, the Accommodator's sacrifice being made willingly because any perceived negative outcomes are deemed acceptable; he or she can live with them. Accommodation may take the form of a manipulated parent "giving in" to his whining and pouting child. In the very noblest situations, however, one party will—not only in a spirit of sincerity but also by way of well-grounded logic—place the other's welfare above his or her own, and suffer genuine change or genuine distress as a result.

5. Compromise

When each party in a conflict agrees to give something up in order to get something in return, Compromise, a "*give and take*" style, is in effect. There are no clear winners and losers with this approach; rather, there is (1) a rationing of the object of conflict (where the object is divisible, like sums of money), or (2) a reward yielded by one party to the other in return for concessions granted. Union-Management negotiations frequently take the Compromise approach, as concessions from one side of the table are mated with concessions from the other in order to reach an agreement.

Using the Model

The great usefulness of this model lies in its ability to define and describe a *variety* of ways to manage conflicts. No one style is appropriate in all business circumstances. Pity the Industrial Relations Manager, for example, who uses Avoidance at the bargaining table...or the Corporate Director of Purchasing who exclusively uses Competition to solve problems among his division executives.

But, while the freedom to choose among conflict-handling styles is attractive (and, indeed, always available to us), research indicates that most of us have a single *preferred style* of handling conflicts. We often fail to regard each conflict we come up against as separate; as requiring an individualized solution. This means that without conscious attention to the model and the options it offers, the likelihood is that we will use the same well-worn style across all situations—often inappropriately.

The following list, summarized from Ken Thomas' article entitled "Toward Multidimensional Values in Teaching: The Example of Conflict Behaviors" (*Academy of Management Review,* July 1977), indicates situations where each different conflict-handling style may be the best choice:

Competition

1. When quick, decisive action is vital.
2. On important issues where unpopular actions must be implemented.
3. Against people who take advantage of non-competitive behavior.

Collaboration

1. To find an integrative solution, when both sets of concerns are too important to be compromised.
2. To merge insights from people with different perspectives.
3. To gain commitment by incorporating the concerns of other parties.

Avoidance

1. When the issue is trivial, or when more important issues are pressing.
2. When the possible disruptions outweigh the benefits of resolution.
3. When other people or future scenarios may be able to resolve the conflict more effectively.

Accommodation

1. When issues are more important to others than to yourself; to satisfy others and maintain their cooperation.
2. To stockpile social credits for later use.
3. To minimize loss when you're outmatched and losing.

Compromise

1. When opponents of equal power are committed to mutually exclusive goals.
2. To achieve temporary settlements on complex issues.
3. To achieve expedient solutions under time pressures.

As leaders, spouses, parents, group members or friends, we encounter the challenge of conflict many times daily. Recognizing and practicing the various approaches to dealing with these conflicts is an essential skill for all of us to master.

Maintaining Job Satisfaction

Are American workers satisfied with their jobs? According to Stephen Robbins, author of the popular management text *Organizational Behavior,* "The answer to this question...is a resounding 'Yes!'" Robbins writes that, based on employee surveys, about 8 out of 10 people say they're satisfied with their jobs. Older workers are most satisfied (92% for those age 65 and over), but figures are impressively high for young people as well (73% for those age 25 and younger). Still, says Robbins, other research demonstrates that only 41% of white-collar employees would again choose to enter their current occupation, and the statistic is only 24% for blue-collar workers.

Satisfaction varies by profession: urban university professors (93%) and mathematicians (91%) rate high, while textile workers (31%), unskilled steelworkers (21%), and unskilled auto workers (16%) are at the low end of the spectrum.

So, how do we account for these disparities? What makes an employee resign from her job? Why is it that one, seemingly disgruntled employee will stay on with a company for decades, while another, apparently content worker will decide to move on after only a few months? What is considered the ideal work setting?

"Job satisfaction" is a very complex matter, comprised of many elements and dimensions that are not easily captured by a simple questionnaire. However, job satisfaction is an important issue to managers for at least three reasons: (1) There is unmistakable evidence linking job dissatisfaction to high absenteeism and turnover; (2) It has been demonstrated that satisfied employees are healthier and live longer lives; and (3) Satisfaction at work carries over to the employee's life away from work.

Managers clearly need to understand the mechanics of job satisfaction and how best to encourage it among their employees.

Job Satisfaction: What Is It?

Job satisfaction is actually a bundle of concrete elements that coalesce into an *attitude* the employee holds about his or her job. Management writers speak of the "A-B" relationship—that is, "Attitudes affect Behavior." The professional manager is well advised to pay attention to the attitudes circulating among employees; auto executives who struggled through the crisis of low morale in their organizations during the 1970s will attest to this fact.

Jobs themselves are more than the actual tasks that define them. Jobs also require interaction with co-workers, are encircled by organizational policies and politics, demand adherence to company or work unit procedures, have performance standards to meet, exist in certain working conditions, and so on. The employee's overall sense of job satisfaction is a subjective tally of his or her reactions to many factors. Instruments designed to measure job satisfaction typically gauge the following core elements:

- *Nature of the work.* Do the requirements and benefits of the job fit the employee's personality, family and social lifestyle, financial needs, growth potential, etc.?
- *Nature of the supervision.* Does the job demand that the worker perform without constant supervision; or, on the other hand, is he suited to the pressures of close scrutiny? Are both supervisor and employee flexible enough to get along?
- *Present pay, and pay in relation to other jobs.* Does the employee feel that his salary is consistent with job difficulty, expected training and education, experience or expertise, and in line with other workers—inside or outside the company—who effectively perform the same task?
- *Promotion opportunities.* Within the company, is there a very real possibility of being promoted to a more prestigious, better paying level? Are the pay and perquisites that go along with advancement worth the hassles of increased responsibility?
- *Relationships with other employees.* Is the worker respected and valued by her peers, both as a fellow employee and as a person?

These seemingly straightforward elements actually comprise an intricate, ever-fluctuating, hard-to-decipher composite picture of job satisfaction.

What Affects a Worker's Job Satisfaction?

Research shows that job satisfaction is heightened or diminished according to how certain important contingencies are dealt with in the work environment. The following is a summary of the most significant variables.

Mentally Challenging Work

Most employees prefer work that allows them to *use and improve their skills and abilities.* They seek a job that offers a variety of tasks and that permits some *autonomy* in decision making. They also like to receive *feedback* on how well they're doing. The presence of these characteristics produces challenging work; their absence, a boring eight-hour day.

Equitable Rewards

Employees want pay systems they perceive as *fair, unambiguous,* and in line with their expectations. They form expectations by measuring their own work against other work in the company (or work unit, or community, or industry), comparing pay rates, and making a subjective assessment of fairness: "Compared to senior programmers and their compensation, I'm paid about right for what I do."

The key to linking pay systems with job satisfaction lies in understanding that only the employee's *perception* of fairness counts in attitude formation. Perceptions can be changed, of course, but managers should approach them as subjective "facts" at first.

Supportive Working Conditions

Working conditions make a difference—it's really that simple. Employees prefer working environments that are *safe* and *comfortable;* temperature, light, noise, smoke control and other environmental factors should be monitored and appropriate. In a larger sense, the working conditions established by a firm communicate a message to its employees: "Here's what we think of you..."

Most people prefer to work relatively close to home, in clean, modern facilities, and with adequate tools and equipment. Contrast, for example, the feelings of a claims clerk who works in hot, cramped surroundings with old typewriters, versus those of a clerk in a modern, air conditioned office that supplies state-of-the-art computers and color monitors.

Constructive Co-worker Relationships

People work for more than money—much more. For most of us the workplace is also an important source of *social interaction,* a place where we receive *validation* as worthwhile people and form long-lasting personal relationships. A work environment with friendly and supportive colleagues contributes to job satisfaction.

Not surprisingly, management behavior is the key determinant in how well employees work together. A manager's responsibility is two-fold: (1) The manager is a *leader* of his or her immediate work group, setting the *tone* for interaction and creating *expectations* regarding acceptable conduct; and (2) The manager is also a *member* of this network of relationships, *interacting* with each employee in either a constructive or destructive way.

Managers can create high job satisfaction when they:

- Are understanding, friendly, and approachable.
- Set clear performance objectives.
- Praise good performance when it is demonstrated.
- Show personal interest.
- Genuinely listen to employee opinions.

What Will Having a Satisfied Employee Buy Me?

Many occupational studies have tried to assess the satisfaction-to-performance linkage. In general terms, findings indicate that satisfaction and productivity are positively related: *the higher the level of job satisfaction, the greater the productivity.* This finding, however, has a number of complex variables that moderate the connection. Upper level employees, for example, are free of the constraints imposed on the machine-paced assembly line worker; consequently, they are better able to demonstrate the effects of satisfaction on performance.

It has also been shown that higher job satisfaction is positively connected to *attendance at work;* but here, too, a number of intervening factors can skew the statistical picture.

In addition to performance and attendance, the third major benefit of job satisfaction involves *turnover*. And, just as common sense would suggest, satisfied employees do tend to stay with a company longer than dissatisfied ones. The connection of job satisfaction with turnover, in fact, is the strongest and most direct of these three.

What job satisfaction attitudes permeate your workplace? Are employees happy with what they do, the facilities, their associates and the rewards connected with their jobs? Knowing and acting on these determinants of satisfaction can lead to greater efforts and effectiveness in worker performance.

Incentives for Productivity

Lincoln Electric is a ninety-year-old company that may be shedding some light on the future. In 1907, the company started using an incentive compensation program with its employees—most of them production line workers who turn out the company's mainstays, arc welding equipment and induction motors. The program's components are unique and effective:

1. Most workers are paid on a piece-rate basis, which means that there is no guaranteed base pay: if a worker is sick for a day, he or she takes home 4 days pay for the week.
2. Workers must repair defective machines on their own time.
3. Employees with over two years of service are guaranteed at least 30 hours of work each week.
4. Overtime is mandatory when orders are backed up.
5. Bonuses are given for teamwork, reliability, and productivity-enhancing suggestions.

At the heart of this management system is a framework that encourages *self-motivation.* Seniority carries little weight, and all employees compete on a merit basis for the few jobs that are not paid on a piece-rate basis. Interestingly, Lincoln's workers have averaged as much as $45,000 per capita earnings a year; further, they own over seventy percent of the company's stock. Turnover has averaged a low six percent per year, and the company hasn't had a layoff since 1951.

On the down-side, some Lincoln employees (and former employees) report that the working environment can be intensely competitive.

Incentives

The main purpose of incentives is to match pay with performance. While incentives can be complex and take many forms, the preceding chart presents four main classes of incentive programs: (1) Individual-based approaches; (2) Group-based approaches; (3) Profit sharing; and (4) Employee ownership. Most of these programs will be discussed here, but first consider some general principles that should be followed in establishing and maintaining any incentive system:

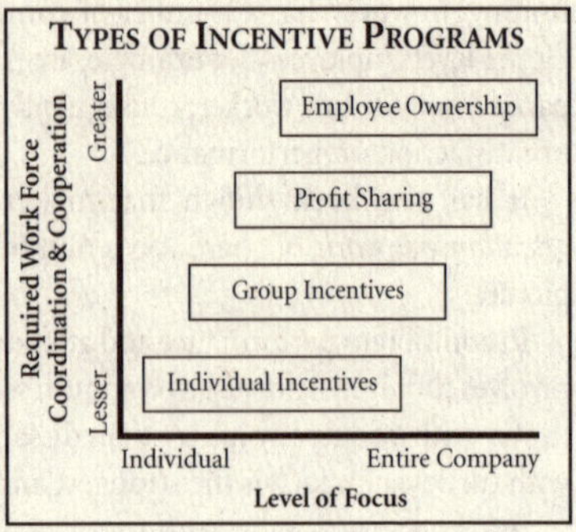

1. ***A Linkage With Performance:*** All incentive programs should tie pay as closely as possible to desired performance. Employees must see a direct relationship between their efforts and their rewards.

2. ***Recognition of Individual Differences:*** People are not all alike, and different people will value different rewards. A variety of appealing incentive programs may have to be developed.

3. ***Recognition of Organizational Factors:*** Incentives have to "fit" the structure, strategy, culture and financial resources of the organization. It is inconsistent, for example, to install a program that requires a high degree of employee participation into a tightly controlled bureaucracy.

4. ***Continuous Monitoring:*** Conditions in organizations change, and incentives need to be adjusted accordingly. New technology on the production line, for instance, may make a previously satisfactory system outmoded overnight. Programs should also be reviewed on a regular basis to ensure they are performing as planned.

Incentives For Individuals

The most basic individual-level incentive is the **piece-rate** system, in which wages are determined by multiplying the number of units produced by the piece-rate for a single unit. A variant of this, the **differential piece-rate** system, builds on the concept by paying employees one piece-rate wage if they produce less than a standard output, and a higher piece-rate wage if they produce more than the standard. The object in this latter case is to encourage workers to produce up to and beyond a pre-set output standard.

Despite their simplicity and incentive value, piece-rate systems are difficult to use in many cases, because the output standards for some jobs are difficult and costly to determine, or because the employee has no control over the number of units produced. For example, paying a bank teller for transactions processed would be inappropriate since the employee has little control over customer traffic.

Commissions are computed as a percentage of sales in units or dollars. There are two common computation methods: (1) ***Straight commissions,*** where the employee receives a percentage of the sales made; and (2) ***Salary-plus-commissions,*** which offer the employee both the stability of a salary and the incentive value of a commission (a common split being 80% salary, 20% commissions for the total compensation package). A national survey reports that about 21% of all sales representatives are paid through commissions only, while over 50% are on a salary-plus-commissions system.

Bonuses are frequently used as incentives at the executive level, although they can be used at lower levels too. Bonuses are organizationally attractive because they provide additional employee income when profits are up, and defer this expense when times are hard. Because of the broad nature of executive-level duties, most traditional bonus systems tie monetary or other rewards to overall corporate or divisional performance. But the same concept can easily apply to smaller groups—or to a total workforce.

Group Incentives

Incentives for groups are a direct result of the growing number of complex jobs requiring *interdependent* effort. Small-group incentive plans can encourage teamwork and enhance overall productivity where interdependence is required. The mechanics of group incentives are similar to those of individual-based plans—piece-rate, commission, and bonus systems. But when considering this approach, two conditions should be considered: (1) Do the tasks require significant *coordination?* and (2) Is the *group size* small?

If the answer to both questions is "yes," then a group incentive system may be appropriate; otherwise, use an individual or organization-based strategy. Most experts agree that group size should be kept under ten for best results from a group incentive plan. And, again, a pattern of interlocking, interdependent tasks is crucial.

Organizational Incentives

Organization-wide incentive systems compensate all employees based on how well the organization, as a whole, performs during a given period. One year at Kodak, for example, 93,000 employees shared $254.3 million in "wage dividends." Individual amounts were determined in part by seniority; the average check was $2,730.

Generally, such plans are most effective when all employees—exempt and non-exempt—are included. Some of the more significant organizational programs are described below.

Improshare (Improved Productivity Through Sharing) is similar to a piece-rate plan, except that it *rewards all company employees.* Input is measured in hours, output in physical units, and bonuses are distributed weekly when a discretionary standard is exceeded.

The Scanlon Plan rests on the premise that *efficiency depends on teamwork and plant-wide cooperation.* It offers two main features: (1) A setup of interdepartmental committees to hear and review cost-saving suggestions, and a separate screening committee which evaluates suggestions presented; (2) A direct incentive for all employees to improve efficiency. Incentive rewards are paid to employees based on pre-established ratios. Common ratios that are used include "labor costs to total sales," "total production," and "total hours to total production." Savings due to differences between *actual* and *expected* ratios are split between employees and the organization.

Profit sharing, as its name implies, distributes a *percentage* of the organization's profits to employees. Southland Corp., the holding company of 7-Eleven, shares 10% of its pre-tax profits with 50,000 employees at 7,000 store locations. Such programs foster within employees both cost-and profit-consciousness.

Linking an employee's earnings to his performance is paramount to improving that performance, and to cultivating overall productivity.

ALLEVIATING WORKER ALIENATION

Citibank recently introduced various programs and systems designed to combat employee alienation and enhance productivity. Among the measures implemented were: (1) Refined communication programs to facilitate and enhance workflow between the operations, marketing, service, and functional departments; (2) Decentralization measures to make it possible for individual employees to handle an entire transaction from beginning to end; and (3) Job redesign efforts to put employees performing a consumer-contact job in direct contact with their customers.

Leaders who implement measures like these recognize that *employee commitment* is a powerful force for growth in organizations, and that *worker alienation* is a ruinous form of corporate cancer. There are many forces and issues that bear upon the alienation—commitment factor in a company; but one of the most telling is the way jobs are designed. *The Job Characteristics Model (JCM)* includes research on how jobs should be designed. This model identifies the job characteristics that are powerful determinants of commitment, and charts their relationship to personal and work-related outcomes. The model may help the professional manager draw implications to fit the right job to the right person.

Core Dimensions

According to the JCM, any job can be described in terms of five core dimensions. They are:

1. Skill Variety: This refers to the number of distinct skills and activities required by the job, allowing an employee to use and improve on a number of his abilities. The owner-operator of a garage that services radiators, repairs automotive air conditioners, services electrical systems, rebuilds engines, and interacts directly with customers, has a high degree of skill variety. A body shop technician who sprays paint eight hours a day has low skill variety.

2. Task Identity: We know that people enjoy tasks that lead to a whole or complete piece of work. The assembly line employee in an automobile factory, who tightens the three bolts of the front bumper, car after car, day after day, has relatively low task identity; while the cabinet maker who designs a piece of fine furniture, builds it, and finishes it to perfection, feels considerably more identity with the product.

3. Task Significance: This describes the degree to which the job has direct perceived impact on the lives or work of others. It involves the sense of "making a difference," by contributing to the company, for example, or by doing jobs that directly benefit others. Among healthcare workers, for instance, doctors, nurses, therapists and social workers usually feel a high degree of task significance. By contrast, employees in hospital housekeeping, who sweep floors, are likely to sense less significance in their work.

4. Autonomy: Most people prefer jobs that offer a substantial amount of discretion and independence. However, the opposite of this ideal is what we find in the typical bureaucracy: job functions that are tightly constrained by regulations and policies, and supervisors whose task it is to see that employees abide by these formalized strictures.

5. Feedback: Ideally, the individual carrying out a task will receive clear, direct and timely feedback on his or her performance, as well as on the results of his or her actions. Again, for contrast, consider the stereotypic bureaucrat who shuffles papers all day with no direct knowledge of the actual impact of her actions. This worker has little feedback; while the electronics worker who assembles a radio and then tests it to find out if it operates properly, sees the direct effects of his work and learns immediately what he has done right or wrong.

The Model

The JCM predicts that the higher a given job ranks in the dimensions of Skill Variety, Task Identity, Task Significance, Autonomy and Feedback, the greater the employee's commitment to his job. Conversely, jobs that offer few of these elements will generate more worker alienation.

The model shown on the next page uses the concepts of the JCM to define the mechanisms of job commitment. This model introduces two ideas:

(1) The design of any job tends to induce certain *critical psychological states* among workers.

(2) Different people have different *growth-need strengths.*

The notion of a "psychological state" is just what it sounds like: Experiences encountered in daily living are processed cognitively and lead to certain states of mind. Studies supporting the JCM indicate that doing *meaningful* work is satisfying to people, as is a *sense of responsibility;* and knowing the *results* of one's actions completes an emotional as well as a cognitive circuit.

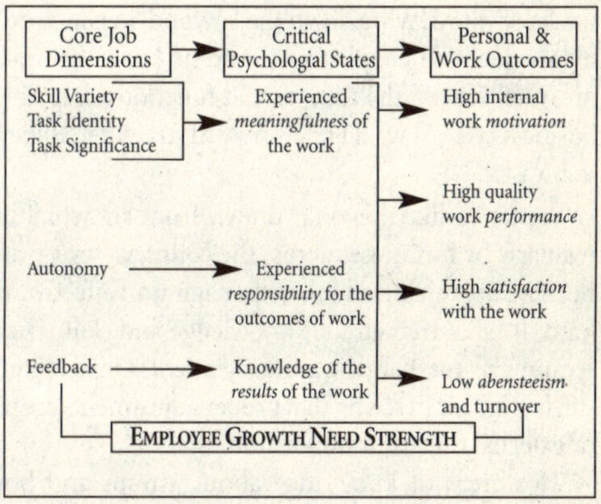

The idea of a "growth need strength" relates to the concept of "self-actualization"—that is, to the business of continually becoming a more fully functioning person. Psychologists suggest that growth (or "actualization")—the acquisition of increasingly refined skills and competencies in all areas of life—is basic to human nature. We grow when we learn to handle difficult relationship situations, solve challenging technical problems or deal with troubling emotions. But it can also be the case that circumstances in a person's life can truncate her "need" for growth, so that she remains stuck at the lower stages of actualization.

The JCM deals with the realities of the workforce and recognizes that different people will enter the workplace with differing levels of growth need, i.e. some people will actively seek challenging assignments, while others will be content to put in their eight hours. An employee's growth need strength modifies the impact of adjustments made to the left side of the model. Thus, employees who have a high growth need will respond to enriched tasks—those high in the core dimensions—more positively than those who have a comparatively low growth need.

Modeling human psychology and predicting behavior are tricky assignments at best.

The JCM helps narrow down the immense range of variables that impinge on employee behavior, and in so doing, makes itself subject to criticism from many sectors. But serious analysis supports the thrust of the JCM and leaves us with two safely drawn conclusions:

(1) People who work on jobs with high core job dimensions are generally more motivated, satisfied, productive and committed than those who do not.

(2) Job dimensions operate through psychological states to influence personal and work-related outcomes rather than influencing them directly.

Perhaps equally compelling is the fact that most corporate job design efforts have been organized around the JCM's basic principles for two decades or more—because they work. Great power can be tapped from a committed and motivated workforce.

Unlocking Your Workteam's Potential

It never fails," Bill muttered to the V.P. "Just when the crunch hits, the Division 3 sales team starts to pull in all directions at once. Nobody cooperates with anybody else, nothing gets done." Bill resigned himself to the fact that, once again, he would have to take time away from his own projects to march into another part of the office, spend two weeks or more laying down the law, and, in effect, do what he was already paying seven highly qualified people to do. And he knew that once they closed the quarter and the pressure was off, the team would function acceptably until the next busy part of their business cycle. "I wish I knew how to straighten things out once and for all," Bill thought to himself.

Scenarios like this one (drawn from an actual business situation) are played out regularly by businesses across the country—every day, every week, all year long. Why? Because organizing and then managing an effective, smooth, high-performing group is hard. It takes tremendous knowledge and skill. The initial organization of any group requires direct, hands-on management. Once organized, the group's leadership must still be vigilant in seeing that proper adjustments are made in response to internal change or external threats or opportunities.

Two areas of knowledge about groups and how they work have helped many managers become more effective. The first involves the stages of development that every group goes through, and the second addresses the individual roles that groups tend to divvy out in order to accomplish their work.

Stages of Group Development

Every group must pass through four distinct stages of development, resolving any number of important social and personal issues along the way, before it can function productively.

The Pre-Group Stage

Here, a number of independent, autonomous individuals exist within the corporate structure. They have no real ties to each other: no common goals, no common interests, no mutual dependencies. Six people who sit within ten feet of each other, day after day, without such ties, fail to constitute a group. A truly united group consists of two or more people who:

- Think of themselves as a unit, distinguishing members from outsiders.
- Share a common fate—that is, they're *interdependent.*
- Are identified by non-members as a group. In other words, they have a *group identity.*
- Have a *common goal.*

Stage 1: Forming

The first stage of group development is characterized by a great deal of *uncertainty* about the group's identity, purpose, structure and leadership. People literally "feel their way" and "test the waters" to determine what kinds of behaviors will be acceptable, what the norms are, what the personalities of those making up the group are like, and so on.

This stage is completed when people begin to think of themselves as part of a group.

Stage 2: Storming

This second stage involves inter-group conflict. People now know that they're included as members of a group, so the new key issue becomes "control": "Who's in charge here?" Groups must confront this issue of leadership. This can lead to either constructive outcomes or to a destructive spiral—a constant struggle for leadership positions.

Stage 2 ends when there is a relatively clear sense of hierarchy and leadership in the group.

Stage 3: Norming

During this stage, group members develop working relationships and a sense of cohesiveness. This cohesion is the result of norms that are explicitly or implicitly set by the members: "We work for an hour and then take a break." "Arguments are left out in the hall." "We'll follow an agenda in each meeting."

By this time there is a strong sense of group identity; and a set of expectations about who, what, where, when, why and how is shared by each member.

Stage 4: Performing

Now that each individual knows his or her place in the group, what to expect, what the rules are, and how problems are tackled, they are ready to function as one; they can go to work. Up to this point, their "work" has dealt more with group issues and solidifying the group's social infrastructure than with the assigned task.

In general, the closer a group comes to Stage 4, the more prepared it is to address work issues.

The important thing for managers to recognize is that *all groups go through these stages.* In fact, a well established *Stage 4* group will cycle through the first three stages every time it meets (though very quickly and with few or no hitches); and this same group can be thrown back to *Stage 2* ("Storming") simply with the introduction of a new member or the promotion of an established one.

Managers can facilitate a group's more rapid development by (1) making authority patterns clear, (2) articulating norms and expectations, and (3) being sure the group has a clear sense of its objectives.

Group Membership Roles

Accompanying the stages of group development is another important phenomenon:

a pattern of roles emerges. These roles are of three basic kinds: (1) *Task-Oriented,* (2) *Group Maintenance,* and (3) *Individual.* The interesting thing is that all groups develop this pattern of roles, and all members necessarily assume one or more functions in each new group interaction.

The following outline shows some of the more common roles and role behaviors observed in business groups. These come in three categories, depending on the particular personality and/or interest of the member:

<u>**Task-Oriented Roles**</u>

Initiator

Offers new ideas or suggests solutions to problems.

Information Seeker

Seeks pertinent facts or clarification of information.

Information Giver

Provides opinions, facts and information.

<u>**Group Maintenance Roles**</u>

Encourager

Promotes cohesiveness, warmth; praises and accepts others' ideas.

Harmonizer

Alleviates tensions; resolves intra-group disagreements.

Standard Setter

Raises questions about group goals; helps set and maintain group objectives and standards.

Follower

Agrees with others' ideas and emulates their actions.

Group Observer

Monitors group progress and operations; gives the group feedback on its performance.

<u>**Individual Roles**</u>

Blocker

Resists stubbornly; is negative; returns to issues already rejected by most group members.

Recognition Seeker

Calls attention to self by boasting; acts as if superior to others.

Dominator

Manipulates the group; interrupts others; looks for and gets attention.

Avoider

Remains apart from others; is passive and uninvolved.

Generally speaking, managers should try to create a balance between Task and Maintenance roles for their groups. A team composed solely of Initiators and Information Givers is a team in trouble: the focus is on the task at hand, but there will be no effort devoted to keeping the group alive and functioning. The converse is also true: exclusive concern with Maintenance roles will result in a happy and smoothly working team, but also a team without a task. In almost every case the Individual roles detract from group effectiveness, disturb the members, and lead to a downgrading of performance.

Working teams must be managed and molded to become effective. Wise management can facilitate a team's success by helping members through the stages of group development and working to strike a balance between Task and Maintenance roles.

ATTITUDES AT WORK

"That was a lousy way for him to treat Darryl. I don't think you should insult a foreman in front of his crew."

"Did you hear that the president of this place made over a million dollars last year? That's ridiculous!"

"I'll put in a day's work and take the paycheck. But don't expect any miracles coming out of my office."

"To me, the best boss is an invisible boss. I don't like anyone breathing down my neck."

Negative statements like these are a regular feature of organizational life. At one level, they are only opinions, but all these opinions reflect deep-seated *attitudes*—attitudes that often shape *behavior*. Because there's no escaping the fact that employees *have* attitudes, and because attitudes and behavior are usually closely related, managers need insight into what influences attitudes and what their impact is at work.

Attitudes: What Are They?

Attitudes are *valuative stances*—favorable or unfavorable—towards specific objects, people, issues or events. They reflect feelings and basic values.

How Are Attitudes Molded?

Attitudes are acquired throughout life from significant others: parents, teachers, friends, leaders, co-workers, etc. In our early years we begin to model attitudes after those we admire, respect, or perhaps, fear. This same process continues in later life (people adopt the behavior and attitudes of popular figures, cult heroes, national figures), though most adults also form attitudes by reasoning through the details of issues or events and responding according to their own personal values, desires, or fears.

Attitudes are unstable entities that can be molded and changed almost day-to-day. Advertising, for example, aims squarely at our attitudes, trying to alter them with the kind of glitz and appeal we see on TV. If an automobile dealer can get you to form a favorable attitude towards her product and dealership, that attitude may lead you to the car lot.

Why Are Attitudes Important?

Attitudes in organizations are important because they can affect job behavior. An employee may possess thousands of attitudes about innumerable topics and objects, but managers are concerned only with those that affect work performance. Three worker attitudes, in particular, have been scrutinized extensively: *job satisfaction, job involvement and organizational commitment.*

Job Satisfaction

An employee with high Job Satisfaction holds positive feelings about his work, while one with low Job Satisfaction is usually full of negative comments (attitudes)—and these are sure to show up on the job. Research reveals that Job Satisfaction is improved, generally, when workers have:

- Mentally *challenging* work
- Equitable *rewards* (as they perceive them)
- A *supportive* working environment
- Good working *relationships* with peers
- A good person-to-job *fit*

Studs Terkel, in his book *Working People Talk About What They Do All Day and How They Feel About What They Do* (Avon, New York, N.Y., 1975), graphically examines workers' attitudes:

...The automated pace of our daily jobs wipes out name and face—and, in many instances, feelings...

"I'm a machine," says the spot-welder. "I'm caged," says the bank teller...

Are these workers' feelings justified? Are corporate profits and governmental job security indeed more important than people? How can we get back in the habit of respecting men and women both for what they do and for what they are, bolstering their attitudes and that of the corporation as a whole?

Terkel concludes that, yes, there are "the happy few who find a savor in their daily job": *the Indiana stonemason, who looks upon his work and sees that it is good; the Chicago piano tuner, who seeks and finds the sound that delights; the bookbinder, who saves a piece of history; the Brooklyn fireman, who saves a piece of life...But don't these satisfactions...tell us more about the person than about his task? Perhaps. Nonetheless, there is a common attribute here: a meaning to their work well over and beyond the reward of the paycheck.*

Studies support the finding that high levels of Job Satisfaction lead to (1) increased productivity, (2) lower absenteeism, and (3) less turnover.

Job Involvement

This term is a recent addition to the manager's vocabulary. It is a measure of the degree to which a person *identifies* psychologically with his job, *"owns"* it, and considers it *important* to his self worth. An employee with a high level of Job Involvement, is "wrapped up" in the work and really cares about what he accomplishes and how well the task is done. High levels of Job Involvement have been found to correlate with fewer absences and lower resignation rates.

Organizational Commitment

While Job Involvement involves a worker's identification with her job, Organizational Commitment reflects her sense of identity with the entire organization and its goals. "Membership" in the organization or "affiliation" with the company are important to her.

As is the case with Job Satisfaction and Job Involvement, high levels of Organizational Commitment lead to, among other things, lower absenteeism and turnover rates. In fact, this factor seems to be a stronger predictor of work performance than either Satisfaction or Involvement.

The A-B Relationship

Attitudes affect behavior. People naturally seek harmony and consistency between their attitudes and behaviors. When one contradicts the other, they try to change either the attitude or the behavior so that the two are in alignment.

Suppose, for example, your friend has always argued that Americans should own American-made cars, because they're superior to imports and they're built by U.S. workers. Then suppose he inherits a Ferrari. His attitudes about foreign cars may suddenly change, or, alternatively, he may sell the car. But the fact remains that he'll experience considerable discomfort—what psychologists call "cognitive dissonance"—while he maintains the original attitude but acts in a contradictory way.

The "A-B" relationship is subject to some moderating variables, however. Research has uncovered at least three reasons or situations where disharmony between attitude and behavior may be tolerated:

(1) When the issues underlying the dissonance are of minimal importance;

(2) When the individual perceives the source of the dissonance to be externally imposed and not under his control;

(3) When rewards are sufficient to make living with the dissonance acceptable.

When one of these three situations is present, a person may very well live with incompatible or mismatched attitudes and behaviors, and the organizational ramifications can be significant. To illustrate, many otherwise honest employees don't think twice about taking home company-owned pens or paper; the matter is perceived to be of minimal importance. But in the same way, a valued accountant may take excellent care of his company's funds for years on end, but jump at the chance to embezzle a million dollars; to him, the potential reward seems worth the risks.

Managers should realize that attitudes can be shaped through *persuasion* (the employee becomes convinced of the attitude's worth) and *modeling* (the employee admires an attitude exhibited by others, and adopts it). Moreover, employee dissonance can be managed: workers may be asked to engage in behaviors that are inconsistent with their attitudes. The dissonant pressure can be lessened, however, when they perceive that it is externally imposed, is beyond their control, or the rewards are significant enough to offset their discomfort.

Involved, committed employees generally have good attitudes—and correspondingly high productivity. In determining the factors that most affect the behaviors of individuals in your company or organization, you would do well to observe closely their work-related behavior and periodically ask them about their feelings concerning the various requirements of their work.

DUAL-CAREER COUPLES

A career is a curious thing. It's something most of us think we merely "have." Yet, we are largely defined—outwardly and in self-worth—by our careers.

Careers can give us a sense of direction in life. But, at the same time, to the extent that we rely on career counselors and organizationally-defined career paths for guidance, we may be giving up our autonomy and self-direction—the very things most of us are seeking in the first place. Thus, our "work career" clearly shares the stage of a balanced, happy life with two other important elements: family involvements and the opportunities for self development.

Today's family structure, however, is not always so simply defined. With increasing numbers of women in the workplace, modern society has seen, not only the emergence of *dual-career couples* (marriages or relationships where both partners pursue important independent work—frequently in separate organizations, and occasionally in separate cities or on both coasts) but now *the majority* of couples come under this heading. Some concept of this more complex relationship is shown below in the Model of the Dual-Career Couple.

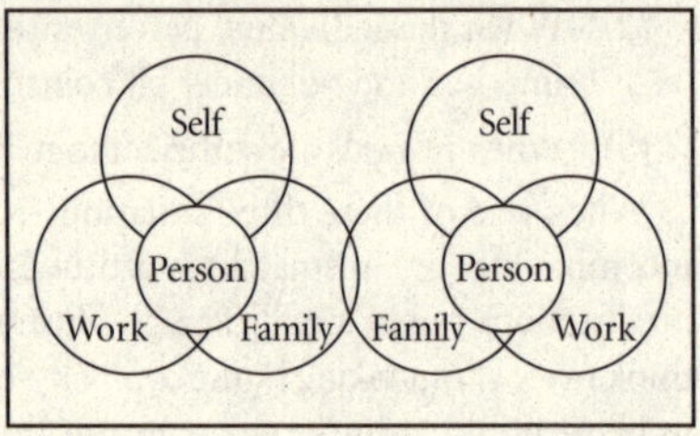

Such relationships, which consist of separate individuals who only overlap in their mutual relation in the family, and who have the added "detraction" of separate careers often pulling them in opposite directions, have the capacity of being potentially disruptive, or highly rewarding, depending on how the couples deal with them.

Dual-Career Relationships

The U.S. Bureau of Statistics reported in 1986 that 54% of all marriages were dual-career. Geographically, the leading areas of growth in this modern phenomenon are the West Coast, Denver, Chicago, New York and the Washington D.C.-Baltimore areas. Since 1970, the number of relationships where both partners are managers, professionals or technicians has doubled. The difficulties this poses for corporate transfers are obvious; these couples are far less mobile than their single-career counterparts.

Some companies, like Procter & Gamble and General Electric, require relatively few transfers for upward mobility. But in most organizations, a move is still the concomitant of advancement. IBM, for example, each year relocates three percent of its employees (some say the initials "IBM" stand for "I've Been Moved"). The Employee Relocation Council estimates that 600,000 annual moves involve dual-career relationships, and that one-half of all corporate transfers affect dual-career couples. The implications these figures have for companies lie primarily in the areas of succession planning and logistics, although scheduling and child care also pose challenges.

Absorption

Obviously, there is more than one model for dual-career relationships: different couples, like different individuals, integrate work into their lives in different ways. One of the main differences affecting dual-career relationships is the concept of *absorption*. A person is absorbed in his or her work to the degree that it takes the lion's share of time, energy and effort, leaving other areas of life correspondingly impoverished. A simple matrix helps to clarify the issues:

Q1: Classic Dual-Career Dynamics— In this quadrant fall relationships where both parties are pursuing their professions or work careers actively and aggressively. Both invest great time, effort and energy in their jobs. Everyday logistics—from coordinating child care and business travel, to simply putting a meal on the table—can result in major problems for these couples. Their mutual absorption in work can also cause headaches for their corporations; i.e. It may be impossible to recruit or transfer one without the other.

Person 1	Person 2: Highly Absorbed	Person 2: Not Absorbed
Highly Absorbed	Quardrant 1	Quardrant 2
Not Absorbed	Quardrant 3	Quardrant 4

Q2 & Q3: One Job, One Career—The more traditional form of relationship predominates in these two quadrants: one partner's work is considered central and important, the other's is considered peripheral and supplementary. One of the partners, with little career investment in the company and with transportable skills (secretarial, construction, etc.), may be readily willing to leave an employer when a spouse is transferred. These relationships experience far less career-related stress than those in quadrant 1, and they are also easier to deal with from the corporate perspective; i.e. It's generally harder to recruit or transfer a comptroller with a lawyer spouse than it is a comptroller and a secretary.

Q4: Two Jobs, Little Investment—Here we find two individuals neither of whom has a serious investment in his work; rather, they both emphasize other areas of life. There are many couples who passionately seek to keep their careers in harmony with their recreation, family, community, church, and so on. A relationship founded on this basis is less likely to encounter work-related stress, and the organizations involved will probably have an easier time managing assignments and transfers as well.

Meeting the Challenge

How do couples and companies cope with the problems inherent in dual-career relationships? The following tried-and-true techniques have proven helpful to many successful dual-career couples:

- ***Develop a joint commitment to both careers.*** Each person agrees to his or her partner's need and right to pursue a career.
- Work at ***becoming flexible***—at home and on the job. Each partner has to be willing to make adjustments and compromises in the interest of the other. This may mean that one of the partners may have to forego an advancement opportunity if it requires a move, which would disrupt the other's career plans. But it is also possible to opt into professions that have built-in flexibility; university professors and medical specialists have more flexibility in their career options than branch-bank managers, for example.
- Develop a number of coping mechanisms to help ***streamline and simplify*** the logistics of the partnership. Shopping for food only once a week can save time and energy for more important things. There may be a need to change priorities attached to particular activities like eating a certain type of meal at a certain time of day. Favorite television programs may of necessity be sacrificed. Both family and individual social calendars might have to be "trimmed." And both partners may chose to forego certain volunteer responsibilities.

• Finally, in order to enhance their careers as well as their marriage, each partner strives to ***develop career competencies***, such as self-assessment, collecting occupational information, goal setting, planning and problem-solving. This approach is necessary to facilitate their mutual career advancement.

SITUATIONAL LEADERSHIP

Choosing the Best Pattern That Matches the Circumstances

"Iacocca Pulls Chrysler Into The Future." "Sculley Leads Apple Turnaround." "How Does Bush's Executive Ability Stack Up?" "Lakers Win Due To Magic's Command of the Court." Newspaper headlines highlight leadership roles; management magazines are rife with tips, tactics and techniques having to do with leadership. Strong leadership is obviously critical to an organization's success.

Consider the company as a coordination-and-control mechanism: managers use various rules, policies, job descriptions, authority hierarchies and other devices to ensure that collective effort becomes something more than individuals working as isolated molecules. Good leadership, however, contributes to coordination and control in ways that formal mechanisms cannot. Leadership is alive and flexible—a dynamic part of daily organizational life.

A Situational Perspective

While all of us acknowledge leadership's importance, there is some debate about how best to go about the job of leading. A leader's moods, attitudes, behaviors, and resources change. So do those of his subordinates and superiors. *Situational leadership* theories stress that leaders work in complex settings where rules, players, problems and objectives can change from hour to hour. It's unlikely that any one tactic or style will fit all these changing conditions; and so the credo for situational theories is: "*There is no one best way.*" Rather, the "best" way is contingent on the situation.

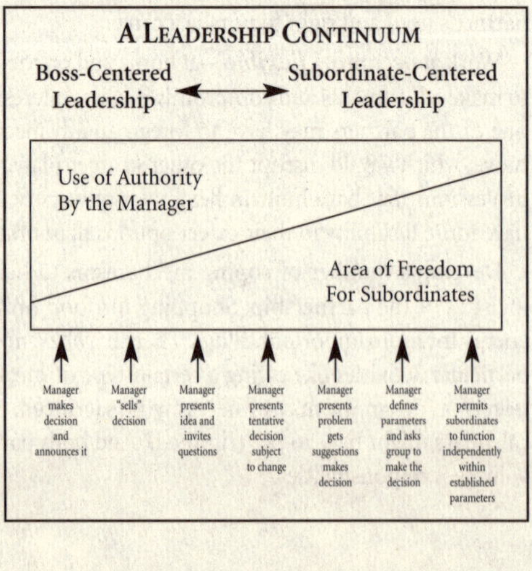

A Continuum of Style

Leadership can be defined as *the exercise of influence.* Business leaders are concerned with moving various organizational stakeholders (subordinates, peers, superiors, stockholders, government officials, etc.) toward company goals. The *Leadership Continuum* diagram presented here illustrates a variety of ways to do this.

At the extreme left of the chart we see that the leader can simply make decisions by fiat; at the extreme right, by delegating authority to subordinates; and toward the middle, by engaging in different forms of participative decision making. The diagonal line suggests the fact that leaders infuse their subordinates with the power to act only by relinquishing a portion of their own *direct* involvement. Note that it is only direct involvement that is given up; the leader's *total* influence on the situation may well be enhanced by inviting participation.

The Hersey-Blanchard Approach

Paul Hersey and Kenneth Blanchard have developed a leadership model that further depicts the spectrum of management styles. Their model has been used as a major training device by such *Fortune 500* firms as BankAmerica, Caterpillar, IBM, Mobil Oil and Xerox, and by all of the military services.

Leaders in this model can exhibit one of two basic types of behavior, depending on their objectives: *task-oriented* (emphasis on the technical or production aspects of the job, with goal accomplishment as the main concern), or *relationship-oriented* (emphasis on interpersonal relations).

The two critical situational variables identified in the Hershey-Blanchard Model are:

(1) The *willingness* of subordinates to do the work; a mixture of personal and professional commitment, motivation, drive, ego and fear of failure....

(2) The *ability* of subordinates to do the work; a mixture of individual knowledge, skills and aptitudes.

These variables, taken together, produce what the authors call the "Maturity Level" of subordinates.

Why this focus on followers? Because regardless of what the leader does, productivity depends on the actions and attitudes of her followers; it is they who accept or reject the leader and carry her strategies forward.

There are four stages of follower Maturity:

- **M1** people are both *unable and unwilling* to take responsibility for the work. They are neither competent nor confident.
- **M2** people are *unable but willing* to do the work. They are motivated, but currently lack the appropriate skills.
- **M3** people are *able but unwilling* to do what the leader wants.
- **M4** people are both *able and willing* to do what is asked of them.

As the Hersey-Blanchard curve indicates, *leaders should adjust their behavioral style according to the Maturity of their followers.* As subordinates reach higher levels of Maturity, the leader responds not only by decreasing direct control

HERSHEY-BLANCHARD LEADERSHIP MODEL

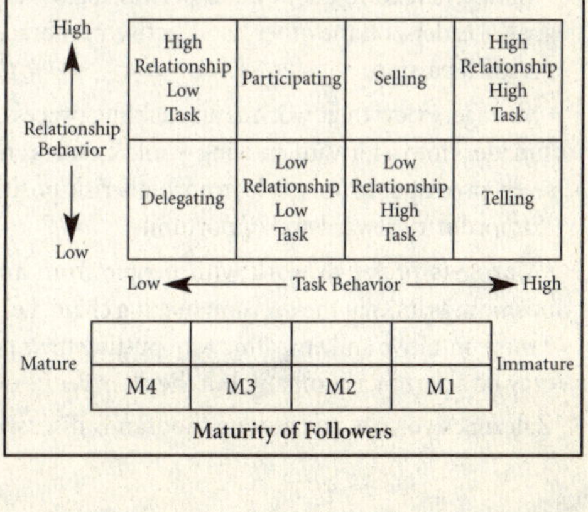

over activities but by decreasing relationship behavior as well. At stage M1, followers need clear and specific directions. Many managers lack the time or patience to handle these situations.

At M2, both high-task and high-relationship behavior is needed. Followers require close supervision of their work, together with trust and encouragement. An M3 situation entails motivational challenges that are best solved by supportive, nondirective, participative leadership. Sometimes M3 followers just need to know that the leader recognizes them, is interested in them and values them as individuals—then they *become* willing. And, finally arriving at this most effective M4 stage, the leader's direct involvement is considerably reduced because subordinates are both able and willing to take on responsibility.

Leaders and Managers: Is There a Difference?

Obviously, not all leaders are managers; but, are all managers, by virtue of their authority positions, leaders? This question has real implications for both the way managers think of themselves and for their resulting behavior. The fact is that any time a manager makes decisions affecting the work lives of subordinates, he is acting as a leader.

Both the Situational (Hersey-Blanchard) Leadership Model and the Leadership Continuum offer useful guidelines. Truly professional managers are always mindful of the impact their behavior has on others. They know that their effectiveness is critically increased when they can define and manage each situation with the appropriate leadership style.

LEADERSHIP: A BEHAVIORAL VIEW

Abraham Zaleznik, a respected management theorist from the Harvard Business School, believes that a manager and a leader are two very different people: different in their motivations, personal history, and in the ways they think and act. He suggests that:

• Managers tend to adopt an impersonal, almost passive attitude toward company goals. Leaders, on the other hand, actively embrace them and often inject a touch of personal passion.

• Managers view their work as an enabling process, one that molds people, resources and ideas into a forward-moving whole. Leaders are mostly concerned with ideas and seem predisposed to work from high-risk positions, especially when they sense extraordinary reward and opportunity.

• Managers prefer to work with people from an organizationally-conferred role position; as links in the decision making chain. Leaders relate to people and events in a more intuitive and empathic way, putting their personal stamp on actions. Leaders may be a part of a company, but they'll never be owned by the company.

Zaleznik's voice is one among thousands discussing some aspect of the leadership phenomenon. No area of management science has received more attention than has leadership (although motivation is a close second). Practicing managers recognize that good leadership is absolutely essential to the success of their businesses, as well as to the success of other institutions that shape our lives.

If leadership is so critical, the question is, "What makes a good leader?" It turns out, according to Zaleznik, that the answer is multifaceted. Most authorities currently recognize a number of factors involved, including: (1) The traits associated with leaders; (2) The behaviors they exhibit; (3) The situations in which they find themselves; (4) The attributions of others in close proximity to the leaders; and (5) The substitutes for leadership that exist in modern business organizations.

Leadership Behavior

"*Leadership: The ability to influence a group toward the achievement of goals.*" This definition seems simple and straightforward. But notice that few of us are able to *consistently* and *effectively* move groups of individuals toward objectives that are only ideas and ideals.

Some argue that the ability to lead stems from the position one holds in an organization. There are many people, however, who have held lofty positions, and yet failed the test of leadership. Conversely, there have been great leaders who have moved masses and mountains without the benefit of an organizational role (Gandhi, for example). Puzzles like this led early researchers to wonder if there was something unique in the way effective leaders behave. Are they more democratic or more autocratic in their interactions with others? What exactly do productive leaders do and say?

Zaleznik points to certain leadership fundamentals that have stood the test of time, both in theory and in practice.

The Early Studies

Beginning in the 1940s, behavioral scientists at Ohio State University and the University of Michigan addressed such questions concerning leadership. The Ohio State researchers studied hundreds of subjects and eventually segregated over a thousand dimensions of leadership behavior into two general categories:

(1) Initiating Structure: The extent to which a leader is likely to define and structure his or her role and those of subordinates.

(2) Consideration: The extent to which a leader is likely to build job relationships characterized by mutual trust, respect for subordinates' ideas, and regard for their feelings.

At about the same time, researchers at the University of Michigan, in their efforts to locate the behavioral characteristics—performance effectiveness—of leaders, came up with two primary "leader types":

(1) Production Oriented Leaders: These individuals tend to focus on the technical or task aspects of the job; their main concern is goal accomplishment, and people are seen as a means to that end.

(2) Employee Oriented Leaders: These emphasize interpersonal relations, take a personal interest in the needs of their subordinates, and accept individual differences among them.

While the Ohio State research indicated that, generally speaking, the most effective leaders were those who achieved "high" Initiating Structure *and* "high" Consideration, the Michigan studies held that higher group productivity was associated with Employee Oriented leadership behaviors. Notice, however, that the categories used by both groups are markedly similar: one emphasizes a "people" dimension, the other one relates to "production" or "task."

The Managerial Grid

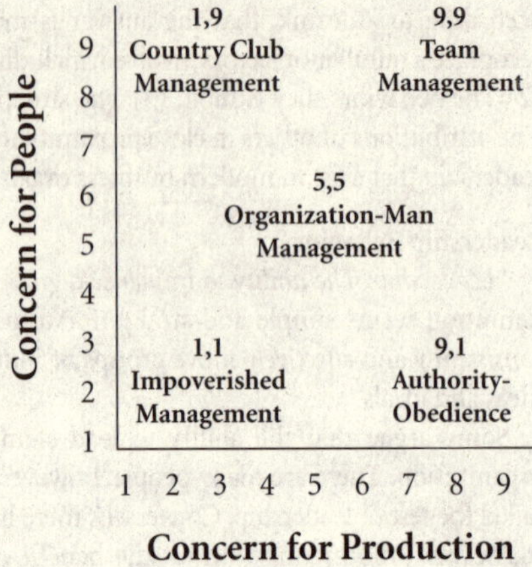

Robert Blake and Jane Mouton developed their Managerial Grid on the heels of these early studies. Where before the two dimensions of leadership were conceptualized as being independent, Blake and Mouton placed them at right angles to one another:

1,9—Country Club Manage-ment: Thoughtful attention is given to the needs of workers. Satisfying relationships lead to a comfortable, friendly environment and work tempo.

9,9—Team Management: Work is accomplished by committed people. Interdependence, created by workers sharing a "common stake" in the organization, leads to relationships of trust and respect.

5,5—Organization-Man Management: Adequate organization perform-ance is made possible through balancing the necessity to get work out with the maintenance of employees.

1,1—Impoverished Management: Exertion of minimum effort to get required work done is appropriate to sustain organization membership.

9,1—Authority-Obedience Management: Efficiency in operation results from arranging conditions of work in such a way that human elements interfere to a minimal degree.

This grid has nine possible positions along each axis, creating eighty-one possible leadership "styles." The five major positions depicted do not show the actual results obtained, but rather the dominant elements in that "style" of leadership. Logically, Blake and Mouton found that the 9,9 style of leadership—*Team Management*—was the most effective.

People, Production, or People-Production

The accumulated evidence from these models is both enlightening and disturbing. On one hand, "Concern for People" and "Concern for Production" orientations seem valid in the steely, cold light of everyday experience; it's easy to look around and find leaders or managers who are skewed one way or the other, and then to catalog resulting achievements, problems and deficiencies in production or morale. It's harder—but possible, in most cases—to think of a manager who seems to exhibit both "people" *and* "production" qualities simultaneously. If you can point to such a person, chances are you'll consider him or her an effective leader: someone who gets the job done while caring about the people who do it.

Interestingly enough, this appealing idea doesn't hold up in all cases or at all times. It does make sense and is a useful general principle, but it fails to take into account the situational factors that complicate the leadership context. Accordingly, subsequent theorists have incorporated situational variables that tend to improve the predictive ability of the People-Production models. But, as always, there's something gained and something lost in such improvements. Increased complexity yields increased scientific precision, but the simple elegance of a potent idea is left by the wayside.

Ponder the People and Production aspects of leadership. If you aspire to a leadership position, what are your own predispositions?

What Do Managers Do...Really?

Some Facts and Fallacies

Try this experiment. Walk into a business, find a typical manager, and ask him what he does. The answer will usually connect with what he learned in school: "I plan, organize, direct, coordinate, and control." Then spend a little time watching this manager. Don't be surprised if what you observe doesn't match with what he reported. In fact, a large body of research shows that most managerial jobs have very little to do with these five principles. This is somewhat surprising when you consider that the management vocabulary most of us know was built on the principles of planning, organizing, directing, coordinating and controlling...artifacts, really, of the early 1900s. It turns out that these principles are *prescriptive*...cloudy tactical objectives that managers have internalized and strive for from day to day. They are not, however, *descriptive* of what really happens on the firing line.

How Should a Manager Manage?

1. Traditionalists tell us that good managers are reflective, systematic, rational, and plan-oriented. In fact, study after study has shown that managers, in the real world, work at an *unrelenting pace*, that their work is characterized by *brevity, variety* and *discontinuity*, and that they are predisposed to *action* and disinclined to engage in mere reflective activity.

A study of CEOs found that half of managers' activities lasted less than nine minutes, and only ten percent exceeded one hour. Ninety-three percent of the verbal contacts were of an ad hoc nature, and only 1 out of 368 conversations was unrelated to a specific issue and could be called "general planning." Studies of foremen in the U.S. show that each averages 583 activities per eight-hour shift, or one every 48 seconds. Another study of 160 British middle and top managers found that they worked for more than one-half hour without interruption *only about once every two days.*

2. Pragmatists argue that managers should spend more time delegating and less time getting directly involved. Good managers are like good conductors: they orchestrate everything in advance and then monitor the results.

The truth is, however, that managers have a number of regular duties that only they can perform; the manager gets involved only because the work demands it. Presidents of small companies regularly do the type of work that staff specialists do for larger companies, and, when absences occur, they perform the duties of operating personnel as well. They have to—small companies are thinly staffed and require their presence and involvement.

Recent studies of successful field salesmen and CEOs suggest that it's a natural part of their jobs to see important customers (assuming they wish to keep those customers). Retirement parties, Christmas dinners, meetings with government officials, serving on the board of a trade association; these and other duties are a part of a manager's job that he neglects at great peril.

3. Organizational technicians inform us that managers need and want all the information the MIS can provide. The vaunted image is that of a manager perched atop a giant organizational pyramid that feeds her all the information needed to manage the enterprise.

But the fact is that, since their introduction in the 1960s, enthusiasm for "total information systems" has waned. They simply don't work. Why? Because they don't fit the way managers actually process information.

Managers have five media at their disposal: documents, the telephone, scheduled meetings, unscheduled meetings, and observational tours. Virtually every study conducted on the matter reports that managers strongly favor verbal media—namely, the telephone and meetings. Henry Mintzberg writes of observing a CEO go through the mail one Saturday morning: "[The CEO processed] 142 pieces of mail in just over three hours, to 'get rid of all the stuff.' This same manager looked at the first piece of 'hard' mail he had received all week, a standard cost report, and put it aside with the comment, 'I never look at this.'"

Information in hard copy—memos, letters, bulletins—simply fails to provide timely, vital information. It loses speed and relevance while traveling over the company's formal communication pathway. Seasoned managers, however, know that the "soft" information they get from gossip, hearsay and the grapevine can be invaluable. Why? Because, while it sometimes has its credibility problems, this type of information has its finger on the pulse of the company's direction.

What Do Managers Do?

Managerial work can be depicted by the following model. (In reality, the ten roles are combined to form a complete managerial job):

Interpersonal Roles
1. Figurehead 2. Leader 3. Liaison

Informational Roles
4. Monitor 5. Spokesman 6. Disseminator

Decisional Roles
7. Entrepreneur 8. Disturbance Handler 9. Resource Allocator 10. Negotiator

Interpersonal Roles

Managers spend a lot of time with people. Three roles under this heading capture most of their activities—

1. *Figurehead:* By virtue of position, every manager performs certain ceremonial duties: the foreman hands out paychecks, the president awards a gold watch, the sales manager dines with an important customer.

2. ***Leader:*** By virtue of formal authority, every manager is called on to make decisions, to motivate subordinates and to chart direction. Employees want and look for direction: "Is this OK?" "Should we do it this way or that?"

3. ***Liaison:*** Managers act as an interface between their unit and others on the same organizational level. They also cultivate contacts up and down the chain of command in an effort to create "cognitive buffers" that mitigate surprises and provide politically astute information to themselves and others.

Informational Roles

Information can be thought of as the lifeblood of an organization, and the manager as its heart. Three roles are identified under this heading—

4. ***Monitor:*** The manager continually scans the environment for information, questions liaison contacts, and obtains unsolicited information from the network of contacts he has built inside the organization. Recall that the manager prefers verbal media, and it is in connection with this role that that preference is most obvious.

5. ***Disseminator:*** Information does little good until it's properly placed in the organization, and in this role the manager passes his information along, when and where it will do the most good.

6. ***Spokesman:*** In this role, the manager sends information to people outside his or her unit. A foreman suggests a production line modification to an engineer, a president makes a speech to a community group, etc. The higher a person is in a business' formal chain of command, the more he acts as a spokesman.

Decisional Roles

Information is not an end in itself, but only an input to decision making. Managers encounter four decisional roles—

7. ***Entrepreneur:*** The entrepreneurial manager stays on the alert for opportunities to improve her work unit, seeks ways to adapt improvements to the company's environment, initiates developmental proposals, and sells her and her team's ideas to top management.

8. ***Disturbance Handler:*** While the entrepreneurial role is that of an initiator of change, this role depicts the manager as responding to pressures, changes, and shifts in the organization. Action is required to maintain the work unit, and only the manager has the position, information and perspective to act in handling problems as they crop up.

9. ***Resource Allocator:*** Managers typically have the responsibility of deciding who gets what in an organization, including money, time, privileges, chances at projects, and other benefits.

10. ***Negotiator:*** Managers spend considerable time in negotiations. These can be between employees, between the company and customers, between departments in the company, with outsiders for new stock issues, and so on. Negotiating becomes an integral part of the manager's job because only he has the authority necessary to commit organizational resources.

Managers have important jobs, ones that are poorly described by the traditional principles of planning, organizing, directing, controlling, and coordinating. The ten roles listed above more accurately describe the work most managers do. Recognizing the true nature of managerial work helps strip away stodgy conceptions to discover the realities of today's administration.

UNDERSTANDING MANAGERIAL COMMUNICATION

Ask an exasperated employee what's wrong at work and 90 percent of the time the answer is, "Poor communication." But what is poor communication? For that matter, what is good communication? Most managers dismiss the issue as superficial; but, considering that we spend nearly 70 percent of our waking hours communicating, it is a key factor in the problems that confront us at work. Poor, distorted or filtered communication has a clear impact on business. No idea (not even a great one) is useful until it is transmitted and understood by others.

Consider the conceptual model below. Also examine some of the common barriers to effective communication and suggested ways to overcome them that follow.

A Communication Model

Communication is the *transfer of meaning:* the idea you have in mind has to somehow make it into the mind of your listener *with the original meaning relatively intact.* The way this occurs can be thought of as a process or flow of events with six key elements.

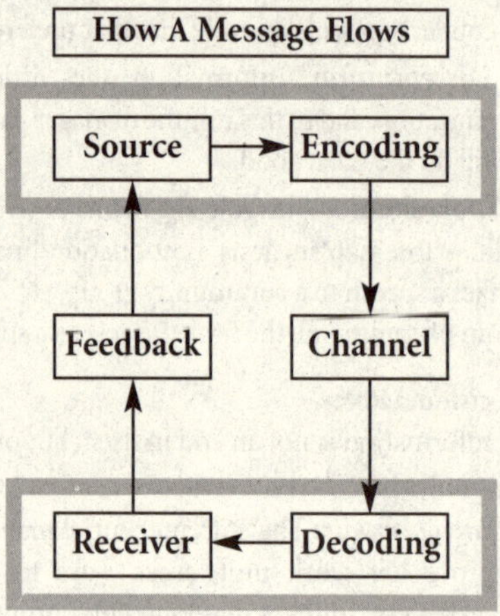

When expressing a thought (initiating a communication) you act as the *source* and begin the communication cycle. The thought you have can be communicated in multiple ways: by speaking, in writing, through non-verbal signals, in English or Spanish...But in one way or another, the mental spark, an "idea," has to be *encoded* into some kind of symbolic form, or else it cannot be received by the world outside one's own mind.

The actual physical product of this encoding is the *message* itself. This message is then sent to the receiver via a *channel,* which in business offices can include such avenues as the formal authority system (memos, presentations, reports), the grapevine, the newsletter, or the after-hours watering hole. Regardless of how it is transmitted, the message must also be *decoded* by the *receiver* for a transfer of meaning to occur. This means, for example, that in a memo the receiver must understand the language, words, nuances and any "techno-jargon." Note that both the encoding and decoding processes are dependent on the skills, attitudes, knowledge and cultural back- ground of the sender and receiver.

The final link in communication is the feedback loop; a check on how successfully the intended meaning was transmitted and received. Feedback, however, is not always given, nor is it always solicited. So, while the feedback loop represents a type of fail-safe mechanism, it only operates if called into play by the sender or receiver.

In the best of all possible situations the source encodes a message that is sent to a receiver who is able to decode the message and extract all of the intended meaning. Unfortunately, this is rarely the case. Each element in this flow has potential communication barriers, which may lead to a complete break down. If the encoding is done carelessly, the message will leave in a distorted state; if the message contains strange and confusing symbols (a word like "obstreperous," for example), meaning may be lost by the receiver. A message can be distorted by a faulty channel (asking your secretary to tell a subordinate to tell the president that sales are off); or the receiver can infuse a message with values or attitudes that were never intended by the source.

Communication Barriers

There are, in fact, far more opportunities to generate problems than there are ways to send and receive a clear, effective message. Below are four of the most common communication barriers.

1. Filtering: Senders sometimes manipulate information to make it look good to a receiver. If a manager tells the vice president what he thinks she wants to hear about a project, he has filtered the information. This is common in organizational life. John DeLorean writes that while he was at GM he witnessed managers providing information "in such a way that they would get the answer they wanted. I know. I used to be down below and do it." In general, filtering proliferates as the number of organizational levels increases.

2. Selective Perception: Communication is an *interpretive* process. Receivers may selectively admit information based on their needs, motivations, experience, background and other personal characteristics. Receivers may also project their interests and expectations into communications as they decode them. The corporate recruiter who *expects* the female applicant to put family before job might interpret many of her communications in this light, when the reverse may actually be the case.

3. Emotions: Our emotional states and our cognitive systems are inseparable. They interact constantly. How a receiver *feels* at the time of a communication will influence how he or she *interprets* it. The same message, received during times of anger, euphoria, or amusement, will be interpreted distinctly—different emotions color the meaning of the message. Extreme shifts in feelings, one side or the other, produce the greatest distortions and make most of us prone to substitute emotional judgments for rational responses.

4. Language: Different words have different meanings for different people. As S.I. Hayakawa remarks, "The meanings of words are *not* in the words; they are in *us*." For this reason, apprentice writers should stick to using simple, widely understood words, and refrain from the type of vocabulary associated with philosophers and nuclear physicists. A company's employees generally come from diverse backgrounds, generating shades of meaning for certain words. Large companies may also employ specialists who have their own jargon, some of which is unintelligible to the lay person.

Overcoming the Barriers

Happily, all is not lost. There are some simple ways to improve communication effectiveness. Three of the most useful methods are to:

- **Use Feedback**—Simply checking to see if the message sent was the message received can alleviate many communication problems. Asking, "Did you understand that?" is a good beginning but usually elicits a simple yes or no answer. It is better to ask a brief set of questions to confirm that the message was decoded in detail. If the sender hears back—and clarifies, if necessary—what he or she intended to send, then understanding and accuracy are enhanced.

(Notice that the receiver can also initiate a feedback cycle: "Here's what I understand so far...")

- **Simplify Language**—In virtually every case, communication is enhanced when the sender uses clear, easily understood words and phrases. Avoid jargon, except when communicating with a specialized receiver or group. "Antecedent conditions," "beta weights," and "leverage" are examples of jargon; "ubiquitous," "magnanimous," and "avuncular" are examples of words that may be "scrambled." When in doubt, keep the language simple.
- **Listen Actively**—The most powerful tool at your disposal is to *work at listening. Listening is a skill. It is hard work.* Consider that most of us speak at a rate of about 150 words per minute, but have the capacity to listen at the rate of over 1,000 words per minute. The gap between these two creates "idle brain time" during which many people's minds wander; they think about a piece of unfinished business or impute meaning where none really exists. Active listening is the active search for meaning: the receiver reserves judgment, weighs the words, and places himself or herself in the sender's position. The goal is to receive as much of the original meaning as possible.

Any manager or employee would do well to avoid communication barriers by keeping messages simple and direct, by actively listening, and by inviting feedback from the receiver.

Communication Skills for Managers

Communication is the common thread that runs through each of the challenges a manager faces every day. A manager is always communicating—sometimes verbally, other times through silence; sometimes through facial expressions or body language, other times with a written letter or memo. Whether a manager's communication is formal or informal, personal or business-like, it should convey and include four elements:

(1) A knowledge of the issues discussed

(2) An attitude of cooperation

(3) Positive and specific statements

(4) A definite purpose (share or seek information, show appreciation, congratulate, request or persuade, offer services, etc.)

Depending on the message sent and the person receiving it, communication can take any of various forms. Some common forms of managerial communication are ranked below, according to the richness of the information transferred. "Richness," in this context, denotes the degree to which the information being transmitted can change understanding within a given period of time.

According to this graphic, the poorest forms of communication include the statistical and formal written approaches; conversely, the closer a communicator can come to relating personally and informally to the other individual, the better the communication.

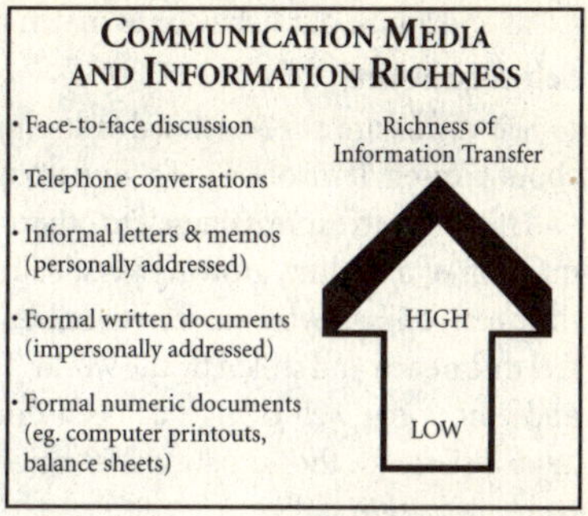

The richest communication method, as the chart points out, is a face-to-face discussion, where the entire range of verbal and non-verbal information is available, and where communicators can instantly check the accuracy of the information being transmitted and received. Roughly 75 percent of all managerial time is spent in verbal, one-on-one exchange.

Discussed below are the three major areas that contribute heavily to the quality of oral communication. They are: (1) *Quality of feedback*, (2) *Level of self-disclosure,* and (3) *Listening effectiveness.*

Feedback

Feedback falls into the categories of supportive (that which reinforces ongoing behavior) and *corrective* (that which indicates a need for change in behavior). Both types of feedback are beneficial when communicators observe these principles:

1) Ideally, feedback is given in an atmosphere of *mutual trust*. An organizational culture characterized by hostility—high competitiveness, emphasis on the use of power to punish and control subordinates, and rigid boss-employee relationships—lacks the level of trust necessary for effective feedback.
2) Feedback should be *specific* rather than general, using clear and, when possible, recent examples. "You are a dominating person," is not as effective as saying, "Just now, when you were talking to John, you didn't listen to what he said. You decided the matter yourself, with no input from him."
3) Feedback should be given when the receiver seems *ready* to accept it. When a person is angry, upset or defensive, it's probably a poor time to bring up new issues via feedback.
4) Feedback should be *audited* to determine if the receiver agrees with it and accepts its validity. The sender can ask the receiver to rephrase the information and see if it matches what the sender intended.
5) Feedback should be geared to the receiver's *capabilities;* that is, it should focus on issues the receiver can do something about.
6) Feedback should include an *appropriate level of information;* no greater detail or complexity should be offered than the receiver can handle at any one time. Anyone may become threatened and defensive after a shotgun blast of feedback about everything he or she does wrong on the job.
7) All employees, including managers, should be trained to understand the role of feedback. They should be shown that the feedback interchange is an important psychological and social checking device. It allows us to see ourselves as others see

us and adjust our behavior to match intentions and expectations.

Self-Disclosure

Self-disclosure can be defined as any information consciously offered by an individual about himself. It involves the ability to communicate *openly and non-defensively.*

The ability to express oneself to others is considered by most psychologists as the sine qua non of a healthy, growing personality. The reverse also holds: people who cloister their real feelings, who are secretive about their inner selves and motivations, generally feel threatened and stifled by the world. The connection between open communication and emotional well-being has been documented for over 40 years. Self-disclosure, appropriate to the situation, is among the most healthy and powerful of all communication skills.

There are two extremes of self-disclosure to recognize and avoid: the overly disclosing model, and the closed, non-disclosing model. The over-disclosing person is out of place and ineffective in a business organization because he shares feelings and thoughts that are inappropriate to the time and place. Offices are formal settings, and people who treat them otherwise (like a family or as a cause celebre, for example) can make others defensive and can actually curtail effective communication. On the other hand, people who never reach out or fail to share even small shards of their inner selves also prove to be ineffective in the workplace. The key is to offer the right amount of appropriate self-disclosure to bolster communication, morale and problem solving, and still maintain a professional attitude. This selective self-disclosure enhances teamwork because it improves camaraderie and stimulates deeper, more meaningful dialogue.

Listening

Possibly the most difficult communication skill to learn, productive listening requires hard work and participation. Active, attentive listening integrates all the physical, emotional and intellectual faculties.

As much as 40% of the workday among office employees is spent listening. Tests of listening comprehension, though, show that most of us only listen at 25% efficiency; 75% of the original message is lost.

There are seven keys to active listening:

1. Good listeners find a *reason or purpose* for listening in each new situation. They search for value and meaning in what is said. Good listeners are interested.

2. Good listeners *suspend judgment* on what is being said, at least initially. Listening requires concentration on the message being sent; attention devoted to forming impressions or developing a rebuttal only detracts from this.

3. Good listeners *resist distractions* such as noises, sights and other people, so that they can focus on the sender and the message.

4. *A pause* before responding to the sender often helps the good listener absorb the meaning of a message.

5. When the message is emotional or unclear, a good listener *restates* it in her own words. She paraphrases the meaning she received and directs it back to the sender for validation.

6. Good listeners search for *themes* in communication—the broad, important premise that the sender wishes to convey.

7. A good listener remembers that there is a time differential between his rate of thought (400-500 words per minute) and the sender's rate of speech (100-150 words per minute). He uses this "extra time" to search for meaning.

Most of these suggestions for improving listening skills are interrelated; it's hard to practice one without improving the others.

As always, it is easier to *understand* these principles of effective communication than it is to *develop* them on a skills level. But experience shows that the effort to communicate through giving and receiving feedback, through self-disclosure, and through active listening pays handsome dividends individually and corporately.

Psychological Contracts

Forces That Bind Managers And Employees

There is an unwritten "contract" existing between employers and employees called the *Psychological Contract* (see the reference to H.G. Baker's *Personnel Bulletin* article which follows). This term refers to the set of expectations found in all organizations; expectations that all managers have of their subordinates, that all employees have of their superiors, and that all co-workers have of their peers. These expectations focus on the behaviors that properly accompany a role, and they can be broad and general (civility in the workplace) or circumscribed and specific (the dress code for a bank teller). Psychological contracts and the impact they have on performance are crucial for the manager to understand.

Roles

When he or she sits down behind a desk at 8:00 A.M., a manager assumes numerous roles, largely defined by the specific organizational structure. A plant manager, for instance, may simultaneously fill the roles of (1) company employee, (2) member of senior management, (3) technical expert in some narrow domain, (4) chair of the executive committee, (5) spokesman to the community, and so on. Away from work, this plant manager again steps into multiple roles (Rotarian, Catholic, tennis player, parent, member of the country club, etc.).

The key that unlocks role behavior lies in understanding that *each of us enacts a given role in a given situation.* When presiding over a budget meeting, the plant manager *should* act in the role of a chairman. If he does not, the incongruities resulting from *expected* versus *actual* behavior usually cause considerable difficulty for others who rely on that role. This, then, begins to get at the meaning of a psychological contract: each member of a company expects other members of that company to act in a way that is consistent with their roles...or, rather, with the role they *should* be assuming at the moment.

Four important concepts, taken together, help clarify and convey the essence of psychological contracts: (1) Role Identity, (2) Role Perception, (3) Role Expectations, and (4) Role Conflict.

Role Identity

Certain attitudes and behaviors are considered consistent with a given role, and these create *role identity*. For example, one research study showed that when union stewards were promoted to supervisory positions, their attitudes changed from pro-union to pro-management within a few months; but when these promotions were rescinded due to economic problems and the new supervisors were demoted back to the union, they once again adopted pro-union attitudes. This shift from a managerial to a pro-union role identity demonstrates that each of us has the ability to shift our behaviors and attitudes to meet the perceived demands of a given function. We are, quite literally, different people in different contexts.

But what if the role is vague or unclear? How do we act when we have no clue how we should act? Another researcher found that former classmates attending high school reunions five, ten, even twenty years after graduation, unfamiliar with each other in their adult roles, assumed the roles they had held as students: football hero, cheerleader, recluse, scholar, etc. So the second important insight regarding role identity is that, when role requirements are ill-defined or clouded, individuals tend to revert to old and familiar patterns of behavior.

A manager's or a worker's role identity and personality, then, are hardly static. They are an ever-changing composite of past assumptions and experiences as well as present assumptions, relationships and circumstances.

Role Perceptions

Each of us has an idea of how we're supposed to act in a particular circumstance, and this is termed *role perception*. It's important for managers to know that their subordinates (and even their superiors) engage in certain kinds of behavior based on how they *believe* they are supposed to act in a given situation. Think of the first-line foreman who has recently returned from a supervisory training program after being taught that motivation is enhanced when clear, challenging and measurable goals are set. This foreman now has an idea of how she's supposed to deal with her employees, and is likely to behave as prescribed.

One of the primary reasons that apprenticeship programs exist in most trade occupations is to allow the novice to watch an "expert" at work, and thus learn new and better techniques; the same can be said for mentoring programs at higher levels.

Role perceptions, however, are not always accurate. Hence, to improve production and teach correct role perceptions, formal training, informal demonstrations, observation, goal-setting, etc. should be employed on a continual basis.

Role Expectations

While role perceptions are defined in terms of how one believes he or she should act in a given situation, *role expectations* are the converse; they are defined as how *others* believe one should act in a given situation.

The foreman, mentioned above, learned role expectations in the company training program—that is, "Set clear, challenging and measurable goals with your crew." But what happens when role expectations aren't met? The psychological contract is violated, and management is forced to take some sort of stance. If the violation has serious performance implications, the response may be counseling or disciplinary action; but if the violator maintains performance objectives, he or she will either be (1) tolerated and considered odd or unique, or (2) regarded as something of a prodigy who has defined a "new way."

Interestingly enough, employees often react in a similar way when a manager transgresses role expectations. But, because of the constraints put on employees, they usually levy a different, less formal kind of "discipline."

In any case, managers help to smooth out the work flow in their companies when they *communicate clearly* what the specific role expectations are for a job (a task the traditional job description only begins to address), and then consistently *reinforce and reward* proper execution.

Role Conflict

An individual experiences *role conflict* when he or she encounters divergent, incompatible, or inconsistent role expectations. Role conflict can result when compliance in one capacity makes it more difficult to comply with another, as when a team leader who is expected to act as a co-worker or mentor has to deliver a performance evaluation. He struggles to be buddy and boss both at the same time. Both roles may be expected as part of the job, yet one tends to conflict with the other.

An extreme case of conflict occurs when two or more role expectations are mutually exclusive, leaving the individual in a classic double-bind. Recall the plant manager described earlier; his role as a husband and father requires stability and time at home, while his position as an executive requires travel, late-night meetings and 80-hour work weeks. In such cases the manager is left with making a choice between one or the other expectation, or, in some cases, compromising both.

The issue of business ethics also illustrates this point. One study (see P.S. Goodman's book referred to below) uncovered the fact that 57 percent of Harvard Business Review readers had faced the dilemma of choosing between profits for their firm and following ethical business practices.

Managers should seek to develop a "feel" for the psychological contracts—both implied and formally stated—that exist in their organizations. They should also recognize that their employees, in genuine attempts to define their niches in the company, will actively search for and try to fill organizational roles.

Understanding the dynamics of Role Identity, Role Perception, Role Expectations and Role Conflicts enhances the manager's ability to develop lasting, effective and clearly defined expectations and working relationships.

EMPLOYEE RECRUITMENT AND SELECTION

I failed to get this job I wanted because I answered one of the questions on the application wrong. The question asked, "Do you advocate the overthrow of the United States Government by revolution or violence?" I chose violence!

—Dick Cavett

Dick Cavett here is poking fun at yet another one of his supposed shortcomings; but employee recruitment and selection is serious business, more important to organizational survival than many managers once realized. With the growing need for corporate competence to meet the pressures of competition, many companies are now taking a harder look at whom they recruit and how they make their selections.

The Recruiting Process

The steps in a typical recruiting approach are identified in the figure below. Ideally, the company already has an ongoing human-resource program that ties in with the company's overall business and strategic planning process.

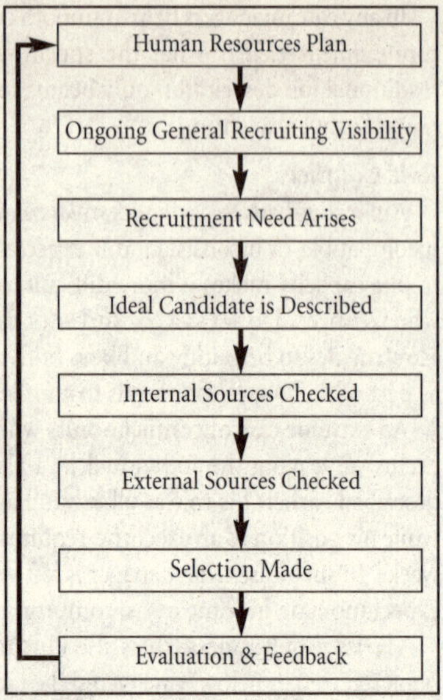

Waste and error in employee selection often result from scurrying around to fill "surprise" openings. Maintaining a company's visibility through a recruitment program—even during periods of reduced hiring—has definite benefits.

Line managers are often the triggers in the hiring process. Managers should work closely with knowledgeable human-resource personnel to list specific desired *qualifications* for the job. Next, it is usually advantageous to search inside the company for available candidates to transfer or promote into the position. If none are found, talented individuals can be recruited from a number of external sources: college campuses, temporary agencies, search firms, trade and other media, and so on.

Ongoing recruitment and episodic hiring are each represented as varying by time and place in the following graphic, with examples given in each quadrant:

Selection: The Attraction ⇨ Retention ⇨ Attrition Cycle

Think of recruitment and selection in terms of three concepts: attraction, retention and attrition. People are not randomly assigned by lottery to work for certain companies. In most cases they're attracted to a particular firm, apply for entry, are selected or rejected, and then either stay or leave. Also, different organizations select and retain different kinds of people. This attraction—selection / retention—attrition cycle leads to a natural but powerful tendency: over time, most companies become more and more homogenous; people who don't "fit in," leave, and those who do, remain and gain influence.

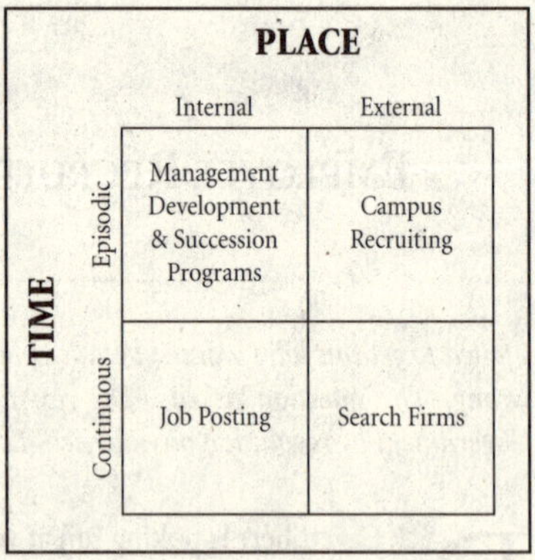

Recruiters and decision makers should keep this "homogeneity" in mind, because it has both positive and negative effects. On one hand, the company may become crippled by too much of the same kind of talent, the same kind of thinking, the same tired visions for the future. On the other hand, "dissidents" and "misfits" can sap a considerable amount of managerial energy as the company tries to cope with ideas and behaviors that are too atypical to be integrated. A balance has to be struck so that a "loyal and constructive cacophony" is heard around the conference table—both rebellion and similitude are avoided.

Tools Used in Hiring

Without a doubt, the most revered and frequently used employee-selection device is the personal interview or series of interviews. There is something about a face-to-face visit that appeals to our human nature. But as the following chart illustrates, research evidence points to better means for predicting job fit, tenure and productivity. (The higher the correlation number, the better the prediction.):

Predictor	Average Validity
Cognitive Ability Tests	.53
(What is the interviewee's learning ability and adaptability?)	
Job Tryout	.44
(What can he actually do?)	
Biographical Inventory	.37
(What is his experience?)	
Reference Checks	.26
GPA	.21
Experience	.18
Interview	.14
Ratings of Training & Experience	.13
Amount of Education	.10
Interest Level	.10

You may be surprised by this list. Notice that the amount of *Education* ties for last place, *Interviewing* is just .04 ahead, and a candidate's high school or college GPA doesn't fare much better in predicting a person's ability and job fit. *References* always have a built-in bias: who would ever think of listing their critics or enemies as references? *Resumes,* interestingly, are notoriously unreliable: one VP of a major corporation estimates that 20% of all resumes contain at least one "factual misstatement," and a firm that checks academic records for companies indicates that 30 to 40 percent of all people simply lie about themselves.

Interviewing

Even though the interviewing process may look inferior on paper, those who do the hiring wouldn't sleep at night without holding interviews. To help these talks be more valuable, here are a few well-documented cognitive biases that affect interviews and the decisions made from them.

1. The Illusion of Completeness: Decision-makers often perceive an information set to be complete, even in the absence of important facts. Short of time and energy, managers typically collect just enough information on candidates to make a decision—one often based on guesswork.

2. Arbitrary Standards: A manager will tend to fill in the gaps of his knowledge about a person by using information from his own past experience with people, places, events, etc. Subjective biases—factors that only "seem" to apply to the individual or issue, but are actually deep-rooted preferences found in the interviewer—creep in. Thus, a large, heavy woman may not be hired as a cosmetics salesperson because high fashion sales representatives are typically slim.

3. Overconfidence: Managers are often more confident in their own judgment than they should be. For example, research shows that a recruiter may make snap judgments about the quality of a candidate in the first four minutes of an interview! She may "triangulate" her considerable historical and current experience to arrive at a "feel" or "sense" for the individual before her—and form a judgment that is incorrect.

4. Confirmatory Bias: All of us operate using our own distinct models and theories about the world. We tend to retain in memory information that supports our personal hypotheses and to criticize and cast away information with which we disagree.

Consider the previous example—the interview that is essentially over in the first four minutes. The remainder of such an interview is usually spent collecting only those facts that will confirm and support the interviewer's initial judgment; and, in her mind, her early views of the candidate are validated.

5. The Law of Small Numbers: Managers sometimes ignore the implications of sample size, attributing greater stability to results obtained from small samples than is warranted. In other words, most managers are poor statisticians.

Suppose a job-seeker is interviewed by you and by five other members of your staff. All the interviews go well except yours, which is a disaster for the candidate. What information will weigh most heavily in your decision? The experience in your own interview, or the favorable reports from the five others?

6. Either-Or Questions: Some types of questions produce more meaningful and revelatory answers than others. Open-ended questions—ones that can't be answered with a "yes" or a "no"—are helpful. Who, what, when, why, how, tell me, which...are all good ways to begin questions that will help draw out a candidate's true experience and knowledge. Also, queries that invite problem-solving and clarifications of job or craft descriptions can function as informal "tests" or "tryouts," which, according to the earlier research chart, are the two top job-performance predictors.

By carefully considering what type of on-the-job experience, education, abilities, and personality that you want in a new employee, and using selection devices that are most valuable in helping you to objectively "see" how he or she will fit in your job opening, a more accurate decision can be made.

Employee and Management Rights

Notes on Whistle-blowing, Drug Testing and Other Controversies

The Constitution and the Bill of Rights provide every American with what most of us consider the fundamental human rights: free speech, due process, and protection from "the tyranny of the majority." But such rights do not necessarily apply in the workplace. In fact, it is not the Constitution but a collection of federal, state and local statutes, along with specific labor-management contracts, that grant employees rights—such as due process—at work. Without such laws in place, the right of management to run its business as it sees fit has often overridden any employee rights.

New laws have changed so many traditional management prerogatives—in areas like safety, sexual harassment, and equal opportunity, for example—that considerable confusion now surrounds the issues. This article discusses some of the larger fields of concern in the unfolding and unresolved arena of employee and management rights.

Rights Defined

A "right" is a power which *belongs to a person by virtue of law, nature or tradition.* Some scholars separate moral and legal rights for clarity; a right in one category may or may not have the same standing in the other. Some employee rights apply both on and off the job; free speech and health and safety are two examples. Others apply only at work or only outside of the workplace, such as the right to smoke at home but not in the office. Additionally, there is a distinction between a "right" and a "privilege," the latter being implied or offered within the employment contract. Following are some important rights affecting persons and companies:

1. ***Employment at Will*** (EAW) is a common-law doctrine giving employers the right to hire, fire, demote and promote whomever they wish, unless there is some covenant to the contrary. EAW is usually advanced by defenders of the free ownership of *private* enterprise. It is, however, an artifact of the industrial revolution. Although many states are enacting restraints on it, the doctrine still enjoys considerable exercise in daily commerce.

Our legal system has recognized three rationales for testing the principle of Employment at Will: (1) Actions against public policy (an employee is fired for refusing to conduct industrial espionage); (2) Actions rebutting the implied employment contract; and (3) Employer actions that fail to demonstrate good faith and fair dealing.

2. ***Implied Contracts*** can exist between employer and employee without any kind of written stipulation. An oral promise or agreement, sometimes even a history of actions, can qualify as an implied contract. The key elements are actions or words that establish employee *expectations,* which then become the basis for the employees' *actions.* Several courts have held, for example, that if an employer hires a person for an indefinite period or promises job security, the employer has lost the right to terminate at will.

Employee handbooks can also become the basis for an implied contract, and most Human Resource executives have their documents reviewed by legal experts to safeguard against unwarranted expectations.

3. ***Due Process*** is guaranteed by the Constitution and is generally spelled out in fine detail by collective bargaining agreements. But at-will employees have greater variability in the protections and procedures afforded them. They do have the right to due process; however, employees must be given the opportunity to present their side of the story during disciplinary hearings.

4. ***Dismissal for Just Cause*** is also specified in union contracts, but is often unclear in an at-will situation. Proving just cause depends on one or more of the following elements: (1) If warnings were given to the employee; (2) If the company's rule was reasonable; (3) If management investigated before applying discipline; (4) If the investigation was fair and reasonable; (5) If there was evidence of guilt; (6) If the rules and discipline were applied in an even-handed fashion; and (7) If the penalty was reasonable, given the offense.

There have also been cases where employers made the work situation so intolerable that the employee was "forced" to resign. Such cases are referred to as Constructive

Discharge and can be treated as a dismissal by the courts.

5. Employees have ***Rights to Records,*** or, the right of access to their personnel files. Specifically, they have: (1) The right of access to personal information; (2) The opportunity to respond to unfavorable information; (3) The right to correct erroneous information; (4) The right to be notified when information is given to a third party; (5) The right to know how information is being used internally; (6) The right to reasonable precautions by the employer so that personal information is safeguarded.

6. ***Substance Abuse and Drug Testing*** are two controversial areas of current employment law. An employer cannot discriminate against an employee because of alcohol or drug dependency if, after reasonable accommodations for this handicap, he or she can do the job. But blood tests, polygraph tests and urinalysis can and are being required of employees. Unless otherwise prohibited by state laws, employers have the right to require such tests of each and every employee.

The two main arguments against drug testing are that they violate employees' rights to privacy and that they are unreliable. To the first objection it must be noted that employers are not constrained by federal statutes regulating search and seizure (which apply only to governmental agents), and are not bound by the criminal standard of "beyond a reasonable doubt." Searches and testing are legal. However, research has shown that drug tests can be notoriously unreliable. The Center for Disease Control found in its ten-year study, that virtually every laboratory conducting drug tests had unacceptably high error rates. This and other complications raise the troubling prospect of a high rate of false accusations.

7. ***Polygraph Tests*** were dubbed "twentieth century witchcraft" by Senator Sam Ervin. But 20 percent of this country's major organizations and 50 percent of all retail establishments use polygraph tests even though studies show that such tests yield erroneous results about 33 percent of the time. The Office of Technology Assessment has determined that the validity of the polygraph can not be determined, and the American Psychological Association has confirmed that an unacceptable number of "false positives" occur. For these reasons there are few courts that will admit polygraph data as evidence.

Many objections to the polygraph test are aimed at its use in screening applicants for jobs. Because of the previously noted problems, 36 states have enacted laws regulating the use of these tests for employment purposes, and several bills have been introduced in Congress to eliminate them completely.

8. ***Whistle-Blowers*** are persons who report a real or perceived wrong done by an employer. The two key issues in the debate on whistle-blowing are:

(1) Do employees have the right to speak out with protection from retribution?

(2) When should employees violate the confidentiality of their jobs?

Many regard whistle-blowing as an important right in that it can shield fellow workers or the general public from employer misdeeds. But, because civil service systems have regulations protecting the whistle-blower, studies show that private sector whistle-blowers are more likely to lose their jobs than their public sector counterparts. The penalties levied against private sector employees by their employers, can be severe—especially if the whistle-blower goes outside of his organization with the information.

One of the few research studies on whistle-blowing gathered nearly 8,000 surveys from federal employees and concluded that parent organizations often lashed out at "stool pigeons," subjecting them to various formal and informal pressures to get back in line. If this represents the general situation, the idea that organizations should encourage valid whistle-blowing may be difficult to implement.

Worker rights may differ from state to state and company to company. Being informed of your rights can lead to greater security and personal confidence in your work.

The Performance Appraisal Process

A division of *Xerox* (the *Reprographic Business Group,* which makes copiers) had used performance appraisals for over 20 years. The system was typical of others around the country, using numbers to rate performance, but it had its problems: 95% of the ratings were 3's or 4's on a five-point scale, and merit increases were usually within one or two percent of each other. Xerox listened to its managers and did something. An employee task force designed a new program with:

(1) Six-month progress reviews
(2) Goal setting
(3) Year-end written appraisals
(4) No numerical ratings
(5) Merit increases separated from appraisal by two months
(6) Focus on coaching and development
(7) Extensive training.

The results were dramatic. Within a year, 81% of those surveyed felt they better understood what objectives their work was supposed to accomplish, 84% felt their appraisals were fair, 70% met their work objectives, and 72% said they understood how merit pay was determined.

A Look At Performance Appraisal

Performance appraisal is easy to define. It involves nothing more than *determining how well employees do their jobs* compared to a set of standards, and then *communicating that information* to employees.

Appraisal systems are in wide use today, for both white- and blue-collar employees (88% of white-collar and 63% of blue-collar organizations use some kind of performance appraisal system). The reasons are simple: effective performance appraisal systems contribute to a company's competitive position; they help to solve problems, improve morale, and ensure that important tasks get the main focus; and they contribute to the bottom line. Additionally, sophisticated appraisal systems help to groom the company's brain-trust, ensuring a steady stream of the *right people* in the *right jobs* at the *right time.*

There are many ways to configure an appraisal system and many methods for structuring the form of the appraisal itself. The chart on the previous page chart illustrates some of the options:

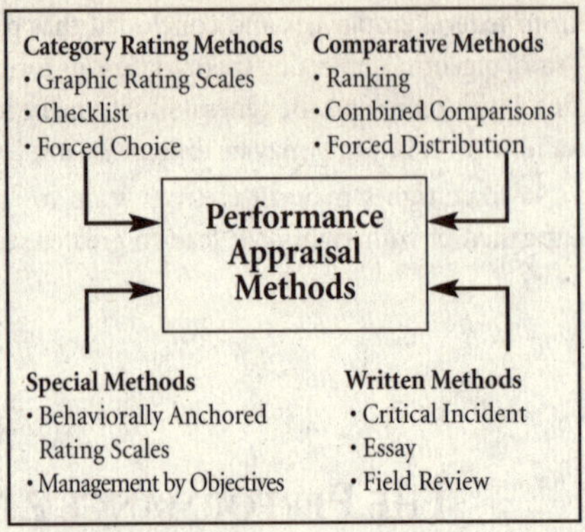

(1) *Category* methods are the simplest; they usually require the manager only to mark an employee's level of performance on a specific form.

(2) *Comparative* methods demand that the manager directly compare the performance of one employee against another's.

(3) *Written* methods ask for documentary and descriptive information on each employee.

(4) Two *"special" systems* that have met with widespread acceptance are BARs, which examines specific employee behaviors, and MBO, which focuses on mutually set goals and objectives.

Common Problems and Errors

There are many sources of potential rating errors in any appraisal system. Some of the better documented ones are listed below:

1. Varying Standards: The manager should strive to keep standards and expectations consistent for all employees' appraisals. Consistency is always difficult, but especially so when ambiguous criteria or subjective weightings are used. And even when standards and criteria are held constant, an employee may not perceive this to be the case—*and it is the employee's perceptions that count.* To be most helpful, the rater must not only use the same standards and weights across employees, but be able to *defend and explain each appraisal* on the basis of fairness.

2. The Recency Problem: Remembering issues and performances that are six or nine months old is difficult; it's much easier to recall incidents that occurred in the last month. But some employees will take advantage of this human foible by "coasting" for months, then delivering exemplary work for a week or two before their appraisal dates. One way of minimizing this practice is through careful and consistent *documentation* of critical incidents and events on the job.

3. Rater Bias: It is not uncommon to see a rater's values, biases and prejudices creeping into an appraisal. This problem can be especially harmful if the appraiser *remains* blind to his own biases. Age, race, religion, personal habits, lifestyle, gender, appearance, and other attributes can easily cloud an otherwise objective assessment of job performance. Carefully designed appraisal methods can cut back on rater bias, as can a review of ratings by a management level person just above the rank of the actual appraiser.

4. Rater Patterns: Different raters will interpret even the best designed appraisal forms and methods differently. One appraiser may conscientiously rank employees on a curve, for example, with the majority rated "average," or somewhere in the 50% range; while another interviewer, accentuating the positive, may consistently rate her employees in the 75% range, or as "above average." Consequently, employee A may be rated as "excellent" by one manager and only "average" by another. Making the rater aware of his or her response patterns is one way of dealing with this problem. Another involves the explicit definition of performance categories in the rating scale itself.

5. Halo Effect: Some managers will rate an employee high or low on all items because of one characteristic. If employee A is consistently tardy, this may become the *overriding image* carried in the manager's head, affecting all other dimensions of the appraisal. Enhancing managerial self-awareness and training in the effective use of an appraisal instrument are the two most valuable means of combating this obstacle to meaningful appraisals.

The Appraisal Interview

Appraisal sessions usually present both an opportunity and an obstacle: the manager has the chance to impart career-advancing and developmental feedback, but the interview itself is often highly charged with emotion. Below are some useful hints for conducting an interview:

- Prepare in advance.
- Focus on future performance and development.
- Don't do all the talking.
- Be specific about reasons for ratings.
- Decide on specific improvement measures.
- Consider your role in the subordinate's performance.
- Allow the employee to disagree on certain points.
- Reinforce and reward the behaviors you want.

Of major concern should be to emphasize the positive aspects of an employee's work performance, while still addressing those ways in which she can improve. This type of "constructive criticism" can be difficult for both parties to handle.

Like their employees, most managers are concerned about the fairness, consistency and usefulness of appraisals. Many managers conducting an appraisal feel as though they're being put in the unwanted position of playing *"God"* with the employee's career, but also see the need to coach, counsel and encourage professional development. This Catch-22 can lead to inconsistency or indecisiveness shown by the manager.

A common reaction to appraisals among employees is to view them as *"zero-sum"* games, where there must be winners and losers. ("In order for me to get high ratings, someone else has to get low ratings.") But, in fact, appraisals don't have to be zero-sum. If the manager frames each interview as a developmental and self-improvement exercise *conducted for the employee's benefit,* everyone can win.

There are a number of other technical and theoretical elements of effective performance appraisals. But by keeping squarely in mind the important objectives of any assessment system, and the tools and attitudes for conducting a helpful interview, managers will greatly multiply their chances of making such a review a successful experience for both themselves and their appraisees.

THE ART OF GROUP DECISION-MAKING
A Guide For The Manager

Many organizations foster group decision-making, even at top levels, to meet varied challenges. *J.C. Penney*, for example, deliberately uses group decision-making at the upper reaches of its organization. A committee of fourteen top managers debates issues such as planning, managerial selection, merchandising, and public relations... and reaches effective decisions. *Penney's* management believes that this mechanism has successfully met some very tough, entrenched challenges, like allocating costs among divisions, determining merchandising mix and corporate staff compensation, expediting the use of computers, and improving overall profits.

Arguments For and Against Groups

The alluring thing about groups is that they can achieve *synergy*, to make 2 + 2 = 5. Unfortunately, if managed poorly, they can also make 2 + 2 = 3. Managers can help groups work synergistically through the applications of specific techniques. Over fifty years of research has been devoted to identifying and refining these techniques, and considerable knowledge now exists on how they work in group situations. Here, we will touch on three of the most celebrated methods for increasing the effectiveness of groups in making business decisions.

To begin with, there are both advantages and disadvantages in using groups for decision-making.

Advantages

(1) ***Input.*** Groups bring more complete information and knowledge to a decision-making situation than any of the individuals separately. Generally speaking, two heads are better than one—and three heads are better than two.

(2) ***Diversity.*** Groups usually guarantee a diversity of views. In addition to providing more raw input, this element of heterogeneity usually stimulates the formation of more approaches and alternatives among individual group members.

(3) ***Acceptance.*** A group decision is more likely to achieve acceptance than one made by an individual. A technically excellent decision may well fall flat when key players instrumental to its implementation are not involved in its development. Group decisions may take longer to make, but they are often carried through more effectively and enthusiastically than hand-me-down orders from "on high."

Disadvantages

(1) ***Time.*** It takes time to assemble a group, and the best-running groups are usually those that have spent months and years finding ways for the personalities to work most cogently together. But even the most seasoned groups can be very inefficient users of time when compared to a single executive. Quick, decisive action in the face of crisis is seldom the hallmark of group decision-makers.

(2) ***Pressures toward conformity.*** There are strong social pressures in groups. People have a desire to be accepted, to appear competent, to be seen as team players. Groups, working with the best of intentions, and with the purpose of eliminating conflict, can bring strong normative pressures to bear on dissenters. Most groups encourage conformity among viewpoints.

(3) ***Domination.*** Groups are composed of personalities who not only contribute different information and view points, but who take on different group roles. Frequently one or more of these personalities will assume leadership and dominate group discussion. If the dominant individual or cohort is of less than stellar ability, the group's overall effectiveness is likely to suffer.

These advantages and disadvantages will weigh differently against each other in different situations, but the fact remains that decisions made by groups tend to be more accurate and creative than those made by individuals. The trick lies in managing the group decision-making process to produce superior results and override potential hurdles.

Group Decision Techniques

The following techniques are time-tested, proven paths to coming up with creative and dynamic group decisions.

1. ***Brainstorming.*** Brainstorming is a technique designed to overcome the adverse pressures toward conformity or "group-think," to generate creative solutions. It does this by focusing on *ideation* (idea-generation) among group members, with the understanding that any evaluation or criticism of ideas will be initially withheld.

In a typical brainstorming meeting the group members sit around a table and the leader states the problem or issue in clear, simple terms. The members then "free wheel" as many alternative solutions as they can for a given period of time. No criticism or evaluation is allowed—something that takes practice for most groups. The members are encouraged to let one idea feed another, and usually some truly ingenious proposals result. These are recorded in one form or another for later analysis and discussion. Many of the benefits of brainstorming can be transferred to more formal groups by simply asking people to refrain from criticizing ideas until later in the meeting.

The strength of brainstorming lies in the free generation of ideas it encourages. The refining process that leads to an actual decision, is the focus of the next two techniques.

2. ***Nominal Group Technique.*** The Nominal Group Technique restricts interpersonal communication during the decision-making process. Group members are all physically present, but they operate independently and fairly autonomously. First, the group convenes and the problem or issue is stated clearly and simply. Then:

a) Before discussion begins, each person writes down his or her ideas relating to the problem.

b) After this period of private ideation, each member in turn presents one of his ideas to the group until all original ideas are exhausted. All contributions are recorded in a master list (often on flip charts or a chalkboard).

c) The group discusses the list of ideas, with a focus on clarifying each contribution, and evaluates them. The list is trimmed of untenable ideas.

d) Each member, silently and independently, rank-orders the consolidated list.

e) The final decision can be determined by selecting the alternative with the highest aggregated ranking. Many groups also find that the top three or four solutions have attractive features which can be fitted or blended into the overall decision.

The main advantage of the Nominal Group Technique is that it allows the group to operate in a formal manner, but doesn't restrict independent thinking or force conformity.

3. ***Delphi Technique.*** This is similar to the Nominal Group Technique, but is more complex, more time-consuming, and does not require the physical presence of the participants. (In fact, it actually prohibits face-to-face interaction.) Again, the process starts with a clear and simple statement of the problem. Then:

a) Members are asked to provide potential solutions through a series of carefully designed questionnaires.

b) Each member anonymously and independently completes the first questionnaire, making sure it reflects her best thinking.

c) The results of this questionnaire are compiled by the administrator, and copies of the amassed results are sent back to each participant.

d) The members each review the results independently, and are then asked to generate fresh solutions or ideas based on their new knowledge. Changes from earlier positions are generally observed at this stage, since participants have the benefit of their colleagues' accumulated best thinking.

e) Steps (c) and (d) are repeated as many times as necessary until consensus—or its acceptable approximation—is achieved.

The Delphi Technique, though time-consuming, insulates group members from the undue influence of others and tries to build on the last, best ideas offered. Since it does not require the physical presence of the participants, it is often used to acquire the best thinking of experts from outside the area, or to accumulate expertise and solve problems in a geographically dispersed company. In contrast to Brainstorming, it has a funneling effect on the alternatives generated.

Groups can serve as a varied, purposeful resource for better, more supportable ideas and decisions. The advantages of using groups usually outweigh the disadvantages when you are willing and able to take the time and effort to involve others in your work.

ON ORGANIZATIONAL CULTURE

"In any organization, there are the ropes to skip and the ropes to know."
—R. Ritti & G. Funkhouser

There is a story about Thomas Watson, Jr., who, while chairman of IBM's board, was one day touring a plant with the usual entourage of managers and senior executives. The group made its way toward a security area of the plant but was stopped short by a twenty-two-year-old female supervisor whose job it was to admit only those wearing proper identification badges. Watson wore an orange badge; unfortunately, it was acceptable in every area of the facility except the one guarded by this young woman. Although she knew Watson by sight, the supervisor also knew her job: "You cannot enter. Your admittance is not recognized." The group gave a collective gasp and one of the senior officials barked, "Don't you know who this is?" But Watson quickly raised his hand for silence, had one of the executives fetch the proper identification, and entered only when the correct badge was clipped to his lapel.

Most IBM employees know this story and retell it with some delight to the company's newcomers. The tale does more than recount a simple incident, though; it imparts a "feeling" for—or "sense" of and "knowledge" about—the fabled IBM culture; a culture that one has to live with to fully understand. The concept of organizational culture is similarly ephemeral—hard to pin down concretely but nevertheless critical to performance. The following brief outline shows some important ways of thinking about organizational culture.

What is Organizational Culture?

Above all, organizational culture refers to a system of shared values held by members of a company. These values are known, communicated, and produce a corporate identity that distinguishes one firm from another.

Three Levels of Culture

Most cultures operate on several levels simultaneously. Edgar Schein has developed this model:

Level I:	*Material, Symbolic, Behavioral Artifacts*
Level II:	*Values*
Level III:	*Basic Assumptions and Beliefs*

The first level of corporate culture is easily observed but hard to interpret without access to deeper levels. Being admitted to the "Million Dollar Roundtable," for instance, is symbolic of high sales achievement in the insurance industry, but carries little meaning outside that group.

The second level stresses the way things *ought to be,* as contrasted with the way they *are.* Successful business people possess convictions about what constitutes proper and effective action in particular situations (that advertising will increase sales, for example, or that a professional code of ethics should guide practice).

The third level—the cultural foundation—consists of basic beliefs and values that guide and construct social reality and the interpretation of "objective" environmental realities. Whether the business person is engaged in individualistic competition (often the case in Western business cultures) or as a member of a communitarian society (as in many Asian companies) is governed by the basic assumptions found at this ground level.

The Strength of a Culture

Business cultures are said to be either "strong" or "weak." Strong cultures characteristically have all three culture levels not only present, but *intensely held and widely shared.* The more the members of a group uniformly accept and use the beliefs, language and symbols of a culture, the stronger it is. Strong cultures (such as the one commonly ascribed to Procter & Gambel) forcefully influence the attitudes and actions of a workforce.

Weak cultures, by contrast, support competing beliefs, dissonant values, vague and multiple symbols of success, which dilute the culture's impact on employee behavior.

What Does A Culture Do?

First and foremost, a culture *yields identity.* "I'm an HP engineer," communicates corporate and professional membership to the incumbent, as well as to outsiders.

Second, the culture sets *boundaries* that distinguish the way things are done "here" as opposed to "everywhere else." Cultures act as a "social glue" that holds employees together, conveying to them expected ways of behaving and working together, and creating a sense of community. Consequently, an organization's culture is often linked to the level of commitment among its employees.

Third, and perhaps most important, a culture *shapes the way its members think* about themselves, each other, and the "realities" that surround them. "Is leveraging a good thing?" "Is diversification feasible?" "If we buy that company, do we have the expertise to manage it?" An organization's culture can sway answers to questions like these.

Creating and Building Culture

Most organizational cultures have their roots in the beliefs and values held by the firm's founders. Think of Walt Disney's impact on Disney Productions, Ray Kroc's influence on McDonald's, Steve Wozniak's vision for Apple Computer. These founders infused their companies with a philosophical base that continues to influence corporate strategy decades later. Once in place, this bedrock of beliefs and values is perpetuated (and modified) by some very concrete choices that managers make.

One of the most useful actions in creating and building culture is the *culture audit*—a strategic assessment of what the company's culture is and what it should be. This is a non-trivial exercise carried out at the highest levels of corporate management and repeated on a regular basis. MBA's are taught the importance of examining the assumptions that underlie a course of action; in some ways this parallels the spirit of a culture audit.

Tactical mechanisms for creating and building culture include:

(1) **Recruitment practices,** where the "right" people are selected, based on their ability to support the cultural ideals.

(2) **Employee orientation programs,** which teach new employees about the company, and thus its cultural norms, values, and beliefs.

(3) **Attention to communication** and its various methods—verbal, written, gestural—all designed to impart meaning. Popular cultural texts tend to emphasize the importance of stories, myths, rituals and material symbols (the logo-adorned Cross pen, for instance), but these are only special cases of the communication imperative. The effective manager recognizes the broad range of communication phenomena. When trying to create a certain type of culture, he supports the effort with multiple forms of communication in harmony with the company's underlying values.

Culture: So What?

Can you afford to forget about the culture concept? Probably not, since every firm has one.

If it did nothing else, the book *In Search of Excellence* made clear the extensive impact culture can have in a company. Your business has a culture. The question is whether the culture contributes to overall productivity or lies unnoticed and untended, like a sea anchor that retards the progress of a ship.

Business Gift-Giving Ideas

(Plus, Some Notions on the Art of Giving)

For the proper reason, and at the timely moment, a gift is a token of sensitivity and refinement. A thoughtful gift might be presented: to say ***thank you*** (for a favor, the hosting of a party or for your stay in a home); to congratulate (on a promotion, an award, the birth of a baby, a good performance or impressive speech); to ***encourage*** (for someone experiencing a new career or job, an illness or accident, a death in the family); to ***apologize*** (for an offense, a missed appointment or forgotten promise, a troublesome incident); to wish ***good luck*** (on an important birthday or anniversary, a move to another city, a marriage, a retirement, a major change, a holiday); or to express ***friendship*** to an employee, boss or client, being careful, of course, to avoid any impropriety—suggestion of a bribe, a bid for influence or any other inappropriate motive.

The thought *does* count in gift-giving. While some situations may demand a more expensive present than others, your thoughtfulness in selection and presentation is much more important than the money spent.

Remembering when to give is vital. A daily calendar with important events noted, a tickler file system (3 x 5 cards or computerized), or a wall or desk calendar will all do the job. Jot down for the year, a week or so in front of each major occasion, all your personal gift-giving dates.

In giving, here are some pointers to keep in mind:

- Select an item with both the *occasion* and the recipient's *tastes* in mind. Give a cooking buff a book on seasonal recipes from around the world for Christmas; give a sports fan a videotape of great moments in football history for a September birthday.
- Buy something he or she can and will *use*. This can be determined by keen observation or by questioning acquaintances or family members.
- The *quality* of a gift is most important. Carefully chosen sale purchases, supermarket items and even some second-hand treasures (books, glass or porcelain pieces, old-fashioned jewelry, etc.) can make excellent gifts. But whatever you get or however much or little you spend, get something good of its kind.
- Demonstrate *high esteem* for the recipient; a "comical" gift may offend. Though a laugh-getting shirt slogan may be fine for a peer whose tastes you know well, joke gifts are, for the most part, taboo. Gifts that are too impersonal, on the other hand, may seem perfunctory.
- Photo albums, bookplates, stationery, and all kinds of leather accessories will mean and express many times more to a recipient when they are personalized with engraved or printed names, initials, designs, etc.
- Along with your gift, include an enclosure card with some brief (even one- or two-word) greeting or wish, hand-written on good note paper, and sealed or placed in an envelope.
- Use *attractive* gift-wrap.
- Use packaging that is reusable and handsome.
- Present the gift in *person* whenever possible.

Some Gift Ideas

Food

Cheeses, easily prepared gourmet dishes, jams and jellies, nuts, cookies, candy, fresh fruit, dried fruit, baked goods, exotic or regional foods, selected sauces, mustards or other condiments, selected teas, small squashes, smoked salmon, fresh lobster, caviar, frozen steaks, distinctive ice creams and toppings, coffees, liquors (wines or champagne).

For Travel

Luggage piece (matching existing pieces), tote bag or briefcase, folding umbrella, first-aid kit, sewing kit, toiletry or cosmetics kit, manicure kit, stationery and stamps, travel iron, magnified folding mirror, wallet, passport case, diary, alarm clock (wound or battery-operated), camera, rolls of film, hair dryer, best-selling novel, dictionary of foreign terms, regional guide or history book, travel game.

For the Office

Clock for desk or wall, desk-top organizer with matching wastebasket, letter opener, magazine subscription, briefcase, latest book on management, pocket calculator, desk calendar, pen-and-pencil set, dictionary/thesaurus set, magazine rack, ashtrays, thermos set with tray, bar accessories (if there's a bar), large standing plant, bookends, attractive jar filled with candies, wall mirror, leather telephone directory cover.

For the Home

Kitchen accessories (cooking equipment, cookbook, favorite recipes, house-hold hint book, knife set, cutting board, condiment set, specialty napkin rings, beverage or dessert set), bath or beach towels, serving tray, guest soaps, barbecue set, picnic basket, cooler, potpourri, bar implements (glasses, tray, pitcher, wine cooler, ice bucket, tongs, coasters), records or tapes, specialty gadgets, books relating to a hobby, games, food or drink, stationery, pieces to augment or complete an existing display or collection.

For a Special Occasion (recognition, retirement...)

Tie clip or brooch, watch or bracelet, other jewelry, fine clock, photograph, plaque, embossed scrapbook (with pictures already mounted, if possible), tickets for an event, trip or cruise, personal presentation or "roasting," piece of antique furniture, work of art (a framed painting, drawing, lithograph, poster, or small statue), a hobby or sports item (painting, golf, tennis...), membership at a country club or health spa. (Many items can be embossed or engraved with the company logo and/or the recipient's name)

For Someone Who Is Ill

Amusing book, flowering plant, taped music or book, cologne, cosmetics or toiletries, room spray, bath soap, game, soft sculpture, robe or bed jacket, slippers, card, poster or cassette tape with individual good wishes from group members, memory book or filled photo album, recorded VCR tapes, hand-work set (needle point, knitting, etc.) if the person is bed bound but feeling quite well, blank note cards or stationery to make his or her time seem productive.

For a New Mother or Baby

Newborn diapers (disposable or cloth), plant or flower arrangement, card, baby quilt, baby mug or spoon, bibs, rattle, soft toy, baby book or journal, baby clothes sized between six and eighteen months, stroller, book on names, baby care booklet (for first babies), high-chair dining set, film, camera, individual or group collection of favorite lullabies, subscription to a parenting magazine offering baby-care or stay-sane mothering/fathering tips, baby travel kit.

For Sensitive Giving (death, serious injury...)

Appropriate book for the time, fresh flowers, large plant, taped music, personal letter or card.

Dressing for Business

It's a fact of life: A businessperson dressed in simple fashion, well groomed, and in clean, quality, appropriate clothing, projects success.

Each company has its own dress code, usually unwritten, but unmistakably clear. The countless subtleties of dress can become apparent through close observation and daily experience. An executive can be creative with clothing, however, and still remain within the framework appropriate for his or her firm.

Select the advice that is helpful to you from the categories below:

Buying Sense

Ask yourself key questions when considering the purchase of a piece of business clothing:

- Is it suitable for my job and company?
- Does it fit properly now and will it fit in the future?
- Is the fabric and cut of top quality for long wear?
- Is it fashionable yet basic enough to stay in style?
- Is it right for my body and personal tastes?
- Are the colors neutral and the patterns and textures complimentary, to match other clothing in my ward-robe?

As you dress each day, combine and accessorize the clothing you've bought in order to feel confident and relaxed. Buying items with your age, body-build and professional position in mind will help keep your daily decision-making simple and anxious-free.

Image Decisions

Dress according to the image you want to project. This image will change somewhat depending on:

- The city you are in.
- The occasion.
- The people you are about to meet.
- The weather.
- The time of day.

Overall, however, your style will be fairly consistent. Aligning your dress with your desired image, may require some "editing." Sources of fashion advice include:

- A department or specialty store consultant.

- A friend with obvious fashion sense.
- A paid-by-the-hour, free-lance or company consultant.

Basic Don'ts

Avoid in business settings:

- Mismatched or clashing ensembles.
- Exaggerated future trends in grooming and apparel.
- Too much fragrance.
- Clothes that are too tight. (Snug clothing can magnify a weight gain—or give the appearance of one. It's best to either lose the weight, buy some new clothes, or have the clothes let out.)
- Wearing running shoes.
- Bragging about or displaying your designer-label clothing.
- Outfits that aren't fundamentally "you." Contrived fashions (for example, western duds on a city person) may look ridiculous.
- For men—socks that allow bare leg to show at the bottoms of slacks.
- For women—dressy fabrics more suitable for evening wear (satin, cut velvet, lame, brocade); also, stocking runs, or slip straps that show.

Jackets

- Select a jacket that is complimented by your shoes, slacks or skirt, shirt or blouse, tie, jewelry or other accessories. Check for color, texture, pattern and overall style compatibility.
- A jacket should either be part of a matching suit or not be too close in color to your pants or skirt. Generally, only one pattern, texture, or type of fabric should prevail.
- Keep a double-breasted jacket buttoned.
- If you normally work without your jacket on, a long-sleeved shirt or blouse looks much better than a short-sleeved one, even with sleeves rolled up to the elbow when it's hot.
- As a sign of deference, put on your jacket when—or before—an outside client or the "big boss" enters your office.

Grooming

You might want to post and consult (especially before important occasions) a grooming checklist to check yourself out before other people do:

Since grooming is the cornerstone of good appearance, consider keeping a grooming kit in the office for "emergencies." The kit might include fragrance, comb or brush, hairspray, mouthwash, toothbrush, toothpaste, mirror, shoe polishing kit, spot-remover, (for men, a razor), (for women, make-up and extra hosiery).

Hair

- In some offices, a man's clean-shaven, beardless face, though not mandatory, may be expected.
- Keep hair combed or brushed at all times, but don't perform the ritual in public.

Grooming Checklist			
	General	**For Men**	**For Women**
HEAD	Clean face, ears and neck	Well-shaven or trimmed facial hair	Make-up carefully applied
	Hair clean, cut and well combed	After-shave or cologne applied	Earrings and/or necklace shined
BODY	Clothing clean, pressed and checked for fraying	Shirt collar and cuffs adjusted	Slip not showing
		Tie neatly tied	No make-up on blouse collar
	Deodorant applied		Fragrance applied sparingly
	Underwear fresh		
	Clothing spot-free, buttoned and checked for lint and dandruff		
HANDS	Washed with nails clean and in good shape		Nail polish well done and in the proper color
	Watchband and rings free from soap film		Hand lotion applied
LEGS & FEET	Shoes in good condition, well polished and free of scuff marks; laces or tassels not broken or frayed	Clean socks pulled up high	Pantyhose run-free and, if seamed, with the seams straight
HANDBAG/ BRIEFCASE	Polished and packed with all necessities for the day		

- Use a minimum of hair-spray—especially if it's perfumed.
- Abstain from the habit of stroking or playing with your hair.
- Avoid wearing curlers in public.
- If a wig or hairpiece is worn, make sure it is conservative, fits properly, is of good quality, and that its color is consistent with your complexion.

Make-up

- Learn to apply make-up to enhance your appearance. A make-up specialist can offer hints to help you more deftly disguise your weaknesses and accentuate your attributes.
- "Subtract something" is a good rule before going out the door. Critique your face, then remove, lighten or blend as needed. Less is truly more.
- It's best to use less make-up in the office than you might use during off hours.
- Types and amounts of make-up needed for the office may include: a moisturizer, a colorless or skin-matching foundation, a light dusting powder, light blush to the cheeks, thin eyeliner (without noticeable color), and eyebrow pencil lightly applied to the contour of your natural brows.
- Thick mascara and eye shadow, beauty marks and false eyelashes are best left for socializing.
- Blot lipstick before a social or meeting where drinks are to be served to avoid getting lipstick on your glass.

Nails

- Well-shaped, clean—and unbitten—nails, along with healthy cuticles, are important to both men and women.

- Brightly colored or excessively long nails tend to be a distraction. A quiet-colored polish on shorter nails is attractive, and is preferred by most businesswomen.

Fragrance

- Buy only quality perfume, after-shave lotion or cologne.
- Apply fragrances lightly so that others are only slightly aware you are using them.

Remember: Good taste is mostly a matter of common sense, mixed with taking the time and thought necessary to constantly improve and refine your appearance.

Business and Executive Etiquette

(Guides to Getting Along and Getting Ahead)

OFFICE RELATIONSHIPS

Relating to others in a courteous, constructive manner is a valuable skill we can all refine. Continually violating the simple rules of civility conveys a lack of education and experience. Conversely, handling awkward moments with charm and grace shows you are in control.

You and Your Associates

- Discover your office's unwritten code of behavior: formality of greetings and dress, expectations for lunch-time fraternizing, rules for maintaining office privacy, etc. Blend common sense with the atmosphere that prevails in your office.
- To introduce two people, speak first to the "superior": "Mrs. Fox, this is Doug Weber, our new assistant editor. Doug, our accountant, Mrs. Fox." Use the titles each will use daily.
- Acknowledging an introduction is done best with a simple, "How do you do."
- Shake hands with any person you meet for the first time.
- Stand to greet anyone who enters your office (excepting co-workers carrying out business matters) and invite them to be seated.
- Escort a guest from your office, and to his or her car if it seems called for.
- Office music should be appropriate and soft.
- Unless you are in a designated smoking area, don't smoke without first asking others, "Would you mind very much if I smoked?"
- If smoking is offensive or irritating to you, do speak up before a smoker lights up.
- Romance and flirting have no place in the office. The smartest advice is: don't!
- Don't snack in front of others unless you can fittingly offer to share.
- Try to avoid bringing pets or children to the office for any extended periods of time. If exceptions are necessary, "guests" must be properly controlled.
- In most offices it is appropriate to use first names between associates and subordinates.

- Depending on office procedure, knock on a closed door and enter only after being invited. Ask if you're interrupting before initiating a conversation or question.
- Speak fairly and politely. Abstain from gossip, threats, sarcasm or arrogance in speech.
- Keep conversations honest and open. However, complaints or personal "fence-mending" should be done in private.
- Choose office friendships wisely, while maintaining good relations with all peers. Too much socializing with co-workers outside of work can prove to be a detriment, as can excessive personal conversation. Disclosing all your opinions, personal hang-ups or plans could hurt you and interfere with work.
- If you and a colleague just can't get along, formal politeness is still expected. It is totally unacceptable to complain openly or act spitefully. A "cease-fire" compromise must be reached, which later may lead to genuine respect.
- Considerately and confidentially offer assistance to colleagues when it is perceived necessary, and only when they are not taking advantage of your good nature.
- Give due credit to others when they have helped you.
- "Talkers" can interfere with work. A response of, "I'm sorry, but I really must get back to work," will usually allow you to do so.

You and Your Boss

- Understand your boss' expectations, time schedule, habits, plans and goals. What's important to him or her? Pay attention; try to sense a supervisor's needs without pandering to them.
- Find out your manager's preferred method of communication (letter, memo, talking face-to-face...) and act accordingly.
- An employer dismisses employees at the end of a meeting.
- Be friendly with your boss, but remember: too much intimacy can backfire on you.
- Keep your boss informed of what you're doing. Follow up on assignments without being reminded.
- Never embarrass an employer, particularly in public.
- Never threaten. Assertiveness often smacks of arrogance.
- Accept criticism graciously, not jokingly or defensively. The best reply: "Is there anything else I should know to help me in my work?"
- Vent disagreements privately. Pre-plan tactful discussions with your superior. Disagree without being disagreeable.
- If an office problem must be issued as a complaint, present it professionally rather than personally. Describe the problem using diplomacy, without placing blame. Have various possible solutions in mind.
- If you feel a raise in salary is in order, organize yourself. Write down your contributions to the company and your accepted responsibilities. Arrange a convenient time to meet your boss to present these facts. Calmly accept the initial response to your request. Ask that he or she "go to bat" for you as a valuable employee, and schedule a later time to discuss the matter further.
- Always be prompt for work, meetings and appointments.

- Being efficient and productive in your job show that you value your company, your colleagues and your employer. Such obvious caring will put you ahead.

When You're the Boss

- Constantly strive to improve relations with employees by being gracious and not too assertive, while still motivating each worker as part of the team. Try to be available and listen.
- Delegate clearly, defining expectations and objectives.
- Welcome opinions and feedback from your workers. Consider them experts at what they do, and refer to them as associates, colleagues, team members, managers or directors.
- Trust employees to work out personal and business problems on their own. At most, become involved only to the extent of listening, counseling and coaching, but leave ultimate solutions to them.
- Build confidence through sincere praise and enthusiasm.

COMMUNICATIONS

Effective communication is what much of business is all about. It is mostly a matter of common sense and courtesy; thinking how your method and manner will affect others. Passing out routine memos, unnecessary copying of forms and letters, passing on paperwork, and unthinking speech not only waste time but may also be viewed as breaches of etiquette.

Written Communication

- Letters should lean toward personal expression and away from stuffiness. They generally include the following parts: heading (your address and date of letter), inside address (person's name and title, company name and address), greeting (Dear Mr. Jones,), body (brief business, stated clearly), closing (Very truly yours, or Sincerely,) and signature (handwritten with typed name and title beneath).
- Personal letters of congratulation, appreciation or condolence are best if they are handwritten, concise, and contain no references to business.
- Business stationery and cards should be conservative.
- In-house, brief information can be written in a memo. A casual yet candid approach is best. Describe in plain language who, what, when, where, why and how.
- Don't waste the readers' time. Choice of words, spelling, grammar and simple sentence structure are vital.
- Convey a positive tone and sincere regard in all writing.

Telephone Etiquette

- Avoid machine-answering of incoming calls.
- Professional, simple courtesy needs to be evident upon answering a call. State your name and what company or department you represent.
- Speak softly and clearly.
- When receiving a call for another, screen it so that your associate may know how to respond: "May I say who is calling?"
- If a secretary places a call for you, be ready to get on the line immediately to avoid

keeping that person waiting. Better yet, place your own calls when possible.

- When calling someone, identify yourself and with whom you would like to speak. "This is Mrs. Jones. May I speak to Dr. Waite, please?"
- If you are unavoidably interrupted during a conversation, say, "Excuse me a minute. I have to handle something." Take care of the problem with the mouthpiece covered, then apologize and resume your business.
- Normally, the call's initiator signs off. However, if you're busy and someone's call interrupts you, say so and indicate a time when you will call back.
- Graciously guard your business hours from "talkers": "I really don't want to take any more of your time, so I'll say goodbye."

Speaking Face-to-Face and in Public

- Recognize that choice of words, tone of voice, body language, gestures, and posture can be powerful tools—or frustrating obstacles—to effective speaking. If you don't speak well, do something about it: listen to and observe others; ask a friend to analyze your skills; take a class or read a book; join Toastmasters or other speaking group...Practice communicating aloud. Use a mirror and an audio or video recorder to diagnose yourself, if these seem helpful.
- Attentive listening is a compliment to any speaker, and can reap great benefits. Refrain from interrupting another or appearing only to be planning your next statement. Lean slightly forward, look at the speaker and focus your thoughts on what is being presented. Your facial expressions and slight nods indicate understanding.
- Verbal signals of agreement ("Yes, I agree completely...") or of disagreement ("I'm not sure about that point," or "You may be right, but...") can be "slipped in" as appropriate.
- Extend a genuine, brief compliment to someone who has impressed you. Avoid flattery or gushing praise.
- Cliches, slang or business jargon often seem insincerely spoken. Don't use "utilize" for "use"; or habitually insert the word "impact" when "affect" will do.
- Use jokes, wisecracks or anecdotes sparingly—or not at all—particularly in meetings. Perceived charlatans or jokers are often passed over on serious assignments.
- Avoid coarse or suggestive language.
- Public speaking will be less frightening and more comfortable if you overly prepare: know your topic; don't memorize your talk, but practice speaking about your subject in a natural way; add appropriate stories and humor; dress conservatively; the day of your speech, relax your mind; breath deeply several times before beginning your address.
- Be sure to stay well within your time limit. Make your point without exhausting either the topic or your audience.
- If you choose to use a specific word or phrase—especially a foreign word /or phrase—be certain of pronunciation and meaning.
- Cultivate a well-modulated voice; not too high-pitched, too loud, or too soft. Enunciate properly. Vary, from time to time, your volume, intonation and speed.

- Practice discretion in all your speech. Consciously refrain from monopolizing meetings or conversations. Make your comments with respect and forethought. Remember Abigail Van Buren's observation: "The less you talk, the more you're listened to."

SOCIAL ETIQUETTE

The business lunch and company party have become common yet important affairs that require social poise and style. Even minor irritants or faux pas can terminate a relationship or a deal.

The Business Lunch

- If you would like to host someone for lunch for a particular purpose, extend the invitation within a phone conversation: "How about lunch next week?" Asking ahead of time will allow you both to calendar a mutually agreeable time.
- To further clarify that this person will be your guest, suggest a location and reconfirm the time.
- Call ahead for reservations, giving the number of guests and, if needed, the desired seating arrangement.
- Frequent one particular restaurant most often. Being recognized and getting quality, personal service make subtle impressions.
- Arrive before your guest. Wait in the lobby to check in coats and to be seated.
- It's best to sit in the nonsmoking section if any nonsmoker is included. If you are entertaining an important client who smokes, and you can tolerate it, it's polite to offer to sit in the smoking section.
- If the lunch involves a man and a woman, watch for cues on how the other person wants to be treated socially. Men usually open doors and offer assistance to remove coats.
- A woman is quite capable of ordering her own meal and drink. Either a man or a woman may order for the other, if requested.
- When asked if you wish to order drinks, put your guest at ease: "Yes, I would. What will you have, Frank?" The drink is a formality. Generally, only one drink (at most two) should be ordered, especially if it is alcoholic. No one, regardless of his drinking habits, wants to be perceived as a heavy drinker.
- Your guest orders his or her meal first.
- While ordering, do not comment about past or present diets.
- Show concern about your guest and his or her meal, without being overly dramatic.
- If you are the guest, remain low key and pleasant.
- During a "working" lunch, the host may be direct and ask, for instance, "Well, shall we discuss the Bailey account?" If you want to be more subtle, start with, "Well, what do you think about...?" or "Tell me what's happening with you."
- When finished, or nearly finished, ask the waiter for the check. If the check is brought to your guest, simply reach over and take it (don't grab it). Look the bill over quickly and carefully and figure the tip. Place the check and your credit card (or money if you must) on the tray, with the check face down.

- The usual tip is 15 to 20 percent. Pennies, nickels or dimes are best not used unless they are from the change brought to you; then, leave all the coins.
- Both guest and host should thank the other for the pleasant time.

Entertaining at Home

- Good planning allows you, the host, to have as much fun as your guests.
- A formal dinner is no longer expected for successful gatherings in the home. Look to plan more personal, individual patio parties or simple buffet dinners.
- Plan the entertainment and meal or refreshments according to the occasion, your budget and the space available.
- Make up the guest list with care. Consider how many people you feel comfortable serving and can comfortably fit in your home. More people can be invited to a party where simple food and drinks are served than for a sit-down dinner. Invite persons who, for business or social reasons, will be compatible.
- Invitations to casual events are generally made by phone.
- For a formal dinner, on white or pastel stationery, hand-write a simple message: "We request the pleasure of your company..." and stating the occasion, date, time, place and appropriate dress. If necessary, request a response to your invitation by placing "RSVP" at the bottom.
- To reply to an invitation, "accept with pleasure..." or "regret that a previous engagement prevents our accepting..." on plain white stationery.
- A call made several days before the event to those who have not responded, is in order. You merely need ask if they are going to attend so that you may plan for them.
- For large parties, organize far in advance. The catering, bartending and serving staff must be sufficient to handle your group; for every 25 guests, one "helper" of each kind is about right. Providing these services frees you to be a more gracious host.
- Decide what you will need to borrow or rent: silverware, glasses, platters, dishes, tables, chairs, linens, bartending supplies, etc. These items may require time for cleaning or polishing.
- Be sure to have enough fresh soap, bathroom tissue, coasters, ash trays, matches, and guest towels on hand.
- Remember extras like candles, decorations, banners, and centerpieces. Dress up serving platters with simple garnishes: sprigs, herbs, cut fruits, baby vegetables, flowers or sauces.
- Food extras, such as nuts, olives, cut vegetables and drinks, make marvelous "unstiffeners" to help guests feel welcome and comfortable when they first arrive. Stock your kitchen with quick-to-fix fare (deli meats, pre-cut or shredded cheese, frozen bread dough, etc.) and munchies (nuts pretzels, cookies, candies, dried fruits, etc.).
- Arrange for food to be prepared in advance, as far as is possible. Choose recipes that can be frozen or refrigerated.
- Spend time greeting your guests. Take coats, or show where they may be taken, and usher new arrivals into the party. Make at least one introduction so newcomers will have an immediate acquaintance. If the gathering is small, they should be introduced to everyone.

- Along with the introduction, you might add something about each person or couple: "Rex, this is Mike and Jan Reid. They just returned from living in Maine. Mike, Jan, this is my business partner, Rex Dome."
- Tactfully guide conversations to include all guests in small visiting pockets. But don't forget to relax. If you enjoy the event, it's more likely your guests will too.
- Artful hints may be required to let guests know it's time to go. While visiting, state warmly, "Well, I hope you had a nice time." However, be prepared to take care of late-stayers, and even to provide an early morning round of food (coffee, eggs, donuts) to departing guests.
- Be a responsible host. If a visitor has had too many drinks, or if you at all question his ability to drive, don't argue. Discreetly arrange for a ride home with another guest, or else call a taxi. Then tell the guest you will bring his car over in the morning.
- If a guest is leaving and comes to thank you for the party (as she should), graciously inquire, "Why so soon?" (even if it's three in the morning). Then thank her for coming and escort her to the door.
- Elderly guests and single women should be escorted to their car or cab..

EATING AND DRINKING

Managing the task of putting food in your mouth can be as important as any business skill. Dinner poise is one more indication of your education and caring. Modern rules are designed to help you show consideration for others and to make eating together an enjoyable, comfortable occasion. Excessive strictness, however, is no longer the norm.

Eating Etiquette

- If you are unsure how to proceed with a dish or which spoon to use, wait a few moments. Someone else at the table will likely initiate the action and you may then nonchalantly follow suit.
- The rules governing the use of flatware are: start from the outside fork or spoon and work in as each course is served; keep used flatware on the plate, not on the tablecloth; place the knife and fork side by side on your plate to indicate to the waiter when you are finished.
- You may find a finger bowl on the table at very formal restaurants, which may appear before or after the meal. Dip only your fingers into the water and dry them with your napkin below table level.
- Place your napkin on your lap shortly after being seated. Unfold it to a comfortable size (usually so that it is still folded in half) and use it as needed to remove crumbs from your mouth before drinking. When finished, place it unfolded to the left of the plate.
- Bread or rolls should be broken in half before buttering, and may be supported in one hand to aid in picking up food. Rolls are not to be used to wipe a plate clean.
- Be seated and unseat yourself quietly, and always from the right of the chair.
- Excuse yourself if you leave the table for any reason.

- Maintain good posture. Don't support yourself with your elbows. An elbow on the table is permissible before and after the meal and between courses, but not while eating.
- A woman wearing lipstick might blot her lips in private before dinner to avoid getting lipstick on her water or wine glasses.
- Refrain from reaching across someone. If an item is not within reach, politely ask for it to be passed.
- To ask for something to be brought, or to request a change in improperly prepared food, firmly yet politely address the waiter or attendant without bringing your request to the attention of other diners.
- Don't slurp, smack your lips, or speak with food in your mouth—errors that are more common than one would think.
- Accidental slurping or spilling is easily handled with a quiet apology.
- Drink slowly and noiselessly after sweeping your lips with your napkin to remove particles that may stick to the glass.
- The soup spoon is moved away from the body during formal dinners. To extract the last bit of soup, tilt the bowl slightly away from you and spoon it out. Then rest the spoon in the bowl or on the plate under it.
- Eat the main course using the large fork and knife. The fork is placed in the left hand (for right-handers) and the knife in the right for cutting. The fork should remain almost horizontal with the tines pointing down and the index finger on top of the handle. Transferring the fork to the right hand (American method) or leaving it in the left (Continental method) to bring food to the mouth are both acceptable. Cut food by moving mainly the wrists, with moderate or no movement of the elbows.
- To remove pits or bones from your mouth, cup your fingers to hide the food, bring the napkin to the mouth, and place particles discreetly on the side of your plate.
- Never spit out food that's too hot. Strategically and calmly take a drink.
- Drenching food with catsup or other bottled sauce can be viewed as an insult. A condiment may be applied directly to an open-faced sandwich or to the side of french fries.
- First transfer pats of butter (using a fork) or jams/jellies (using a spoon) to your plate, then spread them onto breads using the butter knife.
- Stirring or mashing food on your plate is offensive. A baked potato is generally eaten as it is forked from the shell.
- Steer your discussion to topics that won't cause others to feel uncomfortable or squeamish. "Politics" and "religion" might lead to an argument; and an account of your recent surgery or illness might make someone ill.
- A waiter or waitress deserves your respect and an occasional "thank you," especially for extra service. You need not offer thanks for every act.
- If you drop a fork or piece of food, it's best if you don't make even the slightest scene. Casually scoot the article to an out-of-the-way spot, and, if convenient, quietly retrieve it after the meal.
- Never move your own dishes or stack them. This is left for the server to do.

- Toothpicks should not be used in public.
- After being served what to you might be a "tricky" food (lobster, specialty sandwich, etc.), either slow down and notice how others proceed, or speak up and say to a nearby acquaintance, "I've never eaten this. How do I go about doing it?" Most people are pleased to be able to provide instructions.
- Most foods are cut and eaten using the knife and fork. Unless your host decrees otherwise, only at drive-ins and picnics do chicken and french fries become finger-foods. Strawberries, grapes, other fruits, and olives are most often eaten using the fingers.
- Spaghetti should be wound around the tines of the fork using one of several methods.
- The key is to leave no ends hanging that need to be sucked into the mouth. This may be difficult to master, but with some in-home practice you can become expert.
- Relax....Regardless of the pressures you may be under, slow down and enjoy your guests' company—and *enjoy* yourself!

Classics in Personal Effectiveness

A Classic Collection

THE SEVEN HABITS OF HIGHLY EFFECTIVE PEOPLE

by Stephen R. Covey, Simon & Schuster, 1989

I've set and met my career goals and I'm having tremendous professional success. But it's cost me my personal and family life. I don't know my wife and children any more. I'm not even sure I know myself and what's really important to me. I've had to ask myself—is it worth it?"

"There's so much to do. And there's never enough time. I feel pressured and hassled all day, every day, seven days a week. I've attended time management seminars and I've tried half a dozen different planning systems. They've helped some, but I still don't feel I'm living the happy, productive, peaceful life I want to live."

In response to such sentiments, Covey's *Seven Habits of Highly Effective People* defines powerful principles for joyful, effective living. His book is saturated with advice on leadership, life management and relationships, all centered around the "inside-out" concept: behavior is learned, it is not instinctive. Old habits *can* be discarded and replaced by new and more effective habits.

Until 1930 or so, most success literature was based on the *Character Ethic*—the belief that there are basic principles of effective living and that people can only experience true success and enduring happiness as they integrate these principles into their lives. Then shortly after World War I, the central view of success shifted from the Character Ethic to the *Personality Ethic.* Success became a function of persona, of public image, of positive attitudes and behaviors, human-relations skills and techniques. The Personality Ethic is still in wide favor today. And adherents often do find temporary help by practicing these techniques, but sooner or later most realize that the underlying obstacles to happiness still persist.

Paradigms

A *paradigm* is a model or graph of the way we "see" the world—in terms of perceiving, understanding, and interpreting. A paradigm can be compared to a map. Improving behavior, doubling your effort, or thinking more positively would have no effect if you were given a map of Chicago and asked to find an address in Los Angeles. The frustrations you would face would have nothing to do with behavior or attitude: *they would arise out of having the wrong map.*

When *principles*—fundamental values, like fairness, integrity, human dignity and service—are *internalized into habits,* they empower people to formulate a wide variety of practices to deal with different situations. This involves developing an "inside-out" paradigm—maps and models generated of both the way things really are and the way we want them to be—then *following* the maps and *living* the models.

We cannot change all situations, but we can change ourselves—inside-out. "[Inside-out] says if you want to *have* a happy marriage, *be* the kind of person who generates positive energy.... If you want to *have* a more pleasant, cooperative teenager, *be* a more understanding, empathetic, consistent, loving parent. If you want to *have* more freedom, more latitude in you job, *be* a more responsible, a more helpful, a more contributing employee...."

HABIT 1: *Be Proactive (Initiative)*

Four main characteristics separate humans from animals: *imagination, conscience, independent will,* and *self-awareness.* In humans there is an interval between stimulus and response; we have the freedom to *choose,* not just to *react.* Being proactive means making this conscious "choice to choose"; being responsible for our own lives; taking the initiative; acting instead of being acted upon. Proactivity empowers us to *create* circumstances.

Effective people truly lead their lives. Instead of saying, "It's hopeless," they say, "Let's look at the alternatives." Instead of, "If only..." they say, "I will."

Each of us possesses a *circle of concern,* which includes our state of health, our children, problems at work, the national debt, nuclear war....It is apparent that we have a great deal of control over some of these concerns and very little influence over others. The events we do have control over constitute our *circle of influence.* Proactive people focus their time and energy on their circle of influence—those things they can do something about.

HABIT 2: *Begin With the End in Mind (Creativity)*

All successful endeavors are created twice. There's a first, mental or spiritual creation, and a second, physical creation to all things. For example, if you were going to build a home, you wouldn't simply start hammering away. You would look at your budget, carefully plan what you wanted in the house, make a blueprint, and then develop construction plans. The same is true with parenting. If you want to raise responsible, self-disciplined children, you have to keep that end clearly in mind as you daily interact with your children.

Effective leaders *envision* what they want and how to get it. They habitually pick priorities stemming from their basic values.

In our personal lives, if we do not develop self-awareness and become responsible for our own "first creations," we empower other people and circumstances to shape our lives by default. Living "by default," we merely react to the scripts given to us by our family, associates, et al.

HABIT 3: *Put First Things First (Productivity)*

Habit 3 sparks the second, physical creation that fulfills habits 1 and 2. It entails the idea of management, or using our four human endowments (self-awareness, imagination, conscience and will) to accomplish *important* things.

In a time-management matrix, there are four "quadrants":

Quadrant I includes the affairs that are *urgent and important*—crises, pressing problems, deadline-driven projects. We react quickly to urgent matters. However, if we focus on Quadrant I, the "urgent" list tends to get bigger and bigger and we seem to go from one crisis to the next.

Quadrant III includes matters that are *urgent but not important*—some interruptions, phone calls and meetings. Many people spend much of their time reacting to things they deem urgent, assuming that they are also important.

Quadrant IV consists of activities that are *not urgent and not important* such as busy work and some recreation. These could be thought of as the "escape" portions of our lives.

Quadrant II is at the heart of effective personal management. It deals with concerns that are *important but not urgent*—building relationships, long-range planning, exercising...things we know we should do but seldom get around to actually doing.

"Important matters that are not urgent require more initiative, more proactivity. We must act to seize opportunity, to make things happen." We become Quadrant II persons by learning to say no, by defining our roles in life, and by deciding what we want to accomplish in each of these roles.

HABIT 4: *Think Win/Win (Interdependence)*

Win/Win thinking is a frame of mind that constantly *seeks mutual benefit* in all human interactions—agreements or solutions that are satisfying to all involved. Most people are inclined to think in terms of competitive dichotomies: strong or weak, win or lose. But Win/Win thinking centers on the paradigm that there is plenty for everybody, and that one person's success is not achieved at the expense or exclusion of another person.

HABIT 5: *Seek First to Understand, Then to Be Understood (Empathy)*

Suppose you've been having trouble with your eyes and you go to an optometrist. After listening to your complaint, he takes off his glasses and hands them to you: "I've worn these glasses for years now and they've really helped me. I have an extra pair at home; you can wear these." Would you thank him for his generosity?

In the communications process, how often do we *prescribe* before we *diagnose?* We have a tendency to rush in, to fix things up with "good advice," but without deep understanding. Habit 5 involves fostering the habit of empathic listening—making deposits in the other person's "emotional bank account" by sincere validation and appreciation.

HABIT 6: *Synergize (Valuing Differences)*

"Synergy" implies that the whole is greater than the sum of its parts. Synergistic Communication begins with the assumption that cooperating individuals will *share* insights and open their minds and hearts. Then, if the opinions of all parties are valued, momentum will build and new alternatives will emerge where there were only roadblocks before.

HABIT 7: *Sharpen the Saw (Consistency)*

Habit 7 entails preserving, renewing and enhancing the greatest asset you have—*you.* It enables you to move on an upward spiral of growth.

Formulate a personal program to *keep in balance* the four dimensions of your nature—physical, spiritual, mental and social/emotional. To do this, again begin with habit 1—be proactive. Taking the time to regularly "sharpen the saw" is a definite Quadrant II activity.

The *physical dimension* of saw-sharpening involves caring effectively for your body—eating the right foods, and getting sufficient rest, relaxation and exercise.

The *spiritual dimension* gives direction to your life. Find inner peace through daily prayer, meditation, reading from scripture, communing with nature, or habitually immersing yourself in great literature or music. Get up early ("mind over mattress") and live in harmony with the "still small voice" within you.

The *mental dimension* is central to life-long development. Education is a vital source of mental rejuvenation. Sometimes it requires the external discipline of the classroom or a systemized home study program; often it does not.

The *social/emotional dimension* embraces Habits 4, 5, and 6, which center on the principles of interpersonal leadership, empathic communications, and creative cooperation. This dimension is developed through service to others and self-discipline.

The *inside-out, upward spiral, self-renewal* concepts of *Seven Habits* revolve around becoming more self-aware. Only by knowing ourselves can we choose high purposes and principles to live by and find similar unity in our relationships with others. Developing the seven habits won't eliminate mistakes from our lives, Covey insists, but it will make us more able people. To quote Emerson: "*That which we persist in doing becomes easier—not that the nature of the task has changed, but our ability to do has increased.*" And habits centered on correct principles can increase our ability to live peaceful, harmonized, loving, effective lives.

WISHCRAFT

by Barbara Sher, with Annie Gottlieb, Ballantine Books, 1979

I don't care how old you are, or what your past history has been, or what your present circumstances are: you can still do and have and be anything in the world you really want.

Barbara Sher's premise is that within every individual are unique—and unfulfilled—dreams and capabilities. Finding and defining your deepest wishes, then refining them through a "crafting" process, can be an exhilarating experience. And in her thinking, no dream is too far-fetched. Consider these *Wishcraft* precepts.

I. THE CARE AND FEEDING OF HUMAN GENIUS

We can all be winners and bring our dreams to life—from choral singing to writing children's books to selling blue-chip stocks. Winning—experiencing a joy-filled life-style—is a process, not a product. The search for the "lost treasure map of your talents [begins in the] first five precious and mysterious years of life—the greatest learning period you ever had.... All the people we call 'geniuses' are men and women who somehow escaped having to put that curious, wondering child in themselves to sleep....Einstein was able to make great discoveries precisely because he kept alive the originality and delight of a small child exploring its universe for the first time." In fact, all geniuses share three characteristics: great brilliance, original vision, and incredible determination.

Remembering what you loved to do as a child gives clues to the original genius within. Providing a nurturing environment, then, is the only challenge that remains in your unfolding. "All genuinely successful people—the ones who love their lives—have had that environment...or some parts of it...or they've figured out how to create it for themselves."

How well were your wishes nurtured as a child? Were you encouraged to build within yourself your own unique kind of genius? Were you given the freedom to explore your own talents and interests? Were you allowed to complain and make mistakes without feeling guilty?

Thinking about "what might have been" had the childhood conditions been right, is an exercise in cherishing and respecting yourself. Any discomfort you feel while pondering such dreams is a good sign; it shows that you recognize that there is more for you to accomplish. "Your capacity to do will depend on your capacity to dream, so prove that that capacity, at least, has survived intact."

II. WISHING

...Far from being "impractical" or "irresponsible," doing what's closest to your heart is like striking oil: you tap into a surge of energy that will propel you to the heights of success.... You will recognize your own path when you come upon it, because you will suddenly have all the energy and imagination you will ever need.

Three years ago Diane's secret dream was to become a city planner. However, she had no experience in planning, and besides, the city of New York was going broke—it was firing, not hiring, planners. As a 24-year-old secretary "with a B.A. in nothing special," a job she couldn't afford to quit for full-time study, and a pocketbook too drained to accommodate night classes, she felt her dream was impossible.

Still, Diane's favorite pastime was to stroll around the city, savoring the flavors and the architecture of the various neighborhoods. During these times she would brainstorm on what she could do. She began to attend local planning-board meetings and volunteered to help on projects; and her enthusiasm and deep understanding won the trust of city councilmen and other leaders. As a result of their high recommendations, Diane won a full-tuition scholarship to a nearby college and was able to secure part-time work.... Today, despite her original staggering list of obstacles, this determined woman has a high-paying job in a field she loves.

Diane's story proves that with an open mind and the right encouragement, *you can be doing at least some of what you're passionate about doing—right now.* "If your goal is to make your living by doing what you love, start doing it just for love." If you've always wanted to paint landscapes, do it. Don't worry if your first attempts are disastrous; in fact, plan on them to be "bad" paintings. Just paint because you want to, for your own sense of fulfillment—and your work will improve.

A boy of 17 applying for college struck up a conversation with a white-haired seventy-four-year-old man, also in the admissions line. "I'm applying for college," said the old man, smiling. "But...you'll be seventy-eight by the time you graduate," the boy remarked.

"Son," said the old man, "I'll be seventy-eight anyway."

Stylesearch

"Remembering" and "taking note" assist you in finding your intuitive style. There are a thousand clues in your life to help you discover your style. The way you dress, the way you decorate your home, your favorite foods, colors, hobbies, etc.—these preferences declare your deepest self. "Your style is the place where you still exercise the creative power to shape your world and design yourself."

Make a list of twenty things you like to do—anything. Next, ask yourself questions about each activity: Did I do this yesterday, or has it been a long time since I did it? Why? What did it cost? Was it fast-paced, or slow and relaxed? Was it planned, or done spontaneously? Unearth patterns about the kind of life you live—and the kind you'd love to live. Unlock your true nature.

Goalsearch

Using this understanding of your personal style, begin to fantasize about what type of environment would allow your best self to emerge. Imagine what your ideal day would be like if you had no financial or time restraints. Prune that ideal by describing which elements of your day would be "indispensable," which would be "optional but desirable," and which you would consider "frill" activities. This exercise should help re-reveal your dreams, which you can now incorporate into your set of life *goals.*

Goals are the basic units of life design. They are targets, derived from your dream, and motivated by touchstones (insistent needs) and role models. Make your goals measurable and concrete—and make sure you really want the goals you chase.

If you had five lives, what would they be? Pull from each "life" the "something" you most value, and blend those vital parts into the design.

Hard Times, or the Power of Negative Thinking

Sher contends that there is a time and a need for negative thinking. Griping may be constructive, especially once it's out of the way; then you are ready for positive problem-solving, planning and action. Keep a "Problems List," a "Diary of Hard Times," and an "Action and Feelings Journal" to help propel you past negativity, and to remind you of "gained ground"—real progress you can see and savor.

III. CRAFTING: PLOTTING THE PATH TO YOUR GOAL

Here are the three "wishcrafting" strategies:

(1) *Brainstorming* (using human ingenuity) is a time-honored method of exploring all of the avenues leading toward your target. All ideas must be seriously considered, but only those that are workable and suit your style and ultimate destination need be pursued.

(2) *Barn-raising* (using human community), named after the pioneer practice, allows you to gain support, develop contacts, and gauge the strength of present resources that can help you in reaching your goal. In effect, throw a "barn-raising party," inviting all your trusted friends and acquaintances. Together, focus on your dreams and goals, and the steps necessary to turn them into reality. "The seeds of human genius happen to travel by a system of personal contacts."

(3) *Work with time.* The hard part is over; now the work begins. Devise a plan. "The only way to build a dream is brick by brick, action by action, day by day, in real time." Work with time by using six distinct but crucial tools:

a. *A planning wall* (any full-view wall space or bulletin board) helps you map out plans and chart progress across time. It also serves to motivate and remind. Your planning wall will include several of the other planning tools, as well as a picture of your personal *"saint"* who epitomizes your goal (businessman, movie star, singer, etc.) to help inspire and cheer you on.

b. *A flow chart* highlights your planned steps to achievement. Write out your goal, then list some first steps. Follow the steps one by one, day by day. Later, list some second steps and proceed to accomplish them...

c. *A goal calendar* consists of "a large sheet of paper divided into boxes, one box for each month between you and your target date." Appoint landmark *deadlines* (taken from your flow chart) to the months in which they can be realistically met. Setting personal, written deadlines "makes the difference between acting like you have all the time in the world and getting yourself in gear."

d. *A weekly calendar* is the principal tool for filling in the details of your plan. Assign each week's activities (appointments, phone calls, etc.) to specific days and times—and follow through. Also remember to put to good use the "free moments" in your day.

e. A *"tonight/tomorrow" sheet* is used to plan the all-important up-coming hours. Fill out a new sheet at the end of each day. "What do you have scheduled for tomorrow? What do you have to do tonight to prepare for it—lay out your clothes, lay out your paintbrushes and paints, make sure a phone number is in your pocket calendar, rehearse an interview in your mind? Now do it." Reward yourself often—a hot bath, a glass of brandy, a late movie. Self-congratulation is "food for your unfolding self."

f. *A five-year goal scheme* wraps up your plan into a real, year-by-year time frame. "Of course, you have no way of knowing what you'll really be doing—or wanting—in five years. But of all the forces that will be operating on your life over those years—chance and love and loss and luck, health and economics and history—your wish and will, your own unfolding, should be one of the strongest."

With a "head full of brains," "a room full of friends," and a solid plan, you can liberate your thinking and mobilize your efforts to allow you to attain what you want. *Wishing* is the starting point; crafting that wish becomes the continuum. There is no limit to your capabilities. There is no end to your potential. For it is the nature of the human animal to say "What next?" Once self confidence is attained in one thing, the search begins for something new—and you learn how to learn.

No matter how old you are, what your past history has been, or what your present circumstances are, know that "it is the journey, not the arrival, that matters."

PEAK PERFORMANCE PRINCIPLES FOR HIGH ACHIEVERS

by John R. Noe, Berkley Press, 1984

Peak Performance Principles, says its author, sets a new direction in the literature of self-improvement. The hype and cheerleading so often associated with motivational books is notably absent here; concise, inspirational stories take their place. Noe's book reflects his business opinions, his deeply religious views, and his experience as an expert mountain climber. "If a picture is worth a thousand words then reality is worth a thousand pictures," and the best life has to offer comes not only through "high achievement," but through "stopping and smelling the roses along the way."

Noe's first section begins with a warning: "*The ideas in this book are hazardous to your complacency.*" To become a high achiever requires you to break out of personal or societal "comfort zones." High achievement means high adventure; climbing your own mountains; developing your personal potential.

Peak Performance Principles is designed to show the "achiever" how to become a "high achiever"—the difference being that while achievers may set and strive for goals, high achievers are only satisfied with reaching their full potential; they push themselves always just beyond the limits of their bodies and wills.

Ten Questions

In order to show what he means by "high achievers," Noe has devised "10 questions "that, if answered from the heart, can "change your life."

(1) *Do you really want to become a high achiever?* Self-discipline takes desire and personal investment. Most of us are constantly immersed in a world of noise; but creative self-discipline requires a degree of solitude. And since high achievement always involves creativity—breaking new ground—in the last decade of the 20th century high achievers must be willing to break away from their sometimes chaotic "comfort zones" to the silence and solitude of their own thoughts.

High achievers also typically reach out to embrace new situations; they are not afraid of change. The willingness to leave safe and comfortable surroundings in search of something better is their hallmark. Leaving a secure corporate position to start your own business may not be considered wise by statisticians, but it is a risk that high achievers often choose to take.

"To be great," Emerson wrote, "is to be misunderstood." Those who strive for great goals must risk rejection from their peers, and be confident enough to deal with the fact that not everyone will share their vision.

(2) *Do you have a strong inner urge to reach out?* High achievers reach out to new situations and people with enthusiasm, not fear.

(3) *What matters most to you?* "The key question for high achievers is never 'What have you done?' but 'What have you become?'" Material possessions have little meaning to the high achiever. Remember the "great secret" revealed by the fox in *The Little Prince?* "Only that which is invisible is essential." So, for high achievers, the intangible possessions—self-respect, pride of accomplishment, the capacity for love, and a positive outlook—are always paramount, and the primary goal is always to become a better, more able person.

(4) *What are you willing to invest?* High achievement requires an enormous amount of commitment and energy. Questions such as "How much longer will it take?" or "How much further do we have to go?" are self-defeating. The amount of time or effort required to obtain something worthwhile is secondary. The high achiever's answer to Question 4 is, "I am willing to invest whatever it takes."

(5) *What are you willing to endure?* "What a testing of character adversity is!" exclaims Harry Emerson Fosdick. And Noe concurs: "When the going gets tough...the high achiever shifts gears, and keeps going."

(6) *What are you willing to give up?* Society tends to define our comfort levels. But it can also desensitize us to our surroundings and distance us from other people—dangerous situations for even the high achiever. In high-performance driving, for instance, Noe points out that four small tire patches "are the only contact you have with the road.... You must be sensitive to the signals that are picked up by the tires and transferred to the wheels, suspension, car seat, and controls." Regular cars are designed to isolate and desensitize the driver from bumps; the goal is to make the car *comfortable.* High achievement, however, requires that we become, not comfortable and insulated from the bumps of living, but *sensitive* to the bumps of "high-performance living."

(7) *How much responsibility can you handle?* While others may complain when unexpected responsibilities are thrust upon them, the high achiever will simply do her best. "High achievement and responsibility go hand in hand. You cannot have one without the other."

(8) *Are you willing to start where you are?* No one likes to start at the bottom, but high achievers first accept the circumstances in which they find themselves, and then go from

there. Even the most accomplished entrepreneurs, artists and athletes had to begin at the beginning and then move toward their dreams. So, remember: "You can always get to where you want to go, providing you are willing to start from where you are."

(9) *Are you willing to think for yourself?* Hard work is too frequently acclaimed as the whole answer for anyone striving toward a goal. True, there is no substitute for hard work; but the high achiever must develop a balance between hard work and hard, often solitary thought.

(10) *Are you willing to settle for nothing less than your full potential?* Benjamin Franklin wrote that "success has ruined many a man." Once you achieve your dream, don't allow yourself the luxury of becoming complacent—dream again. To be a genuine high achiever is to continue to forge ahead, regardless of what has already been accomplished.

The Six Attitudes of High Achievers

(1) *High achievers make no small plans* ("Big plans attract big people"). But high achievers also realize that small, everyday choices are the agents that ultimately shape the big decisions of our lives. So, seize control of your little choices—How will you spend today? What will you do first? Second? Next?...And, finally, what will you do when you don't have anything to do?

(2) *High achievers are willing to do what they fear.* "You don't conquer fears with cliches, but with actions." Fears and doubts waste time, energy, initiative and potential. Grieving over past decisions or actions is futile. Moreover, "fear is fraud"; only about 8% of our worries are real and legitimate concerns. And the sooner we challenge and act on those that are real, the sooner we resolve them. Noe suggests: "Sit down and make a list of all the things you are afraid to do, within legal, moral, and spiritual limits. Then go out and deliberately make yourself do every one of them. Each time you confront a fear, become sensitive to the atmosphere surrounding it...then fear will no longer control your life."

(3) *High achievers are willing to prepare.* "He profiteth, who hustles while he waits," said Thomas Edison. Organizing, planning, preparing for events is something we can all do. "High achievers get more excited about what they are becoming than what they have done." Preparation involves setting progressively higher intermediate goals, mastering technical skills, building endurance and, along the way, gaining much-needed confidence.

(4) *High achievers are willing to risk failure.* "Failure is not the enemy of success. It is a teacher—a harsh teacher, but the best....If you are going to be a high achiever, you must learn to 'fail' your way to high achievement." Case in point: For three consecutive Olympic Games, beginning in 1952, each decathlon silver medalist went on to win the following Olympics' Gold Medal. We must not expect to win each time out, but let our losses teach and strengthen us. High achievers know the formula for success: "Double your failure rate."

(5) *High achievers are teachable.* The high achiever continually pursues new knowledge and insights. Staying teachable demands three activities—reading, observing, and listening. It also demands the recognition that "the higher you go the more help you need." Keep in mind that high-achievement goals can only be attained with the help of others. Take advantage of the many mentors along the way.

(6) *High achievers have heart.* Conflict is at the root of the plots of all great literature: the old man battling the sea and a great fish; the athlete working against almost impossible odds. However, "real life" struggles don't usually announce themselves as great adventures; they are much more likely to appear under the unglamorous guise of Murphy's-Law—"If anything can go wrong, it will." But the very weight of these burdensome challenges can impel us toward our highest goals. *Heart*—as in "courage," "persistence," "perspective," and "purpose"—will help you overcome the urge to quit the fight.

High Achievement: Putting It Into Action

Noe uses the rules of mountain climbing to illustrate his *Peak Performance* points. He talks of climbing "fully equipped"—prepared beforehand for any eventuality—and of setting your sights on ever higher heights. (A novice climber can't set out to conquer the Matterhorn, but must begin by ascending less rugged mountains or hills.) He also recommends using "goal-climbing momentum"—grabbing on to a goal you have already reached to launch you toward your next intermediate goal.

In mountain climbing it might seem appealing to be able to move from one peak to the next without descending. But this is not only impossible, *it is undesirable.* Without ever having to come down, at least part way, and begin the new adventure from the bottom of the next peak, we wouldn't be able to savor the difficult climb back up. Life is a series of new adventures, not endings. Changing careers, moving to a new city, or retiring, can be exciting, renewing experiences, depending on your outlook.

The straightforward concepts offered in *Peak Performance Principles* emphasize individual commitment and faith in God. Noe believes that if we dedicate ourselves over and over again to the goal of climbing from one peak to the next—resisting the urge to become discouraged by the heaviness of the task—every one of us can become a high achiever.

How to Get Control of Your Time and Your Life

by Alan Lakein, Peter H. Wyden Inc., 1973

How to Get Control of Your Time and Your Life teaches you how to determine what you want in life and how to get it. Alan Lakein, the long-standing guru of time management, has a simple plan for *setting goals* and *prioritizing* them—the heart and soul of time management.

"Time is life"; by wasting our time we waste our lives. Effective use of time means skillfully selecting the foremost tasks to accomplish and accomplishing them in the best way possible. *You* are the one who decides what is the best possible use of your time.

Getting Control

Lakein's key concept is *control.* Controlling time must be done with balance—neither too tight or too loose. Losing balance becomes a liability.

Three groups of people misuse time management principles, and lose control:

(1) ***The over-organized*** person is more interested in *feeling* organized than in accomplishing anything. He spends much of his time planning and little of it doing.

(2) ***The over-doer*** is always *busy* doing things, but seldom takes the time to assess the value of the tasks she is doing. As a result, she gets only a lot of low priority projects completed.

(3) ***The "time nut"*** is so preoccupied with time that he never wastes a second. He knows how to get everything done a couple of seconds quicker.

All three people drive those around them crazy. However, *scheduling* should mean "making time for what you want to do....A too rigid or demanding schedule creates the feeling of being regimented by the clock." The purpose of controlling time is to instill into your life *greater freedom,* not to turn you into a compulsive organizer or clock watcher. In order to gain this freedom, some people work to follow all of the suggestions given in Lakein's book; others pick and choose only those which they believe will help them.

Life is a never-ending stream of possible activities, constantly being replenished by your family, your teachers, your boss, your subordinates, as well as by your own dreams, hopes, desires, and by the need to stay alive and functioning.

There are always more things that we need to do, or would like to do, than we have time to do. It is often difficult to decide what to do first, what can *wait,* and *what doesn't need to be done at all.*

Control Starts With Planning.

"Planning is bringing the future into the present so that you can do something about it now." In order to effectively plan your time you need to ask yourself:

(1) What are my lifetime goals?

(2) *What do I want to accomplish in the next three years?*

(3) *If I had six months to live, how would I live them?*

What are your lifetime goals? If you are not sure, take fifteen minutes and find out. First, write the question "What are my lifetime goals?" on a sheet of paper. Take two minutes and write down everything that comes into your mind that answers the question. Take another two minutes and make any changes you feel are necessary in the first list. It is not necessary to be completely satisfied with the list at this time. Now follow the same procedure for the other two questions.

Once you have spent four minutes on each list, take two additional minutes and review all three lists.

After compiling your list of lifetime goals, select the top three that are most important to you. Label them A-1, A-2 and A-3, in order of their importance. Then take a new sheet of paper and write "My three most important lifetime goals are..." Do the same thing with your "three-year" list and your "six-month" list. Repeat the process the next day and as often as needed to refine your goals. Once you are comfortable with the lists, it is time to get to work.

Accomplishing Your Goals

You cannot carry out goals; you can only carry out *activities*. To reach a goal you need to select activities that will get you there. To determine the best use of your time, brainstorm and be creative; think of as many possible strategies as you can. Go back over the brainstorming list to revaluate your ideas.

Now, *set priorities* for your tasks. Ask: "Am I willing to spend at least five minutes a day on this activity for the next seven days?" If the answer is no, you have just uncovered a low-priority task. Eliminate it. Perform this exercise for each goal. When you have eliminated all of the low-priority items for each goal, combine all of your lists into one list, and then set priorities for your activities.

The next step is to schedule *realistic deadlines* for completing each activity. Do the activities as scheduled by breaking them down into daily tasks pointed toward achieving your goals.

Daily Planning

Start by looking at your "A" activity list. "The A's generally stand out clearly. They should be the attention-getters." Choose only those activities you can do *today*. Then, add to the list everything else you need, or would like, to get done today. Prioritize these tasks using A's (high value), B's (not quite so important), and C's (low value). Next, return to the list and select the highest priority A and label it A-1. Go through all the A's in this way, then do the same with the B's and C's. Don't let the number of items scare you. *You do not need to finish everything on the list.* Start with A-1 and go through the to-do list in the order of your selected priorities. *"People at the top use a to-do list every single day....One of the real secrets of getting more done is to work on the list at the beginning and end of each day, keep it visible and use it as a guide as you go through the day."*

Look for opportunities to get started on activities. Take advantage of "open" minutes: commuting time, coffee breaks, lunch, and "waiting" occasions.

You will find that the 80/20 rule applies to your "to-do" list: Twenty percent of the items on the list will give you eighty percent of the positive results. For this reason, setting priorities is critical.

When planning your daily schedule, it is best to set aside a block of time to work exclusively on "A" activities. Start with fifteen minutes a day and increase it from there. Leave some "holes" in the day to allow for unexpected interruptions that pop up. Flexibility in your schedule will help you avoid frustration.

Be sure to schedule some quiet time for yourself. When you need time to work on projects, schedule appointments with yourself and then honor the appointments as you would any meeting. Lakein also suggests scheduling the times you will be available to others.

How can you deal with the demands other people put on your time? Two helpful suggestions: (1) Learn to say no, and (2) Learn to compromise without giving up control. The best technique for avoiding time thieves is to be honest with them. If someone asks, "Do you have a minute?" tell them you don't, or indicate exactly how many minutes you have available and ask if their discussion can be accomplished in that amount of time.

Possessions and paperwork also rob you of time. Again, A-B-C organizing is the key. Have a place for every item and put it back when you finish using it. Get rid of 20 percent of everything you own and "set a limit on how many things in each category are optimum—say, 20 ties. Then, before you buy a new one, get rid of an old one." With mail, "deal with each piece...only once and make a decision about it. Mail labeled A should always be handy, and the C's should be stashed away....If you wait long enough, they will become obsolete."

A major stumbling block that everyone faces is *procrastination.* How can you overcome it? Lakein offers several ideas: Ask yourself the question "What is the best use of my time right now?" If you have properly planned your day, you can look at your "to-do" list and see how to best use that moment.

When overwhelmed, you might turn to the "Swiss Cheese" approach, which involves punching several holes into a large project. If you cannot force yourself to launch right into it, take five minutes and complete one of the project's small tasks. The purpose is to get you started on a hard-to-face, high-priority undertaking. Generally, once you begin such a task, you find that working on it is not as bad as you had thought.

Other suggestions to thwart procrastination include: giving yourself a pep talk; realizing that delay will only make the problem worse; making a commitment to someone else; and, slowing down the decision-making process and determining why you're avoiding the A-1 project. Recognize that you decided the A-1 task was the best use of your time; as a result, any other task you choose to do, although it may be valuable, is a comparative waste of time.

Lakein submits other little ideas on how to find time you didn't know you had, how to reduce stress, etc. Some tips:

- Perfection is a waste of time when completing lower priority tasks.
- Accept the fact that, at your choosing, some tasks are better left undone.
- Find "prime times" during the day when you characteristically do your best work. Plan your time blocks accordingly.
- Arrange for quiet times, breaks from extended activities, and times to simply do nothing. Balance work and play; you'll get more done in the long run.
- Experiment with reducing your sleep time.
- Train yourself to use your subconscious during sleep to help you solve difficult problems.
- Don't allow guilt or fear of failure to push you into an "escape" habit. Reading, socializing, daydreaming and indulging in over-scrupulous or menial tasks, while not wrong in and of themselves, are sometimes used as escapes from the A-1 activity.
- Wean yourself away from TV.
- Demonstrate willpower in little ways; it will develop your self-discipline and desire to make good use of time.
- "Do your best and consider it a success."

The real key to control—and the one most often ignored—is setting priorities in your life, both for long-term goals and daily planning. Once you get accustomed to setting priorities and schedules, and sticking to them, you will find that you have control of both your time and your life.

How to Put More Time in Your Life

by Dru Scott, Ph.D., Signet Books, 1981

How to Put More Time in Your Life is a "5-step program that puts you in charge of your clock, your calendar, and your life."

Dru Scott insists that while most time management systems are based on accomplishing tasks, the focus of her book is to help you *gain quality time*—time to do what's really important to you.

Scott feels that time management is not merely a matter of *knowing* what to do, but *getting yourself* to do it. At one period of her life, she was teaching and writing about time management, yet found herself always rushing from one appointment to another. Finally she admitted that she was failing to apply in her own work the principles she was teaching to others.

Briefly, these are some underlying themes behind the steps outlined in her book:

I. Clarify priorities: Concentrate on *quality* activities; fulfill your *wants* as well as your objectives; *define* and *do* what really counts.

II. Understand what motivates you: Face up to *mixed feelings* in yourself and others; *reward* and *reinforce* the best in yourself and others; motivate yourself, every day, to do what's important.

III. Do your best with this day: *Don't wait* to live fully; open yourself to the joys of the moment; go ahead, *do it*—the best time is now.

Step 1: Exploring the Psychology of Management (and Mismanagement)

Perhaps we feel out of control because—consciously or sub-consciously—we subscribe to some of the following myths concerning time management:

- "I'm waiting until I have more time."
- "I've already read the book (or taken the course)."
- "You just can't get organized around here."
- "People keep interrupting me."

Hiding behind such myths often allows us to shield ourselves from the real reasons behind our lack of time management. Some people actually mismanage time as a means of achieving unacknowledged "goals"—to get attention, blame others, gain control, escape unpleasant situations or risks, resist change, or to avoid close relationships.

Guilt

Guilt, "a feeling of deviation from a relevant standard"—a standard usually etched during our childhood—can become a major time-waster. *Inappropriate guilt* occurs when we assault ourselves for not doing everything perfectly. Three questions can help deal with guilt:

(1) "Specifically, what am I feeling guilty about?"

(2) "Is this something that is really an essential or central concern to me or someone else?"

(3) "Today, how can I best do what really counts?"

Elements of Time Design

Five elements of design make up your personal style of time management: *Order* (a direction of movement in life); *Balance* (regular, planned activities); *Contrast* (variety); *Unity* (total life "contributions"); and *Harmony* (connections that blend life experiences into a whole). The blend of these elements determines how we individually go about controlling our time.

Compulsive Controllers

Compulsive time control is typically seen in one of five basic personality styles:

1. **Hurry up:** This person puts things off until the last minute and then is forced to rush.
2. **Be perfect:** This person wastes time on trivial, peripheral matters.
3. **Please me:** This person yearns to satisfy everyone, and often over-commits.
4. **Try hard:** This person wants to be recognized for trying hard, even if failure is the end result.
5. **Be strong:** This person doesn't believe in asking anyone for help and must continually declare independence to prove self-worth.

Do you recognize yourself in one or more of these profiles?

Step 2: Choice Time—Getting Yourself Organized

Setting Priorities

Deciding on your broad objectives is essential. Create a list of what you want more of, and less of, in your life. Then do something towards making your "mores" more of a reality every day. Construct short-term objectives that will serve as daily "nudges" toward achieving your lifetime desires. Be *firm* about your *objectives*, but *flexible* about your *activities*.

Set priorities. Divide tasks into three categories: (1) *Marginal* (not important enough to worry about); (2) *Secondary* (worthwhile, but not the greatest time investment); (3) *Central* (areas that reflect your deepest values and desired direction). Decide what your objective is for any given activity, and plan accordingly.

Managing Time Decisions

Fast, effective decisions demand that you first clarify your objective. Compare several alternatives; which will get you closer to where you want to go? Decide, and then act on your decision by listing the workable steps of your task, doing one thing at a time, and finishing each step fully.

Keep a *personal calendar* handy, combined with a daily action sheet. On your daily action ("to do") list, record objectives, listing urgent and central concerns first. Confine yourself to a realistic number of items so you won't feel overwhelmed.

Next, break your activities into "doable" tasks and prioritize them (1,2,3 or A,B,C...). You may then choose to group tasks, separating them into blocks of time.

Interruptions and demands from others are a part of life. For a week or so, track your interruptions on an "interruption sheet." This can help you detect hidden drains on your time, acting then to either curtail or deal with them.

Step 3: Staying Motivated

Each person has different "stimulation levels"—different needs. Some need to be with people; others require privacy. Some are motivated by another's authority; others work better when "self-inspired." We should seek to recognize what our unique stimulation levels are. What motivates and excites you?

Some people thrive on negative stimulation, often by procrastinating. To overcome this habit, analyze your procrastination patterns. When and how do you most often procrastinate? Why do these times or situations cause you discomfort? How do you feel after you've done an important task that you had previously put off? In some combination of the "Three R's"—*repetition* (making a "hard" task a habit), *reinforcement* (finding some type of satisfaction in performing the task), and *reward* (placing some sort of "carrot" at the end of the task)—you can keep yourself moving in the right direction.

When you are overwhelmed and time *refuses* to be managed, there are some emergency measures you can take. First, clear your mind by writing down everything you're feeling. Next, update your wants. Then add reinforcements and rewards. Last, compare your "feelings" list with your updated "wants" list, and decide what five items are most important to do right at that moment.

Step 4: Coping With Everyday Time Demands

Can you relate to any of these time issues?

- Is it hard to get going in the *morning*? To solve this problem requires planning. Determine the number of minutes you need to complete your morning routine, and add 15 minutes as a time cushion. Commit yourself to arising at the designated time. Don't set your alarm for 5:00 if you don't intend to get up until 6:15.
- Decide if time spent *commuting* to work is worth it for you. Realize you do have a choice—about where you live, your job, car-pooling, etc. If you find that commuting is requisite, learn to make this time personally productive (listening to cassette tapes, planning...)
- If you find yourself consistently *running* late, start cultivating punctuality by picking one important daily commitment for which you will be on time. Reward yourself for being early or on time for an appointment. Mentally take note of your planned time of departure.
- Anticipate moments when you will be *waiting*, and be prepared to deal with them without fretting. Confirm your appointments the day before. If someone you have an appointment with is habitually late, call just before you leave to see if they're running on time. Make the most of your waiting time by carrying work or personal projects with you. "Cluster" appointments and errands whenever possible.
- *Shopping and housework* have to be done. Consider whether it's feasible to hire help. Use both a "standard" shopping list (for common weekly purchases) and a "special" list (for "one-time" purchases). For housework, systematically schedule recurring demands. This eliminates time wasted making decisions.
- Discover an *exercise* program that is enjoyable and practical. Add some reinforcements and rewards to keep you motivated.

Step 5: Putting Time to Work

- Realize that *paperwork* is a means, not an end. Separate "vital" papers from those that are "marginal." Set a time frame for keeping different types of documents.
- In a polite way, make *people* aware of the deadlines you need to meet.

- The *telephone* is a tool; it shouldn't control your life. Take hold of phone conversations from the start. State directly what you want. Develop tact and skill in closing a call—"Thanks for your help; I'll be back in touch..."
- Learn—and practice—to *say "no"* without apology. Say "yes" only if the obligation helps you accomplish one of your key objectives.

Remember: time is a gift. Habitual management of this gift can help you live a fuller life.

THE ROAD LESS TRAVELED

A New Psychology of Love, Traditional Values and Spiritual Growth

by M. Scott Peck, M.D., Simon and Schuster, 1978

Life is difficult. *This is a great truth, one of the greatest truths. It is a great truth because once we indeed see this truth, we transcend it. Once we truly know that life is difficult—once we truly understand and accept it—then life is no longer difficult. Because once it is accepted, the fact that life is difficult no longer matters.*

Confronting and solving problems is a painful, difficult process, one most people try to avoid. But complaints and avoidance actually contribute to our problems and hinder our mental and spiritual growth.

Drawing upon his years of experience as a psychiatrist, Dr. M. Scott Peck takes us along the rocky road—the one not often traveled—of confronting and solving our problems, to arrive at a greater understanding of ourselves and our place in the world.

Discipline

Discipline is the key theme throughout *The Road Less Traveled.* Discipline comprises the basic set of tools required to *constructively experience* the pain of problems. Four tools of discipline are: (1) *Delaying gratification.* The willingness to experience pain first, enabling us to go on to experience the pleasures of life; (2) *Accepting responsibility.* Not placing the blame for problems on our parents, friends, or society; being willing to solve our own problems; (3) *Dedication to truth (reality).* Seeing the world as it is in order to effectively deal with it. (We each have a "map" or view of the world which must be continually adjusted as new information is received.); (4) *Balancing.* The flexibility to give something up in order to gain something of transcendent importance.

Love

Love provides the *motivation* for discipline. Love is the will to *extend oneself* for the purpose of nurturing one's own or another's *spiritual growth.*

Love is not only a feeling; love entails *action*. Genuine love is shown by extending our own limits towards one whose growth we want to nurture.

A common fallacy about love is that dependency—wanting someone else to take care of our needs—is love. People who base their relationships on this concept lack self-discipline; they are "passively dependent" on others.

Neither is love self-sacrifice. Whenever we think of ourselves as doing something "for" someone else, we are in a sense denying her of taking responsibility herself. When we do something for someone that she could just as easily do herself, we do it not out of love, but because it fulfills our own needs.

Love is work—and work involves attention. This can sometimes mean just being with someone, but usually it also means listening. There are different levels of listening. "Real" listening—the highest level—demands full, complete, and active attention.

When we extend ourselves in love we assume many risks:

- The risk of giving up our own "self." The self changes when we force ourselves (or are forced) to do things we are not accustomed to doing, and change usually includes some sense of loss, until we find a way to reintegrate the "old" self with the "new" self. But "courage is not the absence of fear; it is the making of action in spite of fear...."
- The risk of standing alone—of facing our own independence. Independence means not relying on parents or other people for our "shoulds" and "wills" and "wants," but upon ourselves. "The highest forms of love are inevitably totally free choices and not acts of conformity."
- The risk of commitment. In Peck's clinical examples, he notes that many parents "failed to commit themselves to their children in any meaningful way....[The children] grew up without experience of commitment." Commitment is necessary for love to develop and to resolve the issues surrounding a relationship.

Growth and Religion

The *understanding* we have of the world *is our religion.* Everyone has a religion, whether he formally belongs to a church or not. Often a person's world-view is only partially conscious; an expanded overview is lacking. The methods of science—stepping back skeptically to question our basic assumptions—can help us discover our personal religion. This, in turn, can lead us to new truths. It is not necessary to disregard everything we have believed in order to come to terms with our religious views; but we *do* need to *question the source* of these views and decide whether they still adequately and usefully serve our present values.

Grace and Miracles

As we become more spiritually aware, we must guard against "tunnel vision" in our seeking to reconcile science with seemingly unexplainable phenomena, such as the healings and miracles that take place in religion.

If we look at life closely we see that frequent "miracles" do occur. It is not remarkable that we get sick; it is amazing that most of the time we are *healthy*. Think of the many examples of people who have overcome overwhelmingly negative factors in their lives and emerged with their physical and mental health intact. By analyzing such occurrences we can come to the understanding of a hidden truth, the answer to a problem, etc. To do this, however, we must remain open to the miraculous, and not dismiss our experiences merely because they don't appear to have a scientific basis.

In this realm lies the *miracle of the unconscious*—the part of our minds which lies beneath our awareness. Often our unconscious mind seizes on a word that suddenly pops into our thoughts, or yields a dream having no known origin. So-called "Freudian slips" (when we say or do something that doesn't make sense on the surface) are an attempt by our unconscious to let out a denied feeling.

Again, there are times when we feel we "re-know" or recognize something which was somehow "known" to us, but unacknowledged, before. Many psychologists feel that people have the innate relevant experiences to unlock this hidden knowledge.

And then there is the miracle of *serendipity*, when some fortunate revelation occurs that seems impossible according to the known laws of nature. This includes so-called "psychic phenomena," where, for example, a person is able to transmit images to the mind of someone sleeping several rooms away. People sometimes have a sense that they should or should not do a certain thing, which results in avoidance of a serious accident. Often we let these small miracles slip by because they do not fit our preconceived "slots" for sorting experience.

Evolution, both physical and spiritual, is clearly a miracle. According to laws of mechanics, evolution should not exist. However, human beings, as well as the whole plant and animal world around us, are living proof that it does exist. In the same vein, the force of entropy (natural disorder, chaos) would seem to preclude man's historical spiritual development. But despite the problems of society, *we do grow*. Our frequent contemporary sense of disillusionment with the human race arises in part from the fact that we expect more of ourselves than our ancestors did.

So, where do miracles and love and discipline come from? Evidence points to the existence of a supreme being who loves us—*God*. God apparently wants us to learn and grow, but what is his *ultimate* goal for us? It could only be for us to *become like him*. This is a frightening idea to many people, because of the tremendous effort involved. We don't want to have to work that hard.

Indeed, the author asserts, the main impediment to attaining love and spiritual growth is *laziness:* "Since love is work, the essence of nonlove is laziness." We must be willing to work to find love and truth.

Peck believes that God is so closely associated with us that he must be *part* of us. God is a part of our unconscious mind. We can think of our unconscious as a rhizome, or hidden root system, which nourishes the small plant of consciousness—the part of us that can think, analyze, and make decisions. In order to become as God, we don't necessarily need to make the conscious and unconscious one entity. Rather, *we may become as God while preserving our consciousness.*

Power

There are two types of power: political and spiritual. Many people are afraid of power, afraid that they will misuse it. This fear can be so strong that it compels them to consciously or unconsciously avoid power—by shying away from job promotions, spousal responsibility, child-rearing, etc.

Most people make decisions without thinking very much. The secret to making wise decisions and using power as a path to enrichment is to become more aware of what we are doing and to enlarge our capacity for awareness. "...Godlike power is the power to make decisions with total awareness." This is a long, uphill process, requiring much work. But gradually, we can develop an inner God-like spiritual power.

What road does the author suggest we travel? The higher, steeper, more disciplined road—the Road Less Traveled—that brings *spiritual power.* Through this power we can receive grace. We cannot *seek* grace; it must come to us. What we can *do* is *prepare* ourselves by becoming wholly loving individuals. We can listen to our unconscious (God) speaking through us and follow those dictates. We can become spiritually evolved individuals of the highest order.

When we "nurture ourselves and others without a primary concern of finding reward, then we will have become loveable, and the reward of being loved, which we have not sought, will find us. So it is with human love and so it is with God's love."

The Different Drum

by M. Scott Peck, M.D., Simon & Schuster, 1987

In and through community lies the salvation of the world. Nothing is more important. Yet it is virtually impossible to describe community meaningfully to someone who has never experienced it—and most of us have never had an experience of true community.... Still, the attempt must be made.

In this book, Dr. Peck attempts to describe the meaning of spiritual community, the stages of its development, and its importance to the individual and to the world.

Bases of Community

Dr. Peck tells us how he first stumbled into the experience of true community. As a boy he attended a prestigious boarding school where competition to belong to the "in" group was keen. For reasons he didn't fully understand, he felt unhappy there, even after finally becoming a member of this group. Peck then transferred to a small Quaker school, where he immediately felt accepted and loved. At this school, the boundaries between people were "soft." There were about two hundred students enrolled, all from different social and economic backgrounds, yet no one was excluded or made fun of for being different.

The disparity in his experiences at these two schools compelled Peck to seek out other "belonging" experiences. In the army, and later while training to become a psychiatrist, he finally found other groups where true community was achieved.

Peck defines community as "a group of individuals who have learned how to communicate honestly with each other, whose relationships go deeper than their masks of composure, and who have developed some significant commitment to rejoice together, mourn together, to delight in each other and make others' conditions their own."

Today we live in relative isolation from others, both physically and emotionally. Often we don't know the names of our next door neighbors. We give the impression of confidence, that we have it all together—because it is considered "weak" to express emotions like anxiety or depression. We feel we must be strong, rugged individualists. But true community helps us overcome these defensive barriers, freeing us to express our true selves.

There are two main characteristics of such a community:

(1) A community is inclusive. Groups that exclude anyone for any reason are not true communities but cliques. Genuine communities always reach out to

extend themselves. Members of a community commit themselves to one another. Decisions that affect the group are arrived at by consensus.

(2) A community emulates the real world. It embraces members with many different points of view, who, as they work their challenges through together, come to share and appreciate the many different facets and dimensions of each situation.

True communities are bonded by an intense *vitality*. Anyone involved in a group crisis—a flood or an earthquake for example—has seen how this works. Suddenly everyone is vitally concerned for others and more than willing to help. However, problems usually crop up once the crisis is over; and the "crisis community" dissolves into one of four self-destructive responses: "flight" (from troublesome issues), "fight" (among group members for control), "pairing" (into alliances that set the community at odds), or "dependency" (choosing leaders). Sometimes all four responses emerge to feed on each other.

Dr. Peck has conducted hundreds of community-building workshops. Participants usually pass through a four-step process as they struggle towards community.

1. PSEUDOCOMMUNITY. Commonly the first response of a group trying to form a community is to *fake* it. In this superficial situation, everyone tries to be pleasant in order to avoid conflict, but people remain evasive, hiding their real feelings. A group of sophisticated professionals, for example, may seem to get along very well, forming an almost "instant community." However, different ideologies and unvoiced resentments are probably hidden under a layer of sophisticated social skills, and may surface rapidly. Without proceeding through the second and third steps, the process of reaching true community is only delayed.

2. CHAOS. "Chaos centers around well-intentioned but misguided attempts to *heal* and convert." In this phase, each person seeks to advance his or her "cause." It is during this stage that individual differences are first brought out in the open. And, unfortunately, groups in chaos frequently seek to overcome personality or philosophical differences by attacking their leaders or by forming sub-committees to solve their problems, instead of facing them and working together. Still, open chaos in a church congregation or company workteam is preferable to pseudocommunity; it's a painful stage, but only by way of this pain comes the understanding that differences must be acknowledged and dealt with at a new level of relationship.

3. EMPTINESS. There are only two ways to do away with chaos: by *organization* (which isn't community) or by *emptiness*. Emptying ourselves involves putting aside any personal feelings that are acting as barriers to communication. Expectations, assumptions, preconceptions, motives, prejudices, ideologies, prefabricated solutions, and the need to heal or convert, fix, solve, or control, are all "given away." When a friend is grieving, we can either be like Job's friends in the Bible, who gave him "curative" advice (which often makes us feel worse), or we can *share* his pain. Just being there to listen is often what really makes a difference.

4. COMMUNITY. When emptiness is finally achieved, the group enters community—a *peaceful* and *trusting* atmosphere of resolution. Individuals are now given the freedom to be vulnerable and genuine as they deal with the various social challenges that present themselves. In this stage, sadness and grief are readily expressed, as are laughter and joy. And finally, a comfortable consensus in decision-making ensues. Group members become individually more eloquent and expressive; as a group they become more gentle.

Communes and Communities

The driving concept behind most communes is that all members should adhere to the same schedules, rules, ideas and behaviors. But the key to creating true communities is to accept and welcome the fact that *we are all different.* It sounds nice to say, "Underneath their skins, Russians are really just like us," but that is simply not true. A Russian's idea of freedom and democracy has been shaped by a cultural hierarchy distinctly different from ours. What is considered *normal* in one culture is considered *abnormal* in another. Even conceptions of good and evil are, to a considerable extent, culturally determined.

But human beings have the unique capacity to change, to be transformed. By exercising this capacity, we can surpass our own individual backgrounds, to both experience and transcend the differences between cultures.

Both personal and collective change occurs through augmented spiritual development, which is cultivated in four stages:

Stage I: *Chaotic, antisocial.* A stage of undeveloped spirituality. The Stage I person is selfish, disordered, and generally incapable of loving others.

Stage II: *Formal, institutional.* The stage II person, typified by many churchgoers, is usually attached to the forms rather than the essence of her religion, and she may quickly take offense at anyone who attacks these forms. Personal stability and outward appearances are very important to her.

Stage III: *Skeptic, individual.* The stage III person is often referred to as a "nonbeliever" because he has given up being "conventional." He thinks independently and is often deeply involved in social causes. An advanced stage III individual is an active truth-seeker.

Stage IV: *Mystic, communal.* This is the stage of unity. A person arriving at stage 4 sees an underlying connectedness between herself, other creatures, and her surroundings. With little or no outside prodding, and as a confident yet humble, self-governing human being, she reaches out to others in recognition of the whole world as part of her community.

"Mystics" comprehend the value of emptiness. Rather than being frightened by the enormity of the unknown, they acknowledge it and immerse themselves ever deeper into it, that they may understand more. Likewise, we can, despite our differences, unite to form communities of caring friends and associates; we can transcend bigotry, selfishness, "ownership," and learn to solve problems in empathy and love.

Many variations exist among individuals in these four phases of spiritual development. Some of us may bounce back and forth between stages; many may feel threatened or intimidated by those functioning in the upper stages (III or IV). Certainly, parents, teachers, ministers, friends, and neighbors—and that includes everyone in some capacity—should be aware of the threat they may represent to those in different stages of spiritual growth. But the paradox remains that it is hard to lift anyone else unless we are already in a more spiritually discerning position than the person we seek to lift.

These four personal spiritual stages are analogous to the development of community. The hardest stage of community formation is to achieve—and return to—emptiness. "Emptiness requires work. It is an exercise of discipline and is always the most difficult part of the process that a group must undergo if it is to become a community....For emptiness always requires a negation of the self...a sacrifice." In order to make a significant change in our lives we must give something up, and consequently must go through a form of depression.

The Solution: An Expanding Community

Inasmuch as small communities have been successfully established, why not extend the idea of community to entire neighborhoods and schools—even to countries and to the world? In fact, progress is being made towards forming a global community. Individuals are slowly becoming more aware that communication is the key to the effective functioning of any group enterprise—a marriage, a corporation, a unified world. Sadly, though, the institutions that can tip the balance between war and peace—the arms-race nations, many charitable organizations, unions, churches—have barely been touched by the concept of community.

Peck notes that in democracies "we the people" elect our leaders. Thus, it is up to us to begin peacemaking—or, community-making. Learn to communicate with peoples of other cultures by first learning to commune with your family and understand your neighbor, urges Peck. Establish peaceful communities where you are, and let your influence spread. "Sell the world on love."

LOVE IS LETTING GO OF FEAR

by Gerald G. Jampolsky, M.D. , Celestial Arts, Berkeley, Ca., 1979

"*There must be another way to go through life besides being pulled through it kicking and screaming,*" says Hugh Prather. Gerald Jampolsky agrees. A former heavy drinker who denied responsibility for his own emotions and actions, Jampolsky overcame his bouts of depression, guilt and anger by finally recognizing the source of his feelings. He found, however, that to follow life's "better path" required of him a willingness to change his goal.

Most of us want to rid ourselves of pain and frustration and experience peace of mind, but, at the same time, we want to control and predict future events and maintain our old self-concept. Consequently, we resist any real change or human contact and continue to feel isolated and unloved.

Jampolsky's book is a compilation of therapeutic methods and practical applications for making a "personal transformation towards a life of giving and Love, and away from getting and fear." We can dissolve fear, it says, through consciously establishing peace as our goal and forgiveness as its vehicle.

Preparation for Personal Transformation

What is real? Too often we accept feedback from our physical senses as the only "reality." However, love, though intangible, is real; and so is the *fear (ego)* that frequently thwarts love.

Our minds constantly replay all our memories, like a videotape. Included are tons of distorted and obsolete guilts and fears, which squeeze out the joy of the present. But "Love is letting go of fear."

Even in the present, our priorities frequently become scattered and filled with conflict, as we try to juggle too much at once. But by choosing a single life goal—that of inner peace—we become better able to focus our energies. Peace of mind, however, demands mind control. Judging people comes naturally; it's more difficult to love them. Yet, if we start by *forgiving* them, it will become more and more apparent that "other people do not have to change for us to experience love and peace of mind."

Jampolsky offers several "themes to live by," centered around peace of mind, forgiveness, inner direction and active choice. He asks us to "retrain" our minds; to make active choice and "self-examination" a daily habit: *Do I choose to find love or find fault? Do I choose to be a love giver or a love seeker?*

Ingredients of Personal Transformation

We are what we believe.

We are always expressing either love or fear. Fear is really a call for help...a request for love.

Fear and love can never be experienced at the same time....By choosing love more consistently than fear, we can change the nature and quality of our relationships.

Such "true concepts," if we are mindful of them, allow us to shake negative thoughts and feelings.

Lessons for Personal Transformation

Below, in brief, are some of Jampolsky's lessons and examples, designed to help us apply true principles of inner peace.

Lesson: All that I Give is Given to Myself. "I was mistaken in believing that I could give anyone anything other than what I want for myself. Since I want to experience peace, love and forgiveness, these are the only gifts I would offer others...."

After visiting with Mother Teresa, Jampolsky asked if he could fly with her on her way to Mexico City. With a gentle smile, she replied, "...I would have no objection about your joining me....But you said you wanted to learn about inner peace. I think you would learn more about inner peace if you would find out how much it costs to fly to Mexico City and back, and give that money to the poor." Hers was a powerful lesson in giving and receiving.

Lesson: Forgiveness is the Key to Happiness. "I cannot forgive myself unless I am willing to forgive others...." Bitterness is a mixture of distorted perceptions. And holding grievances or speaking condemning words doesn't help anyone; it only brings more bitterness. But forgiveness opens new doors in both hearts. Neither "guilt" nor "innocence" should play a part in our forgiveness.

On one occasion, Jampolsky consciously determined to bury his long-kept anger over a client's unpaid bill, informing him that no more bills would be sent. Surprisingly, the man paid the money, and Jampolsky was able to give it to someone who was in real need. Thus, by the vehicle of forgiveness, many hearts were healed.

Lesson: I Am Never Upset for the Reason I Think. It's easy to presume that "the outside world is the cause and we are the effect." But this thinking is backwards. The world doesn't "cause" feelings. "Peace of mind begins with our own thoughts and extends outward."

All negative feelings (jealousy, anger, resentment, etc.) in reality represent some form of fear. And fear frequently triggers other problems. Back pain is sometimes a manifestation of harbored hatred or envy, for instance. So, "...whenever you are tempted to be fearful, remind yourself that you can experience Love instead."

Lesson: I Am Determined to See Things Differently. A "fearful past will extend into a fearful future," making us feel vulnerable and out of control. This cycle of fear holds the assumption "that anger occurs because we have been attacked. It also assumes that counterattack is justified...." But we are not robots; we are free to follow our inner guidance and respond with understanding and love.

Jampolsky once was put in the position of saving a tubercular woman's life by giving her mouth-to-mouth resuscitation. Where before he had felt "attacked" by his patients and lived in continual fear of catching the dreaded disease, now it suddenly dawned on him that he had just learned a valuable lesson: "...When I was totally absorbed in giving, I felt no fear."

Lesson: I Am Not the Victim of the World I See. "Attacks" originate in the mind. Replace thoughts that others are hurting you with love thoughts. "To be consistent in achieving inner peace, we must perceive a world where everyone is innocent....I can see the world differently by changing my mind about what I see."

Often, as we go through our maturing processes, we also tend to learn the art of distrust. We become paranoid of life itself, not to mention distrustful of others (work associates, sales clerks, car dealers, etc.). But when we let go of this sense of "victimization," then our relationships become based on genuine respect and love.

Joe, a fifteen-year-old boy whose head was run over twice by a tractor, was left blind and paralyzed. How does he maintain his optimism? "Oh, I just look at the positive things in everyone—and pay no attention to the negative things, and refuse to believe in the word, 'impossible.'" Joe refuses to feel sorry for himself, and miracles have followed. "He could feel that the world had dealt him a horrible blow. However, he chooses peace instead of conflict."

Lesson: Today I Will Judge Nothing that Occurs. "Tunnel vision": it makes us prone to "pigeon-hole" people upon first meeting them. "We just see a fragment of a person and our mind often interprets what we see as a fault." Faultfinding is a habit; but focusing on the strengths of others is also a habit. "See everyone you meet or think of as either extending love, or as being fearful and sending out a call for help, which is a request for love."

For example, in a restaurant we might feel inclined to correct – or "attack"—a rude waitress. If, instead, some voice whispered the truth in our ear—that the waitress's husband had died two days before, or that she's worried about finances, or that her oldest child was recently arrested for dealing drugs—then we could see the waitress, not as rude, but as fearful and calling out for love. With any person, we have the innate capacity for unconditional love. The highest gift we might be capable of offering is to overlook his or her weaknesses and demonstrate total acceptance.

Lesson: This Instant is the Only Time There Is. As experienced adults, we may find ourselves continually recycling old judgments, vulnerability and guilt. To break this distorted cycle, we must look upon the past as "archeological garbage" with no recycling value. "The past is over...." Peace is found "only in this instant." But in order to concentrate on the present, we must release "others and ourselves from all the errors of past pain and suffering."

The exasperated parents of a chronic schizophrenic thirty-five-year-old son once asked Jampolsky how they could apply the principles of love. "Spend as much time as you can before tomorrow ridding yourself of all the past, painful, guilty, fearful thoughts and experiences you have had with your son," he responded. "Release yourselves from any guilt you have about your son's condition." He urged them to imagine themselves stuffing their built-up pain into a trash can attached to a yellow helium balloon, and letting it float away. "Pay attention to how much lighter you feel. ...Look past what your eyes and ears report. Choose to see your son only through the window of Love...." Soon after, the parents wrote to say that that day they "experienced the most peaceful visit with their son they had ever had."

Lesson: I Could See Peace Instead of This. Is your happiness or unhappiness based on events or people or "luck"? It is a natural response to use blame as a defense, absolving ourselves of responsibility. But when we see the bits and pieces of a fragmented world, it is only a reflection of the chaos we see in ourselves. "Peace of mind is an internal...matter." Accordingly, "whenever you feel that your peace is threatened by anything or anyone," repeat in your mind, "I could see peace instead of this."

In sickness, for example, each of us has the tendency to focus only on our own discomfort—and we complain loudly to reinforce our hopelessness. Jampolsky suggests, rather, that we direct our minds away from our bodies and center all of our attention on serving others. By doing this, we cease to see our own suffering, finding meaning in the maxim, "To give is to receive."

Lesson: I Can Elect to Change All Thoughts that Hurt. One technique to leaving worries and problems behind is to retreat from them. Visualize yourself in a favorite hide-away. Imagination, selectively released, often brings about fresh solutions to problems. Still, remember: "We are never presented with lessons until we are ready to learn them."

Jampolsky perceived a club-wielding psychiatric patient, "gone berserk" one day, as a personal threat. The patient was scared; but when the doctor openly admitted that he too was frightened, a "common bond" was created between the two, and they were able to compose and help each other.

One final, brief ***Lesson—"I Am Responsible for What I See"***—encapsulates *Love is Letting Go of Fear:*

I Am Responsible for What I See
I choose the feelings I experience, and I decide
upon the goal I would achieve.
And everything that seems to happen to me,
I ask for, and receive as I have asked.
Teach only Love, for that is what you are.

PSYCHO-CYBERNETICS

by Maxwell Maltz, M.D., Simon and Schuster, 1960

Doctor Maxwell Maltz, a plastic surgeon, noticed that most of his patients who underwent surgery to correct a major defect experienced an accompanying rise in self-esteem. However, in some cases the patient continued to have feelings of inferiority. This phenomenon led Maltz to conclude that changed physical image was not the only key to the changes he saw in personality. He felt the need to treat the *whole* patient rather than just the defective part that required his surgical skills.

While struggling with these ideas, Dr. Maltz became interested in *cybernetics.* Cybernetics is based on "teleology"—the study of purpose or design—and deals with the goal-striving behavior of mechanical systems. Cybernetics attempts to explain the necessary steps of mechanical processes; to find mechanical analogies that can also be applied to humans. Scientific evidence shows that the brain and nervous system operate harmoniously in a purposeful manner, much like the components of a complex machine. Of course, man is not a machine—but he has and uses the ultimate machine: his brain.

Self-Image and Imagining

Dr. Maltz, ascribing the principles of cybernetics to the brain, created the term (and the success mechanism) *"psycho-cybernetics."* PC, as it is sometimes called, is based on "self-imaging"—imagining successful outcomes. Self-image is the key to human personality and human behavior; *change the self-image and you change the personality and the behavior.* But more than this, self-image sets the boundaries of individual accomplishment. It defines what you can and cannot do. *Expand the self-image and you expand your "area of the possible."*

The development of an adequate, realistic self-image actually does seem to imbue the individual with new capabilities, new talents, and the gifts to literally turn failure into success.

Self-image is altered by *experience.* It is remarkable, but experiences don't have to involve actual events—they may be *synthesized,* proxy experiences created by the mind. Since the nervous system and brain do not distinguish between real and imagined experience, you can exercise your imagination to discover a "success mechanism" within yourself.

We inevitably act in accordance with our self-image. For example, if a student feels he is "dumb" in math, he will live up to that image by avoiding math homework and freezing up on tests. He will be frustrated, feeling there is nothing he can do to improve his ability, when what he really needs is to change the way he *thinks* about himself. *Our self-image prescribes the limits for the accomplishment of our goals.*

A Success Mechanism

A sense of success is a key ingredient of a positive self-image. We know that animals possess instincts that help them survive as "successful" predators, swimmers or nest-makers. In addition to our intellectual, emotional and spiritual endowments, humans also have instincts. We too are survival-oriented, but unlike other animals, whose "goals" are predetermined, we are left to select our own goals. Luckily, we are not left alone; our *creative imagination* allows us to consider many possibilities and goal paths.

In this creative process, the brain and nervous system act as a "servo-mechanism," which "learns" or programs itself as it makes mistakes and receives negative feedback. This can be compared to a guided missile, making its way to a prescribed target; it uses trial and error (mistakes) as guides to correct its course.

The process of arriving at a new mental picture of yourself involves six steps:

(1) Relax.

(2) Imagine success.

(3) "Dehypothesize" yourself from false beliefs.

(4) Visualize goals (targets) as if they were already in existence.

(5) Resolve to be unafraid of making mistakes.

(6) Trust your creative mechanism to do the work.

Hypnotism is an example of the power of imagination. A hypnotized person who is told she is at the North Pole will often start to shiver. If she imagines meeting a bear on her path, she will respond with a typical "fight or flight" syndrome—rapid heartbeat, dilated pupils, etc.

Imagination (really another form of hypnotism) allows us to practice new actions and attitudes. *Visualizing* a successful action—from a masterful golf swing to a favorable job interview—can dramatically improve performance in real life. *Role-playing* and *rehearsal* have also been employed for years to bolster confidence and competence among salespeople and actors. To make your imagination work for you, you must actually *see yourself in your new role.* Maltz suggests imagining yourself acting and reacting appropriately and consistently for thirty minutes each day, until your whole self-image is modified.

We all suffer from certain feelings of inferiority, and each of us is in fact inferior to others in some areas. It is not the *knowledge* that we are inferior, however, but the *feeling* of being somehow "inherently" inferior that increases our negative self-image. To counteract this feeling, remember that there is no one else exactly like you. You are not competing to be better than others; you are striving to develop—and become—*yourself.*

Physical and mental relaxation also may help you counteract the need to compete and conform. Imagine a beautiful and gentle scene in all its detail. Concentrate on it for a short while every day, letting your worries fade and each part of your body loosen up.

But imagination is not all there is to changing a negative complex. Actually, *most learning comes about through trial and error.* And we must also learn to forget our errors once they have taught us their lessons. Don't dwell on failure; remember instead the attempts that finally worked.

Solving Problems and Being Happy

When you doubt your ability to accomplish a task, simply ask yourself why you believe you can't do it. Then examine this belief to see if it is based on actual fact or on a false premise. Ask:

- Is there any rationale for such a belief?
- Could it be that I am mistaken in this belief?
- Would I come to the same conclusion about someone else in a similar situation?

Sometimes it is best to relax your mind in problem-solving; *solutions often come more freely when you are not concentrating on them.* Rational thought must be accompanied by deep feeling and desire—again engendered through imagining. Picture the outcome you would like to see, and go over it again and again in your mind. (We do this very thing the other way around when we worry.) *Focus* on a positive image. Decide what you *want* to happen, not what you don't want. Keep yourself focused on the goal.

Most of us are too hesitant; even after a decision has been made, we often sit and wonder whether we are doing the right thing. But the only way to know this for sure is to act—and find out.

We can be happy (most of the time) only if we *decide* to be happy. The basis of happiness is refusing to allow other people or outside events to control our responses, and dwelling instead on pleasant, joy-producing incidents. *Develop the habit of being happy.*

Mechanisms

Success-oriented personalities embrace the following qualities in their thought mechanisms:

S-ense of direction
U-nderstanding
C-ourage
C-harity
E-steem
S-elf-Confidence
S-elf-Acceptance

Most people, however, have formed emotional scars. They have reacted to harmful or embarrassing events in their lives by developing a thick, tough "skin," resolving to never let anything or anyone hurt them that way again. To rid yourself of emotional scars, cultivate and balance *self-reliance* and *forgiveness* of self and others. Become your real self (a frequently hidden entity); trust your true personality. Stop worrying about what others think of you. Shake inhibitions, worry, and self-criticism by ignoring feedback that is not instructive and realizing that in most situations there is no simple right or wrong way of acting.

More and more people are turning to artificial tranquilizers to help them cope with life. However, your mind can manufacture its own "tranquilizers"; it can be trained to ignore "bells" or "signals" that previously brought on an automatic alarm reflex. A ringing telephone, for example, is a signal that someone wishes to speak with you, but *you can choose* whether to respond (answer it) or to ignore it (let it ring). In the same way, you should consciously understand that you are in control of deciding whether to react to an event immediately, to *ignore* it completely, or to utilize your natural tranquilizer (your mind) to *delay* response until you have rationally, creatively, and peacefully analyzed the situation.

To control your mind, relaxation (again) is crucial. If your days are hectic, a quiet room in which to "escape" may be just what you need. Another healthy method for dealing with difficult circumstances is to practice responses during times when there is no pressure—like going through a fire drill. Visualize and rehearse confident behavior in order to overcome fear in social situations, business meetings, sports, or any other area. "*Non-crisis conditioning*" injects you with a winning feeling and assures that you will be well prepared when it comes to doing the real thing.

Our minds are like a stereo playing a record. We each have the power to choose what kind of music is played. *Psycho-cybernetics* urges you to "mechanize" your responses in life by *setting goals, letting your unconscious and conscious mind cultivate them, conquering negative beliefs and feelings of failure, visualizing your targets through positive experiencing, and, finally, achieving the ultimate life-goal—happiness.*

Understanding

Eliminating Stress and Finding Serenity in Life and Relationships

by Jane Nelsen, Ed.D., Prima Publishing and Communications, Rocklin, California, 1988

Though she was a successful marriage, family and child therapist, Jane Nelsen was dissatisfied with her life; something seemed to be missing. It was not until she applied the principles she later described in *Understanding* that she discovered how to find peace and happiness. In her book, Nelsen confronts the many thoughts, moods and long-held myths that act as barriers to happiness in our personal lives and relationships.

Society defines success as fame, fortune and achievement. We will be happy, we believe, when we finally make our fortune, find the perfect spouse, graduate from college, or end up at the top in our business. But most people who define success in these terms are unhappy, and will likely remain in misery. Happiness really does come from within.

There are four principles that can serve as a treasure map, says Nelsen, which will lead us to true inner happiness. In life's journey, our natural feelings of peace, love and joy frequently become clouded over by negative feelings. These feelings are created by negative thoughts and beliefs implanted along the way. Negative thoughts easily enslave us, and our subsequent reactions to them usually cause a negative outcome (or loss of joy). Built-up stress and insecurity can be eliminated by understanding how we become slaves to our self-created thought systems.

Principle No. 1: *Thinking as a Function*

Truly, thoughts determine attitudes. However, most people believe they are victims of their thoughts rather than *producers* of them. Nelsen counters: "We can think anything we choose to think, and our emotions are then a direct result of what we choose to think." For example, try feeling insecure without thinking thoughts dealing with insecurity. It can't be done.

"Melissa believes she is depressed because life is overwhelming. But life cannot be overwhelming; only what she thinks about life makes it feel overwhelming." The simple solution?: "If you don't like what you are thinking about, stop thinking about it." Don't let your thoughts take control of your life.

Principle No. 2: *Feelings as a Compass*

Try viewing feelings as an indicator or a compass. "Negative feelings tell us it is time to dismiss negative thoughts. Positive feelings tell us we are experiencing life through our natural state of mind, where we have access to our inherent good feelings." To know whether an emotion comes from your true, inner self or from a false thought system, Nelsen advises: "If the feeling comes first, it is from your natural state of mind; if the feeling comes second, it is from your thought system." Thus, "secondary" feelings become a good indicator of the negative or positive thought-systems we are involved with.

The author shares a personal illustration: Her thirteen-year-old son had been suspended from school because cigarettes were found in his locker. As he told it: "I don't know how they got there. I was just putting them in my pocket to take them to the principal when a teacher came by..." She writes:

My thoughts went crazy for a few minutes. "He is lying to us. I'm a failure as a mother. If he is smoking cigarettes, he is probably also using alcohol and drugs. He is going to ruin his life. What will people think?" I was feeling pretty upset, so my feeling compass let me know loud and clear that I was caught up in my thought system and was not seeing things clearly. I dismissed my compass instead of my thoughts for a minute and used more thoughts to argue with my inner wisdom. "Yes, but this is different. These are really terrible circumstances....How could I possibly see them differently? I am going to have to scold him severely, 'ground' him for at least a month, take away all his privileges, and let him know he is ruining his life."

But rather than react immediately, Nelsen used the second principle of *Understanding*. When she dismissed the thought system, her inner wisdom came through:

I then saw the circumstances in a completely different way and felt understanding and compassion....[My son] had just entered junior high school, where the pressure is enormous to follow the crowd rather than to follow common sense.

When I got home I listened to my inspiration and knew what to do. I sat down with my son, put my arm around him, and said, "I'll bet it's tough trying to figure out how to say no to your friends so you won't be called a nerd or a party pooper." He had been expecting my usual craziness and hardly knew how to respond to my sanity. He tentatively said, "Yeah." I went on, "And I'll bet the only reason you would ever lie to us is because you love us so much you don't want to disappoint us." Tears filled his eyes, and he gave me a hug. I responded with tears in my own eyes as we experienced those wonderful feelings of mutual love. I reassured him, "If you think you could ever disappoint us enough to diminish our love, then we are not doing a good enough job of letting you know how much we love you, unconditionally.

Principle No. 3: *Separate Realities*

Each of us interprets life differently. "The reason becomes obvious when we understand that everyone sees through the filters of his or her own unique thought system." But when we stop judging and start *appreciating* people's differences, we can learn from them. Any form of condemnatory judgment, hatred or self-righteousness only contaminates the common sense that could lead to positive action. Allowing negative feelings to persist makes you "become like the thing or person you judge or hate, spreading more negativity in the world." Conversely, "Higher levels of understanding will come naturally from the positive feelings that surface when judgmental thoughts about separate realities are dismissed."

Principle No.4: *Mood Levels*

"When you are in a high mood, you see things one way; when you are in a low mood, you see the same things differently." For example, your natural self might gladly let someone go in front of you at the grocery check-out stand: She's in a hurry and only has two items. But if your thought system takes over, you reason differently: I'm in a hurry; he'll just have to wait. According to the principle of Mood Levels, when you are in a pleasant mood you are living in your natural state of mind and when you are angry or sad you are too often living in your thought system.

Once these four related principles are understood, we can actively change our situational responses. "The secret is knowing that moods are not nearly as bad as the thoughts we have about them; it is our thoughts about low moods that can make them seem really awful. Patiently wait for the mood to pass. A quiet mind is the best cure for a low mood....Quiet is listening without judgment. Sometimes the simple realization that it is just a mood, will be enough to immediately raise your level of consciousness."

Conscious gratitude can help in altering a bad mood. Just by appreciating your health, talents, children or simply a beautiful object, you begin to want to give rather than receive. "Expecting something back is manipulative, conditional giving."

Destructive Myths

We frequently hold false assumptions about relationships. Here are listed a few of these myths.

- *Love is Blind:* Love is not blind. When in love, we notice differences and see them as interesting and endearing rather than as faults.
- *It is important to be compatible:* The notion that people have to think about and enjoy doing the same things to be compatible is simply not true. By respecting differences, we all have the ability to be compatible.
- *We will be happy when circumstances change:* You cannot experience joy by focusing on circumstances and "what is not." Get rid of the "shoulds" and the "should nots" and start seeing what is. A letter to Dear Abby from a woman who complained about her husband's snoring was followed up by another woman's insight: "I used to complain about snoring. My husband is dead now. I would give anything..."
- *Jealousy* (imagined fear, insecurity and possessiveness caused by ego) and *assumptions* (imagined ideas about how another person thinks or feels, which leads to distrust or blame) are two other barriers that limit clear, real, happy thinking.

Another core component of Nelsen's book is a section entitled "Lack of Wisdom, from the Ages." One pearl of false wisdom which many of us have been subjected to growing up is the adage: "Anything worth doing, is worth doing well." Like many myths, this is just not so. If "doing well" simply meant "putting your heart in it" or "enjoying it," the saying would be a positive help to us. But most often we define doing a thing well as executing it perfectly—a judgment of what is ideal. The greatest treasures—joy and serenity in doing—should replace judgment.

"When happiness is more important to you than anything else, you will be happy," Nelsen says, "because there will be no thoughts you will be willing to give up your happiness for....When understanding changes how we see things, everything and everyone in our world looks different. It may seem as though others have changed, but it is our thoughts, and thus our reality, and thus our feelings that have changed. Others often respond to our feeling level. When we give love, we get love—not necessarily because others give it back to us, but because love will emanate from within."

"AS A MAN THINKETH, SO IS HE."

A Whack on the Side of the Head

How You Can Be More Creative

by Roger von Oech, Warner Books, 1990

Roger von Oech packs this book with creative examples and innovative exercises, together with incredible illustrations (by George Willett), all in a framework that is refreshing and imaginative. Though geared to the professional, the work is diverse enough to apply to anyone.

To von Oech, creativity is not only fun but necessary to success and survival in the nineties. But why? "Why be creative? Why challenge the rules? Why run the risk of failing and looking foolish?" For two good reasons: (1) *To discover new solutions to problems...;* (2) *To generate new ideas when old ones become obsolete.*

The inventor-explorer plays with knowledge; he alters his perspective, making "the ordinary extraordinary and the unusual commonplace." Johann Gutenburg observed how grapes were crushed for wine in a wine press, and by combining two previously unconnected ideas invented the printing press and movable type.

An *exercise:* How can two people stand on the same piece of newspaper face to face, unrestrained, and still not be able to touch each other? If you couldn't come up with an answer (the book's answer is to put the newspaper in a doorway—door closed—with the people on opposite sides of the door), chances are, a "mental lock" impeded you from thinking out the solution. You may be imprisoned by a mandate to find "the right answer," for example, to "follow the rules," or to "avoid ambiguity."

So, how do you open your mental locks? One way is to "unlearn" them; temporarily forget that wine presses only squeeze grapes; go in a new direction with a less cluttered mind; "unimprison" yourself from routine and familiarity. *Sometimes, nothing short of a "whack on the side of the head" can dislodge the assumptions that keep us thinking "more of the same."*

"Whacks" come in many forms. Getting fired, having a teacher with a special talent, breaking your leg, or a business success or emergency might force you to "think something different," make you dislodge presuppositions that stifle thinking, and cause you to generate new questions.

Here are some of von Oech's "whacking" techniques to help you snap your mental locks:

"The Right Answer"

Educator Neil Postman said, "Children enter school as question marks and leave as periods." Our educational system channels us to seek "the right answer." We are taught to solve problems, not to recognize opportunities. But, in most arenas, "...if you think there is only one right answer, then you'll stop looking as soon as you find one."

"Look for the second right answer," von Oech recommends. He quotes Linus Pauling: "The best way to get a good idea is to get a lot of ideas." Professional photographers, for instance, take many pictures of a subject so that they can experiment with lighting, different filters, and changes in exposure, in order to find what they're looking for.

- *An idea:* Whack your thinking by changing the original question; play with the wording to approach it from a different angle. Instead of "What type of door can I use to connect these two rooms?" an architect might ask "What sort of passageway should I put here?"

"That's Not Logical"

Logical, analytical thinking is hard thinking. Soft thinking, on the other hand, is divergent, fantastical, visual and often poetic. There is a place for both, but true creativity usually begins with soft thinking, where similarities and connections between objects or situations are explored. Most people have developed a "creative rigor mortis due to excessive hard thinking." They don't give themselves license to use imagination or metaphors.

A metaphor is a "mental map"; a tool to compare something tangible to something abstract. Niels Bohr explained how an atom might look by comparing it to the structure of the solar system, with its central sun (nucleus) and revolving planets (electrons). By showing how dissimilar things are similar, good metaphors enable you "to gain a new perspective on both the unfamiliar and the quite familiar." Try some metaphors of your own: How is motivating a sales force like feeding zoo animals? How is a problem you're dealing with like building a house?...

"Follow the Rules"

Rules, routine, and patterns in life are important. But "...almost every advance in art, cooking, medicine, agriculture, engineering, marketing...has occurred when someone challenged the rules and tried another approach." In sports, if someone hadn't challenged the rules, football wouldn't be a passing game; and in basketball there would still be a jump ball after every field goal.

A rule sometimes outlives the purpose for which it was intended. The typewriter keyboard, for example, was originally positioned with letters in an illogical sequence in order to slow down typists and keep the keys' hammers from hitting each other. Now, although high-tech machines allow for much faster typing without jams, we continue to use this same configuration—only because it's "the rule."

Go after and slay your "sacred cows"—rules that limit your thoughts and actions to one particular approach.

"Be Practical"

Try some exercises in *What-Iffing:* What would happen if gravity stopped functioning for one second every day? How would life be different? What would transportation be like?...

Seeding your imagination with questions like these can help you generate ideas, as well as help you cast off the constraints of the "real" (status-quo) world. Although "what-iffing" doesn't usually lead directly to practical answers, these questions can make excellent "stepping stones" to workable, creative solutions. Fortunately, an engineer's "silly" suggestion to put gunpowder in house paint so that it could be blown off the house when it started to peel, was not discarded as "mental trash," but was used by his team members to launch a search for additives that allowed paint to release when strippers were applied.

- *An idea:* Imagine how Winston Churchill, Mother Teresa, George Patton, the Three Stooges, a plumber, or a banker might solve your problem or perform your task. What expertise would each add? How would they see your situation differently?

"That's Not My Area"

Today we live in a world of specialization—relief pitchers in baseball, specialists in medicine. "So, we have a situation where people know more and more about less and less."

To avoid "tunnel vision," actively search for ideas outside your field; look for history in a hardware store, study fashion at a flea market. Football coach Knute Rockne came up with the concept for his "four horsemen" backfield while watching a burlesque chorus routine. The roll-on deodorant was an adaptation of the ball-point pen. Nature inspired the Velcro fastener and new designs in windmill blades (the hook spine of the common burr and the spinning feature of falling elm seeds).

"Avoid Ambiguity"

On most occasions it helps to be clear and precise. At times, though, you can make ambiguity work for you:

- *Paradoxes.* "The ability to entertain two different, often contradictory notions at the same time" can stimulate thought. Niels Bohr stated this classic paradox: "The opposite of a great truth is another great truth."
- *Oracles.* Consult, not the oracle at Delphi, but the oracle of your own intuition. Take a random word or object and discover how it applies to your situation. Remember, ancient oracles were often deliberately ambiguous, forcing their petitioners to go beyond the literal, obvious answer and find hidden links to interpretations.
- *Dreams* are "naturals" as oracles. "Listening" to what your dream is really telling you, can provide insights into relationships, or even lead you to choosing the "right" pattern or design idea for your living room furniture.

"Don't Be Foolish"

We all tend to "go along with the crowd" to a certain extent; in fact, seeing how others do things is a good way to learn. But "when everyone thinks alike, no one is doing very much thinking."

In classical times, a king would hire a jester-fool to give him insight, which was frequently in direct contradiction to advice given by the "yes-men" of his court. Parody, irreverence, analogy, and offbeat observations were the fool's priceless wares. And today, "thinking like a fool" may be essential to breaking through and jolting your mind. After all, "some of the most foolish ideas from five years ago are now a reality."

- *Some ideas:* Reverse your point of view; disagree with yourself; sometimes do the opposite of what is expected.

Designer Christopher Williams instructed his landscape crew to wait to put sidewalks in around a new cluster of buildings. Over the subsequent months, as the buildings' occupants traversed the grounds, the new lawn became laced with pathways that followed the most efficient curves linking building to building. Only then, in response to user needs, did Williams have the sidewalks paved.

Especially in competitive situations such as sports, warfare, and business, doing the unexpected or seeing yourself from the other side's viewpoint are effective strategies to catch the opposition off-guard.

Some other common mental locks:

"Play is Frivolous." Is it really? Children do most of their learning through play. And "there is a close relationship between the 'ha-ha' of humor and the 'aha' of discovery....The next time you have a problem, play with it."

"To Err Is Wrong." Surely we all want to succeed; but the best stepping stone to real creative success can be failure. "Thomas Edison knew 1,800 ways not to build a light bulb." Keep your "risk muscles" in shape by regularly trying a new recipe or tackling a problem outside your area of expertise. You may fail—but you may also learn a whole new way of looking for answers.

Have fun using these strategic "whacks." Put yourself in a position to be creative: play with knowledge; find "the seventh right answer"; take some risks; open up a new idea.

Then, "don't wait for your idea to happen." Act on it. "If you want to be a singer, go sing. Sing in the shower. Sing for your friends. Join the choir.... " And "after you implement your idea," says von Oech, "give yourself a pat on the back. And then go out and earn another one."

DEVELOPING CRITICAL THINKERS

Challenging Adults to Explore Alternative Ways of Thinking

by Stephen D. Brookfield, Jossey-Bass, San Francisco, California, 1987

Stephen Brookfield established his place as an author in the field of adult education with his award-winning book *Understanding and Facilitating Adult Learning* (Jossey-Bass, 1986). Developing Critical Thinkers continues his exploration of the fascinating phenomenon of thinking. Brookfield is one academic who is unafraid to dissolve theoretical abstractions into practical information; his book is both understandable and useful.

Developing Critical Thinkers covers some interesting ground, with chapters on decision-making, adult learning, creative problem-solving, values clarification, and change. The text is divided into three main sections. Part one focuses on the definition and description of critical thinking; part two deals with practical approaches to development; and the third section concentrates on urging adults to think critically in four major life contexts: the workplace, politics, television, and personal relationships. Through-out, the key issue remains "critical thinking," as defined by two simple principles or activities. People act as "critical thinkers" when they:

(1) Identify and challenge the assumptions underlying their own or another's beliefs and behavior.

(2) Explore and imagine alternatives to current ways of thinking and living.

The first step in critical thinking is to recognize and then scrutinize the assumptions that guide us through life. Philosophers, physicists, psychologists, and scientists in general acknowledge the foundational role that assumptions play in their work. Critical thinking is only possible when "people probe their habitual ways of thinking... for their underlying assumptions—those taken-for-granted values, common-sense ideas, and stereotypical notions about human nature...that underlie our actions."

Getting beneath the surface features of thought or behavior—to the thinking below the thinking—is tricky, but it is possible, and plainly in evidence when, for example, a management consultant asks an executive why she does something a certain way and gets the response, "That's just the way we do things around here." The consultant is questioning the assumptions behind a practice. In the same way, when a father has a heart-to-heart talk with his teenager and they both discover that they hold some erroneous preconceptions, the father and the son are *unearthing assumptions* and *building new insights.* Critical thinking is the essence of such scenarios.

The second step involves becoming aware of alternative perspectives...perspectives that may be as valid as our own. Brookfield writes:

> *...Considering and imagining alternatives, leads to the development of a particularly critical cast of mind, especially where any claims for the universal truth or validity of an idea or practice are concerned. We become suspicious of those who tell us that they have "the answer" to life or the solution to all our problems.*

The message here is that critical thinkers don't automatically accept a particular idea, statement, lifestyle, or solution; rather, they examine the alternatives, make a conscious choice among them, and accept the consequences. The honest critical thinker recognizes that there are many paths to follow, not just his own.

In describing strategies for developing and nurturing critical thinking, Brookfield first outlines a process involving several phases:

(1) ***A Triggering Event:*** something that causes a sense of "inner discomfort and perplexity"

(2) ***Exploration:*** a search for ways of reducing this discomfort

(3) ***Developing Alternative Perspectives:*** the selection of "new roles we wish to play" and the development of "knowledge and skills for the action we wish to take"

(4) ***Integration:*** finding and integrating new ways of thinking and living

The author avers that the most important of these phases is the first. He describes two kinds of triggering events: positive and negative. *Positive triggers* are those that lead us to discover new ways of thinking in pleasant or fulfilling circumstances, as when we accomplish something we assumed we could not do. But far more common are the *negative triggers* of divorce, death, dislocation, and termination, which force us to confront and change dysfunctional assumptions. This explains why professional helpers—psychologists, counselors, therapists—have such a powerful impact on some lives; they intervene just as old assumptions are crumbling and help clients develop fresh assumptions to chart a new course through life.

How does one go about examining the basic assumptions that underlie thought and action? Brookfield lists a variety of tips and techniques, all revolving around a pivotal proposition:

"Challenge is central to helping people think critically."

Critical Questioning—This is questioning designed to bring to the surface basic assumptions and to prompt "reflective analysis"—to allow people to scrutinize the basis for their thinking or actions.

Critical Incident Exercises—Here, the individual identifies a specific incident or event that, for some reason, was of particular significance to her. This milestone is written down and then explored to reveal the assumptions that made it meaningful.

Criteria Analysis—By eliciting and then examining the criteria set for judging specific events, critical thinkers discover more about their unspoken assumptions of right and wrong, good or bad.

Crisis-Decision Simulations—For this exercise, people are asked to imagine themselves in a situation where they are forced to make a decision from among a number of uncomfortable choices. After making their choice, they are asked to justify and elaborate on their reasons for choosing one course of action over others. As they do so, their underlying assumptions become more evident.

Once assumptions have been identified, the next logical step is to develop alternative ways of thinking; to adopt (or become aware of) a different set of assumptions. Again, Brookfield suggests how critical thinking might be enhanced.

(1) Practice being a critical thinker:

(a) Reject *standardized formats* for problem solving.

(b) Cultivate interests in a *wide variety* of related and divergent fields.

(c) Take *multiple perspectives* on a problem.

(d) View the world as *relative* and *contextual* rather than universal and absolute.

(e) Use *trial-and-error*—experimental and experiential—methods in daily living.

(f) *Embrace change* as a valuable developmental opportunity.

(g) *Build self-confidence and trust* in your own judgement.

(Brookfield stresses that these characteristics are developed over time, not overnight.)

(2) **Make decisions by brainstorming,** a respected technique for encouraging structured spontaneity among individuals or groups. Brainstorming follows three basic stages. After the problem is carefully specified:

(a) Generate a free flow of ideas, with *no evaluation or criticism* allowed.

(b) Encourage individuals to *propose outrageous solutions* or ideas.

(c) Attempt to *build on these ideas.*

(3) Heighten critical thinking by using a **futures invention** game. Participants are encouraged to imagine both individual and collective futures they desire (becoming an artist, getting the job of director of marketing, starting a family...). Through a process of revealing, comparing and negotiating visions of what people most desire in their personal and social worlds, a concrete, psychologically magnetic future scenario is generated revolving around four questions:

(a) *Who am I?*

(b) *What do I want to do?*

(c) *How can I do it?*

(d) *What are the grounds for inviting other persons to join me in making these decisions?*

Such a future vision can create, for some people, a "psychological magnetism" that can have great impact on their lives.

Brookfield's book goes on to discuss more ways of understanding and articulating our hidden assumptions and of positing new alternatives. Some methods are highly creative: writing an individual futures history and using "aesthetic triggers" (art, poetry, nature, fantasy or drama) to relax the mind.

In the final section of the book, Brookfield examines the value of critical thinking in different areas of life. In the workplace, critical thinking is a sorely needed commodity; but it can also be dangerous. For example, it is uncommon to see a subordinate publicly question his superior's underlying assumptions about a decision or course of action—although most of us do so privately. However, companies that reward and encourage critical thinking may be significantly more effective than traditional businesses.

This book may appeal to teachers, who might find that its games and techniques stimulate creative thinking in their students. Managers and executives interested in reducing pressures for conformity within their organizations can find new ways of "opening up" business cultures. Counselors and consultants involved in team building can discover valuable ideas for engaging their clients.

"*Critical Thinking*," is the highest and most human of human potentials.

How to Prosper During the Coming Bad Years

by Howard J. Ruff, Times Books, 1979

"*Invest in inflation, it's the only thing that's going up.*" —Will Rogers

Howard Ruff does not believe that the United States is "going under." However, he does feel that the nation is in an increasingly fragile state, where collapses (national, local, or within families) are more and more likely to occur. Ruff's opinion is that we *will* survive the coming economic and social difficulties if we are prepared. Personal preparation is the focus of his timeless book.

Part I: Problems

Odds are, your neighbor spends more than he makes. The same could be said of you, your county government, and most Washington offices. Debt and mortgages are the norm. But the result of spending money we don't have is inflation, and this is the monster creeping up to devour us. Nevertheless, you don't have to be eaten alive if you understand the dangers involved, and make some simple decisions to regulate your assets.

Economic trends indicate, says Ruff, that eventually, whether through inflation or national emergency, the nation's monetary system will forcibly be returned to the gold-backed standard. When that time comes, because our gold reserves have been greatly depleted, the price of metals will skyrocket. Investors in commodities such as precious metals, that either hold their values or go up in value, will not only survive, but prosper during this crisis. These financially shrewd individuals and families will remain "solvent, self-sufficient and panic-proof...."

What are the issues that will threaten your future prosperity? How will you react to these realities? Ruff suggests two possible problems, along with possible scenarios for each:

Inflation

Inflation is the decrease in value of your money. Both history and contemporary national and international crises have shown that inflation can weaken personal pocketbooks and shatter national economies. The world's economic future depends on the U.S. dollar, which is recurrently at risk of collapse.

In like manner, your individual retirement account robs you. The retirement annuity that looked so promising twenty years ago would now reduce you to living at the poverty level. Governmental inflation reduces your spending power, nibbles at your savings, your stocks....In short, most of your assets are diminishing in value.

Who loses money due to inflation?

- The lender (you, if you have a mortgage, a life insurance policy, or bonds)
- The saver (you again, if you put money into a bank or Savings and Loan)
- The pensioner (you, if you have set up an annuity or rely on Social Security, both of which feed on your interest and whose actual purchasing power will be close to nil by the time you cash in on them)

Who are the winners?

- Big borrowers (like the Government)
- Big business
- Mortgage companies
- Those who invest early to hedge potential financial chaos (possibly you!)

City Deterioration

The dearth of safety and services in our major cities, and their preponderance of poor and dissatisfied inhabitants, will make them the first victims of inflation and monetary disruption. The already dangerous climate of our cities is worsening. Crime *does* pay because so few criminals go to jail; welfare rolls swell because there is little economic incentive to work; slums expand; property values plummet; jobs are scarce. When the "crunch" hits, city families and property will be in danger.

Ruff further avows that, besides cities overcrowded with people "on the edge" of poverty, a combination of other factors puts us all at risk: decreasing birth rates and increasing longevity; general distrust, by most citizens, of governments and their economic future; and the reliance of American banks on foreign capital. These risk factors may cause many small breakdowns (materials shortages or a series of unsettled strikes, for instance), or they may lead to one major disaster. "Basically," says Ruff, "I am outlining a new way of helping people become financially secure at a time when the institutions they have come to depend on are clearly failing them."

Parts II and III: Preservation and Strategy

Inflation can be good for you—*if you invest in it.* To make inflation work for you, you must own some of those things which are going up in value as fast or faster than inflation itself is rising.

If you have to periodically buy something on a regular basis, and prices rise, you are hurt by inflation. If you already bought a lot of it when it was cheap, you can watch your wealth increase and you are on good terms with the inflationary monster....[Then,] if you live in the right place and have a reasonable amount of self-sufficiency, and the distribution machine misses a few beats, you'll still be O.K.

Even if the odds favor good times in the coming few years, Ruff submits the following as sound advice. (For emphasis, he leaves his most important recommendation till last.):

- Keep, in a safe deposit box, a bag of "junk" silver (one per person), and, if feasible, an equivalent amount of gold to avoid the hazards of our paper-based economy. Metals hold steady in value even in the worst of times. (However, don't buy from a private mint or on margin.)
- Avoid unnecessary debt. Over-extension causes risks—and accompanying fear. Borrow only to purchase income-producing investments or those that inflate in overall value. Pay off your mortgage completely, if possible.
- Sell big-city or suburban real estate and purchase small-town property. Move there, if you are able. Small-town homes will be the safest in the event of a crisis—riot, disrupted services (water supply, electricity, etc.) or financial depression.
- When buying a home or investment property, either pay in immediate cash or invest as little cash as possible; "Nothing in between makes sense." By choosing one of these two paths, you either avoid the interest of a mortgage, or leave your funds available for other good investments.
- In less urban areas, small-scale residential units (up to a "fourplex") are usually favorable investments. There will always be renters; everybody has to have a place to live. (Of course, remember that being a landlord also takes time and upkeep. Don't invest beyond your resources.)
- Spread your risks among as many inflation-beating investments as possible.
- Be highly self-sufficient. By all means, have some food stored and plant a garden. Keep chickens or rabbits; have a generator, a water well, a modern wood-burning stove and a supply of wood, an underground gas tank, a bicycle or moped. Know how to hunt and fish, and have the needed equipment. Learn practical skills such as home and auto repair.
- Plan your future as if Social Security didn't exist.
- Maintain some cash reserves for emergencies, but don't keep them in savings or checking accounts. Money-funds or Treasury Bills earn better rates and are liquid and safe.
- Have on hand a supply of those items that would likely be scarce in the event of a shortage: food, water, seeds, tools, ammunition, reading material, durable clothing, soap, toilet paper, motor oil, automobile replacement parts, light bulbs, etc. Buy these in quantity when they are at bargain prices. It will surely save you money; and the items you don't use yourself may serve as barter in times of need.

Top, Number One Recommendation:

- Store enough usable food to last one year (dehydrated food is top priority). In Europe during the early 1920s, diamonds, heirlooms, silver sets, and other luxury items were steadily transferred from their upper class owners to the peasants as barter for sacks of potatoes. Panic-proof yourself by having food on hand before the widespread hoarding that commonly accompanies a crisis. Many factors make food a vulnerable commodity—weather conditions, oil supply, transportation and worker demands, for example, not to mention your monetary ability to buy food if the economy goes sour.

Ruff stresses having a proper food supply; after all, "no one can raise prices on food you bought last year," and "food storage is the insurance you can eat." Stored food represents money well invested, and not only prepares you to meet a possible widespread disaster down the road, but hedges you up against personal hardship brought on by an accident or the loss of work.

■■■

How to Prosper in the Coming Bad Years provides details on many other subjects related to basic principles of preparedness: real estate; leveraging of money; metals-buying; negotiation techniques; securing a loan; steps and stages of survival; food production, planning, buying, and storage, etc.

The book's appendices list publications and newsletters that, in Ruff's view, offer good financial advice *(The Wall Street Journal, Business Week, Forbes)*. Also, Ruff endorses certain companies that can help make real progress toward your present goals of future prosperity and peace of mind.

THE RICHEST MAN IN BABYLON

by George S. Clason, Hawthorn Books, New York, N.Y., 1955

The Richest Man in Babylon is a compilation of pamphlets dealing with personal finance, written as parables set in ancient Babylon. The book is based on the adage that "A lean purse is easier to cure than to endure."

Friends of Arkad approached him saying: "You, Arkad, are more fortunate than we. You have become the richest man in Babylon while we struggle for existence." Now these men had all been taught by the same teacher and had played the same games in their youth. They noted that Arkad had not out-performed them in either schooling or the games. So, how could his riches be explained?

Arkad answered his friends: "If you have not acquired more than a bare existence in the years since we were youths, it is because you either have failed to learn the laws that govern the building of wealth, or else you do not observe them." He then revealed how he had recognized early that if he was to achieve his youthful desire to accumulate wealth and put it to good use, two things—*time* and *study*—would be required.

"As for time, all men have it in abundance. You, each of you, have let slip by sufficient time to have made yourselves wealthy...." Arkad said. "As for study, did not our wise teacher teach us that learning was of two kinds: the one kind being the things we learned and knew, and the other being the training that taught us how to find out what we did not know?"

Arkad went on to share with his friends his story:

As a young man, he had found work inscribing clay tablets in the hall of records. One day Algamish, the money lender, ordered a copy of a law which must be ready within a very short time. "Algamish, you are a very rich man," said Arkad. "Tell me how I may also become rich, and all night I will carve upon the clay, and when the sun rises it shall be completed." Algamish smiled and replied, "We will call it a bargain." Arkad worked through the night and fulfilled the task.

Algamish told Arkad: "I found the road to wealth when I decided that *a part of all I earned was mine to keep.* And so will you." By faithfully following this principle, Arkad eventually became the richest man in all Babylon.

Seven Cures for a Lean Purse

After many years of prosperity, Babylon found itself in sore straits. Few people in the city had sufficient money to provide for their needs. The king called Arkad before him, questioned him about his secret of wealth and asked if it could be taught. Arkad responded, "...That which one man knows can be taught to others."

One hundred teachers assembled in the Temple of Learning, where Arkad instructed them in the seven cures for a lean purse.

The First Cure—*Start thy purse to fattening:* "For every ten coins thou placest within thy purse take out for use but nine. Thy purse will start to fatten...and bring satisfaction to thy soul." Arkad ended the first class by declaring: "Which desirest thou the most? Is it the gratification of thy desires of each day? Or is it for substantial belongings? The coins thou takest from thy purse bring the first. The coins thou leavest within it will bring the latter."

The Second Cure—*Control thy expenditures:* "That which each of us calls our 'necessary expenses' will always grow equal to our income unless we protest to the contrary." The key is to institute and observe a budget. "The purpose of a budget is to help thy purse to fatten."

The Third Cure—*Make thy gold multiply:* "Put each coin to laboring that it may reproduce its kind even as the flocks of the field and [bring] a stream of wealth that shall flow constantly into thy purse."

The Fourth Cure—*Guard thy treasures from loss:* The first rule for sound investing is "security for thy principal." Study investments wisely before parting with hard-earned money.

The Fifth Cure—*Make of thy dwelling a profitable investment:* By owning your home you can invest a portion of the nine-tenths of your money that you live on, and make your worth grow more rapidly.

The Sixth Cure—*Insure a future income:* Plan and save now for the time when you do not have the capacity to earn.

The Seventh Cure—*Increase thy ability to earn:* "The more...we know, the more we may earn. That man who seeks to learn more of his craft shall be richly rewarded."

Along with these cures, Arkad continually advised against "overstraining" (trying to save too much) and becoming "niggardly and afraid to spend." He suggested hard work, compassion toward those less fortunate, and making life "rich with things worthwhile and things to enjoy." He also counseled:

Desires must be simple and definite. They defeat their own purpose should they be too many, too confusing, or beyond a man's training to accomplish.

Meet the Goddess of Good Luck

In ancient Babylon, those who sought greater understanding would meet in the Temple of Learning. There, rich and poor alike questioned one another and debated many issues.

On one evening, Arkad presided in the Temple of Learning over a discussion on how a person could attract the Goddess of Good Luck. The men mourned their lack of success—at finding unclaimed valuables, at the gaming tables, and at the race tracks—finding that none of these had made their fortune.

The group then observed those among them who had found good fortune in their professions, and concluded that "good luck can be enticed by accepting opportunity." "Luck" is created by taking action and overcoming procrastination.

The Laws of Gold

A bag heavy with gold or a clay tablet carved with words of wisdom: if thou hadst thy choice, which wouldst thou choose?

This question Kalabab asked of his servants. When they all responded that they would take the gold, Kalabab told them the story of Nomasir, Arkad's son...

The father called Nomasir to stand before him and stated that he would be required to prove himself in order to inherit Arkad's estate. He gave Nomasir a bag of gold and a tablet which had carved upon it five laws of gold.

Nomasir traveled to Ninevah to prove himself to his father. He had terrible experiences with the gold, spending it foolishly and without thought. Soon he had no money. At that point, he turned to the tablets and studied the Five Laws of Gold. Here he read his father's wisdom on reserving one tenth of all earnings and making gold multiply; and here he also found new wisdom:

Gold clingeth to the protection of the cautious owner who invests it under the advice of men wise in its handling....Gold flees the man who would force it to impossible earnings or who followeth the alluring advice of tricksters and schemers or who trusts it to his own inexperience and romantic desires in investment.

When Nomasir discerned and applied the Five Laws of Gold, he was able to increase that which his father had given him many times over.

The Gold Lender of Babylon

Rodan had just received a tribute from the king—fifty pieces of gold. He retired to the gold lender to discuss the desires of family members to borrow the money. The gold lender advised Rodan that if his desire was to help his friends and family, he should do it in a way that would not bring their burdens upon himself, and illustrated this concept in a parable:

This farmer, who could understand what the animals said to each other, did linger in the farm yard each evening just to listen to their words. One evening he did hear the ox bemoaning to the ass the hardness of his lot: "I do labor pulling the plow from morning until night....But you are a creature of leisure. You are trapped with a colorful blanket and do nothing more than carry our master about where he wishes to go. When he goes nowhere you do rest and eat the green grass all the day."

The ass replied,

My good friend, you do work very hard and I would ease your lot. Therefore...in the morning when the slave comes to fetch you to the plow, lie upon the ground and bellow much that he may say you are sick and cannot work.

The ox did as the ass had suggested, whereupon the farmer commanded, "Hitch the ass to the plow for the plowing must go on. All that day the ass, who had only intended to help his friend, found himself compelled to do the ox's task."

A man should not be "swayed by the fantastic plans of impractical men," but every time he allows a gold piece to leave his purse, he must be satisfied that at any time he can reclaim it with a profit.

The Camel Trader of Babylon

When a person is in debt he loses the soul of a free man and becomes a slave. But if he has the determination to regain his soul, the way can be found.

Five clay tablets, Babylonian in origin, were sent to Professor Caldwell to be translated. The tablets were records of a camel trader of Babylon, and contained this man's plan to get out of debt. He had resolved to put away ten percent of his income, live on seventy percent, and pay twenty percent to his creditors. Most of his creditors found this acceptable, because they were sure to ultimately be paid in full.

Professor Caldwell and his wife, who found themselves in financial difficulty, decided to try this approach. They found that the plan which had worked for a humble Babylonian camel trader long ago worked just as well for them today.

Grow Rich Slowly

The Merrill Lynch Guide to Retirement Planning

by Don Underwood and Paul B. Brown, Viking Press, 1993

In their book ***Grow Rich Slowly,*** Don Underwood and Paul B. Brown contend that the only way for America to maintain its "entrepreneurial drive" is to "rediscover the old habits of saving and investing that made us the most affluent nation and the leading economic power on earth." The authors—using a combination of accessible quotes, examples and graphs—go on to outline various strategies for building wealth, saving and investing which they believe will not only help us attain "a financially secure retirement," but will also "keep America on top in an increasingly competitive global economy."

The 4-S Savings Formula

There are no tricks when it comes to planning your retirement, say Underwood and Brown. Americans simply must save. To help you think more clearly about savings strategies, the authors present what they call the "4-S Savings Formula." In essence, the formula shows how to:

1. Save More
2. Save Systematically
3. Save Tax-Advantaged
4. Save Smarter

Save More

The odds are high that you are not saving enough, that a "Savings Gap" exists between what you are putting away today and what you will need tomorrow. It's never too late to start saving, either, because your future is at stake.

People save for a variety of reasons: to enjoy a financially secure retirement, to put children through college, to leave a substantial estate....No matter what your goals are, the point is that you need to give yourself *real* reasons, if you're going to save more, that is.

The authors cite the examples of John and Lori Peters. John, a mid-level manager at the IRS, and Lori, a secretary, have a combined income of $78,000 a year. They share what John describes as a "low-key life-style." Although they are sensible with their money, John and Lori nonetheless worry that their retirement savings won't be sufficient to allow them to do the kind of things that they enjoy doing now—like "going to a concert or the movies."

The authors believe, however, that the Peters have made a good start. Aware that their retirement days are not far off, they have begun to set aside $1500 a month (or 23% of their gross monthly income) to invest in a variety of retirement plans. Moreover, by increasing their house payments by $100 each month, the Peters will be able to pay off the remaining $30,000 of their mortgage six years early.

Save Systematically

Retirement plans are "like noses—[they] come in all sizes and shapes." Whether you fashion a retirement plan that is "huge," "elegant," or "barely there," like a nose, "it is better to have a pension plan than not." And it's even better if you have a *disciplined* plan; a haphazard savings plan will be insufficient if you want a comfortable, worry-free retirement.

Among the numerous retirement plans available today, Underwood and Brown point in particular to the advantages of the *401(k)*. Introduced in the late 1980s, the plan has quickly become a favorite with large and small companies alike. Employers like the plan because it "limits their costs" by fixing the amount of their "retirement contributions." Thus, unlike plans which require employers "to keep paying out benefits" as long as their retired employees live, the *401(k)* enables employers to know in advance exactly how much their contributions will be.

The authors also find that employees are attracted to the plan, though in their case because of its flexibility and portability. For instance, in contrast to traditional company pension plans, the *401(k)* allows employees to direct the growth of their retirement funds by determining the amount of money they wish to contribute—an amount which, in many cases, is then supplemented by employers. Perhaps even more significant in today's job market, the authors suggest, is the fact that contributions to the *401(k)* plan are portable. That is, once employees are "vested" in the plan, they can transfer their retirement contributions from job to job.

Save Tax-Advantaged

Underwood and Brown list several tax advantages employees enjoy with the *401(k)* plan. For instance, with the exception of Social Security taxes, both federal and state taxes on contributions to the *401(k)* can be deferred until retirement benefits are drawn. Thus, the *401(k)* plan can substantially reduce taxable income.

Similarly, any interest, dividends, or capital gains earned from contributions to the fund can also be deferred from federal and state taxes. The authors refer to a hypothetical employee who contributes $2000 a year to a *401(k)*. In this scenario, the employer contributes nothing. Assuming the fund earns 10% interest (compounded annually), the authors calculate that in the space of 30 years the *401(k)* would grow to $361,887. The employee's contribution to the fund would be $60,000, and the tax-deferred interest he would enjoy would amount to $301,887.

Most employers, the authors note, do make contributions to their employees' retirement funds, typically matching every dollar the employee contributes (up to 6%

of the gross salary) with 50 cents of their own. What's more, employer contributions are tax-deferred as well.

Save Smarter

Chances are you already know more about retirement planning than you give yourself credit for. However, say the authors, most of us could raise our "investment sights a notch or two."

One of the ways you can learn to "save smarter" is to consider hiring an investment counselor. One executive mentioned in the book attributes his business success to the fact that "I always hire people smarter than me." When it comes to planning your retirement, Underwood and Brown suggest you do the same: hire people who know more than you do about savings and investments to help you devise a smarter retirement plan.

Profiling Yourself

The book cautions not to lose sight of your own comfort level when you consult a professional for financial advice. An expert "can serve as a guide," but you are the one who has to live with the investments.

To help clarify various investment criteria, the authors identify six basic types of investors.

1. Conservative, focused on preserving capital. This type of investor is most concerned with preserving capital. He does not feel comfortable exposing his investments to risks. The authors observe that this kind of investor tends to keep his money in cash (or cash equivalents), highly rated corporate and government bonds, and even a few stocks.

   However, this strategy involves a frequently overlooked risk: it "works only if inflation doesn't outstrip...earnings."

2. Conservative, concentrating on current income. This investor is "willing to absorb a modest amount of risk" to establish a "*secure* income stream." Her portfolio usually includes "blue chip stocks—shares of big companies...with a long history of paying dividends to their shareholders." Even though blue chips have growth potential, she is more concerned with "the dividend these stocks pay."

3. Conservative, oriented toward growth. This person, though concerned with the principal, accepts the fact that growth stocks are volatile. Consequently, he divides his portfolio between growth stocks and fixed income investments.

   Investing in growth stocks may simply mean that, rather than cashing out, he uses dividend checks to buy more stock and reinvests any interest in money market funds. The fixed income side of his portfolio will likely comprise government securities, high-grade corporate and municipal bonds, and "perhaps some zero coupons."

4. Nonconservative, oriented toward growth tomorrow. This investor is one who is less concerned with earnings today. Instead, she invests in growth stocks that promise "above-average capital gains over a three-to-five-year period." She accepts market volatility, and three quarters of her investment portfolio is made up of stocks. Moreover, the stocks are not simply of the blue chip variety; she also buys stock in "small capitalization companies"—those that often outperform larger companies but whose market value is less than $500 million. The risk here, the authors point out, is that small cap stocks can fall as fast and far as they rise.

5. Nonconservative, oriented toward capital appreciation. This investor looks for capital appreciation. He wants to outperform the market by moving his capital between "asset classes—stocks, bonds, cash—on a regular basis...." Perhaps two-thirds of his portfolio will consist of stocks. A higher percentage of his investments will include not only small cap stocks, but speculative issues as well.
6. Aggressive. Finally, there is the aggressive investor, whose motto is "No risk, no reward." A "long-term" investment to her means one in which her capital is tied up for no more than a year or two. Investments with broader "time horizons," she believes, fail because they don't "take immediate advantage of the changes [in the marketplace]." For instance, if the aggressive investor sees that interest rates are about to fall, she'll move assets from cash to bonds. Similarly, if she sees that bonds are performing poorly, she'll move her capital to "investments with far greater growth opportunities." In short, she is "comfortable with volatility" and is willing to assume large risks.

In ***Grow Rich Slowly***, Underwood and Brown present common-sense, strategic approaches to planning a smarter retirement. Although their emphasis is retirement planning, the basic concepts and suggestions are applicable to anyone, whether they are "big-time" players or those who merely want to dabble on the sidelines.

ONE UP ON WALL STREET

by Peter Lynch, Simon and Schuster, New York, N.Y., 1989

This acclaimed, still-very-applicable personal investment guide, written by one of America's top money managers, offers some unique and effective strategies for using what you already know about finance to make money in the stock market.

PART I: PREPARING TO INVEST

While completing a college internship, Peter Lynch made what to him was a startling discovery: traditional business-school teachings aren't of much use when it comes to picking a good stock—in fact, some of them "could only help you fail." "Wall Street thinks just as the [ancient] Greeks did...[Philosophers] used to sit around for days and debate how many teeth a horse has. They thought they could figure it out by just sitting there, instead of checking the horse. A lot of investors sit around and debate whether a stock is going up, as if the financial muse will give them the answer, instead of checking the company." Yet "it's very hard to support the popular academic theory that the market is irrational when you know somebody who just made a twenty-fold profit in Kentucky Fried Chicken, and...who explained in advance why the stock was going to rise."

Lynch goes out of his way to underscore again and again that there is nothing "mystical" about selecting which stock to invest in. Good stock is "good" only because the particular company offers a good product, is well-managed, and is doing good business. The list of companies meeting these simple criteria is endless: *Subaru, Toys "R" Us, 7-Eleven, Circle K*....Equally endless is the list of companies that may have had an excellent product or service, yet were poorly managed or simply didn't have the foresight to plan for the future. Along with their profit margins, their stock prices—very predictably—soon dropped out of sight.

The real joy in buying stocks is in consistently picking "tenbaggers"—underappreciated and/or undervalued stocks that increase ten times or more in value, not over a period of twenty years, but in five years or less. Lynch points out that this is not an unusual occurrence and that as a small investor you have definite advantages over the conventional professional—if along the way you apply some research and common sense. "With every spectacular stock I've managed to ferret out," he avers, "the virtues seemed so obvious that if 100 professionals had been free to add it to their portfolios, I'm convinced that 99 would have done so. But," Lynch adds, "...There are simply too many obstacles between them and the tenbaggers."

Under the current system, a stock isn't truly attractive until a number of large institutions have recognized its suitability, and an equal number of respected Wall Street analysts (the same researchers who track the individual industries) have put it on the "recommended" list. With so many experts waiting for other experts to make the first move, it's amazing that anything ever gets bought. "Every year...thousands of experts study overbought indicators, oversold indicators, head-and-shoulder patterns, put-call ratios...foreign investment, the movement of the constellations through the heavens, and the moss on oak trees, and they can't predict markets with any useful consistency, any more than the gizzard squeezers could tell the Roman emperors when the Huns would attack."

Lynch uses prominent examples to point out how relatively few brokers are truly aware of the nuts and bolts of picking good stocks:

**Dunkin' Donuts,* between 1977 and 1986, was a 25-bagger (in other words, during that time its stock value rose a whopping 2500%). But even today only two major firms follow *Dunkin's* ups and downs—and neither of these analysts showed the slightest interest at all five years ago.

"...Contrast [this and numerous other examples]," Lynch dares his reader, "with the fifty-six brokerage analysts who normally cover *IBM* or the forty-four who cover *Exxon*." In fact there's an unwritten rule on Wall Street: "You'll never lose your job losing your client's money in IBM." The thinking goes that "if IBM goes bad and you bought it, the clients and the bosses will ask: 'What's wrong with that damn IBM lately?' But if La Quinta Motor Inns goes bad, they'll ask: 'What's wrong with you?'"

As a private investor, however, you are not obliged to answer to a boss; and you are not forced to spend 25% of your time answering to a corporate investor. "If no company seems attractive on the fundamentals, you can...wait for a better opportunity....Most important, you can find terrific opportunities in the neighborhood or at the workplace, months or even years before the news has reached the analysts and the fund managers they advise...."

Historically, stockmarket investments have been much more profitable than any other investment vehicle. "Since 1927, common stocks have recorded gains of 9.8 percent a year on average, as compared to 5 percent for corporate bonds, 4.4 percent for government bonds, and 3.4 percent for Treasury bills....The real return on Treasury bills, known as the most conservative and sensible of all places to put money, has been nil. That's right. Zippo."

Lynch admits that any investment carries with it some risk, and that some are more risky than others. But—even in Las Vegas and at the track—there are those who consistently win:

Once the unsettling act of the risk in money is accepted, we can begin to separate gambling from investing not by the type of activity (buying bonds, buying stocks, betting on the horses, etc.) but by the skill, dedication, and enterprise of the participant. To a veteran handicapper with the discipline to stick to a system, betting on horses offers a relatively secure long-term return, which to him has been as reliable as owning a mutual fund or shares in General Electric. Meanwhile, to the rash and impetuous stockpicker who chases hot tips and rushes in and out of his equities, an "investment" in stocks is no more reliable than throwing away paychecks on the horse with the prettiest mane, or the jockey with the purple silks....

PART II: PICKING WINNERS

The best place to begin looking for the tenbagger is close to home—if not in the backyard then down at the shopping mall, and especially wherever you happen to work. With most of the tenbaggers already mentioned...the first signs of success were apparent at hundreds of locations across the country....The customers in central Ohio where Kentucky Fried Chicken first opened...the mob down at Pic 'N' Save...all had a chance to say, "This is great; I wonder about the stock," long before Wall Street got its original clue....You don't necessarily have to know anything about a company for its stock to go up. But the important point is that (1) the oil experts, on average, are in a better position than doctors to decide when to buy or to sell [oil stock]; and (2) the doctors, on average, know better than oil experts when to invest in a successful drug. The person with the edge is always in a position to out-guess the person without an edge....

By whatever means a potentially good stock has just come to your attention—"whether via the office, the shopping mall, something you ate..."—now what?

Now hold on for a minute, says Lynch. The mere existence of a great new product or service is *not* necessarily a signal to buy. "Just because Dunkin' Donuts is always crowded or Reynolds Metals has more aluminum orders than it can handle doesn't mean you ought to own the stock. Not yet. What you've got so far is simply a lead to a story that has to be developed."

Thus, Lynch unfolds his **Thirteen Characteristics of the Perfect Company:**

1. It sounds dull—or, even better, ridiculous

"Pep Boys—Manny, Moe, and Jack is the most promising name I've ever heard. It's better than dull, it's ridiculous.... What Wall Street analyst or portfolio manager in his right mind would recommend a stock called Pep Boys—Manny, Moe, and Jack—unless of course the Street already realizes how profitable it is, and by then it's up tenfold already."

2. It does something dull

"I get even more excited when a company with a boring name also does something boring. Crown, Cork, and Seal makes cans and bottle caps. What could be duller than that? You won't see an interview with [its] CEO in Time magazine alongside an interview with Lee Iacocca, but that's a plus. There's nothing boring about what's happened to the shares of Crown, Cork, and Seal.

3. It does something disagreeable

"Better than boring alone is a stock that's boring and disgusting at the same time....Take Safety-Kleen. Safety-Kleen goes around to all the gas stations and provides them with a machine that washes greasy auto parts. This saves auto mechanics the time and trouble of scrubbing the parts by hand in a pail of gasoline, and gas stations gladly pay for the service."

4. It's a spinoff

"Large parent companies do not want to spin off divisions and then see those spinoffs get into trouble, because that would bring embarrassing publicity that would reflect back on the parents. Therefore, the spinoffs normally have strong balance sheets and are well-prepared to succeed as independent entities."

5. The institutions don't own it, and the analysts don't follow it

"If you find a stock with little or no institutional ownership, you've found a potential winner. Find a company that no analyst has ever visited, or that no analyst would admit to knowing about, and you've got a double winner."

6. The rumors abound: It's involved with toxic waste and/or the Mafia

"It's hard to think of a more perfect industry than waste management....That's why I got very excited one day when the solid waste executives showed up in my office. They had come to town for a solid waste convention complete with booths and slides—imagine how attractive that must have been. Anyway, instead of the usual blue cotton button-down shirts that I see day after day, they were wearing polo shirts that said 'Solid Waste'....These are the kind of executives you dream about....As you already know if you were fortunate enough to have bought some, Waste Management, Inc. is up about a hundredfold."

7. There's something depressing about it

"In this category my favorite all-time pick is Service Corporation International (SCI), which also has a boring name....Now, if there's anything Wall Street would rather ignore besides toxic waste, it's mortality. And SCI does burials."

8. It's a no-growth industry

"Many people prefer to invest in a high-growth industry, where there's a lot of sound and fury. Not me. I prefer to invest in a low-growth industry like plastic knives and forks....In a no-growth industry...there's no problem with competition....SCI already owns 5 percent of the nation's funeral homes, and there's nothing stopping them from owning 10 percent or 15 percent."

9. It's got a niche

"I'd much rather own a local rock pit than own Twentieth Century-Fox, because a movie company competes with other movie companies, and the rock pit has a niche. Twentieth Century-Fox understood that when it bought up Pebble Beach, and the rock pit with it."

10. People have to keep buying it

"I'd rather invest in a company that makes drugs, soft drinks, razor blades, or cigarettes than in a company that makes toys. In the toy industry somebody can make a wonderful doll that every child has to have, but every child gets only one each."

11. It's a user of technology

"Instead of investing in computer companies that struggle to survive in an endless price war, why not invest in a company that benefits from the price war—such as Automatic Data Processing? As computers get cheaper, Automatic Data can do its job cheaper and thus increase its own profits."

12. The insiders are buying

"There's no better tip-off to the probable success of a stock than that people in the company are putting their own money into it."

13. **The company is buying back shares**

"Buying back shares is the simplest and best way a company can reward its investors. If a company has faith in its own future, then why shouldn't it invest in itself, just as the shareholders do?"

Lynch discusses many more criteria and methods to use in determining stocks that might make worthwhile investments. "All you have to do is put as much effort into picking your stocks as you do into buying your groceries."

PAGE-A-MINUTE MEMORY BOOK

by Harry Lorayne, Holt, Rinehart & Winston, 1985

"There is no such thing as a poor memory! There are only trained and untrained memories."

Harry Lorayne wrote his book by compiling a lifetime of research, seminars, and radio and television demonstrations, and distilling them down to the basics. Lorayne's goal in teaching his techniques and applications is not only to improve your memory, but "to give you memory POWER you never imagined possible"—and to give it to you quickly. He claims that by following his simple systems you can train your memory to an unprecedented degree. "Trying the ideas is the key. Once you try, you'll be hooked, because you'll see immediate results...."

A chapter on "The Business Edge" emphasizes how indispensable memory is in business. An extraordinary memory stands out, gives you an extra edge. "Nothing sells better than facts... at your fingertips."

"All knowledge is but remembrance," said Plato. And to remember is to associate the past with some present stimulus. As Lorayne's "Reminder Principle" states, "We usually remember one thing because we are reminded of it by another thing." Training your memory, then, amounts to consciously controlling these associations.

Examples of association: remember the spelling of the word "piece" by imagining a PIEce of PIE; memorize the names of the five Great Lakes by visualizing many HOMES on the lake shores—**H**uron, **O**ntario, **M**ichigan, **E**rie and **S**uperior.

Thinking is seeing—visualizing pictures in your mind. "If it can be visualized it can be remembered."

You need a *unique* visual association to achieve a lasting memory. When Lorayne's son Robert was about five years old, he was frustrated because he could never remember to say "caterpillar" instead of "catterlipper." "I told him to picture a cat chasing that crawly, hairy thing up a pillow. It worked."

Learning New Words

Silly associations work. "Peduncle" means a flower stalk. If, by chance, you had to learn the word, you could visualize that you owe your uncle money and you pay him with flower stalks instead—you *paid uncle* with flower stalks. This simple association works both left to right and right to left. Needing to recall the biological word for flower stalk, you will be reminded that you paid your uncle with them—peduncle.

This "Substitute Word System" takes advantage of your ability to think of something that sounds like the unfamiliar word—enough to remind you of it. A silly image gives you a needed "slap in the face"—we easily forget commonplace occurrences, but tend to remember the rare, the unusual, or the violent. For example, an "endocarp" is a fruit pie. Picture: *ending* a *carp's* life by hitting it with fruit pies. A "litany" is a form of prayer. Picture: you have set fire to *(lit)* your *knee* and are saying a prayer over it.

You can make your own associations to learn other words. In word association you are using the OAR (Observe, Associate, Remember) method to force attention. This painless method can also be applied to learning foreign words or registering new concepts.

Names and Faces

Forgetting the name of a past business associate can be both embarrassing and a critical mistake. According to Lorayne: "I'm introduced to someone, and a few minutes later—no, seconds later—I've forgotten his or her name!" But this is a lie! You haven't forgotten the name; you simply didn't remember it in the first place.

Again using the Substitute Word System, you can easily recall names such as Wolfe, Rivers, and the like. But other names (Cohen, Betavagnia, Rafferty, Smith) must first be clearly heard and then actively associated with some forceful image. (Cameron = camera on; Carruthers = Car udders...)

Listening attentively and thinking up brief, pictorial "reminders" that will link names to faces, are fundamental to helping your memory do its work. Observe the detailed features of a face, then "lock in" on a particular feature for association. Examples: Mr. Betavagnia—his large nose will be a bent vane on his face; Mr. Brodsky—see the broad skis going down the deep lines in his forehead; Mrs. Smith—you're pounding in the prominent lines between her nostrils and her lips with a blacksmith's hammer.

You might practice this system using pictures in magazines: Look at the name, "christen" the face, apply the system, and after a few faces, see how you do on a self-test.

The Link System

This system is effective in memorizing lists of things or ideas by visually "linking" the items in order—the parts of a speech, shopping list items, school assignments, historical events, etc. Lorayne uses the "Three R's"—Register, Remember, and Recall—to connect items. For instance, to remember the words "book" and "airplane" in sequence, think of a giant book flying like an airplane. Then you can link "airplane" to "eyeglasses" by picturing an airplane wearing glasses, and so on.

Fear of forgetting is the foremost fear in public speaking. By extracting key words from sections of a talk and linking them together visually, you can give a speech without using notes.

Numbers and the Phonic Alphabet

Lorayne teaches that number sequences can be memorized by breaking them down into smaller "units" (i.e. it's harder to remember "2-4-1-7-3" than "twenty-four, one seventy-three"). In a series of "Memory Breaks," he introduces the "Phonic Alphabet System," a technique based on associating the numbers 1 through 0 with sets of similarly grouped sounds and letters:

1 = T, D
2 = n
3 = m
4 = R
5 = L
6 = J, sh, ch, and soft g
7 = K, hard c, and hard g
8 = f, v, ph
9 = P, B
0 = z, s, and soft c

Full understanding and utilization of this complex system requires a careful reading of the related chapters; but the idea is basic: 5 = L, for example, because if you hold up your five fingers, the index finger and thumb form an "L". By creating sentences using the associated sounds and numbers, you can remember even long numerical sequences or multi-digit numbers.

Practical Memory Hints

Absentmindedness: Ever go somewhere and forget why you went, or put down an object and forget where you placed it? Doing things while your mind is "absent" can be time-wasting and aggravating.

To solve this problem, you can associate between item and place. If you put your eyeglasses on the TV in the spare bedroom, for example, envision the antenna penetrating and shattering the lens. It's like the Gracie Allen joke: When you put a large roast in the oven, put a small one in at the same time; when you smell the small one burning, you'll be reminded that the large one is ready.

It's true! Dropping a potholder in the middle of your floor or putting something conspicuously out of place—the old "string on the finger" trick—can remind you of a specific task you need to do at a specific time.

Poor spelling: As already mentioned, you can remember the spelling of a difficult word by connecting the "hard" word with an easier word in a brief sentence: It's ne**CESS**ary to clean a **CESS**pool. I take a **BUS** to my **BUS**iness. My **PET** learns by re**PET**ition. DeSSert comes after diNNer. (Double nn reminds you of double ss.) Expen$e is not expen¢e...

School Memorization Tasks: By using imagery you can make learning a game instead of a boring task. Memorizing the names of state capitals is a good example: A *boy sees* an Idaho potato (*Boise*, Idaho); *Mary lands* on an apple (Annapolis, Maryland); you throw *little rocks* at an ark (Little Rock, Arkansas)...

"Substitute images" can also help you memorize items in sequence. For instance, to learn the U.S. presidents in order, link Washing machine to Adams apple to "d'ja have a son?" (Jefferson), and so forth.

Reading-Recall: Memory systems can also help you visualize and associate while you read. Picturing and connecting key words or thoughts may take some concentration, but soon it becomes a source of fun as well as super recall. "...Effective reading is...the art of boiling down dozens, hundreds, and thousands of words into a few vital thoughts." It's "a search for ideas, thoughts, answers." So when a thought is "located," try to "spear" it out of its surrounding pool of words. Then, "boil" the idea down into a few easily remembered words. This *locate, spear, and boil* concept starts you thinking about what or who is important in your reading. Separate ideas from their "padding"—words that can be eliminated from your mind. And remember, as Lorayne cautions: "How quickly you get through reading material is not as important as how much of the material gets through to you!"

Listening: Attentive listening requires a similar four-step approach: (1) Summarize in a short phrase or sentence what the speaker has said; (2) Anticipate the speaker's next points, and ask yourself questions about them; (3) Listen "between the lines" to grasp hidden meaning; and (4) Ask yourself if you agree with the speaker.

The systems and ideas outlined in the *Page-a-Minute Memory Book* are practical and flexible—"They can solve any memory problem with a slight (common sense) change here or there...." Alexander Smith said, "A man's real possession is his memory. In nothing else is he rich, in nothing else is he poor." Lorayne points out that a rich memory can also make learning and life more fun.

Time-Saving Tips

Seven ways to make the most of your time (plus some ideas for "doubling-up" activities to help you get more done)

Control or eliminate seven common time-wasters, and you can significantly improve your productivity and tranquility. Consider the ways you use your time; then take action against one or more of these robbers that may steal hours from a typical day:

THINGS

"Do I compulsively collect or buy items that I don't need; things that have no particular value, bring no real joy, that I have no place for, or can't even find?" Things demand time: time to store, dust, move, sort, find, sell, replace and protect. What do you have *too much* of—clothes, garden tools, pencils, knickknacks, furniture? Simplify your life and unclutter your home or office by devising a plan to rid yourself of unnecessary articles. Limit the number of pairs of shoes, ties, sweaters, etc. that make their way into your closet; and when you buy a new piece of clothing, make sure one of the old pieces is eliminated from your wardrobe. Follow the same procedure with your kitchen, bathroom, garage and office collections. Handle mail, magazines, articles of clothing, paperwork, etc. only once. Don't stack things up, intending to get to them later. Put them away or throw them away—never pile them away.

TELEVISION

"Is our television on too many hours in the day, inviting me or my family members to collapse at any time for a mindless hour or two?" Many of us waste thousands of hours each year in unplanned, indiscriminate viewing. If you complain of not having enough time to get important things done, *limit* your hours in front of the TV. Choose carefully those programs worth watching. Stick to a schedule, giving thought to how you might better spend your time.

WAITING

"Are five or more minutes of my normal day spent waiting for someone or something: on the phone, in a line at the bank or grocery store, in a doctor's office, or for my friend to pick me up? Do feelings of resentment or nervousness sometimes well up in me due to these delays?" We can either develop the attitude that delays amount only to wasted time or we can welcome the waits as unexpected *gifts*—chances to get certain things done that we've been holding off doing. Establish the habit of carrying a book or magazine, planning book, craft, some postcards, thank-you notes, or other letter-writing materials—anything that can help you use spare time constructively. You never know; today you might be given the opportunity to write that distant friend or to finish the *Sports Illustrated* or *Newsweek* article you had wanted to read.

SAYING "YES"

"Can I say ' no' gracefully, without excuse or embarrassment?" If not, you probably take on too many tasks—some tasks that you shouldn't have agreed to perform in the first place. One of the best ways to save time is to say no. The old adage "If you want a job done, give it to a busy person," is fine, but only to a point.

Most people feel some obligation to please others, and that's OK. But if your days are consumed by "doing for others," then you may be diluting the effectiveness of what you are doing. The cure? Take greater thought when you commit your time. When asked to serve on another committee or to "help out for a few minutes," take a few minutes of your own to ponder the priority of the task. Then get back to the "asker" with a rational reply. Practice not feeling guilty when you say no. You should feel flattered that you were deemed trustworthy and capable of carrying out an undertaking—but you need not accept it: "Sorry, not this year..." or "Thanks for asking, but my time and commitments just won't allow me to do that right now."

PEOPLE

"Do one-way conversations or unexpected drop-ins ever steal minutes from me or make me late for an appointment?" Too much politeness can bring about anxiety, hidden anger, and stressed relationships, in addition to lost time. Be more *honest* about your needs. Tell your friend you'll return his call in a few minutes. Tactfully yet firmly deal with the "talker": "I really don't want to take any more of your time, so I'd better say goodbye." Or inform the "drop-in": "Excuse me, but I really must get back to work." These remarks are not rude or ruthless. They simply and gently signify your needs. They also set a tone about how you use your time.

WORRY

"Do minutes or even hours pass in a day with my mind centered on a problem? Do my small worries grow into larger concerns that cause me to waste both time and needed vitality?" Most worries are groundless; they are merely *perceived* as problems. It takes great insight and self-control to keep from agonizing over either past difficulties or future possibilities. Try to keep in mind that the *present,* this moment, is where you live, and that the only worthwhile thing you can do about your real problems is to make plans for their solution—and then carry out those plans. Also, try talking to others, working, serving, or laughing. Stay busy doing things that are rewarding and bring you joy. Positive activities are good medicine against worries.

PROCRASTINATION

"Are some of my most meaningful, top priority to-do's ever 'put on the shelf' at the expense of busywork? Am I ignoring friends or family, talent-growth potential, more productive job tasks, or even needed car maintenance out of fear, ignorance or lack of time?" Separate the important ways you spend your time from the ways that aren't so important. Prioritize your goals and subsequent activities on a regular basis; then just get started (which is usually the hard part) and follow through. You will soon see real progress in reaching your goals. Be sure to include some time for leisure, exercise and hobbies, but build your days and weeks around your central, top-priority values. Set *deadlines* on the jobs you might tend to put off. Keep a list to remind you of appointments. Manage your tasks; pin down the minutes and use them efficiently. Do your most difficult tasks first, when you're sharp and alert; do the less crucial tasks when you don't need such a high energy level. To help keep decision-making time to a minimum, establish and stick to specific daily routines.

In addition, be realistic about minor problems and odd jobs that have a way, if left unchecked, of turning into major, horrendous "headaches." The spare tire that needs fixing, picking up the golf club left on the lawn, buying the birthday gift—don't put them off. "Do it now!" can be a lifesaving motto when you are confronted with such small but necessary chores.

Wouldn't it be nice if you could double the number of minutes available to you each day? Well, there are many odd jobs and small tasks that can be combined to save time—essentially doubling it. In fact, doing one chore together with another errand, good deed, or enterprise often lifts and stimulates you.

You'll probably be able to come up with many ideas besides the suggestions listed here. Depending on your interests and the assorted settings in which you find yourself, sometimes two things can be accomplished in the time it takes to do one.

- **While watching TV:** Soak your feet or body; do aerobics or lift weights; work on an art, craft or sewing project; polish your shoes or those of a family member; organize a storage box or drawer; during commercial breaks, read from a book or magazine, write a letter, plan, or brainstorm; snack; talk things over with a family member or friend; completely relax all parts of your body (a difficult but very beneficial activity); pay bills; mate socks or fold laundry; dust or straighten the family room...
- **While you're relaxing:** Check out a catalog or magazine; listen to music; watch TV; eat a healthy snack; look over or organize a favorite collection; gaze at your yard and do some mental planning/dreaming; soak in the tub; read a novel; phone a friend or relative...
- **While holding on the phone:** Arrange or dust a shelf or drawer; do hand, arm or leg isometrics, or stretch out and flex your neck and shoulders; open and read mail; cut, file, or polish your fingernails; plan an upcoming birthday or anniversary celebration; balance your checkbook; organize receipts for reimbursement or taxes; write part of a letter; clean out your wallet or purse; make up or add to a to-do list; put an address/phone list in order; read...
- **While brushing your teeth, shaving, applying makeup, or combing your hair:** Mentally repeat and memorize a quote or other selection posted on the mirror; plan in your mind the next few minutes or hours; check your clothing for lint and unbuttoned buttons; water a plant; use the toilet; pick up after yourself (or your children)...
- **While driving (staying alert to avoid an accident, of course):** Listen to motivational

or instructional tapes; enjoy music or a talk show; mentally plan, visualizing your day or an upcoming event; snack; problem-solve or come up with a new thought by observing, by combining the best elements of two distinct objects, or by asking "what-if questions; take a co-worker, spouse or child along with you, if possible, to keep you company...

• **A Few Other Doubling Up Ideas:** Take out the trash on the same trip when you pick up the paper or feed the dog; get in the habit of always carrying something with you when you go up (or down) the stairs or down the hall; pick up and put away several different items at the same time; while doing yard work or housework, listen to music on a walkman; make use of small amounts of free time that spring up unexpectedly to do those chores that take just a few minutes (clear out a tool box, clean one shelf of a closet)...

Now's a good time to take stock of your life and time. You're worth it!

PUTTING SPARK IN YOUR RELATIONSHIPS

Activity Ideas

Dating and romancing, communicating and interacting, doing and sharing, all take time and effort. It is the price a couple, married or not, must pay in order to keep a relationship vibrant. The "classic" activities—movie, dancing, dinner—week after week, limit how close two people can become.

Likewise, family or friend get-togethers can become stale if little or no organizing is done.

But what more is there to do? Lots! At the price of some planning, you and your partner, or you and your group, can creatively grow, together.

Mix and match activity ideas from the different categories below. Make up your own variations. Check your local newspaper for those events taking place near where you live.

Some suggestions are more fit for groups; others are best accomplished as a couple. Some just may not appeal to you at this time—and maybe they never will. The key is to be intuitive and inventive, and to discover things that you enjoy doing together.

First, some planning.

• Remember, everything takes time. Don't plan too much. A simple activity savored is better than a larger agenda hurried or only half enjoyed.

• Understand clearly what your purpose is, i.e. simply being together, accomplishing a goal, getting to know one another, serving someone else, having fun, etc. Plan around one idea. Too many objectives leads to confusion.

IDEA CATEGORY INDEX

(1) Out on the Town

(2) Home for the Night

(3) Fun in the Sun

(4) Sports and Things
(5) Kids' Stuff
(6) Feeling Somewhat Strange?
(7) Holidays and Helping
(8) Food Thoughts

(1) ***Out on the Town***

- Go window shopping. At each store window pick your favorite item. See how your tastes compare with your partner's.
- Take a moonlight walk.
- Attend a planetarium, museum, aquarium or art gallery.
- Play computer or video games at an arcade.
- See a local movie, play, concert, ballet, circus or sporting event.
- Have a quiet dinner at a favorite restaurant.
- Dance at a club or ballroom, or, for a change of pace, go square dancing.
- Take a drive to a place you've never been before.
- Attend an auction, bazaar or estate sale.
- Go midnight bowling; then have an early breakfast.
- Visit an old bookstore or a library. See who can find the strangest book.
- Go to an amusement park, state fair, festival, mall, or exhibit (car or boat show, food fair, antique show...)
- Attend a city council/legislature meeting.
- Tour a historic site in your area.
- See what can be done or purchased on a five- or ten-dollar limit.
- Attend a class at the library or university.
- View a competition: dog show, horse show, etc.
- Take a dance lesson—maybe two!
- Visit a relative or friend you haven't seen in a while.

(2) ***Home for the Night***

- Rent a video, pop some popcorn, make a fire in the fireplace...
- Make a terrarium, holiday decoration, mobile, collage, flower arrangement or craft project.
- Learn a new craft, skill or hobby.
- Write a poem, short story or musical piece.
- Prepare a formal dinner.
- Have your own ping pong or miniature golf tournament.
- Decorate a dance floor and dance in your living room.
- Look for stars and constellations using a star book.
- Use a new recipe to make a food or candy.
- Sculpt using clay, or carve with soap.
- Play charades, TV games, card or board games.
- Go through your photographs; create captions for them and put together an album.
- Read and discuss a book, news article or the comics.

- Debate a world event or problem. Brainstorm for solutions.
- Watch TV—the late show, a cultural or sports event, the news, a favorite nature program, comedy series or movie.
- Find unusual words from a dictionary. Make up three definitions for each and see if others can pick the real meaning.
- Do a chore. Shine all the shoes in the house or go through a junk drawer together.
- Learn about a particular topic or famous person.
- Share and update your joint or individual goals.
- Get out your tape cassettes and record a home-made skit or commercial.
- Invent and write out a series of puns, jokes, "Mad Libs," or fortune-cookie tidbits for use at a future party.

(3) ***Fun in the Sun***

- Take an early morning walk, watch the sun rise, then eat breakfast.
- Prepare a meal at an outdoor grill or fireplace.
- Visit a waterslide, canyon, park or zoo.
- Go for a hot-air balloon or airplane ride.
- Plant a tree or a garden.
- Make and fly kites.
- Gather pine cones, pine nuts, wild flowers, berries, fall leaves, butterflies or shells.
- Hunt for rocks, toadstools or arrowheads.
- Pan for gold.
- Go horseback riding.
- Pick strawberries or other fruits and eat them with cream.
- Drive to a lake and rent a rowboat, skip stones, have an evening beach party, build sandcastles, fish...
- Hike or backpack on a nature trail.
- Visit an archeological or historical site.
- Visit a park and feed the ducks, dodge sprinklers, bicycle, picnic, play a game...
- Go bird-watching in a forest, park or bird refuge.
- Attend an outdoor arts, garden or international festival.
- Visit a cemetery and collect epitaphs, or do crayon rubbings of old headstones.
- Be an amateur photographer. Find artistic settings to take great pictures of nature, other people, or each other.
- Write messages in the sand, in the snow, or on the ground using rocks.
- Draw colored-chalk pictures on your patio, deck or entry walk.
- Drive to a new location (mountains, beach, desert) for a picnic, clambake, bonfire (if allowed), or just to talk.
- Visit a local farm.

(4) ***Sports and Things***

Indoor

- Roller-skate, ice-skate, bowl, lift weights, have a ping pong tournament.
- Spend a day or evening at a gym or spa swimming, playing racket or "wally-ball,"

practicing gymnastics, bouncing on the trampoline...

- Practice volleyball, soccer or basketball skills.
- Play broom hockey in a gym or large, tiled room. Use a tennis ball or chalkboard eraser as a puck.

Outdoor/Summer

- Play tennis, golf, soccer, frisbee, badminton, volleyball, softball, miniature golf, croquet, horseshoes...
- Get some baseball mitts and a ball and play catch.
- Go ice-blocking (slide down a grassy hill on ice blocks).
- Play frisbee golf or frisbee football.
- Ride bikes.
- Rent dirt bikes or four wheelers.
- Swim, scuba dive, surf or body surf.
- Go moonlight sailing or canoeing.
- Do a river run in rafts or inflated tubes.
- Go mountain climbing, rappelling, hang gliding or parachuting.
- Fish, hunt, backpack or hike in a wilderness area.
- Practice your skills at a golf driving range, a go-cart track, or some batting cages.
- Go bird-watching, taking along a bird book from the library, or try the fascinating practice of bug-watching.
- Roller-skate or skateboard at a park.
- Ride horses.
- Target shoot, either with bow and arrows or a rifle.
- Go to the sand dunes for jumping or buggying.
- Jog or enter a road race.
- Fly a kite.
- Organize a complete sports day, in which you do a number of activities.

Outdoor/Winter

- Snowshoe, ski (cross-country or downhill), snowmobile, ice-skate, toboggan, or go sledding/tubing during the day or at night.
- Play snow football, hockey, or other snow games.
- Hike to a snowbound cabin.
- Sculpt using snow.
- Go ice fishing.
- Hunt for the perfect Christmas tree.

(5) ***Kids' Stuff***

- Build a snow fort or snowman.
- Have a grass, pillow, or snow fight.
- Play marbles, jacks, hula hoop, hopscotch, jump rope, tiddlywinks, hide and seek...
- Make a model car or plane.
- Create tin can stilts, a finger painting, or paper snowflakes.
- Do a jigsaw puzzle.

- Fly a kite.
- Make simple puppets and have a show.
- Have a water fight with balloons, hose and squirt guns.
- Tell ghost stories in the dark.
- Show a scary movie in a basement or garage.
- Devise a rope swing over a river.
- Invent a prank to play on someone, then play it. (Be nice!)
- Go to a playground or park and go on the slides, etc.
- Play foosball, air hockey or video games at an arcade.
- Attend a kids' matinee.
- Frost graham crackers, watch TV, color in a coloring book and eat ice cream.
- Run through the sprinklers or practice tumbling on the lawn.
- Design, decorate and fly paper airplanes.

(6) ***Feeling Somewhat Strange?***

- Climb a tree and read together.
- Kidnap another person or couple and take him/them to dinner.
- Stage a bubble contest using chewing gum or soap.
- Hold a tape recording competition. With separate cassette recorders, create or find five or ten different sounds you don't think the other will recognize. Decide on a prize for the winner.
- Organize a treasure hunt, giving directions and number of steps in each direction to find some "treasure."
- Go on a date where no verbal communication is allowed.
- Make up a story from cut-out magazine pictures, or from your own photos.
- Paint a mural on a wall or on butcher paper.
- Cut an old inner tube to make a long tube. Tie off one end with wire, tie the other end to a hose and fill it with water. It makes a fun "bouncing log."
- Have a "mud bowl"; play soccer or tag in a muddy field.
- Blindfold and kidnap your partner. Drive around for a while and end up in one of your favorite spots.
- Tape a "Mission Impossible" message to someone. Mail or deliver it to him/her, having the clues lead to a surprise gift or dinner.
- Paint the icicles on your house.
- Do familiar things blindfolded: decorate a cake, draw, or dance.
- Picnic in an unusual location.
- Play croquet or golf at night (use flashlights or glow-in-the-dark balls).
- Ride a bus for the entire length of its route.
- Test-drive a sports car.
- Play "The Price is Right" at a store, with a candy bar or gum stick as prizes for each closest guess.
- Call a police station, fire station or industry for a tour.
- Sculpt with caramel corn.

- Eat at an odd site: in an empty swimming pool, under a waterfall or tree, in a tent or barn, on a raft, on the floor Japanese style...

(7) ***Holiday and Helping***

General

- Make and send a gift or some goodies to someone—known or unknown to you—far away.
- Color and decorate eggs for any holiday.
- Prepare baskets of fruit or candies to give away.
- Visit shut-ins or hospital patients.

New Year's (Eve/Day)

- Make a pinata.
- Hold your own dance, or go to one already organized.
- Play snow football or other snow game.

Valentines

- Take instant color photos of couples in love on the street and give them the pictures.
- Make Valentine cards from scrap material and paper.
- Have a "sing-in" of old love songs.
- Take Valentines to shut-ins at a hospital or rest home.

Presidents' Day

- Visit a museum.
- Read a historical biography.
- Make a cherry pie.
- Chop wood.
- Read by candle- or firelight.
- Give a political speech to one another.

St. Patrick's Day

- Attend an Irish parade.
- Be a leprechaun—leave a pot of surprises on someone's doorstep.

Easter

- Attend a different religious meeting.
- Color and decorate eggs.
- Set up an Easter egg hunt for neighbor children.
- Do an Easter brunch for someone.
- Set up and dance around a maypole.

Independence Day

- Participate in a parade.
- Write a speech about what liberty means to you.
- Set off fireworks.
- Make homemade ice cream.
- Have a watermelon bust.

Halloween

- Volunteer to help in a school classroom activity.

- Hold a Halloween spook alley or dance.
- Make a miniature paper haunted house and graveyard.
- Carve and decorate pumpkins to deliver to someone.
- Visit acquaintances or shut-ins in costume, as "treaters" rather than trick-or-treaters.

Thanksgiving

- Invite a friend or stranger for the big meal.
- Send "Thanksgiving" cards to people you appreciate.
- Decorate a home with corn stalks, gourds, hay, etc.

Hanukkah

- Visit a Jewish Center and participate in the celebration. (Call ahead to see if it's permitted.)
- Hold your own celebration with dancing, candle-lighting, playing games, etc., all done in Jewish tradition.

Christmas

- Go see Santa.
- Help with a Sub-for-Santa project.
- Carol to elderly neighbors or children in a hospital, giving out small gifts.
- Decorate a Christmas tree for a hospital or retirement home.

(8) *Food Thoughts*

- Cheese and chocolate fondue with cut vegetables and fruits.
- Chinese take-out with chopsticks and fortune cookies.
- Backyard barbecue with lawn games.
- Homemade ice cream, taffy, pie, bread, sandwiches, cookies, scones, chili, soup, pizza...
- Banana splits with many toppings.
- International or regional foods.
- Waffles or crepes with various toppings.
- A surprise breakfast or dinner.
- A progressive dinner, or a feast with friends where course items are mixed up (due to the odd descriptions of the items on the menu, choices may be made out of order).
- A "no utensils" meal.
- A tinfoil "hobo" dinner cooked by a campfire.
- Marshmallows roasted over a fire.
- A vegetarian or low-cal banquet.
- Selections from a Western, Renaissance or Pilgrim menu.
- A meal made from separate—and secret—food items, selections made by each group member.
- Create your own recipe for an omelet, soup, or other main dish.

Quotes and Anecdotes

Quotes and Anecdotes

Work

Doing, Activity, Effort

O Lord,
Thou givest us everything,
At the price
Of an effort *–Leonardo da Vinci*

Opportunity is missed by most people because it is dressed in overalls and looks like work. *–Thomas Edison*

Work is doing what you now enjoy for the sake of a future which you clearly see and desire. Drudgery is doing under strain what you don't now enjoy and for no end that you can now appreciate. *–Richard C. Cabot*

The heights by great men reached and kept
Were not attained by sudden flight,
But they, while their companions slept,
Were toiling upward in the night. *–Henry Wadsworth Longfellow*

God gives every bird its food, but He does not throw it into the nest. *–J.G. Holland*

Every man's work is a portrait of himself.

Effort is only effort when it begins to hurt. *–Jose Ortega Y Gasset*

The beauty of work depends upon the way we meet it, whether we arm ourselves each morning to attack it as an enemy that must be vanquished before night comes—or whether we open our eyes with the sunrise to welcome it as an approaching friend who will keep us delightful company... *–Lucy Larcom*

I wish to preach, not the doctrine of ignoble ease, but the doctrine of the strenuous life. *–Theodore Roosevelt*

Genius is one percent inspiration and 99 percent perspiration. *–Thomas Alva Edison*

The world cares very little about what a man or woman knows; it is what the man or woman is able to do that counts. *–Booker T. Washington*

A widely prevalent notion today seems to demand instant achievement of goals, without any of the wearying, frustrating preparation that is indispensable to any task. As the exemplar of a way of life, the professional—that man or woman who injects every new task or duty, no matter how small, with discipline of mind and spirit—is a vanishing American, particularly among those who too often believe that dreams come true because they ought to and not because they are caused to materialize. *–Jack Valenti*

I have a kind of contempt for intelligence all by itself. Coupled with energy and willingness, it'll go. Alone, it winds up riding the rails. *–John Hersey*

Idle folks have the least leisure. *–John Ray*

The real essence of work is concentrated energy—people who really have that in a superior degree by nature are independent of the forms and habits and artifices by which less able and less active people are kept up to their labors. *–Walter Bagehot*

In order that people may be happy in their work, these three things are needed: They must be fit for it; They must not do too much of it; And they must have a sense of success in it. *–John Ruskin*

Far and away the best prize that life offers is the chance to work hard at work worth doing. *–Theodore Roosevelt*

I am a great believer in luck, and the harder I work the more I have of it. *–Stephen Leacock*

For success: try aspiration, inspiration, and perspiration.

A man who works with his hands is a laborer; a man who works with his hands and his brain is a craftsman; but a man who works with his hands and his brain and his heart is an artist. *-Louis Nizer*

The first man gets the oyster, the second man gets the shell. *–Andrew Carnegie*

I like to work half a day. I don't care if it's the first twelve hours or the second twelve hours. I just put in my half every day. It keeps me out of trouble. *–Kemmons Wilson, CEO, Holiday Inns*

God gave us a world unfinished, so that we might share in the joys and satisfaction of creation. *–Allen Stockdale*

All this will not be finished in the first one hundred days, nor will it be finished in the first one thousand days, nor in the life of this administration, nor even perhaps in our lifetime on this planet. But let us begin. *–John F. Kennedy*

St. Francis of Assisi was hoeing his garden when someone asked what he would do if he were suddenly to learn that he would die before sunset that very day. "I would finish hoeing my garden," he replied. *–Louis Fischer*

The highest reward for a man's toil is not what he gets for it but what he becomes by it. *–John Ruskin*

I never did anything worth doing by accident, nor did any of my inventions come by accident; they came by work. *–Thomas Alva Edison*

He that would have fruit must climb the tree. *–Thomas Fuller*

It is the feeling of exerting effort that exhilarates us, as a grasshopper is exhilarated by jumping. A hard job, full of impediments, is thus more satisfying than an easy job. *–H.L. Mencken*

Of all the unhappy people in the world, the unhappiest are those who have not found something they want to do. True happiness comes to him who does his work well, followed by a relaxing and refreshing period of rest. True happiness comes from the right amount of work for the day. *–Lin Yutang*

Men like to make the wheels go round, which is why so many men go around in circles.

If you have built castles in the air, your work need not be lost; that is where they should be. Now put foundations under them. *–Henry David Thoreau*

When we do the best that we can, we never know what miracle is wrought in our life, or in the life of another. *–Helen Keller*

When I was a young man I observed that nine out of ten things I did were failures. I didn't want to be a failure, so I did ten times more work. *–George Bernard Shaw*

Nothing is really work unless you would rather be doing something else.
–Sir James Barrie

Whatever is worth doing at all, is worth doing well.
–Philip Dormer Stanhope, fourth Earl of Chesterfield, 1774

The reward of a thing well done is to have done it. *–Ralph Waldo Emerson*

The best way to appreciate leisure is to work hard for it.

Few things are of themselves impossible...we lack the application to make them a success rather than the means. *–La Rochefoucauld*

Thank God every morning when you get up that you have something to do that day which must be done, whether you like it or not. *–Charles Kingsley*

I Am Work
I am the foundation of all business.
I am the source of all prosperity.
I am the parent of genius.
I am the salt that gives life its savour...
Loved, I make life sweet, purposeful, and fruitful...
All progress springs from me. *–Anonymous*

My father taught me to work; but he did not teach me to love it. *–Abraham Lincoln*

There's nothing wrong with being a self-made man if you don't consider the job finished too soon. *–John Mooney*

They that sow in tears shall reap in joy. *–The Bible, Psalms 126:5*

Well done is better than well said. *–Benjamin Franklin*

Shallow men believe in luck. *–Ralph Waldo Emerson*

We cannot do everything at once, but we can do something at once.
–Calvin Coolidge

A Poet's Proverb

God's road is all uphill,
But do not tire,
Rejoice that we may still
Keep climbing higher. *–Arthur Guiterman*

The battle is not to the strong alone; it is to the vigilant, the active, the brave. *–Patrick Henry*

Be not simply good; be good for something. *–Henry David Thoreau*

The greatest menace to freedom is an inert people. *–Louis D. Brandeis*

Trouble is only opportunity in work clothes. *–Henry J. Kaiser*

Opportunity doesn't necessarily knock on the door; it may be leaning against the wall waiting to be noticed.

The pessimist sees the difficulty in every opportunity; the optimist, the opportunity in every difficulty. *–L.P. Jacks*

A generation ago there were a thousand men to every opportunity, while today there are a thousand opportunities to every man. *–Henry Ford*

Tenacita! Disciplina! Coraggio! And work!
–Definition of Fascism by Benito Mussolini (The last two words were in English)

The dictionary is the only place where success comes before work. *–Arthur Brisbane*

...Getting ready is the secret of success. *–Henry Ford*

The haves and the have-nots can often be traced back to the dids and the did-nots. *–D.O. Flynn*

When God wanted sponges and oysters, He made them, and put one on a rock, and the other in the mud. When He made men, He did not make him to be a sponge or an oyster; He made him with feet, and hands, and head, and heart, and vital blood, and a place to use them, and said to him, "Go, work!" *–Henry Ward Beecher*

If people really liked to work, we'd still be plowing the ground with sticks and transporting goods on our backs. *–William Feather*

No one ever got very far by working a 40-hour week. Most of the notable people I know are trying to manage a 40-hour day. *–Channing Pollock*

Ambition often puts men upon doing the meanest offices: so climbing is performed in the same posture with creeping. *–Jonathan Swift*

If my sister or I took one of those school examinations where you were required to answer only 10 questions out of 12, Mother's comment on hearing this would be, "I hope you chose the hardest ones." *–Margaret Bourke-White*

I never practice; I always play. *–Wanda Landowska, harpsichord master*

No one knows what he can do till he tries. *–Publilius Syrus, 1st century B.C.E.*

Nothing can come of nothing. *–Shakespeare, "King Lear"*

The best-kept secret in America today is that people would rather work hard for something they believe in than enjoy a pampered idleness. *–John W. Gardner*

I've done my small part to stamp out boredom in certain quarters of this world where it threatened to become rampant. If I accomplish little else, I shall consider my life justified by that one fact. Down with boredom... *–Elsa Maxwell*

Forty years ago people worked 12 hours a day, and it was called economic slavery. Now they work 14 hours a day, and it's called moonlighting. *–Robert Orben*

The world stands aside to let anyone pass who knows where he is going.
–David Starr Jordan

Much of the good work of the world has been that of all the dull people who have done their best. *–Senator George F. Hoar*

A great man leaves clean work behind him, and requires no sweeper up of the chips.
–Elizabeth Barrett Browning

Some people get the breaks; some people make their own.

Let us work without protest; it is the only way to make life endurable.
–Voltair, Candide, 1759

Man is the only creature that consumes without producing.
–George Orwell, Animal Farm

In life as in a football game, the principle to follow is: Hit the line hard.
–Theodore Roosevelt

The sleep of a laboring man is sweet. *–The Bible, Ecclesiastes 5:12*

Blessed is he who has found his work; let him ask no other blessedness. He has...a life-purpose; he has found it, and will follow it. *–Thomas Carlyle*

Where our work is, there let our joy be. *–Tertullian, c. 220*

I don't believe one grows older. I think that what happens early on in life is that at a certain age one stands still and stagnates. *–T. S. Eliot*

Growing old is no more than a bad habit which a busy man has no time to form.
–Andre Maurois

Work! God wills it. That, it seems to me, is clear. *–Gustave Flaubert, 1845*

Behold the turtle: He only makes progress when he sticks his neck out.
–James Bryant Conant

Those who do good as opportunity offers are sowing seeds all the time, and they need not doubt the harvest.

A life spent making mistakes is not only more honorable but more useful than a life spent doing nothing. *–George Bernard Shaw*

He that is busy is tempted by but one devil; he that is idle, by a legion.
–Thomas Fuller, 1732

Wisely, and slow. They stumble that run fast. *–Shakespeare, "Romeo and Juliet"*

Make haste slowly. *–Latin proverb*

The journey of a thousand miles begins with one step. *–Lao-Tse*

If wishes were horses beggars might ride. *–John Ray, 1670*

...Even for the neurotic executive—as for everyone else—work has great therapeutic value; it is generally his last refuge, and deterioration there marks the final collapse of the man.... *–Richard Austin Smith*

We have confused the free with the free and easy. *–Adlai Stevenson*

The test of the artist does not lie in the will with which he goes to work, but in the excellence of the work he produces. *–Thomas Aquinas, c. 1265*

Happiness consists in activity—it is a running stream, not a stagnant pool.
–John Mason Good

Our real problem is not our strength today; it is the vital necessity of action today to ensure our strength tomorrow. *–Dwight D. Eisenhower*

Promise me, boy, if thou get a master, work for him as hard as thou canst. If he does not appreciate all thou do, never mind. Remember, work, well-done, does good to the man who does it. It makes him a better man. *–George S. Clason, The Richest Man in Babylon*

The world is full of willing people; some willing to work, the rest willing to let them.
–Robert Frost

Work is the greatest thing in the world. So we should save some of it for tomorrow.
–Don Herold

...I have always liked bird dogs better than kennel-fed dogs myself—you know, one that will get out and hunt for food rather than sit on his fanny and yell.
–Charles E. Wilson

Give the best that you have to the highest you know—and do it now.
–Ralph W. Sockman

The first thing to do in life is to do with purpose what one proposes to do.
–Pablo Casals, cellist

I am only an average man, but, by George, I work harder at it than an average man....I pity the creature who doesn't work, at whichever end of the social scale he may regard himself as being. *–Theodore Roosevelt*

A government official was discussing Prime Minister Ramsay MacDonald's point of view on peace. "The desire for peace," he said, "does not necessarily ensure peace."

MacDonald replied, "Quite true. Neither does the desire for food satisfy hunger. But at least it gets you started toward a restaurant."

Conviction is worthless unless it is converted into conduct. *–Thomas Carlyle*

When I've had a rough day, before I go to sleep I ask myself if there's anything more I can do right now. If there isn't, I sleep sound. *–L.L. Colbert*

What counts is not the number of hours you put in, but how much you put in the hours.

The art of writing is the art of applying the seat of the pants to the seat of the chair. *–Mary Heaton Vorse*

Nothing is particularly hard if you divide it into small jobs. *–Henry Ford*

I long to accomplish a great and noble task, but it is my chief duty to accomplish humble tasks as though they were great and noble. The world is moved along, not only by the mighty shoves of its heroes, but also by the aggregate of the tiny pushes of each honest worker. *–Helen Keller*

Passivity is fatal to us. Our goal is to make the enemy passive. *–Mao Tse-tung*

I loathe drudgery as much as any man; but I have learned that the only way to conquer drudgery is to get through it as neatly, as efficiently, as one can....A dull job slackly done becomes twice as dull; whereas a dull job which you try to do just as well as you can becomes half as dull. *–Sir Harold Nicolson*

The way to Hell is plastered with good resolutions. *–German proverb*

I feel that the greatest reward for doing is the opportunity to do more. *–Dr. Jonas Salk*

I have tried my best to give the nation everything I had in me. There are probably a million people who could have done the job better than I did it, but I had the job and I always quote an epitaph on a tombstone in a cemetery in Tombstone, Arizona: "Here lies Jack Williams. He done his damndest." *–Harry S Truman*

You can't build a reputation on what you are going to do. *–Henry Ford*

What is the use of health, or of life, if not to do some work therewith? *–Thomas Carlyle, 1836*

ADVERSITY AND PERSEVERANCE

determination, courage, faith, understanding

You gain strength, courage and confidence by every experience in which you really stop to look fear in the face. You are able to say to yourself, "I lived through this horror. I can take the next thing that comes along." ...You must do the thing you think you cannot do.
–Eleanor Roosevelt

Aerodynamically speaking, the design of a bumblebee is a disaster. Too much body weight. Too little wing span. Just can't fly. But it does.

You will do foolish things, but do them with enthusiasm.
–Colette, French novelist, to her daughter

A man's errors are his portals of discovery. *–James Joyce*

One doesn't discover new lands without consenting to lose sight of the shore for a very long time. *–Andre Gide*

I expect to fight that proposition until hell freezes over. Then I propose to start fighting on the ice. *–Senator Russell Long of Louisiana*

I have not yet begun to fight. (Sometimes quoted as "I have just begun to fight.")
–John Paul Jones aboard the Bonhomme Richard, when asked whether he was ready to surrender to the British warship Serapis, 1779.

Ambition should be made of sterner stuff. *–William Shakespeare, "Julius Caesar"*

If at first you don't succeed, you're running about average. *–M. H. Alderson*

A hero is one who knows how to hang on one minute longer. *–Norwegian proverb*

We lay too much stress on stick-to-it-iveness. I once had a professor who wisely hung this sign over his desk: "Oh, Lord, teach me when to let go." *–W. G. Carleton*

The only good luck many great men ever had was being born with the ability and determination to overcome bad luck. *–Channing Pollock*

Keep on going and chances are you will stumble on something....I have never heard of anyone stumbling on something sitting down. *–Charles F. Kettering*

If your bayonet breaks, strike with the stock; if the stock gives way, hit with your fists; if your fists are hurt, bite with your teeth.
–M. I. Dragomiroff: Notes from Soldiers, c. 1890

Where The Determination Is, The Way Can Be Found.
–George S. Clason, The Richest Man in Babylon

Pennies do not come from heaven. They have to be earned here on earth.
–Margaret Thatcher

The race is not to the swift, nor the battle to the strong. *–The Bible, Ecclesiastes 9:11*

Lincoln's Road To The White House
Failed in business in 1831.
Defeated for Legislature in 1832.
Second failure in business in 1833.
Suffered nervous breakdown in 1836.
Defeated for Speaker in 1838.
Defeated for Elector in 1840.
Defeated for Congress in 1843.
Defeated for Congress in 1848.
Defeated for Senate in 1855.
Defeated for Vice President in 1856.
Defeated for Senate in 1858.
Elected President in 1860.

Having chosen our course, without guile and with pure purpose, let us renew our trust in God, and go forward without fear and with manly hearts. *–Abraham Lincoln*

Retreat, Hell! We're just advancing in another direction.
–General O. P. Smith, U.N. Forces Leader, Korean War

At first we hope too much, later on, not enough. *–Joseph Roux*

The only thing that keeps a man going is energy. And what is energy but liking life?
–Louis Auchincloss

The big shots are only the little shots who keep shooting. *–Christopher Morley*

Don't let life discourage you; everyone who got where he is had to begin where he was.
–Richard L. Evans

There is no failure except in no longer trying. *–Elbert Hubbard*

Adversity comes with instruction in his hand. *–Welsh proverb*

Hope is a risk that must be run. *–George Bernanos departure from General Motors*

The art of living is more like wrestling than dancing. *–Marcus Aurelius, c. 160*

Someone asked me...how I felt and I was reminded of a story that a fellow townsman of ours used to tell—Abraham Lincoln. They asked him how he felt once after an unsuccessful election. He said he felt like a little boy who had stubbed his toe in the dark. He said that he was too old to cry, but it hurt too much to laugh.
–Adlai Stevenson, commenting on his defeat by General Eisenhower in the presidential election of 1952

Grief drives men [to] serious reflection, sharpens the understanding and softens the heart.

–John Adams

A man is like a plank of wood—soft until seasoned.

I walked a mile with Pleasure,
She chatted all the way,
But left me none the wiser
For all she had to say.
I walked a mile with Sorrow,
And ne'er word said she'
But, oh, the things I learned from her
When Sorrow walked with me! *–Robert Browning Hamilton*

Good people are good because they've come to wisdom through failure. We get very little wisdom from success, you know....One who doesn't try cannot fail and become wise. *–William Saroyan*

If we were logical, the future would be bleak indeed. But we are more than logical. We are human beings, and we have faith, and we have hope, and we can work.
–Jacques Cousteau

I think and think for months and years. Ninety-nine times, the conclusion is false. The hundredth time I am right. *–Albert Einstein*

Inventors and men of genius have almost always been regarded as fools at the beginning (and very often at the end) of their careers. *–Dostoevsky*

I never have frustrations.
The reason is to wit:
If at first I don't succeed,
I quit!

Never bend your head. Always hold it high. Look the world straight in the face.
–Helen Keller, speaking to a five-year-old blind child

No man or woman is uniformly successful....We must all expect a rather high percentage of failure in the things we attempt. *–Barnaby Keeney*

Happiness is beneficial for the body, but it is grief that develops the powers of the mind.
–Marcel Proust

If I had my whole life to live over again, I don't think I'd have the strength.
–Flip Wilson

Is life so wretched? Isn't it rather your hands which are too small, your vision which is muddled? You are the one who must grow up. *–Dag Hammerskjold*

He banged the door on the way out, and out of that bang came eventually the Chrysler Corporation. *–Alfred P. Sloan, Jr., on Walter Chrysler's*

The Wright Brothers flew right through the smoke screen of impossibility.
–Charles F. Kettering

Damn the torpedoes, full speed ahead!
–Admiral David G. Farragut, 1864, at the Battle of Mobile Bay

Men are failures, not because they are stupid, but because they are not sufficiently impassioned. *–Struthers Burt*

Look around and you'll agree that the really happy people are those who have broken the chains of procrastination, those who find satisfaction in doing the job at hand. They're full of eagerness, zest, productivity. You can be, too.

–Norman Vincent Peale

You must pay the price if you wish to secure the blessings. *–Andrew Jackson*

Is anything too hard for the Lord? *–The Bible, Genesis 18:14*

Our belief at the beginning of a doubtful undertaking is the one thing that insures the successful outcome of our venture. *–William James*

The glory of the star, the glory of the sun—we must not lose either in the other. We must not be so full of the hope of heaven that we cannot do our work on the earth; we must not be so lost in the work of the earth that we shall not be inspired by the hope of heaven.

–Phillips Brooks

Give the American people a good cause, and there's nothing they can't lick.

–John Wayne

The hero is no braver than an ordinary man, but he is brave five minutes longer.

–Ralph Waldo Emerson

The world has no room for cowards. We must all be ready somehow to toil, to suffer, to die. And yours is not the less noble because no drum beats before you when you go out to your daily battlefields, and no crowds shout your coming when you return from your daily victory and defeat.

–Robert Louis Stevenson

It is better to be a coward for a minute than dead for the rest of your life.

–Irish proverb

They conquer who believe they can. He has not learned the first lesson of life who does not every day surmount a fear. *–Ralph Waldo Emerson*

Cannon to right of them,
Cannon to left of them,
Cannon in front of them
Volley'd and thunder'd;
Storm'd at with shot and shell,
Boldly they rode and well,
Into the jaws of Death,
Into the mouth of Hell,
Rode the six hundred.

–Alfred Tennyson,
"The Charge of the Light Brigade"

When the going gets tough, the tough get going.

–Maxim adopted by Joseph P. Kennedy

"Cast Your Vote"
Never be afraid to stand with the minority when the minority is right, for the minority which is right will one day be the majority.... *–William Jennings Bryan*

Ah, great it is to believe the dream
As we stand in youth by the starry stream;
But a greater thing is to fight life through,
And say at the end, "The dream is true!" *–Edwin Markham*

We must not hope to be mowers,
And to gather the ripe gold ears,
Unless we have first been sowers
And watered the furrows with tears.
It is not just as we take it,
This mystical world of ours,
Life's field will yield as we make it
A harvest of thorns or of flowers. *–Goethe*

Rapture's self is three parts sorrow. *–Amy Lowell*

Pain nourishes courage. You can't be brave if you've only had wonderful things happen to you. *–Mary Tyler Moore*

I shall grow old, but never lose life's zest,
Because the road's last turn will be the best. *–Henry Van Dyke*

There are some men whom a staggering emotional shock, so far from making them mental invalids for life, seems, on the other hand, to awaken, to galvanize, to arouse into an almost incredible activity of soul. *–William McFee*

The lowest ebb is the turn of the tide. *–Henry Wadsworth Longfellow*

Perseverance is the most overrated of traits, if it is unaccompanied by talent; beating your head against a wall is more likely to produce a concussion in the head than a hole in the wall. *–Sydney J. Harris*

Diligence is the mother of good luck. *–Benjamin Franklin*

The only life worth living is the adventurous life. Of such a life the dominant characteristic is that it is unafraid. It is unafraid of what other people think....It does not adapt either its pace or its objectives to the pace and objectives of its neighbors. It thinks its own thoughts, it reads its own books, it develops its own hobbies, and it is governed by its own conscience. The herd may graze where it pleases or stampede where it pleases, but he who lives the adventurous life will remain unafraid when he finds himself alone.

–Raymond B. Fosdick

The world is round and the place which may seem like the end may also be only the beginning. *–Ivy Baker Priest*

We do not stop playing because we are old. We grow old because we stop playing.

'Tis sweet to think on what was hard t'endure. *-Robert Herrick, 17th century*

...Let us remember that the times which future generations delight to recall are not those of ease and prosperity, but those of adversity bravely borne.
–Charles W. Eliot, Harvard President, 1877

Happy is the man whom God correcteth: therefore despise not the chastening of the Almighty. *–The Bible, Job 5:17*

Most people spend more time and energy in going around problems than in trying to solve them. *–Henry Ford*

Writing is a difficult trade which must be learned slowly by reading great authors; by trying at the outset to imitate them; by daring then to be original; by destroying one's first productions; by comparing subsequent works to recognized masterpieces and, once more, by destroying them; by crossing out whole passages; by weeping from despair; by being more severe with oneself than even the critics will be. After ten years of such arduous activity, if one has talent, one may begin to write in an acceptable manner.
–Andre Maurois

Every mile is two in Winter. *–George Herbert on perspective, 1640*

Every new adjustment is a crisis in self-esteem.... *–Eric Hoffer*

Some griefs are medicinal. *–William Shakespeare*

If I miss one day's practice, I notice it. If I miss two days, the critics notice it. If I miss three days, the audience notices it.*–Ignance Paderewski, Polish pianist-statesman*

Perseverance is more prevailing than violence; and many things which cannot be overcome when they are together, yield themselves up when taken little by little.
–Plutarch, c. 100

The difficult we do immediately; the impossible takes a little longer.
–Attributed variously to George Santayana, Fridtjof Nansen and the U.S. Army Corps of Engineers.

No great thing is created suddenly, any more than a bunch of grapes or a fig. If you tell me that you desire a fig, I answer that there must be time. Let it first blossom, then bear fruit, then ripen. *–Epictetus, c. 1st Century*

The true value of a human being is determined primarily by the measure and the sense in which he has attained liberation from the self. *–Albert Einstein*

A diamond is a piece of coal that stuck to the job.

If I set for myself a task, be it ever so trifling, I shall see it through. How else shall I have confidence in myself to do important things?
–George S. Clason, The Richest Man in Babylon

That is the light grief which can take counsel. *–Seneca, c. 60*

Thine was the prophet's vision, thine
The exaltation, the divine
Insanity of noble minds,
That never falters nor abates,
But labors and endures and waits,
Till all that it forsees it finds,
Or what it cannot find creates. *–Henry Wadsworth Longfellow*

I am an optimist. It does not seem too much use being anything else.

–Winston Churchill

Good news weakens me. *–Charles F. Kettering*

After he had finished a concert and had gone backstage, violinist Fritz Kreisler heard someone say, "I'd give my life to play as you do!" He turned and looked at the lady and said, "Madam, I did."

If one defines the term "dropout" to mean a person who has given up serious effort to meet his responsibilities, then every business office, government agency, golf club and university faculty would yield its quota. *–John W. Gardner*

After you've done a thing for two years, you should look at it carefully. After five years, look at it with suspicion. After ten years, throw it away and start all over.

–Alfred E. Perlman

It is the character of a brave and resolute man not to be ruffled by adversity and not to desert his post. *–Cicero, 78 B.C.E.*

...What counts is not necessarily the size of the dog in the fight—it's the size of the fight in the dog. *–Dwight D. Eisenhower*

Touch a thistle timidly, and it pricks you; grasp it boldly, and its spines crumble.

–William S. Halsey

Of all the traps and pitfalls in life, self-disesteem is the deadliest, and the hardest to overcome; for it is a pit designed and dug by our own hands, summed up in the phrase, "It's no use—I can't do it." ...It is that good hard second look—taken not just for one's own sake but for everyone else's too—that very often reveals that the "impossible" task is quite possible after all. *–Dr. Maxwell Maltz*

The man of character finds an especial attractiveness in difficulty since it is only by coming to grips with difficulty that he can realize his potentialities.

–Charles de Gaulle

Paul Galvin at the age of thirty-three had failed twice in business. He attended an auction of his failed storage-battery business and with his last $750 bought back the battery eliminator portion of it. That part became Motorola. When he retired in the 1960s he said, "Do not fear mistakes. You will know failure. Continue to reach out."

Problems are the price of progress. Don't bring me anything but trouble.

Living is like licking honey off a thorn.

The worst bankrupt in the world is the man who has lost enthusiasm. Let him lose everything but enthusiasm and he will come through again to success.

Life is like playing a violin solo in public and learning the instrument as one goes on.
–Samuel Butler

Hardships, poverty and want are the best incentives and the best foundation for the success of a man. *–Bradford Merrill*

They tried their best to find a place where I was isolated. But all the resources of a superpower cannot isolate a man who hears the voice of freedom, a voice I heard from the very chamber of my soul. *–Anatoly B. Shcharansky, Soviet dissident*

Truly a little body often harbors a great soul.
–Nikita Khrushchev, on the U.S. Communist Party

If Winter comes, can Spring be far behind? *–Shelley*

That which is bitter to endure may be sweet to remember. *–Thomas Fuller, 1732*

The curtain is lifting. We can have triumph, or tragedy, for we are the playwrights, the actors and the audience. *–John Macauley, Chairman, League of Red Cross Societies*

"Stubborn Ounces"
To one who doubts the worth of doing anything if you can't do everything.
You say the little efforts that I make
will do no good: they never will prevail
to tip the hovering scale
where Justice hangs in balance.
I don't think
I ever thought they would.
But I am prejudiced beyond debate
in favor of my right to choose which side
shall feel the stubborn ounces of my weight. *–Bonaro W. Overstreet*

Self-pity is our worst enemy and if we yield to it, we can never do anything wise in the world. *–Helen Keller*

Defeat isn't bitter, if you don't swallow it.

A President has to expect those things. The only thing you have to worry about is bad luck. I never have bad luck. *–Harry S Truman, on his assassination attempt, 1950*

Time and thinking tame the strongest grief.
–English proverb, borrowed from the Latin

Trouble is only opportunity in work clothes. *–Henry J. Kaiser*

It is, of course, a trite observation to say that we live "in a period of transition." Many people have said this at many times. Adam may well have made the remark to Eve on leaving the Garden of Eden. *–Harold MacMillan, British Prime Minister*

Act as if the whole election depended on your single vote... *–John Wesley*

A battle sometimes decides everything; and sometimes the most trifling thing decides the fate of a battle. *–Napoleon Bonaparte*

If thou faint in the day of adversity, thy strength is small. *–The Bible, Proverbs 24:10*

We're eye-ball to eye-ball and the other fellow just blinked.
–Dean Rusk, on the 1962 Cuban missle crisis

Adversity introduces a man to himself.

When I was 40, my doctor advised me that a man in his forties shouldn't play tennis. I heeded his advice carefully and could hardly wait until I reached 50 to start again.
–Hugo Black, Supreme Court Associate Justice

You've got to be a man to play baseball for a living, but you've got to have a lot of little boy in you, too. *–Roy Campanella*

Any man who has had the job I've had and didn't have a sense of humor wouldn't still be here. *–Harry S Truman*

I have chosen thee in the furnace of affliction. *–The Bible, Isaiah 48:10*

Progress needs the brakeman, but the brakeman should not spend all his time putting on the brakes. *–Elbert Hubbard*

Writing a book is an adventure; to begin with it is a toy and an amusement, then it becomes a master, and then it becomes a tyrant; and...just as you are about to be reconciled to your servitude—you kill the monster and fling him...to the public.
–Winston Churchill

I have been driven to my knees many times because there was no place else to go.
–Abraham Lincoln

You're only young once. How long that once lasts is the question.

Most people say that as you get old, you have to give up things. I think you get old because you give up things.
–Senator Theodore Francis Green of Rhode Island, at 87

Let every nation know, whether it wishes us well or ill, that we shall pay any price, bear any burden, meet any hardship, support any friend, oppose any foe to assure the survival and the success of liberty. *–John F. Kennedy*

A man can fail many times but he isn't a failure until he begins to blame somebody else.

What's gone and what's past help

Should be past grief. *–William Shakespeare, "The Winter's Tale"*

Khrushchev reminds me of the tiger hunter who has picked a place on the wall to hang the tiger's skin long before he has caught the tiger. This tiger has other ideas.
–John F. Kennedy

If you have an important point to make, don't try to be subtle or clever. Use a pile driver. Hit the point once. Then come back and hit it again. Then hit it a third time—a tremendous whack. *–Winston Churchill*

A ball player's got to be kept hungry to become a big-leaguer. That's why no boy from a rich family ever made the big leagues. *–Joe DiMaggio*

It circulated for five years, through the halls of 15 publishers, and finally ended up with Vanguard Press, which as you can see, is rather deep into the alphabet.
–Patrick Dennis (Edward Everett Tanner), on his novel, Auntie Mame

Every great discovery I ever made, I gambled that the truth was there, and then I acted on it in faith until I could prove its existence.
–Arthur H. Compton, Nobel Prize physicist

What one approves, another scorns,
And thus his nature each discloses;
You find the rosebush full of thorns,
I find the thornbush full of roses. *–Arthur Guiterman*

Worry never robs tomorrow of its sorrow; it only saps today of its strength.
–A. J. Cronin

I am an old man and have known a great many troubles, but most of them have never happened. *–Mark Twain*

Courage is armor
A blind man wears;
The calloused scars
Of outlived despairs:
Courage is fear
That has said its prayers. *–Karle Wilson Baker, "Courage"*

ACHIEVEMENT

Success, Greatness, Excellence

It is no use saying, "We are doing our best." You have got to succeed in doing what is necessary. *–Winston Churchill*

Getting something done is an accomplishment; getting something done right is an achievement.

Success is to be measured not so much by the position that one has reached in life as by the obstacles which he has overcome while trying to succeed. *–Booker T. Washington*

Doubt is a thief that often makes us fear to tread where we might have won.
–Popular version of a Shakespeare quote

I always turn to the sports pages first, which record people's accomplishments. The front page has nothing but man's failures. *–Chief Justice Earl Warren*

He that will not sail until all dangers are over must never put to sea. *–Thomas Fuller*

You can't steal second base and keep one foot on first.
–A 69-year-old junior executive

Ladder of Achievement
100%–I did. 90%–I will. 80%–I can. 70% I think I can. 60%–I might. 50%–I think I might. 40%–What is it? 30%–I wish I could. 20%–I don't know how. 10%–I can't. 0%–I won't.

They keep saying that what really matters is not whether you win or lose, but how you played the game. The trouble is that the best way to determine how you played the game is by whether you won or lost.

He who comes up to his own idea of greatness must always have had a very low standard of it in his mind. *–William Hazlitt*

If at the end one can say, "This man used to the limit the powers that God granted him; he was worthy of love and respect and of the sacrifices of many people, made in order that he might achieve what he deemed to be his task," then that life has been lived well and there are no regrets. *–Eleanor Roosevelt*

The best part of success is that, whether we know it or not, all of us have been successful at something, perhaps many times, during our lives. The most difficult part of success is knowing when it is really ours.

I think this is the most extraordinary collection of talent, of human knowledge, that has ever been gathered together at the White House—with the possible exception of when Thomas Jefferson dined alone.
–President John F. Kennedy, at a dinner for U.S. winners of the Nobel Prize in 1962

Two roads diverged in a wood, and I
I took the one less traveled by,
And that has made all the difference. *–Robert Frost, "The Road Not Taken"*

Everyone is trying to accomplish something big, not realizing that life is made up of little things. *–Frank A. Clark*

Desires must be simple and definite. They defeat their own purpose should they be too many, too confusing, or beyond a man's training to accomplish. *–George S. Clason*

For success, try aspiration, inspiration, and perspiration.

There ain't no man can avoid being born average. But there ain't no man got to be common. *–Satchel Paige*

God will not look you over for medals, degrees, or diplomas, but for scars.
–Elbert Hubbard

The door to the room of success swings on the hinges of opposition.

In this country, success is commonly regarded as an exclusively American product, and it is advertised on matchbook covers and in the back pages of adventure magazines, accessible by way of high-school education or a new truss. It is thought by some to have a distinctly bitter taste, not unlike a mouthful of dimes. But its smell is generally conceded to be sweet. *–Stephen Birmingham*

We are more ready to try the untried when what we do is incon-sequential. Hence the remarkable fact that many inventions had their birth as toys. *–Eric Hoffer*

If A equals success, then the formula is A equals X plus Y plus Z. X is work. Y is play. Z is keep your mouth shut. *–Albert Einstein*

I don't know the key to success, but the key to failure is to try to please everyone. *–Bill Cosby*

Every great man is unique. *–Ralph Waldo Emerson*

...The average man who wins what we call success is not a genius. He is a man who has merely the ordinary qualities that he shares with his fellows, but who has developed those ordinary qualities to a more than ordinary degree. *–Theodore Roosevelt*

A man is rich according to what he is, not according to what he has.

Our business in life is not to get ahead of other people, but to get ahead of ourselves. *–Maltbie D. Babcock*

Superior achievement, or making the most of one's capabilities, is to a very considerable degree a matter of habit. This was the reason why Joe used to say to the children, "We don't want any losers around here. In this family we want winners." They were encouraged to be winners, leaders, and victors in whatever they set their hand to...to develop the habit. *–Rose Fitzgerald Kennedy*

Metaphors—Life is currently described in one of four ways: a journey, a battle, a pilgrimage, or a race. Select your own metaphors, but the necessity of finishing is all the same. For if life is a journey, it must be completed. If life is a battle, it must be finished. If life is a pilgrimage, it must be concluded. And if life is a race, it must be won. *–The War Cry*

Hitch your wagon to a star. *–Ralph Waldo Emerson*

Ideals are like stars. You will not succeed in touching them with your hands; but, like the seafaring man, you choose them as your guides, and, following them, you will reach your destiny. *–Carl Schurz*

Glory gives herself only to those who always dreamed of her. *–Charles de Gaulle*

We succeed only as we identify in life, or in war, or in anything else, a single overriding objective, and make all other considerations bend to that one objective. *–Dwight D. Eisenhower*

The two hardest things to handle in life are failure and success.

Nothing splendid has ever been achieved except by those who dared believe that something inside them was superior to circumstance. *–Bruce Barton*

As far back as I remember, long before I could write, I had played at making stories. But not until I was seven or more, did I begin to pray every night, "O God, let me write books! Please, God, let me write books!" *–Ellen Glasgow*

The superior man makes the difficulty to be overcome his first interest; success comes only later. *–Confucius, c. 500 B.C.E.*

I believe in the tragic element of history. I believe there is the tragedy of a man who works very hard and never gets what he wants. And then I believe there is the even more bitter tragedy of a man who finally gets what he wants and finds out that he doesn't want it. *–Henry Kissinger*

I knew very well what I was undertaking, and very well how to do it, and have done it very well. *–Samuel Johnson, Speaking of his Dictionary, 1779*

Success is not a harbor but a voyage with its own perils to the spirit. The game of life is to come up a winner, to be a success, or to achieve what we set out to do. Yet there is always the danger of failing as a human being. The lesson that most of us on this voyage never learn, but can never quite forget, is that to win is sometimes to lose. *–Richard M. Nixon*

Some are born great, some achieve greatness, and some have greatness thrust upon them. *–William Shakespeare: Twelfth Night, c. 1601*

That individuals have soared above the plane of their race is scarcely to be questioned; but, in looking back through history for traces of their existence we should pass over all biographies of "the good and the great," while we search carefully the slight records of wretches who died in prison, in Bedlam, or upon the gallows. *–Edgar Allen Poe*

In America, anyone can become President. That's one of the risks you take. *–Adlai Stevenson*

Meet success like a gentleman and disaster like a man. *–Lord Birkenhead*

True success is overcoming the fear of being unsuccessful. *–Paul Seeney*

The man of true greatness never loses his child's heart.` *–Mencius, c. 300 B.C.E.*

They don't sing about racing for the moon any more, because that boat has landed.

On how she became an internationally famous aviatrix, Jacqueline Cochran explained: "I wanted to go higher than Rockefeller Center, which was going to cut off my view of the sky....I might have been born in a hovel, but I determined to travel with the wind and the stars.

Dwight D. Eisenhower, when told that his birthday would make him the oldest President to serve in office, said: I believe it's a tradition in baseball that when a pitcher has a no-hitter going, no one reminds him of it.

Do not commit the error, common among the young, of assuming that if you cannot save the whole of mankind you have failed. *–Jan de Hartog*

The riders in a race do not stop short when they reach the goal. There is a little finishing canter before coming to a standstill. There is time to hear the kind voices of friends and to say to one's self, "the work is done." *–Oliver Wendell Holmes, Jr.*

I sincerely regret all my divorces because I don't like anything to be unsuccessful. *–John Paul Getty*

Men may be divided almost any way we please, but I have found the most useful distinction to be made between those who devote their lives to conjugating the verb "to be," and those who spend their lives conjugating the verb "to have." *–Sydney J. Harris*

...I want it said of me by those who knew me best, that I always plucked a thistle and planted a flower where I thought a flower would grow. *–Abraham Lincoln*

A modest man often seems conceited because he is delighted with what he has done, thinking it better than anything of which he believed himself capable, whereas the conceited man is inclined to express dissatisfaction with his performances, thinking them unworthy of his genius. *–Hesketh Pearson*

A great man will not trample upon a worm, nor sneak to an emperor. *–Thomas Fuller, 1732*

That man is a success who has lived well, laughed often and loved much; who has gained the respect of intelligent men and the love of children; who has filled his niche and accomplished his task; who leaves the world better than he found it, whether by an improved poppy, a perfect poem or a rescued soul; who never lacked appreciation of earth's beauty or failed to express it; who looked for the best in others and gave the best he had. *–Robert Louis Stevenson*

The farmer's son said, "Good-bye, Dad, I'm off to the big city so my talents can flower."
"Same reason the corn stays here," said the farmer.

The lure of the distant and the difficult is deceptive. The great opportunity is where you are. *–John Burroughs*

All you need in this life is ignorance and confidence, and then success is sure. *–Mark Twain*

J. Paul Getty sent the following to a magazine requesting a short article explaining his success: "Some people find oil. Others don't." *–J. Paul Getty*

The mere absence of war is not peace. The mere absence of recession is not growth. *–John F. Kennedy*

Hell begins on the day when God grants us a clear vision of all that we might have achieved, of all the gifts which we might have wasted, of all that we might have done which we did not do. *–Gian-Carlo Menotti*

Lord, I confess I am not what I ought to be, but I thank you, Lord, that I'm not what I used to be. *–Maxie Dunnan*

A man who had been bypassed for promotion went to the president and complained, saying he had fifteen years of experience with the firm.
The president answered him, "Not so. You have had one year of experience fifteen times."

When you can, always advise people to do what you see they really want to do....Doing what they want to do, they may succeed; doing what they don't want to do, they won't.
–James Gould Cozzens

A hundred times every day I remind myself that my inner and outer life depend on the labors of other men, living and dead, and that I must exert myself in order to give in the same measure as I have received and am still receiving. *–Albert Einstein*

Skillful pilots gain their reputation from storms and tempests. *–Epicurus*

Nothing succeeds like the appearance of success. *–Christopher Lasch*

[The great society] is a place where men are more concerned with the quality of their goals than the quantity of their goods. *–Lyndon B. Johnson*

When has lasting greatness ever been achieved by one who sought greatness for itself rather than allowing it to move quietly upon him as he worked for others...? What did Dooley, or what did Rusk, or Kendall or Schweitzer set out to do but help his neighbor in the way he knew best? *–Dr. George Fister*

Not often in the story of mankind does a man arrive on earth who is both steel and velvet, who is as hard as rock and soft as drifting fog, who holds in his heart and mind the paradox of terrible storm and peace unspeakable and perfect.
–Carl Sandburg, on 150th anniversary of Abraham Lincoln's birth

If there is a single quality that is shared by all great men, it is vanity. But I mean by "vanity" only that they appreciate their own worth... *–Yussef Karsh, photographer*

The lure of succeeding grandly before an audience is what keeps the performer alive. It was once aptly described by the late high-wire artist Karl Wallenda, who said: "Life is on the wire. All the rest is waiting around." *–Michael Fedo*

...Applause. Enjoy it—but never quite believe it. *–Robert Montgomery*

The bird of paradise alights only upon the hand that does not grasp. *–John Berry*

I am proud but also, I must admit, awe-struck at your decision to include me. I do hope you are right. I feel we are both running a considerable risk and that I do not deserve it. But I shall have no misgivings if you have none.
–Winston Churchill, accepting Nobel Prize for Literature

I am very happy for any writer who deserves it to get the prize. I am sorry about any writer who deserves it and doesn't get it. This makes me very humble in accepting it.
–Ernest Hemingway, accepting Nobel Prize for Literature

Charles Lawrence, at a dinner honoring him for the development of the engine for Charles Lindbergh's historic non-stop flight to Paris, said: "This is nice and I appreciate it very much. But who ever heard of Paul Revere's horse?"

Recipe For Greatness—To bear up under loss; To fight the bitterness of defeat and the weakness of grief; To be victor over anger; To smile when tears are close; To resist disease and evil men and base instincts; To hate hate and to love love; To go on when it would seem good to die; To look up with unquenchable faith in something ever more about to be. That is what any man can do, and be great. *–Zane Grey*

In his book, *Speaking of Bridge*, Marshall Smith describes the ideal player: "[He] has the conceit of a peacock, night habits of an owl, rapacity of a crocodile and the sly inscrutability of a snake. Along with these he needs the memory of an elephant, the boldness of a lion, endurance of a bulldog and killer instinct of a wolf. In such company, the average bridge player is nothing but a kibitzing monkey."

More worship the rising than the setting sun. *–Plutarch, c. 100*

The graveyards are full of indispensable men. *–Charles de Gaulle*

The toughest thing about success is that you've got to keep on being a success.

–Irving Berlin

Show me a thoroughly satisfied man, and I will show you a failure. *–Thomas Edison*

To be successful is to achieve an objective, but to be a success is always to have yet another objective in mind....

Columbus set out to find a passage to the Indies and failed; he found America instead. Ponce de Leon looked for the fountain of youth and found Florida. The greatest explorers seem to find something other than what they are looking for.

The measure of success is not whether you have a tough problem to deal with, but whether it's the same problem you had last year. *–John Foster Dulles*

Aviation is proof that, given the will, we have the capacity to achieve the impossible.

–Eddie Rickenbacker

Ah, but a man's reach should exceed his grasp, or what's heaven for?

–Robert Browning

There is nothing noble in being superior to some other man. The true nobility is in being superior to your previous self. *–Indian proverb*

Philadelphia Phillies baseball star Mike Schmidt grew up in a sleepy, tree-lined, middle-class neighborhood in Dayton, Ohio. At the age of five he climbed a tree in his backyard and grabbed a 4000-volt power line. Knocked unconscious by the shock, he fell limp to the ground. The impact restarted his heart.

"I've never thought that I was given a second chance because I was supposed to do something great in my life," Schmidt says. "But I've looked back and wondered why that stupid little kid didn't die. Maybe that's the reason I've always worked so hard, because I don't want to think that I wasted that chance."

–Phil Axelrod, in Pittsburgh Post-Gazette

People are always blaming their circumstances for what they are. I don't believe in circumstances. The people who get on in this world are the people who look for the circumstances they want, and if they can't find them, make them.

–George Bernard Shaw

Being powerful is like being a lady. If you have to tell people you are, you aren't.

–Margaret Thatcher

Leadership

Management Skills, Delegation, Government

You done splendid. *–Casey Stengel, an accolade reserved for his best players*

If you want a track team to win the high jump, you find one person who can jump seven feet, not seven people who can jump one foot. *–Louis Terman*

A leader is best when people barely know he exists. Not so good when people obey and acclaim him. Worse when they despise him. But of a good leader who talks little when his work is done, his aim fulfilled, they will say "We did it ourselves."
–Lao-tzu, c. 550 B.C.E.

A first-rate organizer is never in a hurry. He is never late. He always keeps up his sleeve a margin for the unexpected. *–Arnold Bennett*

I never give them hell. I just tell the truth, and they think it is hell. *–Harry S Truman*

The price of greatness is responsibility. *–Winston Churchill*

If we were all determined to play the first violin we should never have an ensemble. Therefore, respect every musician in his proper place.
–Robert Schumann, composer

Certainly a leader needs a clear vision of the organization and where it is going, but a vision is of little value unless it is shared in a way so as to generate enthusiasm and commitment. Leadership and communication are inseparable.
–Claude I. Taylor, Chairman of the Board, Air Canada

Judge a leader by the followers.

Confidence is contagious. So is lack of confidence. *–Michael O'Brien*

A leader is a dealer in hope. *–Napoleon Bonaparte*

The American people want leadership which believes in them, not leadership which berates them. *–Lyndon B. Johnson*

The spirited horse, which will try to win the race of its own accord, will run even faster if encouraged. *–Ovid, c. 9 A.C.E.*

I consider my ability to arouse enthusiasm among people the greatest asset I possess.

I never use a score when conducting my orchestra....Does a lion tamer enter a cage with a book on how to tame a lion? *–Dimitri Mitropolous*

The boss drives his men; the leader coaches them. The boss depends upon authority; the leader on good will. The boss inspires fear; the leader inspires enthusiasm. The boss says "I"; the leader "we." The boss fixes the blame for the breakdown; the leader fixes the breakdown. The boss says "go"; the leader says "let's go!"
–H. Gordon Selfridge, merchant

The marksman hitteth the target partly by pulling, partly by letting go. The boatsman reacheth the landing partly by pulling, partly by letting go. *–Egyptian proverb*

Excellence is to do a common thing in an uncommon way. *–Booker T. Washington*

Message to corporate leaders: Bring your corporation out of the organizational swamp...; spell out your twenty-to-twenty-five-year vision; get your organization structures right; and...create an environment in which everyone has the opportunity to do work which matches his potential capability and for which an equitable differential reward is provided. *–Elliott Jaques*

Big jobs usually go to the men who prove their ability to outgrow small ones.
–Ralph Waldo Emerson

No man is fit to command another that cannot command himself.
–William Penn, "No Cross, No Crown," 1669

A good presentation has as many questions as answers.

People ask the difference between a leader and a boss....The leader works in the open, and the boss in covert. The leader leads, and the boss drives. *–Theodore Roosevelt*

There is a singular quality about Abraham Lincoln which sets him apart from all our other Presidents...a dimension of brooding compassion, of love for humanity; a love which was, if anything, strengthened and deepened by the agony that drove lesser men to the protective shelter of callous indifference. *–Lyndon B. Johnson*

Not often in the story of mankind does a man arrive on earth who is both steel and velvet, who is as hard as a rock and soft as drifting fog, who holds in his heart and mind the paradox of terrible storm and peace unspeakable and perfect.
–Carl Sandburg, spoken on the 150th anniversary of Lincoln's birth

During the Civil War, when someone complained to him that General Grant was a heavy drinker, President Lincoln is supposed to have said, "Find out what brand he drinks, so I can send some to my other generals."

I've met a few people in my time who were enthusiastic about hard work. And it was just my luck that all of them happened to be men I was working for at the time.
–Bill Gold

By working faithfully eight hours a day, you may eventually get to be a boss and work 12 hours a day. *–Robert Frost*

I am more afraid of an army of 100 sheep led by a lion than an army of 100 lions led by a sheep. *–Talleyrand*

I make progress by having people around who are smarter than I am—and listening to them. And I assume that everyone is smarter about something than I am.
–Henry J. Kaiser

The chief executive who knows his strengths and weaknesses as a leader is likely to be far more effective than the one who remains blind to them. He also is on the road to humility—that priceless attitude of openness to life that can help a manager absorb mistakes, failures, or personal shortcomings. *–John Adair*

Any man who has had the job I've had and didn't have a sense of humor, wouldn't still be here. *–Harry S Truman*

Asked what his secret was for lasting so long and being so successful as the president of the University of Michigan, Dr. James R. Angell explained: "Grow antennae, not horns." Preparation makes for leadership, and leadership is service to man.

–Dr. Douglas Southall Freeman

The best executive is the one who has sense enough to pick good men to do what he wants done, and the self-restraint to keep from meddling with them while they do it.

–Theodore Roosevelt

A matchmaker requested an experienced fighter for a match with the local boxing champion. On the day of the fight a middle-aged man with a much broken nose, a punch-drunk manner and two huge cauliflower ears arrived to enter the ring. The matchmaker was aghast. "I asked for an experienced fighter," he complained, "but not a damaged one."

A strong and secure man digests his experiences (deeds and misdeeds alike) just as he digests his meat, even when he has some bits to swallow. *–Friedrich Nietsche*

Experience is largely non-transferable

There are two kinds of men who never amount to much—those who cannot do what they are told and those who can do nothing else. *–Cyrus H.K. Curtis*

Respect a man, he will do the more. *–James Howell, 1659*

Authority without wisdom is like a heavy ax without an edge, fitter to bruise than polish.

–Anne Bradstreet, c. 1670

Most people like hard work. Particularly when they are paying for it.

–Franklin P. Jones

Every great man is always being helped by everybody, for his gift is to get good out of all things and all persons. *–John Ruskin, 1846*

Show me a man who cannot bother to do little things and I'll show you a man who cannot be trusted to do big things. *–Lawrence D. Bell*

While I am not in favor of maladjustment, I view this cultivation of neutrality, this breeding of mental neuters, this hostility to eccentricity and controversy with grave misgiving. One looks back with dismay at the possibility of a Shakespeare perfectly adjusted to bourgeois life in Stratford, a Wesley contentedly administering a country parish, George Washington going to London to receive a barony from George III, or Abraham Lincoln prospering in Springfield with nary a concern for the preservation of the crumbling Union. *–Adlai Stevenson*

Every great advance in natural knowledge has involved the absolute rejection of authority. *–Thomas Huxley, 1870*

There is no necessary connection between the desire to lead and the ability to lead, and even less the ability to lead somewhere that will be to the advantage of the led....

–Bergen Evans

...Government should do only those things the people cannot do for themselves.

–Ronald Reagan

That government is the strongest of which every man feels himself a part.

–Thomas Jefferson

Those who expect to reap the blessings of freedom must...undergo the fatigue of supporting it. *–Thomas Paine*

A man who wants to lead the orchestra must turn his back on the crowd.

–James Crook

Legislators who are of even average intelligence stand out among their colleagues....A cultured college president has become as much a rarity as a literate newspaper publisher. A financier interested in economics is as exceptional as a labor leader interested in the labor movement. For the most part our leaders are merely following out in front; they [only] marshal us in the way that we are going. *–Bergen Evans*

There's plenty of room at the top, but there's no room to sit down. *–Helen Downey*

The man whose authority is recent is always stern.

–Aeschylus, Prometheus Bound, c 490 B.C.E.

The house shows the owner. *–George Herbert, 1651*

A good government produces citizens distinguished for courage, love of justice, and every other good quality; a bad government makes them cowardly, rapacious, and the slaves of every foul desire. *–Dionysius of Halicarnassus, 20 B.C.E.*

...I would rather have a first-class manager running a second-rate business than a second-class manager running a first-rate business.

–Jack E. Reichert, President and CEO, Brunswick Corp.

The same ambition can destroy or save, and makes a patriot as it makes a knave.

–Alexander Pope, 1732

Early in life, I had to choose between honest arrogance and hypocritical humility. I chose honest arrogance and have seen no occasion to change.

–Frank Lloyd Wright, architect

Nothing motivates a man more than to see his boss putting in an honest day's work.

–Wain

I offer neither pay, nor quarters, nor provisions; I offer hunger, thirst, forced marches, battles and death. Let him who loves his country in his heart and not with lips only, follow me. *–Giuseppe Garibaldi, Italian patriot*

Follow me if I advance! Kill me if I retreat! Revenge me if I die!

–Ngo Dinh Diem, battle cry on becoming President of Vietnam in 1954

In enterprise of martial kind,
When there was any fighting,
He led his regiment from behind,
He found it less exciting.

–W.S. Gilbert

The lash may force men to physical labor; it cannot force them to spiritual creativity.
–Sholem Asch

It is not a government's obligation to provide services, but to see that they are provided.
–Mario Cuomo, Governor of New York

Walt Disney seldom surveyed his animators' work while they were creating. He understood the fragile nature of the creative process, and he wouldn't intrude. But there was nothing to stop him after the animator had left for the day. Walt's nighttime visits to the offices became legendary, and animators often left their best work on the drawing table overnight, anticipating that Walt would inspect it. But sometimes they arrived in the morning to find crumpled sheets of paper rescued from wastebaskets and pinned on a storyboard with the notation in the unmistakable Disney script: "Quit throwing the good stuff away."
–Bob Thomas

The day before my inauguration President Eisenhower told me, "You'll find that no easy problems ever come to the President of the United States. If they are easy to solve, somebody else has solved them."
–John F. Kennedy

A great leader molds public opinion; a wise leader listens to it.

When Leo Durocher was manager of the Dodgers he was booed for pulling a pitcher out in the eighth inning of a close game. A reporter later asked him how he felt about the crowd's reaction. He replied, "Baseball is like church. Many attend, few understand."

For every quarterback on the field, there are a thousand in the stands.

Trust men and they will be true to you; treat them greatly, and they will show themselves great.
–Ralph Waldo Emerson

Most of us can learn to live in perfect comfort on higher levels of power. Everyone knows that on any given day there are energies slumbering in him which the incitements of that day do not call forth. Compared with what we ought to be, we are only half awake. It is evident that our organism has stored-up reserves of energy that are ordinarily not called upon—deeper and deeper strata of explosible material, ready for use by anyone who probes so deep. The human individual usually lives far within his limits.
–William James

Gentleness is a divine trait: nothing is so strong as gentleness, and nothing is so gentle as real strength.
–Ralph W. Sockman

Upon what meat doth this our Caesar feed,

That he is grown so great?
–William Shakespeare, Julius Caesar

No one is fit to be trusted with power....No one....Any man who has lived at all knows the follies and wickedness he's capable of. If he does not know it, he is not fit to govern others. And if he does know it, he knows also that neither he nor any man ought to be allowed to decide a single human fate.
–C.P. Snow

...I will not equivocate—I will not excuse—I will not retreat a single inch and—I will be heard.
–William Lloyd Garrison

Government has been a fossil; it should be a plant.
–Ralph Waldo Emerson

All well-governed states and wise princes have taken care not to reduce the nobility to despair, nor the people to discontent. *–Machiavelli, The Prince, 1513*

I have no ambition to govern men. It is a painful and thankless office.

–Thomas Jefferson

The world is ruled by a certain few, even as a little boy of twelve years old rules, governs, and keeps a hundred great and strong oxen upon a pasture. *–Martin Luther, 1569*

A committee is a group that keeps minutes and loses hours. *–Milton Berle*

You can delegate authority, but you can never delegate responsibility for delegating a task to someone else. If you picked the right man, fine, but if you picked the wrong man, the responsibility is yours—not his.

–Richard E. Krafve, President, Raytheon Company

For forms of government let fools contest:
Whate'er is best administr'd is best. *–Alexander Pope, 1733*

The leader must know, must know that he knows, and must be able to make it abundantly clear to those about him that he knows.

–Clarence B. Randall, retired chairman, Inland Steel Co.

In framing a government which is to be administered by men over men...you must first enable the government to control the governed, and in the next place, oblige it to control itself. *–Alexander Hamilton, 1788*

Government never shrinks.

The three great ends which a statesman ought to propose to himself in the government of a nation are: (1) security to possessors; (2) facility to acquirers; and (3) hope to all.

–Samuel Coleridge

P. J. Proudhon, in his Confessions of a Revolutionary (1849) stated: "To be governed is to be watched, inspected, spied upon, directed, law-ridden, regulated, penned up, indoctrinated, preached at, checked, appraised, seized, censured, commanded, by beings who have neither title, nor knowledge, nor virtue. To be governed is to have every operation, every transaction, every movement noted, registered, counted, rated, stamped, measured, numbered, assessed, licensed, refused, authorized, endorsed, admonished, prevented, reformed, redressed, corrected."

Every man who takes office in Washington either grows or swells, and when I give a man an office, I watch him carefully to see whether he is swelling or growing.

–Woodrow Wilson

It may be laid as a universal rule that a government which attempts more than it ought will perform less. *–T.B. Macaulay: 1841*

It's a lot tougher to be a football coach than a President....A coach doesn't have anyone to protect him when things go wrong. *–Harry S Truman*

With public sentiment, nothing can fail; without it, nothing can succeed.

–Abraham Lincoln

A static hero is a public liability. Progress grows out of motion.
–Admiral Richard E. Byrd, Arctic explorer

Government is merely an attempt to express the conscience of...the nation....If the government is going faster than the public conscience, it will presently have to pull up; if it is not going as fast as the public conscience, it will presently have to be whipped up.
–Woodrow Wilson

To make laws that man cannot, and will not obey, serves to bring all law into contempt.
–Elizabeth Cady Stanton

Here I am at the end of the road and at the top of the heap. *–Pope John XXIII*

The best compliment to a child or a friend is the feeling you give him that he has been set free to make his own inquiries, to come to conclusions that are right for him, whether or not they coincide with your own. *–Alistair Cooke*

What does it take to be an Archbishop of Canterbury? The strength of a horse—and the ability to be a cart horse one day and a race horse the next. *–Geoffrey Fisher*

Psychology is the science of predicting how people behave—and explaining why they don't.

Until philosophers take to government, or those who now govern become philosophers, so that government and philosophy unite, there will be no end to the miseries of states.
–Plato, c. 370 B.C.E.

Too often our Washington reflex is to discover a problem and then throw money at it, hoping it will somehow go away. *–Senator Kenneth B. Keating*

Those who do well, like criticism; those who do not do well, resent it.

The deterioration of every government begins with the decay of the principles on which it was founded. *–C.L. De Montesquieu*

There are two ways of spreading light: to be the candle, or the mirror that reflects it.
–Edith Wharton

...Leadership is a word and a concept that has been more argued than almost any other I know....I would rather try to persuade a man to go along, because once I have persuaded him he will stick. If I scare him, he will stay just as long as he is scared, and then he is gone. *–Dwight D. Eisenhower*

Why has government been instituted at all? Because the passions of men will not conform to the dictates of reason and justice without constraint.
–Alexander Hamilton, 1788

Nobody knows who devised the first flag, but there is a myth telling how it happened. Seems that one warrior got hurt in a fight between two tribes and held up his bloody garment to show that he needed help, and everybody followed him. That's why so many flags use the color red...

Great men are rarely isolated mountain peaks; they are the summits of ranges.
–T.W. Higginson, 1871

...What is a committee? A group of the unwilling, picked from the unfit, to do the unnecessary. *–Richard Harkness*

The refreshing definition of a camel: a horse planned by a committee.
–Vogue Magazine, July 1958

Society in every state is a blessing, but government, even in its best state, is but a necessary evil; in its worst state an intolerable one. *–Thomas Paine, 1776*

Laws too gentle are seldom obeyed; too severe, seldom executed.
–Benjamin Franklin

Only a man with the common touch would get his picture on the penny.

What sets American democracy apart is the abiding prejudice against party professionals. Wise candidates advertise themselves as ordinary citizens innocent of the dark arts. In this no one has been more successful than Ronald Reagan...the most artfully camouflaged politician in the business. *–Karl E. Meyer*

It often happens that I wake at night and begin to think about a serious problem and decide I must tell the Pope about it. Then I wake up completely and remember that I am the Pope. *–Pope John XXIII*

Once upon a time my political opponents honored me as possessing the fabulous intellectual and economic power by which I created a world-wide depression all by myself. *–Herbert Hoover, on the depression days*

Ideally, the umpire should combine the integrity of a Supreme Court justice, the physical agility of an acrobat, the endurance of Job and the imperturbability of Buddha.
–Time Magazine, August 25, 1961

A President's hardest task is not to do what is right, but to know what is right.
–Lyndon B. Johnson

It's great to work with somebody who wants to do things differently. *–Keith Bellows*

No matter how humble a man's beginnings, he achieves the stature of the office to which he is elected. *–Nikita Khrushchev*

The public demands that the [university] president be everywhere at all times. He is thought to be omniscient, omnipresent, and Mr. Chips all rolled into one.
–Whitney Griswold

It annoys me to see business people characterized as tight-lipped politicos who write memos that never express an opinion and who never say anything in meetings that deviates from the company line. It bothers me even more to think there are young people who believe that's the way to get ahead. In really good companies, you have to lead. You have to come up with...big ideas and express them forcefully.

I've always been encouraged—or sometimes forced—to confront the very natural fear of being wrong. I was constantly pushed to find out what I really thought and then to speak up. Over time, I came to see that waiting to discover which way the wind is blowing is an excellent way to learn how to be a follower.
–Roger Enrico, President and CEO of Pepsi-Cola, on corporate stereotypes

No government can be maintained without the principle of fear as well as of duty. Good men will obey the last, but bad ones the former only. *–Thomas Jefferson*

It was the nation and the race dwelling all 'round the globe that had the lion's heart. I had the luck to be called upon to give the lion's roar. I also hope that I sometimes suggested to the lion the right place to use his claws.

–Winston Churchill, on the outcome of World War II

Whenever you are to do a thing, though it can never be known but to yourself, ask yourself how you would act were all the world looking at you, and act accordingly.

–Thomas Jefferson

When asked what kind of leader's hat he wears, Lech Walesa answers: My hat will always be a worker's hat and it will always hang on a nail. It's a leader's hat but it shall always be a common hat, used by common people for common purposes.

A bore is a fellow who opens his mouth and puts his feats in it. *–Henry Ford*

If everyone is thinking alike then somebody isn't thinking. *–George S. Patton*

Leadership: the art of getting someone else to do something you want done because he wants to do it. *–Dwight D. Eisenhower*

Leadership is the capacity to translate vision into reality. *–Warren G. Bennis*

Where Example keeps pace with Authority, Power hardly fails to be obey'd.

–William Penn

The best leaders...almost without exception and at every level, are master users of stories and symbols. *–Tom Peters*

Managers are people who do things right, and leaders are people who do the right things.

–Warren G. Bennis

My definition of a leader...is a man who can persuade people to do what they don't want to do, or do what they're too lazy to do, and like it. *–Harry S Truman*

The Hall was the place where the great lord used to eat....He ate not in private, except in time of sickness....Nay, the king himself used to eat in the Hall, and his lords sat with him, and he understood men. *–John Selden, about 1620*

Character is power. *–Booker T. Washington*

Business

Commerce, Occupations, Business Success

Drive thy business; let it not drive thee. *–Benjamin Franklin*

To business that we love we rise betime,
And go to't with delight. *–William Shakespeare*

The brain is a wonderful organ; it starts the moment you get up in the morning and does not stop until you get to the office. *–Robert Frost*

Businesses are successful because someone makes the sacrifices others are unwilling to.
–Ki-Jung Kim, Korean businessman

It takes twenty years to make an overnight success.

We're losing all across the board—steel, textiles, electrical machinery, paper, lumber—you name it. And...when you're losing a war, the first thing you do is to try for a truce before you bleed to death. Right now we're playing innocents abroad in a trade world that is definitely not innocent.
–Lee A. Iacocca, Chairman of the board and CEO, Chrysler Corp.

Never say no when a client asks for something—even if it is the moon. You can always try, and anyhow there is plenty of time afterward to explain that it was not possible.
–Caesar Ritz, Swiss cow herder who later created hotels bearing his name

You have offered to trade us an apple for an orchard. We do not do that in this country.
–John F. Kennedy

Entrepreneurs are simply those who understand that there is little difference between obstacle and opportunity and are able to turn both to their advantage.
–Victor Kiam, CEO, Remington

If you spend money on it, it's a hobby; if you make money on it, it's a business.

The business executive is by profession a decision maker. Uncertainty is his opponent. Overcoming it is his mission. Whether the outcome is a consequence of luck or of wisdom, the moment of decision is without doubt the most creative and critical event in the life of the executive. *–John McDonald*

Beware of little expenses: A small leak will sink a ship. *–Benjamin Franklin*

Working people have a greatness. Given reasonable leadership they are all too willing to follow, do what is asked of them, and give their best to their employers. They are people. They are complex. They are not willing to be treated like indentured servants. Good business leadership can create and generate the work spirit, the wish to cooperate.
–Arthur E. Imperatore, Chairman of the board, APA Transport Corp.

Excellent firms don't believe in excellence—only in constant improvement and constant change. *–Tom Peters*

A business was failing and a consultant was asked to make a survey....He recommended: "Start advertising, and use three media: radio, direct mail, and courtesy. The first two will cost money. The third is free, but it is the most important."

The secret of business is to know something that nobody else knows.

–Aristotle Onassis

And while I at length debate and beat the bush, there shall step in other men and catch the birds. *–John Heywood*

If the profession you have chosen has some unexpected inconveniences, console yourself that no profession is without them, and that all of the perplexities of business are softness compared with the vacancy of idleness. *–Samuel Johnson*

A message for businessmen: "Whatever happens, never happens by itself."

–Sally Rand

I don't meet competition. I crush it. *–Charles Revson*

I want workers to go home at night and say, "I built that car."

–Pahr G. Gyllenhammar, Chairman, Volvo

A friend said to a man who had a frankfurter stand by the side of the road, "If you put up a sign advertising your stand a mile up the road so people see it before they get here, they might be influenced to stop." The man put up the sign and it worked; so as time went on he put up more signs further and further away on the road, and more and more people bought the frankfurters and the owner was able to send his son to the finest university.

When the son returned he said, "You're spending too much money on your advertising. You don't need all those signs." So the father took down some of the signs; the business went down a little, but so did the expense for advertising. With less business, they decided to cut down a little more on the advertising, and the business went down a little more, until finally they were back to a little frankfurter stand without any signs on the road at all.

...If you are quiet about your business, your business is apt to be quiet, too.

The smaller the role of marketing, the greater the possibility that the firm operates its marketing activities on a project, crisis, and fragmented basis.

–Joel R. Evans and Barry Berman

Doing business without advertising is like winking at a girl in the dark. You know what you are doing, but nobody else does. *–Stuart Henderson Britt*

In some advertising, the selling message ends with a period. In other advertising, the selling message ends with a sale. In either, it costs the advertiser just as much to run a poor ad—as it does to run a good one. *–Young & Rubicam, Inc.*

The faults of advertising are only those common to all human institutions. If advertising speaks to a thousand in order to influence one, so does the church. And if it encourages people to live beyond their means, so does matrimony. Good times, bad times, there will always be advertising. In good times, people want to advertise; in bad times, they have to. *–Bruce Barton, chairman, Batten, Barton, Durstine, & Osborne*

A good manager is a man who isn't worried about his own career but rather the careers of those who work for him....Don't worry about yourself. Take care of those who work for you and you'll float to greatness on their achievements.

–H.S.M. Burns, president, Shell Oil Co.

Progress is a continuing effort to make the things we eat, drink and wear as good as they used to be. *–Bill Vaughan*

[Ours is] a program whose basic thesis is not that the system of free private enterprise has failed...but that it has not yet been tried. *–Franklin D. Roosevelt*

A manpower policy should lead us to a society in which every person has full opportunity to develop his—or her—earning powers, where no willing worker lacks a job, and where no useful talent lacks an opportunity. *–Lyndon B. Johnson*

A vice-president in an advertising agency is a "molehill man." A molehill man is a pseudo-busy executive who comes to work at 9 a.m. and finds a molehill on his desk. He has until 5 p.m. to make his molehill into a mountain. An accomplished molehill man will often have his mountain finished even before lunch. *–Fred Allen*

A bad workman never gets a good tool. *–Thomas Fuller*

Let a man practice the profession which he best knows. *–Cicero, c. 50 B.C.E.*

I am rather like a mosquito in a nudist camp; I know what I ought to do, but I don't know where to begin. *–Stephen Bayne*

People will buy anything that's one to a customer. *–Sinclair Lewis*

Any woman who has a career and a family automatically develops something in the way of two personalities, like two sides of a dollar bill, each different in design. But one can complement the other to make a valuable whole. Her problem is to keep one from draining the life from the other. *–Ivy Baker Priest, U.S. Treasurer*

Once upon a time there was a little girl who always said "Thank you" at birthday parties; who called friends of the family "Aunt" Helen and "Uncle" Jim; and who passed out free cookies the day her lemonade stand opened. When this little girl grew up she didn't go to heaven. She went into public relations. And learned that what to her had always been unconscious art is now classified as a science—"the engineering of consent"—worth a hundred a week to her and millions in good will to her clients. *–Mary Anne Guitar*

The business of America is business. *–Calvin Coolidge*

Few people do business well who do nothing else. *–Lord Chesterfield*

Have the mental equipment to do your job, then take the job seriously, yourself not too seriously. *–Francis Willis, U.S. Ambassador to Switzerland*

If I would be a young man again and had to decide how to make my living, I would not try to become a scientist or scholar or teacher. I would rather choose to be a plumber or a peddler, in the hope to find that modest degree of independence still available under present circumstances. *–Albert Einstein*

If you have a job without aggravations, you don't have a job. *–Malcom Forbes*

The harder I work, the luckier I get. *–Samuel Goldwyn*

The worst crime against working people is a company which fails to operate at a profit.
–Samuel Gompers

A young man asked Bernard Baruch if there was a sure way to make a million dollars. Baruch told him that there was one. "All you need to do is purchase a million bags of flour at one dollar and sell them for two dollars each." Apparently the young man took him seriously. He was August Hecker, the founder of a flour mill company that became the largest of its kind.

Most men would feel insulted if it were proposed to employ them in throwing stones over a wall, and then in throwing them back, merely that they might earn their wages. But many are no more worthily employed now. *–Henry David Thoreau*

Some who are not paid what they are worth ought to be glad.

Too many people quit looking for work when they find a job.

Without the element of uncertainty, the bringing off of even the greatest business triumph would be a dull, routine, and eminently unsatisfying affair. *–J. Paul Getty*

When you go to buy use your eyes, not your ears. *–Czech proverb*

Being in your own business is working 80 hours a week so that you can avoid working 40 hours a week for someone else. *–Ramona E.F. Arnett*

Business is never so healthy as when, like a chicken, it must do a certain amount of scratching for what it gets. *–Henry Ford*

When a child smiles, he gives pleasure…so relax. When a business man smiles, he intends to be pleased—so don't relax.

...Courtesy is as important within an organization as in dealing with outsiders.
–Swift and Co.

You can close more business in two months by becoming interested in other people than you can in two years by trying to get people interested in you. *–Dale Carnegie*

There is one major reason why private companies make investments in the developing world: profit. Governments may make investments for political reasons. Companies do it for profit. So, a reasonable greed level is expected.... *–Frank G. Zarb*

I was made to work; if you are equally industrious, you will be equally successful.
–Johann Sebastian Bach

It is naught, it is naught, saith the buyer: but when he is gone his way, then he boasteth.
–The Bible, Proverbs 20:14

He who speaks ill of the mare, will buy her. *–Benjamin Franklin*

The buyer buys for as little as possible; the seller sells for as much as possible. (Emptor emit quam minimo potest, venditor vendit quam maximo potest.) *–Legal Maxim*

My sole inspiration is a telephone call from a producer. *–Cole Porter*

The trouble with the rat race is that even if you win you're still a rat. *–Lily Tomlin*

It is necessary to relax your muscles when you can. Relaxing you brain is fatal.
–Stirling Moss, British racing-car driver

Winston Churchill, in reply to a post-war speech in the House of Commons, said, "The substance of the eminent Socialist gentleman's speech is that making a profit is a sin. It is my belief that the real sin is taking a loss."

The story is told of a multimillionaire who insisted on doing business in a genteel but very shabby office. His lawyer said to him, "A man of your position and resources should really have a better furnished office."
"Why?" asked the multimillionaire. "Everybody will charge me more for what I buy."

Keep thy shop and thy shop will keep thee. *–Benjamin Franklin*

You never get promoted when no one else knows your current job. The best basis for being advanced is to organize yourself out of every job you're put into. Most people are advanced because they're pushed up by the people underneath them rather than pulled up by the top. *–Donald David, former dean, Harvard Business School*

The thing that really worries businesses today is the great number of people still on their payroll who are unemployed.

Put all your eggs in the one basket and—WATCH THAT BASKET *–Mark Twain*

The idea of public relations is that if you lead a horse to water, even if you can't make him drink, maybe you can make him swim.

We have witnessed in modern business the submergence of the individual within the organization, and yet the increase to an extraordinary degree of the power of the individual who happens to control the organization. Most men are individuals no longer so far as their business, its activities, or its moralities are concerned. They are not units but fractions. *–Woodrow Wilson*

It is a great art to know how to sell wind. *–Baltasar Gracian, 1647*

All business sagacity reduces itself in the last analysis to a judicious use of sabotage.
–Thorstein Veblen

Secrecy is the soul of business. *–Spanish proverb*

Education is one of the keys to survival for large corporations in the remaining few years of the twentieth century. We are in transition from an industrial economy to a post-industrial economy where more people are involved in managing information than in producing goods.
–Gordon F. MacFarlane, Chairman and CEO, British Columbia Telephone Co.

Then there was the man whose life was so tied up in his business that his family organized a union so he'd have to meet them around the table.

Quite a few people are already working a four-day week. Trouble is, it takes 'em five or six days to do it. *–Earl Wilson*

Call upon a man of business during hours of business only to transact your business. Then go about your business and give him time to attend to his business.

Country judge, chairman of a committee, President of the U.S.; they are all the same kind of jobs. It is the business of dealing with people. *–Harry S Truman*

There is no such thing as "soft sell" and "hard sell." There is only "smart sell " and "stupid sell."
–Charles Brower

This is the great era of the goof-off, the age of the half-done job. The land from coast to coast has been enjoying a stampede away from responsibility. It is popularized with laundry men who won't iron shirts, with waiters who won't serve, with carpenters who will come around some day maybe, with executives whose mind is on the golf course, with teachers who demand a single salary scale so that achievement cannot be rewarded, with students who take cinch courses.... *–Charles Brower*

I encourage boldness because the danger of our seniority and pension plans tempt a young man to settle in a rut named security rather than find his own rainbow.
–Conrad Hilton

We have gone completely overboard on security. Everything has to be secured, jobs, wages, hours—although the ultimate in security is jail, the slave labor camp and the salt mine. *–Cola Parker, President, National Association of Manufacturers*

In the tiny space of twenty years, we have bred a whole generation...who take it for granted that they will never be out of a job or go a single year without a salary increase.
–K.K. DuVall, President, Chicago Merchandise National Bank

[The way] a young man spends his evenings is a part of that thin area between success and failure. *–Robert R. Young*

This is an industry of ideas and imagination, and what we are selling is hope.
–Steve Mayham, fragrance executive

There is nothing as universal in this world as human thirst....Our market is as big as the world and the people in it.
–Lee Talley, on being elected President of Coca-Cola

The phenomenon I refer to...is the tidal wave of craving for convenience that is sweeping over [us]. Today convenience is the success factor of just about every type of produce and service that is showing steady growth.
–Charles Mortimer, President, General Foods Corporation

One of the symptoms of an approaching nervous breakdown is the belief that one's work is terribly important. *–Bertrand Russell*

Success is that old ABC—ability, breaks, and courage.
–Charles Luckman, manufacturing executive and architect

He who does not teach his son a trade teaches him to be a robber. *–Hebrew proverb*

Creativity is our single product. And heaven help the agency management that does not recognize that fact of life. They may wind up as unemployed as Zeppelin pilots.
–Ernest A. Jones

The merchants will manage commerce the better, the more they are left free to manage for themselves. *–Thomas Jefferson*

A skillful trade is better than an inherited fortune. *–Welsh proverb*

The good workman receives the bread of his labor with boldness; the lazy and careless cannot look his employer in the face. *–St. Clement*

I have no complex about wealth. I have worked hard for my money, producing things people need. I believe that the able industrial leader who creates wealth and employment is more worthy of historical notice than politicians or soldiers. *–John Paul Getty*

You will discover that while the patient wants the best and most modern treatment available, he is also badly in need of the old-fashioned friend that a doctor has always personified and which you must continue to be. In his mind's eye, the patient sees you as in the old paintings or in his real memories—rumpled and kindly, roused from your bed at 3 in the morning to come to his home and pull him through a crisis. But...you will treat him in the clinic or the hospital whenever possible because the care you can give is far better in those facilities. You will try to avoid night calls because you know you can diagnose better with your eyes open. *–Dr. Gunnar Gundersen*

Their dedication is to competitive creativity—a deep desire within the consciousness of man to create something better today than yesterday's best.
–John Orr Young, on what makes an advertising agency great

The only thing that matters is caring, deep caring....The way to make your plans and your products and your themes and your campaigns and your shows and your letters and your programs more solid, more effective, is to go back to Main Street, your memory source of the things that are deepest and truest and greatest. Be the man or the woman you have it in you to be—and you won't be false to Main Street.
–Jean Rindlaub, Vice President, Batten, Barton, Durstine & Osborn

The growth of bigness has resulted in ruthless sacrifices of human values. The disappearance of free enterprise has submerged the individual in the impersonal corporation. When a nation of shopkeepers is transformed into a nation of clerks, enormous spiritual sacrifices are made.
–William O. Douglas, Supreme Court Associate Justice

The dinosaur's eloquent lesson is that if some bigness is good, an overabundance of bigness is not necessarily better.
–Eric Johnson, President, U.S. Chamber of Commerce

Business more than any other occupation is a continual dealing with the future; it is a continual calculation, an instinctive exercise in foresight. *–Henry R. Luce*

In many businesses, today will end at five o'clock. Those bent on success, however, make today last from yesterday right through tomorrow.
–Lawrence H. Martin, Boston banker

People who work sitting down get paid more than people who work standing up.
–Ogden Nash

Your mental health will be better if you have lots of fun outside of that office.
–Dr. William Menninger

A perfume manufacturer who ran out of superlatives and phrases to describe his product finally used this phrase in his advertising: "As we could not improve our product, we improved the box."

Those who scorn business never say it should not exist—rather that it should not exist for profit, but simply to do more for more people and be better and better at doing it. Being better is the eternal pursuit of the businessman. In fact, it might be easy to demonstrate that without the striving of business for an earned profit, there could be no "better."

–Anonymous

The marvels of modern technology include the development of a soda can which, when discarded, will last forever, and a $7,000 car which, when properly cared for, will rust out in two or three years. ***–Paul Harwitz***

The man who has a trade may go anywhere. ***–Spanish proverb***

Jack of all trades and master of none. ***–Maria Edgeworth***

We are all apprentices in a craft where no one ever becomes a master.

–Ernest Hemingway

The gambling known as business looks with austere disfavor on the business known as gambling. ***–Ambrose Bierce***

Do not let what you cannot do interfere with what you can do.

–John Wooden, former UCLA basketball coach

Polishing the client's apple is no way to improve his advertising. Polishing a good idea is. And polishing. And polishing. Until good becomes better. And better becomes best.

–Young & Rubicam, Inc.

You're only as good as the people you hire. ***–Ray Kroc***

One's lifework, I have learned, grows with the working and the living. Serve others as if your life depended on it, and the first thing you know, you'll have made a life out of it. A good life, too.

In war, you win or lose, live or die—and the difference is just an eyelash.

–General Douglas MacArthur

Coming together is a beginning; keeping together is progress; working together is success. ***–Henry Ford***

Never tell people how to do things. Tell them what to do and they will surprise you with their ingenuity. ***–George S. Patton***

I believe that the true road to preeminent success in any line is to make yourself master of that line. ***–Andrew Carnegie***

Money

Wealth, Prosperity, Resourcefulness

Thousands upon thousands are yearly brought into a state of real poverty by their great anxiety not to be thought poor. *–William Cobbett*

We forget what gives money its value—that someone exchanged work for it. *–Neal O'Hara*

Make all you can, save all you can, give all you can. *–John Wesley*

Don't knock the rich. When did a poor person give you a job? *–Dr. Laurence J. Peter*

The safe way to double your money is to fold it over once and put it in your pocket. *–Frank "Kin" Hubbard*

Annual income twenty pounds, annual expenditure nineteen six, result happiness. Annual income twenty pounds, annual expenditure twenty pound ought and six, result misery. *–Charles Dickens, David Copperfield*

One of the hardest things to teach our children about money matters is that it does. *–William Randolph Hearst*

After the first million, it doesn't matter. You can only eat three meals a day—I tried eating four and I got sick. You can't sleep in more than one bed at night. Maybe I have twenty suits, but I can only wear one at a time, and I can't use more than two shirts a day. *–Joseph Hirshhorn, multimillionaire*

We all have the means to become prosperous. We have to find the balance between our wealth and our needs. *–Robert Bourassa*

The trick is to make sure you don't die waiting for prosperity to come. *–Lee Iacocca*

Money is like muck, not good unless spread. *–Francis Bacon, 1625*

Many enjoy a feeling of wealth no matter how little money they have. Wealth well used is a delight to observe; wealth unused is sad to see. Wealth...is not in the having, but in the using.

I was born into it and there was nothing I could do about it. It was there, like air or food or any other element....The only question with wealth is what you do with it. *–John D. Rockefeller, Jr.*

Our child will not be raised in tissue paper!...We don't want her to even hear the word princess. *–Juliana, Princess of the Netherlands, on engaging a nurse for her first child*

We should not be like misers, who never enjoy what they have but only bewail what they lose. *–Plutarch*

Money is like manure. If you spread it around, it does a lot of good. But if you pile it up in one place, it stinks like hell. *–Clint Murchison, Jr.*

The human race has had long experience and a fine tradition in surviving adversity. But we now face a task for which we have little experience, the task of surviving prosperity.
–Alan Gregg

Funny how a dollar can look so big when you take it to church, and so small when you take it to the store. *–Frank Clark*

If ignorance paid dividends, most...could make a fortune out of what they don't know about economics. *–Luther Hodges, Secretary of Commerce*

Alexander Woollcott went to visit Moss Hart at his estate in Pennsylvania. Hart had every inch of the grounds completely landscaped. He asked Woollcott what he thought of the place. His answer: "Well, it only shows what God could do if He had enough money."

If you want to know whether you are destined to be a success or a failure in life, you can easily find out. The test is simple and it is infallible. Are you able to save money? If not, drop out. You will lose....You will lose, as sure as you live. The seed of success is not in you. *–James J. Hill*

There is nothing in saving money. The thing to do with it is to put it back into yourself, into your work, into the thing that is important, into whatever you are so much interested in that it is more important than money. *–Henry Ford*

Money can't buy happiness, but it certainly doesn't discourage it.

Necessity never made a good bargain.

There are more fools among buyers than among sellers. *–French proverb*

True luck consists not in holding the best of the cards at the table: Luckiest is he who knows just when to rise and go home. *–John Hay*

I don't think you can spend yourself rich. *–George Humphrey*

Advice given by George S. Clason in *The Richest Man in Babylon*:

I found the road to wealth when I decided that a part of all I earned was mine to keep. And so will you. Budget thy expenses that thou mayest have coins to pay for thy necessities, to pay for thy enjoyments and to gratify thy worthwhile desires without spending more than nine-tenths of thy earnings.

That what each of us calls our "necessary expenses" will always grow to equal our incomes unless we protest to the contrary. Confuse not...necessary expenses with...desires.

Study carefully, before parting with thy treasure....Be not misled by thy own romantic desires to make wealth rapidly.

Consult with wise men. Secure the advice of those experienced in the profitable handling of gold. Let their wisdom protect thy treasure....

...Humans in the throes of great emotions are not safe risks for the gold lender.

In order to get a loan, you must first prove you don't need it.

If you think the world owes you a living—hustle out and collect it.

A status symbol is anything you can't afford, but did. *–Harold Coffin*

If a man runs after money, he's money-mad: if he keeps it he's a capitalist; if he spends it, he's a playboy; if he doesn't get it, he's a ne'er-do-well; if he doesn't try to get it, he lacks ambition. If he gets it without working for it, he's a parasite; and if he accumulates it after a lifetime of hard work, people call him a fool who never got anything out of life.

–Vic Oliver

Americans have an abiding belief in their ability to control reality by purely material means. Hence...airline insurance replaces the fear of death with the comforting prospect of cash. *–Cecil Beaton*

Personally I do not feel that any amount can properly be called a surplus as long as the nation is in debt. I prefer to think of such an item as a reduction on our children's inherited mortgage. *–Dwight D. Eisenhower*

Old men are always advising young men to save money. That is bad advice. Don't save every nickel. Invest in yourself. I never saved a dollar until I was 40 years old.

–Henry Ford

A light purse is a heavy curse. *–Benjamin Franklin*

Gertrude Berg of CBS Television, recalls: I always remember the first script that I wrote [on The Goldbergs]. Jake came home for supper with a little ambitious bug in his brain. He wanted to go into business and he told this to Molly and Molly had some money she had put away anticipating just such a time and she gave it to him, and as they sat down to the dinner table he said to her, "Molly, darling, some day we will be eating out of golden plates," and Molly turned to him and said, "Jake, darling, will it taste any better?" I always remember that.

Great is he who uses earthenware as if it were silver; no less great is he who uses silver as if it were earthenware. *–Seneca, c. 63*

When Benjamin Franklin was seven years old, a visitor gave him some small change. Later, seeing another boy playing with a whistle, young Benjamin gave the boy all his money for it. He played the whistle all over the house, enjoying it until he discovered that he'd given four times as much as the whistle was worth. Instantly, the whistle lost its charm. As he grew older, Franklin generalized this principle. When he saw a man neglecting his family or business for political popularity, or a miser giving up friendships for the sake of accumulating wealth, he'd say, "He pays too much for his whistle."

–Thomas Fleming

Asked when a wealthy man has enough money to be happy, J.P. Morgan replied, "When he has made the next million."

One man's wealth is another man's pocket money.

A billion here, a billion there—pretty soon it adds up to real money.

–Everett Dirksen, speaking to fellow Senators on government spending

Willful waste brings woeful want. *–Thomas Fuller*

Mention money and the whole world is silent. *–German proverb*

Why is there so much month left at the end of the money?

Always live within your income, even if you have to borrow money to do so.
–Josh Billings

There's no money in poetry, but then there's no poetry in money either.
–Robert Graves

Money itself isn't the primary factor in what one does. A person does things for the sake of accomplishing something. Money generally follows. *–Colonel Henry Crown*

For every talent that poverty has stimulated it has blighted a hundred.
–John W. Gardner

Increased means and increased leisure are the two civilizers of man.
–Benjamin Disraeli, 1872

No men living are more worthy to be trusted than those who toil up from poverty...
–Abraham Lincoln

An elderly man said, "Thank God for my sons. My first is a doctor, the second a lawyer, the third a chemist, the fourth an artist, and the fifth a writer." He was asked, "What do you do?" He replied, "I have a dry goods store. Not a big one, but I manage to support them all." *–Gordon Dakins*

I've never been poor, only broke. Being poor is a frame of mind. Being broke is only a temporary situation. *–Mike Todd, theatrical entrepreneur*

Just about the time you think you can make both ends meet, somebody moves the ends.
–Pansy Penner

No one is ever hanged with money in his pocket. *–Russian proverb*

Sam Levenson often describes the funny and warm incidents of growing up in a family that was hard pressed for a decent income. He explains it by saying: "We didn't know we were poor."

There is inherited wealth in this country and also inherited poverty.
–John F. Kennedy

A man who shows me his wealth is like the beggar who shows me his poverty; they are both looking for alms, the rich man for the alms of my envy, the poor man for the alms of my guilt. *–Ben Hecht*

The share-the-wealth movement appeals the most to those with the least to share.

George Raft earned and disposed of about ten million dollars in the course of his career. "Part of the loot went for gambling," he explained, "part for horses, and part for women. The rest I spent foolishly."

There is no dignity quite so impressive, and no independence quite so important, as living within your means. *–Calvin Coolidge*

Wealth is not his that has it, but his that enjoys it. *–Benjamin Franklin*

Money and time are the heaviest burdens of life, and the unhappiest of all mortals are those who have more of either than they know how to use.

Our economy is the result of millions of decisions we all make every day about producing, earning, saving, investing, and spending. *–Dwight D. Eisenhower*

So often we rob tomorrow's memories by today's economies. *–John Mason Brown*

The chief value of money lies in the fact that one lives in a world in which it is overestimated. *–H.L. Mencken*

In suggesting gifts: Money is appropriate, and one size fits all.
–William Randolph Hearst

There are a handful of people money won't spoil and we count ourselves among them.
–Mignon McLaughlin

Never steal more than you actually need, for the possession of surplus money leads to extravagance, foppish attire, frivolous thought. *–Dalton Trumbo, on stealing*

The men who have earned five million dollars have been so busy earning it that they have not had time to collect it; and the men who have collected five million dollars have been so busy collecting it that they have not had time to earn it.
–William Jennings Bryan

It requires a great deal of boldness and a great deal of caution to make a great fortune, and when you have got it, it requires ten times as much wit to keep it.
–Ralph Waldo Emerson

In a country well governed, poverty is something to be ashamed of.
In a country badly governed, wealth is something to be ashamed of.
–Confucius, c. 500 B.C.E.

The rich who are unhappy are worse off than the poor who are unhappy; for the poor, at least, can cling to the hopeful delusion that more money would solve their problems....
–Sydney J. Harris

Fortune does not change men. It only unmasks them.

The reason the Yankees never lay an egg is because they don't operate on chicken feed.
–Dan Parker

Money has become the grand test of virtue. *–George Orwell*

A man is never so on trial as in the moment of excessive good fortune.
–Lew Wallace, Ben-Hur

I have no complex about wealth. I have worked hard for my money, producing things people need. I believe that the able industrial leader who creates wealth and employment is more worthy of historical notice than politicians or soldiers. *–J. Paul Getty*

There is none so poor as he who knows not the joy of what he has.

It's a terribly hard job to spend a billion dollars and get your money's worth.
–George Humphrey

There are people who have money and people who are rich. *–Coco Chanel*

I am not fond of money, or anxious about it. But, though every day makes me less and less eager for wealth, every day shows me more and more strongly how necessary a competence is to a man who desires to be either great or useful.

–T.B. Macaulay: Letter to Hannah M. Macaulay, Aug. 17, 1833

Whoso has sixpence is sovereign...over all men; commands cooks to feed him, philosophers to teach him, kings to mount guard over him—to the length of sixpence.

–Thomas Carlyle, 1836

The more you get, the more you got to take care of. *–Alice K. Dormann*

How did a fool and his money get together in the first place?

Money, material though it be, does lie at the base of the most useful work you do. In itself nothing, it is the basis of much of the best effort which can be made for spiritual purposes. *–Arthur J. Balfour*

Money begets money. *–Giovanni Torriano, 1666*

...Money can beget money, and its offspring can beget more. *–Benjamin Franklin*

When a feller says it ain't the money but the principle of the thing, it's the money.

–Abe Martin

Thanks a thousand. *–Nelson Rockefeller*

After Clarence Darrow had solved a client's legal problem, the client asked, "How can I ever show my appreciation?" The lawyer replied, "My good friend, ever since the Phoenicians invented money, there has been only one answer to that question."

Money: a blessing that is of no advantage to us excepting when we part with it.

–Ambrose Bierce

Lack of money is the root of all evil. *–George Bernard Shaw*

October. This is one of the peculiarly dangerous months to speculate in stocks. The others are July, January, September, April, November, May, March, June, December, August, and February. *–Mark Twain*

When prosperity comes, do not use all of it. *–Confucius*

A gentleman...is one who has money enough to do what every fool would do if he could afford it:...consume without producing. *–George Bernard Shaw*

Money-giving is a good criterion of a person's mental health. Generous people are rarely mentally ill people. *–Dr. Karl Menninger*

Learn to give
Money to colleges while you live.
Don't be silly and think you'll try
To bother the colleges, when you die,
with codicil this, and codicil that,
That Knowledge may starve
while Law grows fat... *–Oliver Wendell Holmes*

One day a rich man of a miserly disposition visited a rabbi, who took him by the hand and led him to a window. "Look out there," he said. "What do you see?" "I see men and women and little children," the man replied.

Again the rabbi took him to a mirror. "What do you see now?" "I see myself," was the answer.

"Behold, in the window there is glass and the mirror is glass also. But the glass of the mirror is covered with silver. No sooner is silver added than you cease to see others and see only yourself."

Let me tell you about the very rich. They are different from you and me. They possess and enjoy early, and it does something to them, makes them soft where we are hard, and cynical where we are trustful, in a way that, unless you were born rich, it is very difficult to understand. *–F. Scott Fitzgerald*

A man builds a fine house; and now he has a master, and a task for life: he is to furnish, watch, show it, and keep it in repair the rest of his days. *–Ralph Waldo Emerson*

What a lot of people are saving for a rainy day is somebody else's umbrella.
–Caroline Clark in the Saturday Evening Post

The impoverished son of an impoverished family was asked how he could have managed to live so pennilessly for so long. "You must remember," he said, "I had a head start."

Costly thy habit as thy purse can buy,
But not express'd in fancy; rich, not gaudy;
For the apparel oft proclaims the man. *–Shakespeare, "Hamlet"*

LEARNING

Experience, Education, Discipline, Training

There is no lack of opportunity for learning among us. What is lacking is a respect for it...an honest respect such as we now have for technical competence or business success....We honor learning, but do not believe in it....Rather than submit to it ourselves, we hire substitutes; rather than cultivate our own brains, we pick theirs. We spend as much time and energy on short-cuts to learning and imitations of learning as we do on learning itself. *–Whitney Griswold*

It wasn't until quite late in life that I discovered how easy it is to say, "I don't know."
–Somerset Maughm

The farther backward you can look, the farther forward you are likely to see.
–Winston Churchill

What you don't know can hurt you.

Men are wise in proportion not to their experience but to their capacity for experience.
–James Boswell, 1791

Every child is an artist. The problem is how to remain an artist after growing up.
–Pablo Picasso

A college education seldom hurts a man if he's willing to learn a little something after he graduates.

I am still learning. (Ancora imparo.) *–Favorite saying of Michelangelo*

Experience is a good school. But the fees are high. *–Heinrich Heine*

Learning is acquired by reading books; but the much more necessary learning, the knowledge of the world, is only to be acquired by reading men, and studying all the various editions of them. *–Lord Chesterfield, 1752*

I cannot live without books. *–Thomas Jefferson*

Books are good enough in their way, but they are a mighty bloodless substitute for life.
–Robert Louis Stevenson

What we learn after we know it all, is what counts.
We know so many things that aren't so.
A little learning is a dangerous thing;
Drink deep, or taste not the Pierian spring:
There shallow draughts intoxicate the brain,
And drinking largely sobers us again. *–Alexander Pope: 1711*

Judith Swanson tells about how she learned a great lesson:

From the day we entered the ninth-grade health class, one blackboard was covered with the names and locations of the major bones and muscles of the human body. The diagram stayed on the board throughout the term, although the teacher never referred to it. The day of the final exam, we came to class to find the board wiped clean. The sole test question was: "Name and locate every major bone and muscle in the human body."

The class protested in unison: "We never studied that!"

"That's no excuse," said the teacher. "The information was there for months." After we struggled with the test for a while, he collected the papers and tore them up. "Always remember," he told us, "that education is more than just learning what you are told."

What school, college, or lecture bring to men depends on what men bring to carry it home in. *–Ralph Waldo Emerson*

If you spend your time playing bridge, you will be a good bridge player; if you spend it in reading, discussing, and thinking of things that matter, you will be an educated person. *–Sydney Smith, President, University of Toronto*

Men learn while they teach. *–Seneca, c. 63*

Experience is the name everyone gives to their mistakes. *–Oscar Wilde*

When you're through learning, you're through.
–Vernon Law, pitcher, Pittsburgh Pirates

Asked what he thought should be taught to children first, Samuel Johnson replied that "it is no matter what you teach them first, any more than what leg you shall put into your breeches first. Sir, you may stand disputing which is best to put in first, but in the mean time your breech is bare. Sir, while you are considering which of two things you should teach your child first, another boy has learnt them both."

Knowledge and timber shouldn't be much used till they are seasoned.
–Oliver Wendell Holmes

A young man must let his ideas grow, not be continually rooting them up to see how they are getting on. *–William McFee*

It is the province of knowledge to speak and it is the privilege of wisdom to listen.
–Oliver Wendell Holmes

A new graduate rushed out of his college on graduation day and shouted, "Here I am, world. I have my A.B.!" The world answered: "Sit down, young man, and I'll teach you the rest of the alphabet."

A man could retire nicely in his old age if he could dispose of his experience for what it cost him.

If I had my life to live again, I'd make the same mistakes, only sooner.
–Tallulah Bankhead

If you plan for a decade, plant trees. If you plan for a century, teach the children.

Professionals built the Titanic—amateurs the ark. *–Frank Pepper*

Every man is a damn fool for at least five minutes every day; wisdom consists in not exceeding the limit. *–Elbert Hubbard*

We ought to hear at least one little song every day, read a good poem, see a first-rate painting, and if possible speak a few sensible words. *–Johann Von Goethe*

History is the rear view mirror on the road of life.

When you reread a classic you do not see more in the book than you did before; you see more in you than there was before. *–Clifton Fadiman*

The test and the use of man's education is that he finds pleasure in the exercise of his mind. *–Jacques Barzun*

You can learn good manners from the bad manners of others.

It has been said that we have not had the three R's in America, we have had the six R's: remedial readin', remedial 'ritin', and remedial 'rithmetic. *–Robert M. Hutchins*

The latter part of a wise man's life is taken up in curing the follies, prejudices, and false opinions he contracted in the former. *–Jonathan Swift, 1706*

Modern cynics and skeptics...see no harm in paying those to whom they entrust the minds of their children a smaller wage than is paid to those to whom they entrust the care of their plumbing. *–John F. Kennedy*

Learning makes the wise wiser and the fool more foolish. *–John Ray, 1670*

Every citizen of this country, whether he pounds nails, raises corn, designs rockets or writes poetry, should be taught to know and love his American heritage; to use the language well; to understand the physical universe, and to enjoy the arts. The dollars he gains in the absence of [this] enlightenment will be earned in drudgery and spent in ignorance. *–Calvin Gross, superintendent, New York City public schools*

None so deaf as those who will not hear. *–English proverb*

For my confirmation, I didn't get a watch and my first pair of long pants, like most Lutheran boys. I got a telescope. My mother thought it would make the best gift.
–Wernher Von Braun, rocket scientist

A guidance counselor who has made a fetish of security, or who has unwittingly surrendered his thinking to economic determinism, may steer a youth away from his dream of becoming a poet, an artist, a musician, or any other of thousands of things, because it offers no security, it does not pay well, there are no vacancies, it has no "future." Among all the tragic consequences of depression and war, this suppression of personal self-expression through one's life work is among the most poignant. *–Henry Wriston*

Teaching is not a lost art, but the regard for it is a lost tradition.
–Jacques Barzun, dean, Columbia University

I am quite sure that in the hereafter she will take me by the hand and lead me to my proper seat. I always have a great reverence for teachers...both lay and clerical....
–Bernard Baruch, recalling one of his early teachers

A Socrates in every classroom.
–Whitney Griswold, President, Yale University,
on his ambitious standard for building a faculty

Wisdom consists in knowing what to do with what you know.

We have two ears and only one tongue in order that we may hear more and speak less.
–Diogenes Laertius, about 150 B.C.E.

Learn to unlearn. *–Benjamin Disraeli*

To be fond of learning is to be at the gate of knowledge. *–Chinese proverb*

When you read, read! Too many students just half read....The art of memory is the art of understanding. *-Roscoe Pound, dean emeritus, Harvard Law School*

The longer the island of knowledge, the longer the shore line of wonder.
–Ralph W. Sockman

It has been said that the only thing we learn from history is that we do not learn.
–Chief Justice Earl Warren, in the eulogy of John F. Kennedy

The aims of pure basic science, unlike those of applied science, are neither fast flowing nor pragmatic. The quick harvest of applied science is the useable process, the medicine, the machine. The shy fruit of pure science is Understanding.
–Lincoln Barnett, science writer, on Einstein's completion
of the mathematical formula for the Unified Field Theory

Old age is like climbing a mountain. You climb from ledge to ledge. The higher you get, the more tired and breathless you become, but your views become more intensive.
–Ingmar Bergman

Nothing ever becomes real till it is experienced. *–John Keats*

Memory is the mother of all wisdom. *–Aeschylus, 5th Century B.C.E.*

Each day I learn more
Than I teach;
I learn that half knowledge of another's life
Leads to false judgment;
I learn that there is a surprising kinship
In human nature;
I learn that it's a wise father who knows his own son;
I learn that what we expect we get;
I learn that there's more good than evil in this world;
That age is a question of spirit;
That youth is the best of life
No matter how numerous its years;
I learn how much there is to learn. *–Virginia Church*

Knowledge is the food of the soul. *–Plato*

Learning is a treasure which will follow its owner everywhere. *–Chinese proverb*

We can draw lessons from the past, but we cannot live in it. *–Lyndon B. Johnson*

The trouble with experience is that it sometimes teaches you too late.

Experience is the dividend you get from your mistakes.

One thorn of experience is worth a whole wilderness of warning.
–James Russell Lowell

...A page of history is worth a volume of logic. *–Oliver Wendell Holmes*

I still find each day too short for all the thoughts I want to think, all the walks I want to take, all the books I want to read, and all the friends I want to see. The longer I live the more my mind dwells upon the beauty and the wonder of the world.
–John Burroughs

He is educated who knows how to find out what he doesn't know. *–George Simmel*

A person who has had a bull by the tail once has learned 60 or 70 times as much as a person who hasn't. *–Mark Twain*

A man of learning is never bored. *–Jean Paul Richter*

The great difficulty in education is to get experience out of ideas. *–George Santayana*

You don't set a fox to watching the chickens just because he has a lot of experience in the hen house. *–Harry S Truman,*
on Vice President Nixon's candidacy for the presidency in 1960

Learning is ever young, even in old age. *–Aeschylus, c. 490 B.C.E.*

My definition of an educated man is the fellow who knows the right thing to do at the time it has to be done....You can be sincere and still be stupid. *–Charles F. Kettering*

Education is a kind of continuing dialogue, and a dialogue assumes, in the nature of the case, different points of view... *–Robert M. Hutchins*

A man is never too old to learn. *–Thomas Middleton, Mayor of Quinborough, 1651*

Experience is not what happens to you; it is what you do with what happens to you. *–Aldous Huxley*

The secret of education lies in respecting the pupil. *–Ralph Waldo Emerson*

A half century of living should put a good deal into a woman's face besides a few wrinkles and some unwelcome folds around the chin. *–Frances Parkinson Keyes*

...There is a case for keeping wrinkles. They are the long-service stripes earned in the hard campaign of life....Wrinkles are the dried-up riverbeds of a life-time's tears. Wrinkles are the nostalgic remnants of a million smiles. Wrinkles are...crannies and footholds on the smooth visage of life on which man can cling and gain some comfort and security. *–Daily Mail, London, Jan. 20, 1961*

All a child's life depends on the ideal it has of its parents. Destroy that and everything goes—morals, behavior, everything. Absolute trust in someone else is the essence of education. *–E. M. Forster*

You send your child to the schoolmaster, but 'tis the schoolboys who educate him. *–Ralph Waldo Emerson*

Work'em hard, play'em hard, feed'em up to the nines, and send'em to bed so tired that they are asleep before their heads are on the pillow.
–Frank Boyden of Deerfield Academy, on how to run a successful prep school.

A book is like a garden carried in the pocket. *–Arab proverb*

All that mankind has done, thought, gained or been...is lying as in magic preservation in the pages of books. *–Thomas Carlyle*

Age is only a number, a cipher for the records. A man can't retire his experience. He must use it.... *–Bernard Baruch*

To exclude from positions of trust and command all those below the age of 44 would have kept Jefferson from writing the Declaration of Independence, Washington from commanding the Continental Army, Madison from fathering the Constitution, Hamilton from serving as Secretary of the Treasury, Clay from being elected Speaker of the House, and Christopher Columbus from discovering America.
–Senator John F. Kennedy, replying to ex-presidenzt Harry Truman's assertion that he might not be mature enough for the presidency

The best cosmetic in the world is an active mind that is always finding something new. *–Mary Meek Atkeson*

Reading is one of our bad habits....We read, most of the time, not because we wish to instruct ourselves, not because we long to have our feelings touched and our imagination fired, but...because we have time to spare. *–Aldous Huxley*

I do not know what I may appear to the world. But, to myself, I seem to have been only like a boy playing on the seashore, diverting myself in now and then finding a smoother pebble or a prettier shell than the ordinary, whilst the great ocean of truth lay all undiscovered before me. *–Sir Isaac Newton, among his last words.*

A good scare is worth more to a man than good advice. *–E.E. Howe*

The enormous multiplication of books in every branch of knowledge is one of the greatest evils of this age...it presents one of the most serious obstacles to the acquisition of correct information, by throwing in the reader's way piles of lumber in which he must painfully grope for...scraps of useful matter.... *–Edgar Allen Poe*

He that would govern others, first should be the master of himself.
–Philip Massinger, 1624

The close observer soon discovers that the teacher's task is not to implant facts but to place the subject to be learned in front of the learner and, through sympathy, emotion, imagination, and patience, to awaken in the learner the restless drive for answers and insights which enlarge the personal life and give it meaning. *–Nathan Pusey*

A wise man will hear, and will increase in learning. *–The Bible, Proverbs 1:5*

The growth of wisdom may be gauged accurately by the decline of ill-temper.
–Freidrich Nietzche

If you have knowledge, let others light their candles at it. *–Thomas Fuller*

Wisdom is the reward you get for a lifetime of listening when you'd have preferred to talk. *–Doug Larson*

An optimist is a person who sees a green light everywhere. The pessimist sees only the red light. But the truly wise person is color blind. *–Albert Schweitzer*

Samuel Taylor Coleridge was involved in a discussion about religion. The other person believed that children should not be given formal religious education of any kind. They would then be free to select their own religion when they were old enough to decide. Coleridge did not bother to debate the point, but invited the man to see his rather neglected garden.

"Do you call this a garden?" asked his visitor. "There are nothing but weeds here."

"Well, you see," said Coleridge, "I did not wish to infringe on the liberty of the garden in any way. I was just giving the garden a chance to express itself and choose its own production."

The clouds may drop down titles and estates; wealth may seek us; but wisdom must be sought. *–Edward Young, 1744*

In proportion as the structure of a government gives force to public opinion, it is essential that public opinion should be enlightened. *–George Washington*

Where the press is free and every man able to read, all is safe. *–Thomas Jefferson*

Youth is...sure the rules have changed. Age is sure they haven't. Youth feels it knows how far it can go. Age is deeply aware of the danger. Youth feels it can always apply the brakes in time to save itself. Age knows it isn't always so. *–Richard L. Evans*

The differences in human life depend, for the most part, not on what men do, but upon the meaning and purpose of their acts. All are born, all die, all lose their loved ones, nearly all marry and nearly all work, but the significance of these acts may vary enormously. The same physical act may be in one situation vulgar and in another holy. The same work may be elevating or degrading....Wisdom about life consists in taking the inevitable ventures which are the very stuff of common existence, and glorifying them.

–Elton Trueblood

We do not succeed in changing things according to our desire, but gradually our desire changes. The situation that we hoped to change because it was intolerable becomes unimportant. We have not managed to surmount the obstacle, as we were absolutely determined to do, but life has taken us round it, led us past it, and...if we turn round to gaze at the remote past, we can barely catch sight of it, so imperceptible has it become.

–Marcel Proust

Wise men don't need advice. Fools won't take it. *–Benjamin Franklin*

To everyone, life in the first person is a mystery.

Recognizing what we have done in the past is a recognition of ourselves. By conducting a dialogue with our past, we are searching how to go forward. *–Kiyoko Takeda*

The only fool bigger than the person who knows it all is the person who argues with him.

I have walked with people whose eyes are full of light but who see nothing in sea or sky, nothing in city streets, nothing in books. It were far better to sail forever in the night of blindness with sense, and feeling, and mind, than to be content with the mere act of seeing. The only lightless dark is the night of darkness in ignorance and insensibility.

–Helen Keller

Learning by study must be won;
'Twas ne'er entail'd from son to son. *–John Gay, 1727*

The heart has its reasons, which reason cannot know. *–Blaise Pascal*

He who remembers from day to day what he has yet to learn, and from month to month what he has learned already, may be said to have a love of learning. *–Confucius*

Pain makes man think. Thought makes man wise. Wisdom makes life endurable.

–John Patrick

Wear your learning, like your watch, in a private pocket; and do not pull it out and strike it, merely to show that you have one. If you are asked what o'clock it is, tell it; but do not proclaim it hourly and unasked, like the watchman.

-Lord Chesterfield: Letter to his son, 1748

Train up a child in the way he should go: and when he is old, he will not depart from it.

–The Bible, Proverbs, 22:6

Learning without wisdom is a load of books on an ass's back. *–Japanese proverb*

Experience is a hard teacher because she gives the test first, the lesson afterwards.

–Vernon Law, pitcher, Pittsburgh Pirates

The greatest dangers to liberty lurk in insidious encroachment of men of zeal, well-meaning but without understanding.

–Louis D. Brandeis, Supreme Court Associate Justice, 1928

We do not remember days, we remember moments. *–Cesare Pavese*

Education is the ability to listen to almost anything without losing your temper or your self-confidence. *–Robert Frost*

My advice to young players is to see as much good tennis as possible and then attempt to copy the outstanding strokes of the former stars. *–William T. Tilden, player & coach*

The simplest schoolboy is now aware of truths for which Archimedes would have given his life. *–Ernest Renan, 1883*

That some good can be derived from every event is a better proposition than that everything happens for the best, which it assuredly does not. *–James K. Feibleman*

The library is not a shrine for the worship of books. It is not a temple where literary incense must be burned or where one's devotion to the bound book is expressed in ritual. A library, to modify the famous metaphor of Socrates, should be the delivery room for the birth of ideas—a place where history comes to life. *–Norman Cousins*

A handful of good life is better than a bushel of learning. *–George Herbert, 1640*

Any piece of knowledge I acquire today has a value at this moment exactly proportioned to my skill to deal with it. Tomorrow, when I know more, I recall that piece of knowledge and use it better. *–Mark Van Doren*

...I was still learning when I taught my last class.

–Claude Fuess, on retirement after 40 years as a teacher

One of the wisest things my daddy ever told me was that "so-and-so is a damned smart man, but the fool's got no sense." *–Lyndon B. Johnson*

History not used is nothing, for all intellectual life is action, like practical life, and if you don't use the stuff—well, it might as well be dead. *–Arnold Toynbee*

It would have been too bad to miss our mistakes that taught us so much about living. Just as we enjoyed the terror of the roller coaster when we were kids, we must enjoy the terror of life's errors and mistakes. The challenges we meet are the shapers...of our lives.

"Before you get to the three R's," said Grandpa, "you've got to master the three L's—look, listen and learn."

Never learn to do anything. If you don't learn, you will always find someone else to do it for you. *–Mark Twain*

Some books are to be tasted, others to be swallowed, and some few to be chewed and digested. *–Francis Bacon, 1597*

All books are divisible into two classes: the books of the hour, and the books of all time.

–John Ruskin

How many a man has dated a new era in his life from the reading of a book.

–Henry David Thoreau

Books give not wisdom where was none before,
But where some is, there reading makes it more. *–Sir John Harington, 1613*

Go to school. I tell you to go to school. I'm well known and I made a lot of money and I lost a lot of money. I'd be better off if I had gone to school longer, and so will you.
–Joe Louis, Heavyweight boxing champion

What you bring away from the Bible depends to some extent on what you carry to it.
–Oliver Wendell Holmes

Knowledge begets knowledge. The more I see, the more impressed I am—not with what we know—but with how tremendous the areas are that are as yet unexplored.
–Lt. Col. John H. Glenn, Jr.

...It was in making education not only common to all, but in some sense compulsory on all, that the destiny of the free republics of America was practically settled.
–James Russell Lowell, 1870

The Bible is like a telescope. If a man looks through his telescope, then he sees worlds beyond; but if he looks at his telescope, then he does not see anything but that. The Bible is a thing to be looked through, to see that which is beyond; but most people only look at it; and so they see only the dead letter. *–Phillips Brooks*

Wisdom is ofttimes nearer when we stoop
Than when we soar. *–William Wordsworth*

Training is everything. The peach was once a bitter almond; cauliflower is nothing but cabbage with a college education. *–Mark Twain*

To be conscious that you are ignorant is a great step to knowledge.
–Benjamin Disraeli

School ends, but education doesn't.

Great minds are like eagles, and build their nest in some lofty solitude.
–Arthur Schopenhauer

Knowledge is power. *–Sir Francis Bacon, 1597*

'Tis education forms the common mind:
Just as the twig is bent the tree's inclined. *–Alexander Pope, 1731*

Ignorance is the curse of God,
Knowledge the wing wherewith we fly to heaven.
–William Shakespeare, "Henry VI"

Knowledge is the antidote to fear. *–Ralph Waldo Emerson*

To be proud of knowledge is to be blind with light. *–Benjamin Franklin*

No man really becomes a fool until he stops asking questions. *–Charles P. Steinmetz*

Knowledge is proud that it knows so much;
wisdom is humble that it knows no more. *–William Cowper*

Knowledge is happiness, because to have knowledge—broad deep knowledge—is to know true ends from false, and lofty things from low. To know the thoughts and deeds that have marked man's progress is to feel the great heart-throbs of humanity through the centuries; and if one does not feel in these pulsations a heavenward striving, one must indeed be deaf to the harmonies of life. *–Helen Keller*

Many books require no thought from those who read them, and for a very simple reason; they made no such demand upon those who wrote them. *–Charles Caleb Colton*

College is a storehouse of learning because so little is taken away.

Only the educated are free. *–Epictetus, 1st century*

Education: that which discloses to the wise and disguises from the foolish their lack of understanding. *–Ambrose Bierce*

If you think education is expensive, try ignorance.
–Derek Bok, President, Harvard University

Aristotle was asked, "What is the difference between an educated and an uneducated man?" He replied, "The same difference as between being alive and being dead."

Books are the quietest and most constant of friends; they are the most accessible and wisest of counsellors, and the most patient of teachers. *–Charles W. Eliot*

Books have to be read. It is the only way of discovering what they contain. A few savage tribes eat them, but reading is the only method of assimilation revealed to the West.
–E.M. Forster

...The love of learning, the sequestered nooks,
And all the sweet serenity books. *–Henry Wadsworth Longfellow*

It is rare that one cannot learn from another or from life's experiences, if the effort is made. Perhaps that is the secret of achieving a peaceful society: searching for each other's unique and special knowledge.

Problem Solving

Creativity, Thought, Teamwork

Making up your mind is the hard part—the rest is just pure work.

The second assault on the same problem should come from a totally different direction.
–Tom Hirshfield

Whenever I think, I make a mistake. *–Roger Stevens*

I am enthusiastic over humanity's extraordinary and sometimes very timely ingenuities. If you are in a shipwreck and all the boats are gone, a piano top buoyant enough to keep you afloat may come along and make a fortuitous life preserver. This is not to say, though, that the best way to design a life preserver is in the form of a piano top. I think that we are clinging to a great many piano tops in accepting yesterday's fortuitous contrivings as constituting the only means for solving a given problem.

–R. Buckminster Fuller

I have never seen a bad television program, because I refuse to. God gave me a mind, and a wrist that turns things off. *–Jack Paar*

I have one yardstick by which I test every major problem—and that yardstick is: Is it good for America? *–Dwight D. Eisenhower*

When nobody around you seems to measure up, it's time to check your yardstick.

–Bill Lemley

You may have to fight a battle more than once to win it. *–Margaret Thatcher*

After you've done a thing the same way for two years, look it over carefully. After five years, look at it with suspicion. And after ten years, throw it away and start all over.

–Alfred Edward Perlman

Become a possibilitarian. No matter how dark things seem to be or actually are, raise your sights and see possibilities—always see them, for they're always there.

–Norman Vincent Peale

Sometimes I think it sounds like I walked out of the room and left the typewriter running. *–Gene Fowler, on his own written work*

The invention of I.Q. did a great disservice to creativity in education....Individuality, personality, originality, are too precious to be meddled with by amateur psychiatrists whose patterns for a "wholesome personality" are inevitably their own.

–Joel Hildebrand, professor of chemistry

Many a man has fallen in love with a girl in a light so dim he would not have chosen a suit by it. *–Maurice Chevalier*

Two brothers went to a judge to settle their dispute on the division of the estate left to them by their father. The judge ruled: "Let one brother divide the estate, and let the other brother have first choice."

Writers have two main problems. One is writer's block, when words won't come at all, and the other's logorrhea, when the words come so fast that they hardly get to the wastebasket in time. *–Cecilia Bartholomew*

A new idea is delicate. It can be killed by a sneer or a yawn; it can be stabbed to death by a quip and worried to death by a frown on the right man's brow. *–Charles Brower*

All the really good ideas I ever had came to me while I was milking a cow.

–Grant Wood

The time to repair the roof is when the sun is shining. *–John F. Kennedy*

Brand-new ideas are rare; good new ideas are even rarer.

The best time for planning a book is while you're doing the dishes. ***–Agatha Christie***

Anyone can look for fashion in a boutique or history in a museum. The creative person looks for history in a hardware store and fashion in an airport. ***–Robert Wieder***

When I examine myself and my methods of thought, I come to the conclusion that the gift of fantasy has meant more to me than my talent for absorbing positive knowledge. ***–Albert Einstein***

Mrs. Albert Einstein visited Mount Wilson Observatory in California and pointed to a complex piece of equipment and asked what it was used for. The guide said it was used to determine the shape of the universe. "Oh," she said, not impressed, "my husband uses the back of an old envelope to work that out."

We require from buildings, as from men, two kinds of goodness: first, doing their practical duty well; then that they be graceful and pleasing in doing it. ***–John Ruskin, 1851***

There is nothing more difficult for a truly creative painter than to paint a rose, because before he can do so he has first to forget all the roses that were ever painted. ***–Henri Matisse***

Nothing is particularly hard if you divide it into small jobs. ***–Henry Ford***

The best way to have a good idea is to have a lot of ideas. ***–Linus Pauling***

Concentration is my motto—first honesty, then industry, then concentration. ***–Andrew Carnegie***

Thinking well is wise: planning well, wiser: doing well, wisest and best of all. ***–Persian proverb***

If you are attempting the impossible, you will fail.

Morale is when your hands and feet keep on working when your head says it can't be done. ***–Admiral Ben Morrell***

The best way out of a difficulty is through it.

Few men during their lifetime come anywhere near exhausting the resources dwelling within them. There are deep wells of strength that are never used. ***–Admiral Richard Byrd***

If you have built castles in the air, your work need not be lost; that is where they should be. Now put foundations under them. ***–Henry David Thoreau***

A committee is a cul-de-sac down which ideas are lured and then quietly strangled. ***–Sir Barnett Cocks***

The only reason some people get lost in thought is because it's unfamiliar territory. ***–Paul Fix***

Every act of creation is first an act of destruction. ***–Pablo Picasso***

My words fly up; my thoughts remain below. Words without thoughts never to heaven go. *–William Shakespeare, "Hamlet"*

Too many decisions are measured with a micrometer, marked with chalk, and cut with an ax.

We ought to spend more time "wondering" than "doubting whether." Wondering is the key to progress. *–Gerald Horton Bath*

When written in Chinese, the word "crisis" is composed of two characters. One represents danger, and the other represents opportunity. *–John F. Kennedy*

The only angle from which to approach a problem is the try-angle

The greatest discovery of my generation is that a human being can alter his life by altering his attitude. *–William James*

You will never stub your toe standing still, but the faster you go, the more chance you have of getting somewhere. *–Charles F. Kettering*

The doctor can bury his mistakes but an architect can only advise his client to plant vines. *–Frank Lloyd Wright*

Full bellies make empty skulls. *–H.G. Bohn, 1855*

What good is a new-born baby? *–Benjamin Franklin, when somebody asked what good was served by the first balloon ascension in Paris*

You can't see the good ideas behind you by looking twice as hard at what's in front of you. *–Andrew Mercer*

All rivers do what they can for the sea. *–Thomas Fuller*

"Where is your story on the big game today?" the editor asked the new reporter. "I did not write it," said the reporter, "because the game was called off when the stadium collapsed." "Then where is the story on the collapse?" "That wasn't my assignment."

An idea is not worth much until a man is found who has the energy and the ability to make it work.

Creative thinking may simply mean the realization that there is no particular virtue in doing things the way they have always been done. *–Rudolph Flesch*

Honest differences are often a healthy sign of progress. *–Mahatma Gandhi*

Too many people think they are being creative when they are just being different.

Luck is what happens when preparation meets opportunity. *–Elmer G. Leterman*

A man who works with his hands is a laborer; a man who works with his hands and his brain is a craftsman; but a man who works with his hands and his brain and his heart is an artist. *–Louis Nizer*

Facts, as such, never settled anything. They are working tools only. It is the implications that can be drawn from the facts that count, and to evaluate these requires wisdom and judgment that are unrelated to the computer approach to life. *–Clarence B. Randall*

...Man is still the most extraordinary computer of all. *–John F. Kennedy*

Why worry? 40% of my worries will never happen, for anxiety is the result of a tired mind;
30% concern old decisions which cannot be altered;
12% center in criticisms, mostly untrue, made by people who feel inferior;
10% are related to my health, which worsens while I worry;
and only 8% are "legitimate," showing that life does have real problems which may be met head-on when I have eliminated senseless worries.

A widely prevalent notion today seems to demand instant achievement of goals, without any of the wearying, frustrating preparation that is indispensable to any task. As the exemplar of a way of life, the professional—that man or woman who invests every new task or duty, no matter how small, with discipline of mind and spirit—is a vanishing American, particularly among those who too often believe that dreams come true because they ought to and not because they are caused to materialize. *–Jack Valenti*

Before everything else, getting ready is the secret of success. *–Henry Ford*

All you can do is try to use the best of your ability, and with all the input and knowledge you get, then hope that the decisions you make are based on what is morally right.
–Ronald Reagan

When in danger or when in doubt,
Run in circles, scream and shout! *–Clint*

One loss is good for the soul. Too many losses are not good for the coach.
–Knute Rockne

Those who dare, do: those who dare not, do not.
Writing isn't hard; no harder than ditch-digging. *–Patrick Dennis*

Believe you are defeated, believe it long enough, and it is likely to become a fact.
–Norman Vincent Peale

It's not easy taking my problems one at a time when they refuse to get in line.
–Ashleigh Brilliant

Ah, good taste! What a dreadful thing! Taste is the enemy of creativeness.
–Pablo Picasso

Inspiration starts with aspiration.

Common sense is not so common. *–Voltaire*

As regards intellectual work, it remains a fact, indeed, that great decisions in the realms of thought and momentous discoveries and solutions of problems are only possible to an individual, working in solitude. *–Sigmund Freud*

When you try to formalize or socialize creative activity, the only sure result is commercial constipation....The good ideas are all hammered out in agony by individuals, not spewed out by groups. *–Charles Brower*

In relation to society and government it may be repeated that new ideas are rare; in regard to the latter, perhaps not more than two really large and new ideas have been developed in as many millenniums. *–Henry Cabot Lodge*

Between midnight and dawn, when sleep will not come and all the old wounds begin to ache, I often have a nightmare vision of a future world in which there are billions of people, all numbered and registered, with not a gleam of genius anywhere, not an original mind, a rich personality, on the whole packed globe. The twin ideals of our time, organization and quantity, will have won forever. *–J.B. Priestley*

The function of genius is not to give new answers, but to pose new questions which time and mediocrity can resolve. *–H.R. Trevor-Roper*

I wonder whether art has a higher function than to make me feel, appreciate, and enjoy natural objects for their art value? So, as I walk in the garden, I look at the flowers and shrubs and trees and discover in them an exquisiteness of contour, a vitality of edge or a vigor of spring as well as an infinite variety of color that no artifact I have seen in the last sixty years can rival....Each day, as I look, I wonder where my eyes were yesterday. *–Bernard Berenson*

Intuition—the supra-logic that cuts out all routine processes of thought and leaps straight from problem to answer. *–Robert Graves*

In the power and splendor of the universe, inspiration waits for the millions to come. Man has only to strive for it. Poems greater than the "Iliad," plays greater than "Macbeth," stories more engaging than Don Quixote await their seeker and finder. *–John Masefield*

Thinking is the hardest work there is, which is probably the reason why so few engage in it. *–Henry Ford*

Composers should write tunes that chauffeurs and errand boys can whistle....That which penetrates the ear with facility and quits the memory with difficulty. *–Sir Thomas Beecham*

We shall succeed only so far as we continue that most distasteful of all activity, the intolerable labor of thought. *–Judge Learned Hand*

If you keep on saying things are going to be bad, you have a good chance of being a prophet. *–Isaac Bashevis Singer*

You can think about your problems or you can worry about them, and there is a vast difference between the two. Worry is thinking that has turned toxic. It is jarring music that goes round and round and never comes to either climax or conclusion. Thinking works its way through problems to conclusions and decisions; worry leaves you in a state of tensely suspended animation. When you worry, you go over the same ground endlessly and come out the same place you started. Thinking makes progress from one place to another; worry remains static. The problem of life is to change worry into thinking and anxiety into creative action. *–Harold B. Walker*

Worry is a thin stream of fear trickling through the mind. If encouraged, it cuts a channel into which all other thoughts are drained. *–Arthur Somers Roche*

First ask yourself: What is the worst that can happen? Then prepare to accept it. Then proceed to improve on the worst. *–Dale Carnegie*

...There is no new thing under the sun. *–The Bible, Ecclesiastes 1:9*

Youth is the time for adventures of the body, but age for the triumphs of the mind.
–Logan Pearsall Smith

Polishing the client's apple is no way to improve his advertising. Polishing a good idea is. And polishing. And polishing. Until good becomes better. And better becomes best.
–Young & Rubicam, Inc.

I had a monumental idea this morning, but I didn't like it. *–Samuel Goldwyn*

You will find that at the times when life becomes most real, in the great times of life, almost every man or woman becomes a poet at heart, as when in love or in...moments of great loss or bereavement.... *–John Hall Wheelock*

Trust in God—and do something. *–Mary Lyon*

All good things which exist are the fruits of originality. *–John Stuart Mill*

Every book is like a purge; at the end of it one is empty...like a dry shell on the beach, waiting for the tide to come in again. *–Daphne du Maurier*

Did you ever think how much labor went into inventing a labor-saving device?

Don't find a fault. Find a remedy. *–Henry Ford*

No man can think clearly when his fists are clenched *–George Jean Nathan*

Let us never negotiate out of fear but let us never fear to negotiate. *–John F. Kennedy*

The imagination is the very eye of faith. *Henry Ward Beecher*

I have often thought morality may perhaps consist solely in the courage of making a choice. *–Leon Blum*

In composing, as a general rule, run your pen through every other word you have written; you have no idea what vigor it will give to your style. *–Sydney Smith*

The successful man will profit from his mistakes and try again in a different way.
–Dale Carnegie

The most beautiful thing we can experience is the mysterious. It is the source of all true art and science. He to whom this emotion is a stranger, who can no longer pause to wonder and stand rapt in awe, is as good as dead: his eyes are closed.
–Albert Einstein

Any new formula which suddenly emerges in our consciousness has its roots in long trains of thought; it is virtually old when it first makes its appearance among the recognized growths of our intellect. *–Oliver Wendell Holmes*

Inspiration is sometimes another name for desperation.

Every problem has in it the seeds of its own solution. If you don't have any problems, you don't get any seeds. *–Norman Vincent Peale*

I don't know anything about art, but I know what I like. *–American proverb*

The banker asks, "How much?" The scientist asks, "How come?"

...I meditate and put on a rubber tire with three bottles of beer. Most of the time I just sit picking my nose and thinking.

–Writer James Gould Cozzens, on what he does in his study

I can't write five words but that I change seven. *–Dorothy Parker*

I write at high speed because boredom is bad for my health. It upsets my stomach more than anything else. I also avoid green vegetables. They're grossly overrated.

–Noel Coward

Mas Tiempo para el Amor. (Translation: "More Time For Love.")

–Advertising slogan credited with swift sale of washing machines in Spain

Less is more, in architectural design. *–Mies Van Der Rohe, on restraint*

You must treat a work of art like a great man: stand before it and wait patiently till it deigns to speak. *–Arthur Schopenhauer*

Get a good idea and stay with it. Dog it, and work at it until it's done, and done right.

–Walt Disney

Time and Life

Growth, Goals, Planning

The older I get, the more wisdom I find in the ancient rule of taking first things first—a process which often reduces the most complex human problems to manageable proportions. *–Dwight D. Eisenhower*

In the absence of clearly defined goals, we are forced to concentrate on activity and ultimately become enslaved by it. *–Chuck Coonradt*

Never confuse motion with action. *–Ernest Hemingway*

Along with being forever on the move, one is forever in a hurry, leaving things inadvertently behind—friend or fishing tackle, old raincoat or old allegiance.

–Louis Kronenberger

Time is really the only capital that any human being has, and the only thing he can't afford to lose. *–Thomas Edison*

When Mrs. Smith was asked about her two children in elementary school, she answered: "The doctor is in the third grade and the lawyer is in the first!"

We are condemned to kill time: thus we die bit by bit. *–Octavio Paz*

There are three ingredients in the good life: learning, earning, and yearning.
–Christopher Morley

Dreams are the stuff of progress.

Those who dare, do; those who dare not, do not.

Life is full of internal dramas, instantaneous and sensational, played to an audience of one. *–Anthony Powell*

The time which we have at our disposal every day is elastic; the passions that we feel expand it, those that we inspire contract it; and habit fills up what remains.
–Marcel Proust

He who every morning plans the transaction of the day and follows out that plan carries a thread that will guide him through the labyrinth of the most busy life....But where no plan is laid, where the disposal of time is surrendered merely to the chance of incidents, chaos will soon reign. *–Victor Hugo*

We should all be concerned about the future because we will have to spend the rest of our lives there. *–Charles F. Kettering*

God asks no man whether he will accept life. That is not the choice. You must take it. The only choice is how. *–Henry Ward Beecher*

When to the sessions of sweet silent thought
I summon up remembrance of things past,
I sigh the lack of many a thing I sought,
And with old woes new wail my dear time's waste. *–William Shakespeare*

Take care of the minutes, for the hours will take care of themselves.
–Lord Chesterfield

Besides the noble art of getting things done, there is the noble art of leaving things undone. The wisdom of life consists in the elimination of nonessentials. *–Lin Yutang*

Let the past drift away with the water. *–Japanese saying*

To every thing there is a season, and a time to every purpose under the heaven:
A time to be born, and a time to die; a time to plant, and a time to pluck up that which is planted....
A time to get, and a time to lose; a time to keep, and a time to cast away...
A time to love, and a time to hate; a time of war, and a time of peace.
–The Bible, Ecclesiastes 3:1–8

We should take from the past its fires and not its ashes. *–Jean Juares*

If spring came but once a century instead of once a year, or burst forth with the sound of an earthquake and not in silence, what wonder and expectation there would be in all hearts to behold the miraculous change. *–Henry Wadsworth Longfellow*

God, give us grace to accept with serenity the things that cannot be changed, courage to change the things which should be changed, and the wisdom to distinguish one from the other. *–Reinhold Niebuhr*

The greatest assassin of life is haste, the desire to reach things before the right time—which means overreaching them. *–Juan Ramon Jimenez*

Does't thou love life? Then do not squander time, for that is the stuff life is made of. *–Benjamin Franklin*

Time cannot be expanded, accumulated, mortgaged, hastened, or retarded.

Eternity is...
...keeping a smile on your face till the shutter clicks.
...waiting for the tow truck to show up.
...listening for the sound of a key in the lock at 2 a.m.
...trying to find a six-cent error in your bank balance.
...20 minutes of aerobic exercises.
...not peeking till the popovers are done.
...awaiting the result of a pregnancy test.
...listening to a six-year-old relate the plot of this neat movie.
...looking for a freeway exit when you're headed in the wrong direction.
...housebreaking a new puppy.
...the second hour of Monopoly.
...waiting for the light to turn green when you've spotted an empty parking space across the intersection. *–Jane Goodsell*

In one McGuffey's Reader there is a story about the clock that had been running for a long, long time on the mantelpiece. One day the clock began to think about how many times during the year ahead it would have to tick. It counted up the seconds—31,536,000 in the year—and the old clock just got too tired and said, "I can't do it!" and stopped right there. When somebody reminded the clock that it did not have to tick the 31,536,000 seconds all at one time, but rather one by one, it began to run again and everything was all right. *–Nenien C. McPherson, Jr.*

Time is dead as long as it is being clicked off by little wheels; only when the clock stops does time come to life. *–William Faulkner*

Hell, by the time a man scratches his ass, clears his throat, and tells me how smart he is, we've already wasted fifteen minutes. *–Lyndon B. Johnson*

The trouble with life in the fast lane is that you get to the other end in a awful hurry. *–John Jensen*

Progress is a continuing effort to make the things we eat, drink and wear as good as they used to be. *–Bill Vaughn*

Humanity...is like people packed in an automobile which is traveling down hill, without lights, on a dark night at terrific speed and driven by a four-year-old child. The signposts along the way are all marked "Progress." *–Lord Dunsany*

You can save time, but you can't bank it.

Civilization is a stream with banks. The stream is sometimes filled with blood from people killing, shouting and doing things historians usually record, while on the banks, unnoticed, people build homes, make love, raise children, sing songs, write poetry and even whittle statues. The story of civilization is the story of what happened on the banks. Historians...ignore the banks of the river. *–Will Durant*

This time, like all times, is a very good one, if we know what to do with it.
–Ralph Waldo Emerson

...Time is money *–Benjamin Franklin*

The trouble with our age is all signposts and no destination. *–Louis Kronenberger*

I am not young enough to know everything. *–J.M. Barrie*

Young men think old men are fools, but old men know young men are fools.
–George Chapman, 1605

I never think of the future. It comes soon enough. *–Albert Einstein*

We think our fathers fools, so wise we grow;
Our wiser sons, no doubt, will think us so. *–Alexander Pope, 1711*

We succeed only as we identify in life, or in war, or in anything else, a single overriding objective, and make all other considerations bend to that one objective.
–Dwight D. Eisenhower

...If one advances confidently in the direction of his dreams, and endeavors to live the life which he has imagined, he will meet with success unexpected in common hours.
–Henry David Thoreau

Perhaps it would be a good idea, fantastic as it sounds, to muffle every telephone, stop every motor, and halt all activity for an hour some day, to give people a chance to ponder for a few minutes on what it is all about, why they are living and what they really want.
–James Truslow Adams

Next to the dog, the wastebasket is a man's best friend.

Every step forward is made at the cost of mental and physical pain to someone.
–Frederick Nietzsche

Make no little plans; they have no magic to stir men's blood and probably themselves will not be realized. Make big plans; aim high in hope and work, remembering that a noble, logical diagram once recorded will never die, but long after we are gone will be a living thing, asserting itself with ever-growing insistency. *–Daniel H. Burnham*

The art of progress is to preserve order amid change and to preserve change amid order.
–Alfred North Whitehead

The civilized man has built a [carriage], but has lost the use of his feet. He is supported on crutches, but lacks...support of his muscle. He has a fine Geneva watch, but he fails of the skill to tell the hour by the sun. *–Ralph Waldo Emerson*

The tragedy of the world is that men have given first class loyalty to second class causes, and these causes have betrayed them. *–Lynn Harold Hough*

No horse gets anywhere until he is harnessed. No steam or gas ever drives anything until it is confined. No Niagra is ever turned into light and power until it is tunneled. No life ever grows great until it is focused, dedicated, disciplined. *–Harry Emerson Fosdick*

Change is one thing, progress is another. "Change" is scientific, "progress" is ethical; change is indubitable, whereas progress is a matter of controversy. *–Bertrand Russell*

That some good can be derived from every event is a better proposition than that everything happens for the best, which it assuredly does not. *–James K. Feibleman*

Growth for the sake of growth is the ideology of the cancer cell. *–Edward Abbey*

The desire to be well thought of makes people reluctant to say no to anyone regarding anything. We should cultivate an ability to say no to activities for which we have no time, no talent, and in which we have no interest or real concern. If we learn to say no to many things, then we will be able to say yes to things that matter most.

Spontaneity is the quality of being able to do something just because you feel like it at the moment, of trusting your instincts, of taking yourself by surprise and snatching from the clutches of your well-organized routine a bit of unscheduled pleasure.
–Richard Iannelli

Great historical movements are never begun for the attainment of remote and imperfectly comprehended ends. They demand something concrete to work for; they need clearly defined, particular aims. *–J. L. JarÄs*

May you live all the days of your life. *–Jonathan Swift*

I find the great thing in this world is not so much where we stand as in what direction we are moving. *–Oliver Wendell Holmes*

Human nature craves a certain amount of variety. We plant several kinds of flowers in our gardens. We enjoy our meals most when the selection of food is varied from day to day. The same principle applies to our daily activities. *–Harold Shryock*

Time rushes toward us with its hospital tray of infinitely varied narcotics, even while it is preparing us for its inevitably fatal operation. *–Tennessee Williams*

Retirement is the time where there is plenty of it, or not enough.

If people start letting me know how old I am, and I listen, I might start playing like an old man. So, I don't listen. *–Pete Rose, near the end of his baseball career*

The greatest use of life is to spend it for something that will outlast it.
–William James

They say such nice things about people at their funerals that it makes me sad to realize that I'm going to miss mine by just a few days. *–Garrison Keillor*

The years in your life are less important than the life in your years.

I shall pass through this world but once; any good things, therefore, that I can do, or any kindness that I can show to any human being, or dumb animal, let me do it now. Let me not deter it or neglect it, for I shall not pass this way again. *–John Galsworthy*

The years teach what the days never know. *–Ralph Waldo Emerson*

Life should be measured by its breadth, not its length.

Three things return not, even for prayers and tears -
The arrow which the archer shoots at will;
The spoken word, keen-edged and sharp to sting;
The opportunity left unimproved.
If thou would'st speak a word of loving cheer,
Oh speak it now. This moment is thine own. *–Anonymous*

Nothing is free. Even age. Age is the fee God charges for life.

Lost yesterday, somewhere between sunrise and sunset, two golden hours, each set with sixty diamond minutes. No reward is offered, for they are gone forever.
–Horace Mann

One today is worth two tomorrows.
I always wake up in the morning a young man. *–Carlos Pena Romulo*

Winston Churchill once suggested that history would deal gently with him. "Because," he added, "I intend to write it."

Never before have we had so little time in which to do so much.*–Franklin D. Roosevelt*

Time is both common and rare; we either have too much or too little. None of us believe we use it as well as we should. But unlike all the other ingredients in life, some time is for flavor and some time is just to give support to all the other ingredients we mix in. Time's importance is measured from where we sit when we do the measuring. Unfortunately, we frequently think to measure it after it is used rather than before. Then we realize that time is not a common luxury at all—but a rare and valuable gem.

No man is so methodical as a complete idler, and none so scrupulous in measuring out his time as he whose time is worth nothing. *–Washington Irving*

"How do you explain the relativity of time?" the professor was asked. "Well," he said, "if I am rushing to catch a plane, and the check-in clerk is so slow that I miss it, the extra two minutes don't mean much to him but they sure make a difference to me. That's relativity."

I have no Yesterdays,
Time took them away;
Tomorrow may not be—
But I have today. *–Pearl Yeadon McGinnis*

My mother was given to a typical question: "We have always done this. Why should we do anything else?" But my wife's typical question was "We have always done this. Why don't we do it another way or, better still, why not do something else?"
–John D. Rockefeller, Jr.

Perfection of planning is a symptom of decay. During a period of exciting discovery or progress, there is no time to plan the perfect headquarters.

–C. Northcote Parkinson

Those who cannot remember the past are condemned to repeat it.

–George Santayana

...Time is a circus—always packing up and moving away. *–Ben Hetch*

Life has a certain ending and uncertain timing.

Life's a pretty precious and wonderful thing. You can't sit down and let it lap around you....You have to plunge into it; you have to dive through it! And you can't save it, you can't store it up; you can't horde it in a vault. You've got to taste it; you've got to use it. The more you use, the more you have....That's the miracle of it! *–Kyle Chrichton*

It is a mistake to look too far ahead. Only one link in the chain of destiny can be handled at a time. *–Winston Churchill*

The history of free men is never really written by chance but by choice—their choice.

–Dwight D. Eisenhower

...Luddites were those frenzied traditionalists of the early 19th century who toured [England] wrecking new weaving machines on the theory that if they were destroyed...old jobs and old ways of life could be preserved....

At certain times in his life, each man is tempted to become a Luddite, for there is always something he would like to go back to. But to be against all change—against change in the abstract—is folly. *–James A. Michener*

There are parts of a ship which taken by themselves would sink. The engine would sink. The propeller would sink. But when the parts of a ship are built together, they float. So with the events of my life. Some have been tragic. Some have been happy. But when they are built together, they form a craft that floats and is going someplace. And I am comforted. *–Ralph W. Sockman*

Work expands so as to fill the time available for its completion....

–C. Northcote Parkinson

If a man constantly aspires, is he not elevated? *–Henry David Thoreau*

Every day has been so short, every hour so fleeting, every minute so filled with the life I love, that time for me has fled on too swift a wing. *–Aga Khan*

While all other sciences have advanced, that of government is at a standstill—little better understood, little better practised now than three or four thousand years ago.

–John Adams

An elderly lady told me, "When I was younger I never went anywhere without a thermometer, a hot water bottle, a raincoat, and a parachute. Now that I'm older I wish I had walked more in my bare feet, had gone more places, and spent more time picking daisies." *–Roberta Figer*

...Take time to absorb and enjoy the lovely world in which you live and come to know its inhabitants with affectionate amusement. You would do well to budget your time as follows: one-half in work, taking care of personal belongings, etc.; one-fourth in social pastimes with...both young and old; and one-fourth as an interested, pleased observer of life. *–William B. Terhune*

Practical people would be a lot more practical if they were just a little more dreamy. *–J.P. McEvoy*

In America half an hour is forty minutes *–German Proverb*

Not so long ago, when I was a student in college, just flying an airplane seemed a dream. But that dream turned into a reality. *–Charles A. Lindbergh*

Only in growth, reform and change, paradoxically enough, is true security to be found. *–Anne Morrow Lindberg*

The pace of events is moving so fast that unless we can find some way to keep our sights on tomorrow, we cannot expect to be in touch with today. *–Dean Rusk*

Reach high, for stars lie hidden in your soul.
Dream deep, for every dream precedes the goal. *–Ralph Vaull Starr*

Life is a fatal adventure. It can only have one end. So why not make it as far ranging and free as possible? *–Alexander Eliot*

Time is a dressmaker specializing in alterations. *–Faith Baldwin*

RELATIONSHIPS

Companionship, Equity, Respect

Treat people as if they were what they ought to be, and you help them to become what they are capable of being. *–Goethe*

How much more grievous are the consequences of anger than the causes of it. *–Marcus Aurelius, c.170*

Offerings of food have been breaking down barriers for centuries.–Estee Lauder

If a man does not make new acquaintances as he advances through life he will find himself alone. Man...should keep his acquaintances in constant repair. *–Samuel Johnson*

There is great comfort and inspiration in the feeling of close human relationships and its bearing on our mutual fortunes—a powerful force, to overcome the "tough breaks" which are certain to come to most of us from time to time. *–Walt Disney*

He drew a circle that shut me out
Heretic, rebel, a thing to flout.
But Love and I had the wit to win;
We drew a circle that took him in! *–Edwin Markham*

Peace is more precious than a piece of land. *–Anwar al-Sadat*

When evil men plot, good men must plan. When evil men shout ugly words of hatred, good men must commit themselves to the glories of love. *–Martin Luther King, Jr.*

I respect those who resist me, but I cannot tolerate them. *–Charles de Gaulle*

The surest bond of friendship is having enemies in common.

Forgive your enemies, but never forget their names. *–John F. Kennedy*

If you wish to be brothers, drop your weapons. *–Pope John Paul II*

When a man points a finger at someone else, he should remember that four of his fingers are pointing at himself. *–Louis Nizer*

Hold a true friend with both your hands. *–Nigerian proverb*

Your own safety is at stake when your neighbor's house is burning. *–Horace, about 10 B.C.E.*

Then there's the man who puts a sign on his front door when he goes off on vacation, reading: Attention thieves; do not bother to enter here; everything of value has already been borrowed by my neighbors.

The impersonal hand of government can never replace the helping hand of a neighbor. *–Hubert H. Humphrey*

A true friend is someone who is there for you when he'd rather be anywhere else. *–Len Wein*

You can make more friends in two months by becoming interested in other people than you can in two years by trying to get other people interested in you. *–Dale Carnegie*

The best next-door neighbor is the one who overlooks things.

Be kind. Remember, everyone you meet is fighting a hard battle. *–Thompson*

I can't make people like me, but if I wasn't me, I would like me. *–Third-grader*

You cannot be friends upon any other terms than upon the terms of equality. *–Woodrow Wilson*

Commandment Number One of any truly civilized society is this: Let people be different. *–David Grayson*

Some people can stay longer in an hour than others can in a week. *–William Dean Howells*

Tale-bearers are as bad as tale-makers. *–Sheridan*

A gossip was complaining about her neighbor to a visiting friend. Her neighbor was so dirty, it was a disgrace to the neighborhood. "Just look, those clothes she has on the line and sheets and pillowcases all have black streaks up and down them." Her guest said, "It appears, my dear, that the clothes are clean; the streaks you see are on your windows."
Peace may cost as much as war, but it's a better buy.

If civilization is to survive, we must cultivate the science of human relationships—the ability of all peoples, of all kinds, to live together, in the same world at peace.
–Franklin D. Roosevelt

Friends are made by many acts—and lost by only one.

Eating words has never given me indigestion. *–Winston Churchill*

I shall pass through life but once. Let me show kindness now, as I shall not pass this way again. *–William Penn*

Forgiveness does not change the past, but it does enlarge the future. *–Paul Boese*

It is easier to forgive an enemy than to forgive a friend. *–William Blake*

He who cannot forgive breaks the bridge over which he himself must pass.
–George Herbert

Loneliness and the feeling of being unwanted is the most terrible poverty.
–Mother Teresa

Grief can take care of itself, but to get the full value out of a joy you must have somebody to divide it with. *–Mark Twain*

If you want your friends to remember you, borrow something from them.

The most exhausting thing in life, I have discovered, is being insincere. That is why so much social life is exhausting; one is wearing a mask.–Anne Morrow Lindbergh

Hatred is blind as well as love. *–Thomas Fuller, 1732*

When you hear that someone has gossiped of you, kindly reply that he did not know the rest of your faults or he would not have mentioned only these.

The only gracious way to accept an insult is to ignore it; if you can't ignore it, top it; if you can't top it, laugh at it; if you can't laugh at it, it's probably deserved.
–Russell Lynes

A Washington lady explained how to be a successful hostess: When your guests arrive say, "At last!" And when they leave, "So soon!"

We like someone *because.* We love someone *although.* *–Henri De Montherlant*

If a man does not keep pace with his companions, perhaps it is because he hears a different drummer. Let him step to the music which he hears, however measured or far away. *–Henry David Thoreau*

I believe every person has a heart, and if you can reach it, you can make a difference.
–Uli Derickson

Robert Mueller shares this telling and tragically true human relations experience: "I asked a Burmese why women, after centuries of following their men, now walk ahead. He said there were many unexploded land mines since the war."

No one can be wrong with man and right with God. *–Harry Emerson Fosdick*

You learn to speak by speaking, to study by studying, to run by running, to work by working; and just so you learn to love God and man by loving. Begin as a mere apprentice and the very power of love will lead you on to become a master of the art.
–St. Francis De Sales

Real friends are those who, when you've made a fool of yourself, don't feel you've done a permanent job.

When you see a worthy person, endeavor to emulate him. When you see an unworthy person, then examine your inner self. *–Confucius*

Folks never understand the folks they hate. *–James Russell Lowell, 1862*

Laugh at yourself first, before anybody else can.
–Elsa Maxwell, quoting death-bed advice of her father

When I was a young man, I met Franklin Roosevelt and Harry Truman. I remarked to Mr. Truman that I thought Mr. Roosevelt was a wonderful man. Mr. Truman agreed. "Franklin likes me despite my shortcomings in my work, and I like him because he has none." *–Henry O. Dormann*

Be generous with kindly words, especially about those who are absent. *–Goethe*

Some people find fault as if it were buried treasure. *–Francis O'Walsh*

Love your enemies, for they will tell you your faults. *–Benjamin Franklin*

On a cold winter's day, a group of porcupines huddled together to stay warm and keep from freezing. But soon they felt one another's quills and moved apart. When the need for warmth brought them closer together again, their quills again forced them apart. They were driven back and forth at the mercy of their discomforts until they found the distance from one another that provided both a maximum of warmth and a minimum of pain.

In human beings, the emptiness and monotony of the isolated self produces a need for society. This brings people together, but their many offensive qualities and intolerable faults drive them apart again. The optimum distance that they finally find and that permits them to coexist is embodied in politeness and good manners. Because of this distance between us, we can only partially satisfy our need for warmth, but at the same time, we are spared the stab of one another's quills. *–Arthur Schopenhauer*

If you hate a person, you hate something in him that is part of yourself. What isn't part of ourselves doesn't disturb us. *–Hermann Hesse, Demian*

If you join little cliques, you will be self-satisfied; if you make friends widely, you will be interesting. *–Sydney Smith*

To wrong those we hate is to add fuel to our hatred. Conversely, to treat an enemy with magnanimity is to blunt our hatred for him. *–Eric Hoffer*

The best cure for anger is delay. *–Seneca, c. 63*

Thank you all from the bottom of my heart for your hospitality and, as we say in Russia, for your bread and salt. Let us have more and more use for the short American word "O.K." *–Nikita Khrushchev, concluding his first visit to U.S.*

I feel the necessity of deepening the stream of life; I must cultivate privacy. It is very dissipating to be with people too much. *–Henry David Thoreau*

...The most important phase of living with a person: the respect for that person as an individual. *–Millicent Carey McIntosh*

In expressing love we belong among the underdeveloped countries. *–Saul Bellow*

The first duty of love is to LISTEN. *–Paul Tillich*

To be humble to superiors is duty, to equals, courtesy, to inferiors, nobleness. *–Benjamin Franklin*

I'd rather deal with a God-loving person than with a God-fearing one.

When the mouse laughs at the cat, there is a hole nearby. *–Nigerian proverb*

Being taken for granted can be a compliment. It means that you've become a comfortable, trusted element in another person's life. *–Dr. Joyce Brothers*

There are two statements about human beings that are true: that all human beings are alike, and that all are different. On those two facts all human wisdom is founded. *–Mark Van Doren*

Each of us has his own little private conviction of rightness and almost by definition, the Utopian condition of which we all dream is that in which all people finally see the error of their ways and agree with us. And underlying practically all our attempts to bring agreement is the assumption that agreement is brought about by changing people's minds—other people's. *–S.I. Hayakawa*

A gentleman saw a blind woman standing on a busy city corner waiting for someone to help her cross the intersection. He stepped up to her and asked, "May I go across with you?"

Practice smiling. Smile at lamp posts and mail boxes. Don't be modest—this isn't the time. Always eat a snack before going to a luncheon meeting so you can spend your time charming, not chewing. *–Jacque Mercer, former Miss America, on how to win a beauty contest*

Some men still have their first dollar. The man who is really rich is the one who still has his first friend.

The acid test of hospitality is the uninvited guest.

Withdraw thy foot from thy neighbor's house; lest he be weary of thee, and so hate thee.
–The Bible, Proverbs 25:17

It is equally offensive to speed a guest who would like to stay and to detain one who is anxious to leave. *–Homer, The Odyssey*

Fish and guests smell at three days old. *–Danish proverb*

Friendship increases in visiting friends, but in visiting them seldom. *–Thomas Fuller*

Go often to the house of thy friend, for weeds choke the unused path.
–Ralph Waldo Emerson

For any American who had the great and priceless privilege of being raised in a small town there always remains with him nostalgic memories....And the older he grows the more he senses what he owed to the simple honesty and neighborliness, the integrity that he saw all around him in those days.... *–Dwight D. Eisenhower*

When there is room in the heart there is room in the house.

The time to win a fight is before it starts. *–Frederick W. Lewis*

I have made a ceaseless effort not to ridicule, not to bewail, not to scorn human actions, but to understand them. *–Spinoza*

In mixed doubles the mix is very important.

A man cannot be said to succeed in this life who does not satisfy one friend.
–Henry David Thoreau

He who forgives, ends the quarrel.
If I knew you and you knew me,
If both of us could clearly see,
And with an inner sight divine
The meaning of your heart and mine.
I'm sure that we would differ less,
and clasp our hands in friendliness,
Our thoughts would pleasantly agree
If I knew you and you knew me. *–Nixon Waterman*

You punch me, I punch back. I do not believe it is good for one's self-respect to be a punching bag. *–Edward Koch*

He that strives not to stem his anger's tide
Does a wild horse without a bridle ride. *–Colley Cibber, 1696*

All is well with him who is beloved by his neighbors. *–George Herbert*

Am I united with my friend in heart,
What matters if our place be wide apart? *–Anwar-I-Suheili, Persian poet*

When you are down and out, something always turns up—and it is usually the noses of your friends. *–Orson Welles*

Friendship makes prosperity more shining and lessens adversity by dividing and sharing it. *–Cicero, 44 B.C.E.*

The only way to have a friend is to be one. *–Ralph Waldo Emerson*

Check the neighbors before you buy the house.

...Six hundred men all thinking a great deal of themselves and very little of each other.
–Sir James Cassels, on the House of Commons

The love of humanity...is mitigated by violent dislike of the next-door neighbor.
–Alfred North Whitehead

Before borrowing money from a friend, decide which you need more.
–Addison H. Hallock

Let us endeavor so to live that when we come to die even the undertaker will be sorry.
–Mark Twain

The touch of human hands
Not vain, unthinking words,
Not that cold charity
Which shuns our misery;
We seek a loyal friend
Who understands,
And the warmth, the pulsing warmth
Of human hands. *–Thomas Curtis Clark*

Can two walk together, except they be agreed? *–The Bible, Amos 3:3*

Oh, the comfort, the inexpressible comfort of feeling safe with a person; having neither to weigh thoughts nor measure words, but to pour them all out, just as they are, chaff and grain together, knowing that a faithful hand will take and sift them, keep what is worth keeping, and then, with the breath of kindness, blow the rest away.
–George Eliot

A friend is someone who stimulates me and to whom I am stimulated to talk....When the stimulation no longer occurs, it is spent and exhausted friendship, and continues as a burden and a bore....Unfortunately in a long life one gets barnacled over with the mere shells of friendship and it is difficult without hurting one's self to scrape them off.
–Bernard Berenson

All the world's a stage,
And all the men and women merely players:
They have their exits and their entrances;
And one man in his time plays many parts... *–William Shakespeare, As You Like It*

I don't really feel my poems are mine at all. I didn't create them out of nothing; I owe them to my relations with other people. *–Robert Graves*

The first general rule for friendship is to be a friend, to be open, natural, interested; the second rule is to take time for friendship. Friendship, after all, is what life is finally about. Everything material and professional exists in the end for persons.

–Nels F. S. Ferre

I sought to hear the voice of God
And climbed the topmost steeple,
But God declared: "Go down again
I dwell among the people." *–John Henry Newman*

I cannot help believing that the world will be a better and a happier place when people are praised more and blamed less; when we utter in their hearing the good we think and also gently intimate the criticisms we hope may be of service. For the world grows smaller every day. It will be but a family circle after a while. *–Francis E. Willard*

If a wife always laughs at her husband's jokes, is he funny or she smart?

Prejudice is the child of ignorance. *–William Hazlitt*

True generosity requires more of us than kindly impulse. Above all it requires imagination—the capacity to see people in all their perplexities and needs, and to know how to expend ourselves effectively for them. *–I.A.R. Wylie*

Politeness is the art of selecting among one's real thoughts. *–Madame de Stael*

Who gossips to you will gossip of you.

We praise a man who is angry on the right grounds, against the right persons, in the right manner, at the right moment, and for the right length of time.

–Aristotle, c.340 B.C.E.

No man is an island, entire of itself; every man is a piece of the continent, a part of the main....Any man's death diminishes me, because I am involved in mankind; and therefore never send to know for whom the bell tolls; it tolls for thee.

–John Donne, 1624

Thou canst not joke an enemy into a friend, but thou may'st a friend into an enemy.

–Benjamin Franklin

No one can make you feel inferior without your consent. *–Eleanor Roosevelt*

If the happiness of the mass of mankind can be secured at the expense of a little tempest now and then, or even of a little blood, it will be a precious purchase.

–Thomas Jefferson in a letter to Ezra Stiles, 1786

I wish she was smart enough to teach second grade, too, next year.

–William Goumas, first-grade pupil, in his "favorite teacher" essay

A friend is...a second self. *–Cicero*

Always do what you say you are going to do. It is the glue and fiber that binds successful relationships. *–Jeffry A. Timmons*

You can't hold a man down without staying down with him. *–Booker T. Washington*

I always wanted to be somebody. If I made it, it's half because I was game enough to take a lot of punishment along the way and half because there were a lot of people who cared enough to help me. *–Althea Gibson*

The longer we live, and the more we think, the higher value we learn to put on the friendship and tenderness of parents and of friends. Parents we can have but once; and he promises himself too much, who enters life with the expectation of finding many friends. *–Samuel Johnson, 1766*

My own business always bores me to death; I prefer other people's. *–Oscar Wilde*

Friendship, of itself a holy tie,
Is made more sacred by adversity. *–John Dryden, 1687*

The average man is more interested in a woman who is interested in him than he is in a woman—any woman—with beautiful legs. *–Marlene Dietrich*

Most of the trouble in the world is caused by people wanting to be important.
–T.S. Eliot

I've always believed in writing without a collaborator, because where two people are writing the same book, each believes he gets all the worries and only half the royalties.
–Agatha Christie

...Closer together than the hands of a clock at twenty minutes of eight.
–Robert Bedingfield, on the brothers John and Clint Murchison

The holy passion of friendship is of so sweet and steady and loyal and enduring a nature that it will last through a whole lifetime, if not asked to lend money.
–Mark Twain

We are all crazy when we are angry. *–Philemon, c. 300 B.C.E.*

Am I not destroying my enemies when I make friends of them?
–Abraham Lincoln

Make no friendships with an angry man. *–The Bible, Proverbs 22:24*

All government, indeed every human benefit and enjoyment, every virtue, and every prudent act, is founded on compromise and barter.
–Edmund Burke, on conciliation with America, 1775

You don't ever ask a barber whether you need a haircut. *–Greenberg*

Blame-all and praise-all are two blockheads. *–Benjamin Franklin*

The only normal people are the ones you don't know very well. *–Joe Ancis*

God bears with imperfect beings...even when they resist His goodness. We ought to imitate this merciful patience and endurance. It is only imperfection that complains of what is imperfect. The more perfect we are, the more gentle and quiet we become toward the defects of other people. *–Francois de Fenelon*

The first human being who hurled an insult instead of a stone was the founder of civilization. *–Attributed to Sigmund Freud*

To put the world right in order, we must first put the nation in order; to put the nation in order, we must first put the family in order; to put the family in order, we must first cultivate our personal life; we must first set our hearts right. *–Confucius*

COMMUNICATION

Speech, Diplomacy, Advice, Public Speaking

Use soft words in hard arguments. *–H.G. Bohn, 1855*

...It is always well to accept your own shortcomings with candor but to regard those of your friends with polite incredulity. *–Russell Lynes*

Only if we can restrain ourselves is conversation possible. Good talk rises upon much self-discipline. *–John Erskine*

It is only the intellectually lost who ever argue. *–Oscar Wilde*

We cannot learn from one another until we stop shouting at one another—until we speak quietly enough so that our words can be heard as well as our voices.
–Richard M. Nixon

A diplomat is a person who can tell you to go to hell in such a way that you actually look forward to the trip. *–Caskie Stinnett*

Speak when you are angry and you will make the best speech you will ever regret.
–Ambrose Bierce

A gossip is one who talks to you about others; a bore is one who talks to you about himself; and a brilliant conversationalist is one who talks to you about yourself.
–Lisa Kirk

People who know the very least seem to know the loudest.

All the great speakers were bad speakers at first. *–Ralph Waldo Emerson*

One of the best ways to persuade others is with your ears—by listening to them.
–Dean Rusk

Great public speakers listen to the audience with their eyes.

Exhaust neither the topic nor the audience.

In order to speak short upon any subject, think long. *–H. H. Brackenridge*

O Lord, please fill my mouth with worthwhile stuff, and nudge me when I've said enough.

A wise man will not communicate his differing thoughts to unprepared minds, or in a disorderly manner. *–Benjamin Whichcote, 1753*

A reporter, coming upon a big story, telegraphed his editor. The editor replied, "Send six hundred words." The reporter wired back, "Can't be told in less than twelve hundred words." The editor replied, "Story of creation of world told in six hundred. Try it."

President William Howard Taft was requested to attend a banquet and make a speech. The person inviting him said, "Just a brief one, Mr. President, since we can imagine how busy you must be—perhaps five minutes." The president declined. "Do you realize that to prepare even a five-minute speech would take several hours to plan, to draft, to rewrite, to pass through channels for clearance? I'm afraid that I just haven't got the time." The host persisted. "Well, as far as that goes, we'd be delighted to have you speak for an hour." President Taft replied, "Gentlemen, I am ready now!"

All propaganda has to be popular and has to accommodate itself to the comprehension of the least intelligent of those whom it seeks to reach. *–Adolf Hitler*

We are fighting in the quarrel of civilization against barbarism, of liberty against tyranny. Germany has become a menace to the whole world. She is the most dangerous enemy of liberty now existing. She has shown herself utterly ruthless, treacherous, and brutal. When I use these words, I use them with scientific precision. *–Theodore Roosevelt*

Better to remain silent and be thought a fool than to speak out and remove all doubt. *–Abraham Lincoln*

A "no" uttered from the deepest conviction is better and greater than a "yes" merely uttered to please, or what is worse, to avoid trouble. *–Mahatma Gandhi*

Silence is often misinterpreted, but never misquoted.

Baloney is the unvarnished lie laid on so thick you hate it. Blarney is flattery laid on so thin you love it. *–Fulton Sheen*

Anyone who thinks the art of conversation is dead ought to tell a child to go to bed. *–Robert Gallagher*

True, lasting peace cannot be secured through the strength of arms alone. Among free peoples, the open exchange of ideas ultimately is our greatest security. *–Ronald Reagan*

Some people mistake weakness for tact. If they are silent when they ought to speak and so feign an agreement they do not feel, they call it being tactful. Cowardice would be a much better name. Tact is an active quality that is not exercised by merely making a dash for cover. Be sure, when you think you are being extremely tactful, that you are not in reality running away from something you ought to face. *–Sir Frank Medlicott*

Tact is the knack of making a point without making an enemy. *–Howard W. Newton*

A fool uttereth all his mind. *–The Bible, Proverbs 29:11*

Let your discourse with men of business be short and comprehensive.
–George Washington

In the mid-1960s, FBI director J. Edgar Hoover was proofreading a letter he had just dictated to his secretary. He didn't like the way she had formatted it, so he wrote the words, "Watch the borders" at the bottom of the letter and asked her to retype it. The secretary did as she was told and sent it off to all top agents. For the next two weeks FBI agents were patrolling the Canadian and Mexican borders in droves as requested by their leader.

That which we are capable of feeling, we are capable of saying. *–Cervantes, 1613*

The friend who can be silent with us in a moment of despair or confusion, who can stay with us in an hour of grief and bereavement, who can tolerate not knowing, not curing, not healing, and face us with the reality of our powerlessness, that is the friend who cares. *–Henri Nouwen*

Do not the most moving moments of our lives find us all without words?
–Marcel Marceau, pantomimist

The late Sam Goldwyn is credited with devising the all-purpose answer when someone closely connected with a new film comes up to you after the preview to ask what you thought of it. Say "What a picture!" and leave fast.

The art of acceptance is the art of making someone who has just done you a small favor wish that he might have done you a greater one. *–Russell Lynes*

Wit is a treacherous dart. It is perhaps the only weapon with which it is possible to stab oneself in one's own back. *–Geoffrey Bocca*

I'm not capable of blathering pap. I'm not happy or comfortable engaging in mush statements. If I'm going to say something, it's going to be substantive and at least provocative. Hopefully, it will also have some humor. That's my style. It's me.
–Edward Koch

Flattery is from the teeth out. Sincere appreciation is from the heart out.
–Dale Carnegie

A good speech is like a pencil; it has to have a point.

A true sonnet goes eight lines and then takes a turn for better or worse and goes six or eight lines more. *–Robert Frost*

New Englanders' lack of loquaciousness is legendary, as perhaps is this story of a New England President named Calvin Coolidge, who was asked what had been the subject of the pastor's sermon in church that Sunday and said, "Sin." "What did the preacher say?" "He's agin it," said Mr. Coolidge.

Talk low, talk slow, and don't say too much. *–John Wayne, on acting*

A 5th-century barber asked King Archelaus how he would like his hair cut. "In silence," replied the king.

A man stopped in a small town on his journey through Vermont and decided to join a group of men sitting on the porch of the general store. They were quiet. After several tries at starting a conversation and not succeeding, he asked, "Is there a law against talking in this town?"

One of them replied, "There's no law against talking, but we have an understanding that one doesn't speak unless he is sure he can improve on the silence."

Let thy speech be better than silence, or be silent. *–Dionysius the Elder*

First learn the meaning of what you say, and then speak. *–Epictetus*

If you have an important point to make, don't try to be subtle or clever. Use a pile driver. Hit the point once. Then come back and hit it again. Then hit it a third time—a tremendous whack. *–Winston Churchill*

Every time a controversial issue came up at the town meeting, the town dissenter said "We'll stage a demonstration." Finally one of the elders lost his temper. "You don't accomplish anything by your demonstrations," he said. "They always end up in a riot, and what good is that?" "Well," said the dissenter, "it gets a lot more attention than when I talk in the town meeting."

The opposite of talking isn't listening. The opposite of talking is waiting.
–Fran Lebowitz

Hear the other side. *–St. Augustine*

Eating words has never given me indigestion. *–Winston Churchill*

A good citizen is one who doesn't always keep his mouth shut.

...I have made this letter longer because I lack the time to make it shorter.
–Blaise Pascal, 1656

...I have found that the greatest help in meeting any problem with decency and self-respect and whatever courage is demanded, is to know where you yourself stand. That is, to have in words what you believe and are acting from.
–William Faulkner, letter to a University of Alabama student during riots over enrollment of a black student

The right of every person "to be let alone" must be placed in the scales with the right of others to communicate. *–Chief Justice Warren E. Burger*

The newly-arrived immigrant drove his host crazy by talking about how much better food was in the old country, and how much better the weather was and how much better everything was back where he came from. Finally his host said, "If everything was so much better there, why did you come here?" And the immigrant answered, "Because if I said over there that something was better elsewhere they would have shot me. The one thing that's better here is that now I can complain."

Don't flatter yourself that friendship authorizes you to say disagreeable things to your intimates. The nearer you come into relation with a person, the more necessary do tact and courtesy become. *–Oliver Wendell Holmes*

During World War II, the Civil Defense authorities had posters printed which read: "Illumination must be extinguished when premises are vacated." When he saw these signs, President Franklin Roosevelt exclaimed, "Damn, why can't they say 'Put out the lights when you leave'?" *–Franklin D. Roosevelt*

To say nothing often reflects a fine command of the English language.

Do not say things. What you are stands over you the while and thunders so that I cannot hear what you say to the contrary. *–Ralph Waldo Emerson*

Channing Cox, who succeeded Calvin Coolidge as governor of Massachusetts, visited the vice-president. Cox asked him how he could see his visitors every day and manage to leave his office at five, while Cox could rarely leave before nine P.M. Coolidge replied, "You talk back."

He who slings mud generally loses ground. *–Adlai Stevenson*

Never answer a letter while you are angry. *–Chinese proverb*

I was angry with my friend:
I told my wrath, my wrath did end.
I was angry with my foe:
I told it not, my wrath did grow. *–William Blake, c. 1792*

When you are angry say nothing and do nothing until you have recited the alphabet.
–Ascribed to Athenodorous Cananites, 1st century B.C.E.

When angry, count ten before you speak; if very angry, a hundred.
–Thomas Jefferson

When angry, count four; when very angry, swear. *–Mark Twain*

To speak ill of others is a dishonest way of praising ourselves...let us be above such transparent egotism. *–Will Durant*

Having served on various committees, I have drawn up a list of rules: Never arrive on time; this stamps you as a beginner. Don't say anything until the meeting is half over; this stamps you as being wise. Be as vague as possible; this avoids irritating the others. When in doubt, suggest that a sub-committee be appointed. Be the first to move for adjournment; this will make you popular; it's what everyone is waiting for.
–Harry Chapman

Dentopedalogy is the science of opening your mouth and putting your foot in it. I've been practicing it for years. *–Prince Philip*

A bishop was to make his first sermon at the court of Queen Victoria. He asked Disraeli for advice. "How long do you think my first sermon should last, Mr. Prime Minister?" Disraeli replied, "If you preach for forty minutes, Her Majesty will be satisfied; for thirty minutes, she will be delighted. If you preach for only fifteen minutes, Her Majesty will be enthusiastic!"

A scatterbrain is one who never has an unspoken thought.

I can go on forever. To me, one thought becomes five hundred sentences.
–*Alice K. Dormann*

A bore is a fellow who opens his mouth and puts his feats in it. –*Henry Ford*

Blessed is he who, having nothing to say, refrains from giving wordy evidence of the fact.

The boor is of no use in conversation. He contributes nothing worth hearing, and takes offense at everything. –*Aristotle, c. 340 B.C.E.*

Definition of a bore: A person who talks when you wish him to listen.
–*Ambrose Bierce*

Wisdom is divided into two parts: (a) having a great deal to say, and (b) not saying it.

The wise man, even when he holds his tongue, says more than the fool when he speaks.
–*Thomas Fuller, 1642*

There is no greater mistake than the hasty conclusion that opinions are worthless because they are badly argued. –*Thomas Huxley*

Sometimes a fool makes a good suggestion. –*Nicolas Boileau, 1674*

'Tis wisdom sometimes to seem a fool. –*Thomas Fuller,1642*

Nothing is often a good thing to say, and always a clever thing to say. –*Will Durant*

To listen well is as powerful a means of communication and influence as to talk well.
–*Chief Justice John Marshall*

The less you talk, the more you're listened to. –*Abigail Van Buren*

No one means all he says, and yet few say all they mean. For words are slippery and thought is vicious. –*Henry Brooks Adams*

In the dark days and darker nights when England stood alone—and most men save Englishmen despaired of England's life—he mobilized the English language and sent it into battle. The incandescent quality of his words illuminated the courage of his countrymen.
–*John F. Kennedy, conferring honorary citizenship on Winston Churchill, 1963*

Civility costs nothing, and buys everything. –*Lady Mary Wortley Montague, 1756*

Only a brilliant man knows whether the applause for his words is politeness or appreciation.

To the press alone, checkered as it is with abuses, the world is indebted for all the triumphs which have been gained by reason and humanity over error and oppression.
–*Thomas Jefferson*

I know what I say at times is not very diplomatic. –*Nikita Khrushchev*

Diplomacy is the language of international relations, which can say one thing that has two absolutely opposite meanings: A diplomat is one who can tell a man he's open-minded when he means he has a hole in his head.

Let the lie be delivered full-face, eye to eye, and without scratching of the scalp, but let it, for all its simplicity, contain one fantastical element of creative ingenuity.

–Dalton Trumbo, on lying

In 1931, Charlie Chaplin and Albert Einstein drove down a street together. Pedestrians waved and cheered. Chaplin explained all of this: "The people are applauding you because none of them understands you, and applauding me, because everybody understands me."

I'm going to speak my mind because I have nothing to lose. *–S.I. Hayakawa*

His enemies might have said before that he talked rather too much; but now he has occasional flashes of silence that make his conversation perfectly delightful.

–Syndey Smith writing on Thomas Macaulay, Scottish author and statesman

When Jimmy Carter of Georgia was elected President, a common comment in the South was that he was the first President in more than a hundred years who "spoke English without an accent."

If you can't get people to listen to you any other way, tell them it's confidential.

Cynicism is the intellectual cripple's substitute for intelligence. It is the dishonest businessman's substitute for conscience. It is the communicator's substitute, whether he is advertising man or editor or writer, for self-respect. *–Russell Lynes*

It is not necessary to understand things in order to argue about them.

–Caron De Beaumarchais, The Barber of Seville, 1775

A man's judgment cannot be better than the information on which he has based it. Give him no news, or present him only with distorted and incomplete data, with ignorant, sloppy, or biased reporting, with propaganda and deliberate falsehoods, and you destroy his whole reasoning process and make him somewhat less than a man.

–Arthur Hays Sulzberger

The story is told of the way Secretary of State William M. Evarts began a Thanksgiving dinner speech. He said, "You have been giving your attention to a turkey stuffed with sage; you are now about to consider a sage stuffed with turkey."

It is better to advise than upbraid, for the one corrects the erring; the other only convicts them. *–Epictetus, 2nd century*

Advice is less necessary to the wise than to fools, but the wise derive most advantage from it. *–Francesco Guicciardini, 1564*

I was a code clerk in Washington...when we received an urgent message that twelve code clerks were needed by President Wilson at the Versailles Peace Conference. What they really wanted were twelve code books, but somebody got the message mixed up.

–James Thurber, on his first trip to Paris

He can compress the most words into the smallest idea of any man I ever met.

–Abraham Lincoln

Senator George H. Moses complained to President Calvin Coolidge that a man being considered for a Republican senatorial nomination was an "out-and-out S.O.B."

"That may be," agreed Coolidge, "but there's a lot of those in the country and I think they are entitled to representation in the Senate."

Be wiser than other people if you can; but do not tell them so.
–Lord Chesterfield in a Letter to his son, 1745

Never answer a question, other than an offer of marriage, by saying Yes or No.
–Susan Chitty

A powerful agent is the right word. Whenever we come upon one of those intensely right words in a book or newspaper the resulting effect is physical as well as spiritual, and electrically prompt. *–Mark Twain*

Never tell all that you know, or do all that you can, or believe all that you hear.
–Portuguese proverb

I narrow-mindedly outlawed the word "unique." Practically every press release contains it. Practically nothing ever is. *–Fred Hechinger, editor*

Few sinners are saved after the first 20 minutes of a sermon. *–Mark Twain*

If you haven't struck oil in five minutes, stop boring.
–George Jessel, on after-dinner speakers

Here comes the orator with his flood of words and his drop of reason
–Benjamin Franklin

When the main portion of the meal was finished, the presiding person whispered to the first speaker, "Shall we let the people enjoy themselves a little longer, or would you like to deliver your speech now?"

Be sure your brain is in gear before engaging your mouth.

Eloquence: saying the proper thing and stopping. *–Francois de la Rochefoucauld*

The heart of a fool is in his mouth, but the mouth of a wise man is in his heart.
–Benjamin Franklin

Governor Claude A. Swanson of Virginia had made a long and rambling speech. Afterwards a woman came up to...shake his hand. "How did you like my speech?" he asked. She answered, "I liked it fine. But it seems to me you missed several excellent opportunities." Swanson was puzzled. "Several excellent opportunities to do what?" "To quit," she replied.

Hearts may agree though heads differ. *–Thomas Fuller, 1732*

A fanatic is one who can't change his mind and won't change the subject.
–Winston Churchill

In every fat book there is a thin book trying to get out.

The covers of this book are too far apart. *–Ambrose Bierce*

A man of few words, Calvin Coolidge explained why: "I found out early in life that you never have to explain something you haven't said."

Scholarship is polite argument.
–Philip Rieff, associate professor, University of California

The grand aim of all science is to cover the greatest number of empirical facts by logical deduction from the smallest number of hypotheses or axioms. ***–Albert Einstein***

"For the first six months, you should listen and not become involved in debate," Disraeli advised a newly-elected member of Parliament. "But," the man replied, "my colleagues will wonder why I do not speak." "Better they should wonder why you do not speak," explained Disraeli, "than why you do."

The best way I know of to win an argument is to start by being in the right.
–Lord Hailsham

There is a story in Arabic which tells of a pupil asking a wise man how he could become a good conversationalist. The sage replied, "Listen, my son." After waiting a while, pupil said, "I am listening, Please continue your instruction." The sage smiled. "There is no more to tell."

Man does not live by words alone, despite the fact that sometimes he has to eat them.
–Adlai Stevenson

...Rhetoric that rolls like a freight train over a bridge.
–David Brinkley, NBC commentator, on speechmaking of union czar John L. Lewis

When dealing with people, remember you are not dealing with creatures of logic, but with creatures of emotion. ***–Dale Carnegie***

Writers have two main problems. One is writer's block, when the words won't come at all, and the other is logorrhea, when the words come so fast that they can hardly get to the wastebasket in time. ***–Cecilia Bartholomew***

I took a course in speed reading and was able to read War and Peace in twenty minutes. It's about Russia. ***–Woody Allen***

The most stringent protection of free speech would not protect a man in falsely shouting fire in a theatre and causing a panic. ***–Associate Justice Oliver Wendell Holmes, Jr.***

Thank you for sending me a copy of your book. I'll waste no time reading it.
–Moses Hadas, in a letter

It's a strange world of language in which skating on thin ice can get you into hot water.
–Franklin P. Jones

I don't care what is written about me so long as it isn't true.
–Katharine Hepburn, on gossip and publicity

The American arrives in Paris with a few French phrases he has culled from a conversational guide or picked up from a friend who owns a beret. He speaks the sort of French that is really understood only by another American who also has just arrived in Paris. ***–Fred Allen***

How often do we search in vain for a word to bring a thought properly to paper?...Admire words well used: They are living monuments to the power of the minds of men.

One day, while shaving, Mark Twain cut himself. He recited his entire vocabulary of swear words. His wife, hoping to stun him, repeated all the swear words. Then, Twain turned and said, "You have the words, my dear, but you don't know the tune."

If I had kept my mouth shut, I wouldn't be here. ***–Sign under a mounted fish***

Talk is cheap because supply exceeds demand.
A word, once let out of the cage, cannot be whistled back again. ***–Horace***

Nobody talks much who doesn't say unwise things—things he did not mean to say. Talk, to me, is only spading up the ground for crops of thought. I can't answer for what will turn up. ***–Oliver Wendell Holmes***

Anjelica Huston remembers what it was like growing up as John Huston's daughter: Because of his intellect, he didn't suffer fools gladly. Once, at the dinner table, the subject of van Gogh came up. I said somewhat flippantly that I didn't like van Gogh. "You don't like van Gogh?" he countered. "Then name six of his paintings and tell me why you don't like them." I couldn't, of course. And he said, "Leave the room, and until you know what you're talking about, don't come back with your opinions to the dinner table."
–Mark Morrison in the Los Angeles Times Magazine

"When you shout obscenities, you downgrade the game, the public—and the way you're going to be remembered," says Rod Laver, the two-time winner of tennis' Grand Slam. Asked the worst thing he ever said to an umpire, Laver replies, "It would have to have been, 'Are you sure?'"

The trouble with most of us is that we would rather be ruined by praise then saved by criticism. ***–Norman Vincent Peale***

FAMILY LIFE

Marriage, Children, Home

Good family life is never an accident but always an achievement by those who share it.
–James H.S. Bossard

The great man is he who does not lose his child's heart. ***–Mencius***

He that would the daughter win,
Must with the mother first begin. ***–Old English proverb***

Perhaps the greatest blessing in marriage is that it lasts so long. The years, like the varying interests of each year, combine to buttress and enrich each other. Out of many shared years, one life. In a series of temporary relationships, one misses the ripening, gathering, harvesting joys, the deep, hard-won truths of marriage. *–Richard C. Cabot*

Youth fades, love droops, the leaves of friendship fall;
a mother's secret hope outlives them all. *–Oliver Wendell Holmes*

How can I teach, how can I save,
This child whose features are my own,
Whose feet run down the ways where
I have walked? *–Michael Roberts*

Respect the child. Be not too much his parent.
Trespass not on his solitude. *–Ralph Waldo Emerson*

How selfhood begins with a walking away,
And love is proved in the letting go. *–C. Day-Lewis*

Fatherhood is pretending the present you love the most is soap-on-a-rope.
–Bill Cosby

God knows that a mother needs fortitude and courage and tolerance and flexibility and patience and firmness and nearly every other brave aspect of the human soul. But because I happen to be a parent of almost fiercely maternal nature, I praise casualness. It seems to me the rarest of virtues. It is useful enough when children are small. It is important to the point of necessity when they are adolescents.
–Phyllis McGinley

After his introduction at Baylor University, President Lyndon Johnson remarked: "This is a moment I deeply wish my parents could have lived to share. My father would have enjoyed what you have so generously said of me—and my mother would have believed it."

Home is the one place in all this world where hearts are sure of each other. It is the place of confidence. It is the place where we tear off that mask of guarded and suspicious coldness which the world forces us to wear in self-defense, and where we pour out the unreserved communications of full and confiding hearts. It is the spot where expressions of tenderness gush out without any sensation of awkwardness and without any dread of ridicule. *–Frederick W. Robertson*

Heaven lies about us in our infancy! *–William Wordsworth*

My most brilliant achievement was my ability to be able to persuade my wife to marry me. *–Winston Churchill*

The most important thing a father can do for his children is to love their mother.
–Reverend Theodore Hesburgh, president, Notre Dame University

I would like to have engraved inside every wedding band, "Be kind to one another." This is the Golden Rule of marriage, and the secret of making love last through the years.
–Randolph Ray

It is better to advise than upbraid, for the one corrects the erring; the other only convicts them. *–Epictetus*

We must combine the toughness of the serpent and the softness of the dove, a tough mind and a tender heart. *–Martin Luther King, Jr.*

Before I got married I had six theories about bringing up children; now I have six children, and no theories. *–John Wilmot, Earl of Rochester*

Train up a child in the way he should go: and when he is old, he will not depart from it. *–The Bible, Proverbs 22:6*

To bring up a child in the way he should go,
travel that way yourself once in a while. *–Josh Billings*

Children need models more than they need critics. *–Joseph Joubert*

What harsh judges fathers are to all young men! *–Terence, c. 180 B.C.E.*

A daughter: The companion, the friend, and confidant of her mother, and the object of a pleasure something like the love between the angels to her father. *–Richard Steele, 1710*

The suspicious parent makes an artful child. *–Thomas G. Halliburton*

The hardest part of raising children is teaching them to ride bicycles. A father can run beside the bicycle or stand yelling directions while the child falls. A shaky child on a bicycle for the first time needs both support and freedom. The realization that this is what the child will always need can hit hard. *–Sloan Wilson*

Never lend your car to anyone to whom you have given birth. *–Erma Bombeck*

For there is no friend like a sister
In calm or stormy weather;
To cheer one on the tedious way,
To fetch one if one goes astray,
To lift one if one totters down,
To strengthen whilst one stands. *–Christina Rossetti*

As a boy handed his father a poor report card, he asked, "Father, what do you think is my trouble—heredity or environment?"

I have found the best way to give advice to your children is to find out what they want and then advise them to do it. *–Harry S Truman*

Keeping house is like stringing beads with no knot in the end of the thread.

Children sweeten labors, but they make misfortunes more bitter. They increase the cares of life, but they mitigate the remembrance of death. *–Francis Bacon, 1597*

Children are certain cares and uncertain comforts. *–English proverb*

After all, what is a pedestrian? He is a man who has two cars—one being driven by his wife, the other by one of his children. *–Robert Bradbury*

...A family...is a little kingdom, torn with factions and exposed to revolutions.
–Samuel Johnson, 1759

You may give them your love but not your thoughts, for they have their own thoughts. You may house their bodies but not their souls, for their souls dwell in the house of tomorrow, which you cannot visit, not even in your dreams. You may strive to be like them, but seek not to make them like you. For life goes not backward nor tarries with yesterday. You are the bows from which your children as living arrows are sent forth.
–Kahlil Gibran

The greatest thing in family life is to take a hint when a hint is intended—and not to take a hint when a hint isn't intended. *–Robert Frost*

If you want your children to keep their feet on the ground, put some responsibility on their shoulders. *–Abigail Van Buren*

The best years of a man's life are when the kids are old enough to shovel the snow but too young to drive the car.

Give a little love to a child and you will get a great deal back. *–John Ruskin*

Love your children with all your hearts, love them enough to discipline them before it is too late.... Praise them for important things, even if you have to stretch them a bit. Praise them a lot. They live on it like bread and butter and they need it more than bread and butter. *–Lavina Christensen Fugal*

A teacher, noticing how courteous and polite one of her pupils was, wished to praise her and teach the class a lesson. She asked, "Who taught you to be so polite?" The girl laughed and answered, "Really, no one. It just runs in our family."

If you must hold yourself up to your children as an object lesson...hold yourself up as an example and not as a warning. *–George Bernard Shaw*

We think our fathers fools, so wise we grow;
Our wiser sons, no doubt will think us so. *–Alexander Pope*

When I was a boy of fourteen, my father was so ignorant I could hardly stand to have the old man around. But when I got to twenty-one, I was astonished at how much he had learned in seven years. *–Mark Twain*

Mothers are the hardest to forgive;
Life is the gift they long to give us....

The commonest fallacy among women is that simply having children makes them a mother—which is as absurd as believing that having a piano makes one a musician.
–Sydney J. Harris

The most valuable gift you can give your family is a good example.

I think parents should forget the genius bit—what you want is a human being, a mensch, not a genius. *–Jerome Bruner*

If you have never been hated by your child, you have never been a parent.
–Bette Davis

If you bungle raising your children, I don't think whatever else you do well matters very much. *–Jacqueline Kennedy Onassis*

No success can compensate for failure in the home. *–David O. McKay*

The happiest moments of my life have been the few which I have passed at home in the bosom of my family. *–Thomas Jefferson*

A woman, speaking about her family's adjustment to having had to stay home more in order to take care of her dying father, said, "...You know what? It made us realize that we were hardly ever home together before."

Above all, I would teach him to tell the truth.... Truth telling, I have found, is the key to responsible citizenship. The thousands of criminals I have seen in 40 years of law enforcement have had one thing in common: every single one was a liar.
–J. Edgar Hoover, "What I Would Tell A Son"

Speaking of his ancestry, Lincoln once remarked, "I don't know who my grandfather was, but I am much more concerned to know what his grandson will be."

I can't help detesting my relations. I suppose it comes from the fact that none of us can stand other people having the same faults as ourselves. *–Oscar Wilde*

I never reprimand a boy in the evening—darkness and a troubled mind are a poor combination. *–Frank Boyden*

Perhaps host and guest is really the happiest relation for father and son.
–Evelyn Waugh

Certainly the time when the young are to be seen and not heard is gone in America—and gone for good. *–Richard M. Nixon*

We cannot always build the future for our youth, but we can build our youth for the future. *–Franklin D. Roosevelt*

Children today are tyrants. They contradict their parents, gobble their food, and tyrannize their teachers. *–Socrates, c. 420 B.C.E.*

There are times when parenthood seems nothing but feeding the mouth that bites you.
–Peter de Vries

Parenting is disruptive, with the possibility of harm, but also the possibility of growth.
–Frederick Grossman

You never can tell about a marriage from the outside, said the old philosopher. Some couples hold hands because they're afraid that if they let go they'd kill each other.

Before marriage, a man will lie awake thinking about something you said; after marriage, he'll fall asleep before you finish saying it. *–Helen Rowland*

The most difficult year of marriage is the one you're in. *–Franklin P. Jones*

A successful marriage is an edifice that must be rebuilt every day. *–Andre Maurois*

Perhaps the greatest social service that can be rendered by anybody...to mankind is to bring up a family. But...because there is nothing to sell, there is a very general disposition to regard a married woman's work as no work at all, and to take it as a matter of course that she should not be paid for it. *–George Bernard Shaw*

What a father says to his children is not heard by the world, but it will be heard by posterity. *–Jean Paul Richter*

A child is fed with milk and praise. *–Mary Lamb*

Home is a place where, when you go there,
They have to take you in. *–Robert Frost*

A man's home may seem to be his castle on the outside; inside, it is more often his nursery. *–Clare Boothe Luce*

Peace, like charity, begins at home. *–Franklin D. Roosevelt*

Teenage means perpetual emotion.

The father is always a Republican toward his son, and his mother's always a Democrat. *–Robert Frost*

He has quit the awkward stage; he is out of the teens. *–Terence, 166 B.C.E.*

Four is too big for his breeches,
Knows infinitely more than his mother,
Four is a matinee idol
To Two-and-a-Half, his brother.
Four is a lyric composer,
Raconteur extraordinaire,
Four gets away with murder,
Out of line, and into hair.
Where Four is, there dirt is also,
And nails and lengths of twine,
Four is Mr. Fix-it
And all of his tools are mine.
Four barges into everything
(Hearts, too) without a knock.
Four will be five on the twelfth of July,
And I wish I could stop the clock. *–Elsie Gibbs*

God sends children to enlarge our hearts, and to make us unselfish and full of kindly sympathies and affections. *–Mary Howitt*

Television is the third parent. *–Buckminster Fuller*

Television has proved that people will look at anything rather than each other. *–Ann Landers*

On Thanksgiving Day all over America, families sit down to dinner at the same moment—halftime.

There's always room for improvement, you know—it's the biggest room in the house. *–Louise Heath Leber*

...Perhaps a child who is fussed over gets a feeling of destiny; he thinks he is in the world for something important and it gives him drive and confidence. *–Dr. Benjamin Spock*

Could I climb to the highest place in Athens, I would lift my voice and proclaim, "Fellow citizens, why do you turn and scrape every stone to gather wealth and take so little care of your children to whom one day you must relinquish it all." *–Socrates, c. 420 B.C.E.*

It is a wise father that knows his own child. *–William Shakespeare, The Merchant of Venice*

Men are what their mothers made them. *–Ralph Waldo Emerson*

Parents who are afraid to put their foot down usually have children who step on their toes. *–Fortune-cookie proverb*

The universal language of children is called "gimme," otherwise known as "I wanna."

As is the mother, so is her daughter. *–The Bible, Ezekiel 16:44*

There is something frightful in the way in which not only characteristic qualities, but particular manifestations of them, are repeated from generation to generation. *–Oliver Wendell Holmes*

If you know his father and grandfather you may trust his son. *–Moroccan proverb*

A child tells in the street what its father and mother say at home. *–The Talmud*

I attribute my success in life to the moral, intellectual and physical education which I received from my mother. *–George Washington*

The best way to keep children home is to make the home a pleasant atmosphere—and let the air out of the tires. *–Dorothy Parker*

I wish I would have put as much emotion into my relationships with my mom and dad as I do now in my memories of them. We should pay more attention when we are making our memories. If we did, we wouldn't have so many regrets when all we have is memories. *–Elderly woman*

A parent's training starts when that future parent is still a child.

The family is one of nature's masterpieces. *–George Santayana*

"If..."
If a child lives with criticism,
He learns to condemn.
If a child lives with hostility,
He learns to fight.
If a child lives with ridicule,
He learns to be shy.
If a child lives with shame,
He learns to feel guilty.
If a child lives with tolerance,
He learns to be patient.
If a child lives with encouragement,
He learns confidence.
If a child lives with praise,
He learns to appreciate.
If a child lives with fairness,
He learns justice.
If a child lives with security,
He learns to have faith.
If a child lives with approval,
He learns to like himself.
If a child lives with acceptance and friendship,
He learns to find love in the world. *–Dorothy Law Nolte*

There are three degrees of filial piety. The highest is being a credit to our parents, the second is not disgracing them; the lowest is being able simply to support them.
–Confucius

Parents should be their children's parents first, their children's friends later.

Most of all the other beautiful things in life come by twos and threes, by dozens and hundreds. Plenty of roses, stars, sunsets, rainbows, brothers and sisters, aunts and cousins, but only one mother in the whole world. *–Kate Douglas Wiggin*

When I was young, my parents told me what to do; now that I am old, my children tell me what to do. I wonder when I will be able to do what I want to do.

One of the mysteries of life is how the boy who wasn't good enough to marry the daughter can be the father of the smartest grandchild in the world.

..If either side feels aggrieved, comfort rests in the knowledge that time will eventually even all scores. For yesterday's sittee is today's sitter. Today's employer of a sitter is tomorrow's parent of a sitter. And the sitter herself, incredibly soon, will have her own child to be sat for. *–Jean Libman Block*

Some women work so hard to make good husbands that they never manage to make good wives.

My wife and I tried breakfast together, but we had to stop or our marriage would have been wrecked. *–Winston Churchill*

"Cat's in the Cradle"

A child arrived just the other day,
He came to the world in the usual way.
But there were planes to catch and bills to pay.
He learned to walk while I was away.
He was talkin' before I knew
And as he grew he was saying:
"I'm gonna be like you, Dad.
You know I'm gonna be like you."

Well my son turned ten just the other day.
He said, "Thanks for the ball, Dad, let's play.
Can you teach me to throw?"
I said, "Not today; I got a lot to do—"
He said, "That's O.K." and he walked away.
He walked away, but his smile never dimmed.
It said, I'm gonna be like him, yeah.
You know, I'm gonna be like him.

Well, I've long since retired and my son's moved away.
I called him up just the other day.
I said, "I'd like to see you if you don't mind."
He said he'd love to if he could find the time.
"You see, my new job is a hassle and the kids have the flu,
But it's sure nice talking to you, Dad,
It's been sure nice talking to you."

And as he hung up the phone it occurred to me
He'd grown up just like me;
My boy was just like me. *–Story Songs Ltd. (sung by Harry Chapin)*

Keep your eyes wide open before marriage, half shut afterwards.
–Benjamin Franklin

A man in love is incomplete until he has married. Then he is finished.
–Zsa Zsa Gabor

We never know the love of our parents for us till we have become parents.
–Henry Ward Beecher

Nobody's family can hang out the sign, "Nothing the matter here."
–Chinese proverb

One good turn gets most of the blanket. *–Ellenberg*

Science has established two facts meaningful for human welfare: first, the foundation of the structure of human personality is laid down in early childhood; and second, the chief engineer in charge of this construction is the family. *–Meyer Francis Nimkoff*

Love is an act of endless forgiveness, a tender look which becomes a habit.
–Peter Ustinov

Children can have no better inheritance than believing parents. Religion can become real in the midst of the family as in practically no other way. Many of us have inherited great riches from our parents—the bank account of their personal faith and family prayers.
–Nels F.S. Ferre

A lady of 47 who has been married 27 years and has six children knows what love really is and once described it for me like this: "Love is what you've been through with somebody." *–James Thurber*

A suburban mother's role is to deliver children obstetrically once, and by car for ever after. *–Peter de Vries*

.Security is when I'm very much in love with somebody extraordinary who loves me back. *–Shelley Winters*

There are two stages for parents—when your children ask all the questions and when they think they know all the answers.

The greatest aid to adult education is children. *–Charlie T. Jones and Bob Phillips*

A man travels the world over in search of what he needs, and returns home to find it.
–George Moore

In loco parentis—Latin for "Children can drive their parents crazy."

I never thought that you should be rewarded for the greatest privilege in life.
–May Robert Coker, on being named Mother of the Year, 1958

Marriage may be compared to a cage: the birds outside frantic to get in and those inside frantic to get out. *–Montaigne, 1588*

The only thing worse than a husband who never notices what you cook or what you wear, is a husband who always notices what you cook and what you wear.
–Sandra Litoff

Marriage is not just spiritual communion and passionate embraces; marriage is also three meals a day, sharing the workload and remembering to carry out the trash.
–Dr. Joyce Brothers

A marriage without conflicts is almost as inconceivable as a nation without crises.
–Andre Maurois

The two things children wear out are clothes and parents.

Never grow a wishbone, daughter, where your backbone ought to be.
–Clementine Paddleford, quoting advice from her mother

Parents are wise to overlook seemingly disrespectful outbursts from time to time....The point must get across the idea that "I love you always, but sometimes I do not love your behavior." *–Amy Vanderbilt, on teenagers*

To know after absence the familiar street and road and village and house is to know again the satisfaction of home. *–Hal Borland*

Children have never been good at listening to their elders, but they have never failed to imitate them. *–James Baldwin*

Example is not the main thing in influencing others. It is the only thing. *–Albert Schweitzer*

A boy is a magical creature—you can lock him out of your workshop, but you can't lock him out of your heart. You can get him out of your study, but you can't get him out of your mind. Might as well give up—he is your captor, your jailer, your boss, and your master—a freckled-faced, pint-sized, cat-chasing bundle of noise. But when you come home at night with only the shattered pieces of your hopes and dreams he can mend them like new with two magic words—"Hi, Dad!"

Little girls are the nicest things that happen to people. They are born with a little bit of angelshine about them, and though it wears thin sometimes, there is always enough left to lasso your heart—even when they are sitting in the mud, or crying temperamental tears, or parading up the street in mother's best clothes. *–Alan Beck*

Teach your child to hold his tongue; he'll learn fast enough to speak. *–Benjamin Franklin*

All our dreams can come true—if we have the courage to pursue them. *–Walt Disney*

Let our children grow tall and some taller than others if they have it in them to do so. *–Margaret Thatcher*

Honest differences are often a healthy sign of progress. *–Mahatma Gandhi*

The time to repair the roof is when the sun is shining. *–John F. Kennedy*

We can do no great things—only small things with great love. *–Mother Teresa*

To maintain a joyful family requires much from both the parents and the children. Each member of the family has to become, in a special way, the servant of the others. *–Pope John Paul IIr*

Integrity

Character, Service, Loyalty

We can't put our faults behind us until we face them.

Father taught us that opportunity and responsibility go hand in hand. I think we all act on that principle; on the basic human impulse that makes a man want to make the best of what's in him and what's been given him. *–Laurence Rockefeller*

How many cares one loses when one decides not to be something, but to be someone.
–Gabrielle "Coco" Chanel

All that is essential for the triumph of evil is that good men do nothing.
–Edmund Burke

It's a matter of having principles. It's easy to have principles when you're rich. The important thing is to have principles when you're poor. *–Ray Kroc*

The measure of a man's real character is what he would do if he knew he would never be found out. *–Thomas Macaulay*

There's one way to find out if a man is honest—ask him. If he says "yes," you know he is crooked. *–Groucho Marx*

They go forth [into the world] with well-developed bodies, fairly developed minds and undeveloped hearts. An undeveloped heart—not a cold one. The difference is important.... *–E. M. Forster, novelist, on British public school boys*

...Of those to whom much is given, much is required. And when at some future date the high court of history sits in judgment on each one of us—recording whether in our brief span of service we fulfilled our responsibilities to the state—our success or failure, in whatever office we may hold, will be measured by the answers to four questions—were we truly men of courage...were we truly men of judgment...were we truly men of integrity...were we truly men of dedication? *–John F. Kennedy*

The herd may graze where it pleases or stampede where it pleases, but he who lives the adventurous life will remain unafraid when he finds himself alone.
–Raymond B. Fosdick

The world's best reformers are those who begin on themselves.

Think positively about yourself, keep your thoughts and your actions clean, ask God who made you to keep on remaking you. *–Norman Vincent Peale*

The wicked flee when no man pursueth; but the righteous are bold as a lion.
–The Bible, Proverbs 28:1

This above all: to thine own self be true,
And it must follow, as the night the day,
Thou canst not then be false to any man. *–William Shakespeare*

Let unswerving integrity ever be your watchword.
–Bernard Baruch, recalling his "most enduring lesson" from his father

Our scientific power has outrun our spiritual power. We have guided missiles and misguided men. *–Martin Luther King, Jr.*

I do not pray for success. I ask for faithfulness. *–Mother Teresa*

Beloved Pan, and all ye other gods who haunt this place, give me beauty in the inward soul; and may the outward and inward be at one. *–Socrates*

God frees our souls, not from service, not from duty, but into service and into duty, and he who mistakes the purpose of his freedom mistakes the character of his freedom. He who thinks that he is being released from the work, and not set free in order that he may accomplish that work, mistakes the condition into which his soul is invited to enter.

–Phillips Brooks

Do something for somebody every day for which you do not get paid.

–Albert Schweitzer

Our humanity were a poor thing were it not for the divinity that stirs within us.

–Francis Bacon

Let then our first act every morning be to make the following resolve for the day: I shall not fear anyone on earth. I shall fear only God. I shall not bear ill will toward anyone. I shall not submit to injustice from anyone. I shall conquer untruth by truth. And in resisting untruth I shall put up with all suffering. *–Mahatma Gandhi*

Men are valued, not for what they are, but for what they seem to be.

–E.G. Bulwer-Lytton, 1840

One man practicing sportsmanship is far better than a hundred teaching it.

–Knute Rockne

Nearly all men can stand adversity, but if you want to test a man's character, give him power. *–Abraham Lincoln*

The more he talked of his honor the faster we counted our spoons.

–Ralph Waldo Emerson

The ability to think straight, some knowledge of the past, some vision of the future, some skill to do useful service, some urge to fit that service into the well-being of the community—these are the most vital things education must try to produce. If we can achieve them in the citizens of our land, then...we shall have brought to America the wisdom and the courage to match her destiny. *–Virginia Gildersleeve*

A man has made at least a start on discovering the meaning of human life when he plants shade trees under which he knows full well he will never sit.

–Elton Trueblood

Heaven will be inherited by every man who has heaven in his soul. *–Confucius*

The farther a man knows himself to be from perfection, the nearer he is to it.

–Gerard Groote

Courage is the first of human qualities because it is the quality which guarantees all the others. *–Winston Churchill*

So long as a man is angry he can't be in the right. *–Chinese proverb*

The anger of a good man lasts an instant; that of a meddler two hours; that of a base man a day and a night; and that of a great sinner until death. *–Sanskrit proverb*

Abou Ben Adhem (may his tribe increase!)
Awoke one night from a deep dream of peace,
And saw within the moonlight in his room,
Making it rich and like a lily in bloom,
An angel writing in a book of gold;
Exceeding peace had made Ben Adhem bold,
And to the Presence in the room he said,
"What writest thou?" The vision raised its head,
And with a look made of all sweet accord,
Answered, "The names of those who love the Lord."
"And is mine one?" said Abou. "Nay, not so,"
Replied the angel. Abou spoke more low,
But cheerily still, and said, "I pray thee, then,
Write me as one that loves his fellow-men."
The angel wrote, and vanished. The next night
It came again with a great wakening light,
And showed the names whom love of God had blessed;
And, lo! Ben Adhem's name led all the rest! *–Leigh Hunt*

The size of a man can be measured by the size of the thing that makes him angry.
–J. Kenfield Morley

Beautiful thoughts hardly bring us to God until they are acted upon. No one can have a true idea of right until he does it. *–William R. Inge*

The best way to break a habit is to drop it. *–Bartig*

Conviction is worthless unless it is converted into conduct. *–Thomas Carlyle*

U-turn if you want to. This lady's not for turning. *–Margaret Thatcher*

...In a large sense we cannot dedicate, we cannot hallow this ground. The brave men, living and dead, who struggled here, have consecrated it far above our poor power to add or detract.... *–Abraham Lincoln's Gettysburg Address, 1863*

...The workshop of character is everyday life. The uneventful and commonplace hour is where the battle is lost or won. *–Maltbie D. Babcock*

Little white lies are for golfers.

Courage and cowardice are antithetical. Courage is an inner resolution to go forward in spite of obstacles and frightening situations; cowardice is a submissive surrender to circumstance. Courage breeds creative self-affirmation; cowardice produces destructive self-abnegation. Courage faces fear and thereby masters it; cowardice represses fear and is thereby mastered by it. Courageous men never lose the zest for living even though their life situation is zestless; cowardly men, overwhelmed by the uncertainties of life, lose the will to live. We must constantly build dykes of courage to hold back the flood of fear.
–Martin Luther King, Jr.

No man is free who is not master of himself. *–Epictetus*

The ablest man I ever met is the man you think you are. *–Franklin D. Roosevelt*

He who thinks he has no faults—has one.

When it comes to giving, some people stop at nothing. *–Sheetz*

Every man has three friends—children, money, and his good deeds. When the time comes for him to leave the world, he calls upon his children, who reply, "Don't you know that no one can conquer death?" Then he calls upon his money, saying, "Day and night I have worked for you. Save me now." The money replies, "Wealth cannot deliver you from death." He next calls on his good deeds and they reply, "Go in peace. By the time you arrive in the next world, we will be there before you to offer you help."

–The Talmud

I've never signed a contract, so I never have a deadline. A deadline's an unnerving thing. I just finished a book, and if the publisher doesn't like it that's his privilege. There've been many, many rejections. If you want to write in your own way, that's the chance you take. *–Marchette Chute*

Diplomats are useful only in fair weather. As soon as it rains they drown in every drop.

–Charles de Gaulle

After Benjamin Franklin had received a letter thanking him for having done a kindness, he replied: "As to the kindness you mention, I wish I could have been of more service to you than I have been, but if I had, the only thanks that I should desire are that you would always be ready to service any other person that may need your assistance, and so let good offices go around, for mankind are all of a family. As for my own part, when I am employed in serving others I do not look upon myself as conferring favors but paying debts."

I cannot tell you how much I love to play for people. Would you believe it—sometimes when I sit down to practice and there is no one else in the room, I have to stifle an impulse to ring for the elevator man and offer him money to come in and hear me.

–Arthur Rubenstein

A good example is the best sermon. *–Herbert J. Taylor*

Anger is never without a reason, but seldom with a good one. *–Benjamin Franklin*

'Tis better to suffer wrong than do it. *–Thomas Fuller*

Character is something each one of us must build for himself, out of the laws of God and nature, the examples of others, and—most of all—out of the trials and errors of daily life. Character is the total of thousands of small daily strivings to live up to the best that is in us. Character is the final decision to reject whatever is demeaning to oneself or to others and with confidence and honesty to choose the right. *–General Arthur G. Trudeau*

The question is not what man can scorn, or disparage, or find fault with, but what he can love, and value, and appreciate. *–John Ruskin*

Loyalty is an animal instinct; we can take lessons in it from dogs.

Youth is not entirely a time of life; it is a state of mind. Nobody grows old by merely living a number of years. People grow old by deserting their ideals. You are as young as your faith, as old as your doubt; as young as your self-confidence, as old as your fear; as young as your hope, as old as your despair. *–Douglas MacArthur*

Always fall in with what you're asked to accept. Take what is given, and make it over your way. My aim in life has always been to hold my own with whatever's going. Not against: with. *–Robert Frost*

We live in a society where the sin is getting caught.

I've helped some people. *–Anna Mary "Grandma" Moses' reply at 93 when asked what she was proudest of in her life*

In spite of everything, I still believe that people are really good at heart.
–Anne Frank, Dutch-Jewish teenage diarist, 1944

During the Occupation, but before his imprisonment, King Christian X of Denmark noticed a Nazi flag flying over a Danish public building. He called the German commandant and demanded that the flag be immediately removed. The commandant refused. "Then a soldier will go and take it down," said the king. "He will be shot," replied the commandant. "I think not," retorted the king, "for I shall be the soldier." The flag was removed.

Blessed are those who can give without remembering and take without forgetting.
–Elizabeth Bibesco

Gratitude is not only the greatest of virtues, but the parent of all others.
–Cicero, 54 B.C.E.

Thanks is sometimes a mask for ingratitude. True gratitude is expressed in deeds rather than words.

Life is an exciting business and most exciting when it is lived for others.
–Helen Keller

There may be times when we are powerless to prevent injustice, but there must never be a time when we fail to protest. *–Elie Wiesel*

The entire object of true education is to make people not merely to do the right things, but to enjoy them; not merely industrious, but to love industry; not merely learned, but to love knowledge; not merely pure, but to love purity; not merely just, but to hunger and thirst after justice. *–John Ruskin*

We must have many Lincoln-hearted men. *–Vachel Lindsay*

As for charity, it is a matter in which the immediate effect on the persons directly concerned, and the ultimate consequence to the general good, are apt to be at complete war with one another. *–John Stuart Mill*

Civilization is just a slow process of learning to be kind. *–Charles L. Lucas*

Right is more precious than peace. *–Woodrow Wilson*

The weak can never forgive. Forgiveness is the attribute of the strong....Hatred can be overcome only by love. *–Mahatma Gandhi*

When a man blames others for his failures, it's a good idea to credit others with his successes. *–Howard W. Newton*

A gentleman is one who thinks more of other people's feelings than of his own rights; and more of other people's rights than of his own feelings.
–Matthew Henry Buckham

Men show their characters in nothing more clearly than in what they think laughable.
–Goethe

I have four things to learn in life: To think clearly without hurry or confusion; To love everybody sincerely; To act in everything with the highest motives; To trust in God unhesitatingly. *–Albert Schweitzer*

It is a grand mistake to think of being great without goodness; and I pronounce it as certain that there was never yet a truly great man that was not at the same time truly virtuous. *–Benjamin Franklin*

A man can stand a lot as long as he can stand himself. He can live without hope, without friends, without books, even without music, as long as he can listen to his own thoughts.
–Axel Munthe

A saint is one who makes goodness attractive. *–Laurence Housman*

A test of any man's character is how he takes his praise.

Not that I would not, if I could, be both handsome and well-dressed and a great athlete, and make a million a year, be a wit, a bon vivant, and a lady killer, as well as a philosopher, a philanthropist, a statesman, warrior, and African explorer, as well as a "tone poet" and a saint. The thing is simply impossible. The millionaire's work would run counter to the saint's; the bon vivant and the philanthropist would trip each other up; the philosopher and the lady killer could not well keep house in the same tenement....
–William James

If all that Americans want is security they can go to prison. They'll have enough to eat, a bed and a roof over their heads. But if an American wants to preserve his dignity and his equality as a human being, he must not bow his neck to any dictorial government.
–Dwight D. Eisenhower

He errs as other men do, but errs with integrity.
–Thomas Jefferson, speaking of George Washington

A politician thinks of the next election—a statesman, of the next generation.
–James Freeman Clarke

"The worst thing that can happen to a youngster starting school," said the lawyer, "is to be caught cheating." "Not at all," said the clergyman, "the worst thing at the start of a person's life is to cheat and not get caught."

We will be remembered not for the power of our weapons but for the power of our compassion, our dedication to human welfare. *–Hubert H. Humphrey*

Morality is a personal thing. Each of us, through the teachings of our childhood and our experience with others, has developed an unwritten list of criteria of behavior.

Too frequently I find that a person's morality is a code by which he believes others should perform toward him, rather than a code guiding his behavior toward others. It is our actual day-to-day behavior that determines and defines our morality.

We have grasped the mystery of the atom and rejected the Sermon on the Mount.
–General Omar Bradley

If a man be gracious, and courteous to strangers, it shows he is a citizen of the world....
–Sir Francis Bacon, 1597

An old grouch, about to enter a building, found that the door was being held open for him, with considerable effort, by a little boy. "Never mind that," said the old grouch, "I don't need your help." The little boy smiled up at him and said, "You're welcome."

A people that values its privileges above its principles soon loses both.
–Dwight D. Eisenhower

The roots of responsibility run out to the ends of the earth and we can no more isolate our consciences from world issues than we can fence off our oyster beds from the tides of the ocean. *–Ralph W. Sockman*

Men make counterfeit money; in many more cases, money makes counterfeit men.
–Sydney J. Harris

Knowing what's right doesn't mean much unless you do what's right.

There are a large number of well-meaning ambassadors...what I call the pink-tea type, who merely reside in the service instead of working in the service.
–Theodore Roosevelt

You will never be sorry—
for thinking before acting,
for hearing before judging,
for forgiving your enemies,
for being candid and frank,
for helping a fallen brother,
for being honest in business,
for thinking before speaking,
for being loyal to your church,
for standing by your principles,
for stopping your ears to gossip,
for bridling a slanderous tongue,
for harboring only pure thoughts,
for sympathizing with the afflicted,
for being courteous and kind to all. *–Anonymous*

The art of being yourself at your best is the art of unfolding your personality into the man you want to be....Be gentle with yourself, learn to love yourself, to forgive yourself, for only as we have the right attitude toward ourselves can we have the right attitude toward others. *–Wilfred Peterson*

Non-violence and truth are inseparable and presuppose one another. There is no god higher than truth. *–Mahatma Gandhi*

My kind of loyalty was loyalty to one's country, not to its institutions or its office-holders. *–Mark Twain*

There are those who give little of the much they have—and they give it for recognition and their hidden desire makes their gifts unwholesome.

And there are those who have little and give it all.

These are the believers in life and the bounty of life, and their coffer is never empty.

There are those who give with joy, and that joy is their reward. And there are those who give with pain, and that pain is their baptism.

And there are those who give and know not pain in giving, nor do they seek joy, nor give with mindfulness of virtue; They give as in yonder valley the myrtle breathes its fragrance into space. Through the hands of such as these God speaks, and from behind their eyes He smiles upon the earth. *–Kahlil Gibran*

Enlightened loyalty requires that each citizen take the trouble to learn about, to discuss, to think through, the crucial issues of our time. *–Lyndon B. Johnson*

I don't want any yes-men around me. I want everybody to tell me the truth even if it costs them their jobs. *–Samuel Goldwyn*

I decline to accept the end of man. It is easy enough to say that man is immortal simply because he will endure: that when the last ding-dong of doom has clanged and faded from the vast worthless rock hanging tideless in the last red and dying evening, that even then there will still be one more sound: that of his puny inexhaustible voice, still talking. I refuse to accept this. I believe that man will not merely endure: he will prevail. He is immortal, not because he alone among creatures has an inexhaustible voice, but because he has a soul, a spirit capable of compassion and sacrifice and endurance.

–William Faulkner, 1962 Nobel Prize acceptance speech

...In about the same degree as you are helpful, you will be happy.–Karl Reiland

We are a nation of many nationalities, many races, many religions—bound together by a single unity, the unity of freedom and equality. *–Franklin D. Roosevelt*

One of the worst things that can happen in life is to win a bet on a horse at an early age. *–Danny McGoorty*

Presidents learn—perhaps sooner than others—that our destiny is fashioned by what all of us do, by the deeds and desires of each citizen, as one tiny drop of water after another ultimately makes a big river. *–Lyndon B. Johnson*

Liberty is not free; it is paid for with good citizenship.

And so, my fellow Americans: ask not what your country can do for you—ask what you can do for your country. *–John F. Kennedy*

Ask not what your country can do for you, but rather what you can do for your country. *–Marcus Tullius Cicero, Roman orator and statesman, 63 B.C.E.*

Self-respect cannot be hunted. It cannot be purchased. It is never for sale. It cannot be fabricated out of public relations. It comes to us when we are alone, in quiet moments, in quiet places, when we suddenly realize that, knowing the good, we have done it; knowing the beautiful, we have served it; knowing the truth, we have spoken it. *–Whitney Griswold, president, Yale University*

My importance to the world is relatively small. On the other hand, my importance to myself is tremendous. I am all I have to work with, to play with, to suffer and to enjoy. It is not the eyes of others that I am wary of, but my own. I do not intend to let myself down more that I can possibly help, and I find that the fewer illusions I have about myself or the world around me, the better company I am for myself. *–Noel Coward*

It takes good manners to put up with bad ones.

To let [yourself] be bound by a duty from the moment you see it approaching is a part of the integrity that alone justifies responsibility. *–Dag Hammarskjold, UN Secretary General*

Not what we give, but what we share,—
For the gift without the giver is bare;
Who gives himself with his alms feeds three,—
Himself, his hungering neighbor, and Me. *–James Russell Lowell*

Heroism is the brilliant triumph of the soul over the flesh: that is to say, over fear: fear of poverty, of suffering, of calumny, of sickness, of isolation, and of death. *–H. F. Amiel, 1849*

Thomas Jefferson's Decalogue
I. Never put off till tomorrow what you can do today.
II. Never trouble another for what you can do yourself.
III. Never spend your money before you have it.
IV. Never buy what you do not want...because it is cheap; it will be dear to you.
V. Pride costs us more than hunger, thirst, and cold.
VI. We never repent of having eaten too little.
VII. Nothing is troublesome that we do willingly.
VIII. How much pain have cost us the evils which have never happened.
IX. Take things always by their smooth handle.
X. When angry, count ten before you speak; if very angry, a hundred.

The foundation of morality is to have done, once and for all, with lying. *–T.H. Huxley*

We cannot get grace from gadgets. In the bakelite house of the future, the dishes may not break, but the heart can. Even a man with ten shower baths may find life flat, stale and unprofitable. *–J.B. Priestley*

The tumult and the shouting dies;
the captains and the kings depart:
still stands thine ancient sacrifice,
an humble and a contrite heart.
Lord God of hosts, be with us yet,
Lest we forget—lest we forget! *–Rudyard Kipling*

The strongest man in the world is he who stands alone. *–Henrik Ibsen*

Happy is he who has finished the labors of life. *–Euripides, 5th century B.C.E.*

Rare is the person who can weigh the faults of others without his thumb on the scale.
–Byron Langfeld

The most difficult thing in the world is to know how to do a thing and to watch someone else doing it wrong, without commenting. *–T.H. White*

Marie Antoinette's last words, reputedly spoken to her executioner on whose foot she had accidentally stepped: "I beg your pardon. I did not do it on purpose."

Life is what we are alive to. It is not length but breadth. To be alive only to appetite, pleasure, pride, money-making, and not to goodness, kindness, purity, love, history, poetry, music, flowers, stars, God, and eternal hope is to be all but dead.
–Maltbie D. Babcock

Twelve Things To Remember

1. The value of time
2. The success of perseverance
3. The pleasure of working
4. The dignity of simplicity
5. The worth of character
6. The power of kindness
7. The influence of example
8. The obligation of duty
9. The wisdom of economy
10. The virtue of patience
11. The improvement of talent
12. The joy of originating *–Anonymous*

Happiness

Satisfaction, Contentment, Confidence, Life's Joys

Happiness is essentially a state of going somewhere, wholeheartedly, one-directionally, without regret or reservation. *–William H. Sheldon*

If you can't change facts, try bending your attitude.

Wear a smile and have friends: wear a scowl and have wrinkles. *–George Eliot*

Happiness comes of the capacity to feel deeply, to enjoy simply, to think freely, to risk life, to be needed. *–Storm Jameson*

Nobody can make you feel inferior without your consent. *–Eleanor Roosevelt*

Laugh at yourself first, before anyone else can. *–Elsa Maxwell*

Just think how happy you'd be if you lost everything you have right now—and then got it back again.

To be without some of the things you want is an indispensable part of happiness.
–Bertrand Russell

The happiest people are those who discover that what they should be doing and what they are doing are the same thing.

No one could be more unhappy than a man who has never known affliction.
–Ascribed to Demetrius Phalerens, c. 300 B.C.E.

It is a kind of happiness to know to what extent we may be unhappy.
–La Rochefoucauld, 1665

It is wrong to assume that men of immense wealth are always happy.
–John D. Rockefeller, Sr.

Walter Hagen, the highly successful golf professional, offered his secret of success: "You're here for only a short visit, so don't hurry, don't worry, and be sure to smell the flowers along the way."

Some cause happiness wherever they go; others whenever they go.

Laugh and the world laughs with you; Weep and you weep alone...
–Ella Wheeler Wilcox, 1883

This is the true joy in life, the being used for a purpose recognized by yourself as a mighty one; the being thoroughly worn out before you are thrown on the scrap heap; the being a force of Nature instead of a feverish selfish little clod of ailments and grievances complaining that the world will not devote itself to making you happy.
–George Bernard Shaw

Laughter is more contagious than tears.

You can't feel down in the mouth with the corners up.

If you are happy you can always learn to dance. ***–Balinese Saying***

Where ambition ends happiness begins. ***–Hungarian proverb***

A merry heart doeth good like a medicine.... ***–The Bible, Proverbs 17:22***

Some people are happy remembering the past, and some happy forgetting it.

There is no duty we so much underrate, as the duty of being happy.
–Robert Louis Stevenson

The secret of happiness is this: let your interests be as wide as possible, and let your reactions to the things and persons that interest you be as far as possible friendly rather than hostile. ***–Bertrand Russell***

Success is getting what you want; happiness is wanting what you get. ***–Dale Carnegie***

The essentials for happiness are: Something to do, someone to love, and something to hope for.

What life means to us is determined not so much by what life brings to us as by the attitude we bring to life; not so much by what happens to us as by our reaction to what happens. ***–Lewis L. Dunnington***

People are constantly clamoring for the joy of life. As for me, I find the joy of life in the hard and cruel battle of life—to learn something is a joy to me. ***–August Strindberg***

It is not easy to find happiness in ourselves and it is not possible to find it elsewhere.
–Agnes Repplier

The hands of those I meet are dumbly eloquent to me. I have met people so empty of joy that when I clasped their frosty fingertips it seemed as if I were shaking hands with a northeast storm. Others there are whose hands have sunbeams in them, so that their grasp warms my heart. It may be only the clinging touch of a child's hand, but there is as much potential sunshine in it for me as there is in a loving glance for others.
–Helen Keller

If something is wrong, fix it if you can. But train yourself not to worry. Worry never fixes anything. ***–Mrs. Ernest Hemingway***

Happiness is possible only when one is busy. The body must toil, the mind must be occupied, and the heart must be satisfied.

Writing music is my one and only passion and joy. ***–Mozart, 1777***

Happiness consists in activity—it is a running stream, not a stagnant pool.
–John Mason Good

There must be more to life than having everything.
–Maurice Sendak, children's book author and illustrator

The Triple-A formula for experiencing happiness begins by accepting the moment, appreciating it, and adapting to its opportunities.

One of the most tragic things I know about human nature is that all of us tend to put off living. We are all dreaming of some magical rose garden over the horizon instead of enjoying the roses that are blooming outside our windows today. *–Dale Carnegie*

Happiness is good health and a bad memory. *–Ingrid Bergman*

There are as many nights as days, and the one is just as long as the other in the year's course. Even a happy life cannot be without a measure of darkness, and the word "happy" would lose its meaning if it were not balanced by sadness. *–Dr. Carl Jung*

One would suffer a great deal to be happy. *–Mary Wortley Montague, 1759*

Labor, if it were not necessary for existence, would be indispensable for the happiness of man. *–Samuel Johnson, c. 1770*

It is the inalienable right of all to be happy. *–Elizabeth Cady Stanton, 1861*

Man is the artificer of his own happiness. *–Henry David Thoreau*

One of the sanest, surest, and most generous joys of life comes from being happy over the good fortune of others. *–Archibald Rutledge*

Happiness, or misery, is in the mind. It is the mind that lives.
–William Cobbett, 1819

How to Live a Hundred Years Happily

1. Do not be on the lookout for ill health.
2. Keep usefully at work.
3. Have a hobby.
4. Learn to be satisfied.
5. Keep on liking people.
6. Meet adversity valiantly.
7. Meet the little problems of life with decision.
8. Above all, maintain a good sense of humor, best done by saying something pleasant every time you get a chance.
9. Live and make the present hour pleasant and cheerful. Keep your mind out of the past, and keep it out of the future. *–John A. Schindler*

Happiness is the only good. The time to be happy is now. The place to be happy is here. The way to be happy is to make others so. *–Robert G. Ingersoll*

It gives me a deep comforting sense that "things seen are temporal and things unseen are eternal." *–Helen Keller*

Gratitude is a fruit of great cultivation; you do not find it among gross people.
–Samuel Johnson on his journey to the Hebrides Islands, 1773

...There is only one way to achieve happiness on this terrestrial ball, and that is to have either a clear conscience or none at all. *–Ogden Nash*

Wings

Be like the bird
That, pausing in her flight
Awhile on boughs too slight,
Feels them give way
Beneath her and yet sings,
Knowing that she hath wings. *–Victor Hugo*

True happiness is of a retired nature, and an enemy to pomp and noise; it arises, in the first place, from the enjoyment of one's self, and in the next, from the friendship and conversation of a few select companions. *–Joseph Addison, 1711*

Life's greatest happiness is to be convinced we are loved. *–Victor Hugo*

Ten Spiritual Tonics

1. Stop worrying. Worry kills life.
2. Begin each day with a prayer. It will arm your soul.
3. Control appetite. Over-indulgence clogs body and mind.
4. Accept your limitations.
5. Don't envy. It wastes time and energy.
6. Have faith in people. Cynicism sours the disposition.
7. Find a hobby. It will relax your nerves.
8. Read a book a week to stimulate imagination and broaden your view.
9. Spend some time alone for the peace of solitude and silence.
10. Try to want what you have, instead of spending your strength trying to get what you want. *–Abraham L. Feinberg*

We need to find God, and he cannot be found in noise and restlessness. God is the friend of silence. *–Mother Teresa*

Be unselfish. That is the first and final commandment for those who would be useful and happy in their usefulness. If you think of yourself only, you cannot develop because you are choking the source of development, which is spiritual expansion through thought for others. *–Charles W. Eliot*

Happiness doesn't come from doing what we like to do but from liking what we have to do. *–Wilfred Peterson*

All men have happiness as their object: there is no exception. However different the means they employ, they all aim at the same end. *–Blaise Pascal*

If you observe a really happy man you will find him building a boat, writing a symphony, educating his son, growing double dahlias in his garden, or looking for dinosaur eggs in the Gobi desert. He will not be searching for happiness as if it were a collar button that has rolled under the radiator. He will not be striving for it as a goal in itself. He will have become aware that he is happy in the course of living life twenty-four crowded hours of the day. *–W. Beran Wolfe*

If one only wished to be happy, this could be easily accomplished; but we wish to be happier than other people, and this is always difficult, for we believe others to be happier than they are. *–Montesquieu*

Disdain for history is symptomatic of the malaise of today's youth culture and of the larger society which nurtured it. Resenting death, we murdered time. Almost too late we see that what we have slain is not time but our sense of ourselves as humans. To reject the past is to deprive today of its meaning tomorrow. To evade the significance of time is to empty life of its significance. It is that meaninglessness which pervades this age of instant gratification and instant results and permanent dissatisfaction.

–William V. Shannon

Real joy comes not from ease or riches or from the praise of men, but from doing something worthwhile. *–Wilfred T. Grenfell*

Oh, how bitter a thing it is to look into happiness through another man's eyes.

–William Shakespeare

Gratitude is the heart's memory. *–French proverb*

Gratitude is not only the greatest of virtues, but the parent of all the others.

–Cicero, 54 B.C.E.

The voluntary path to cheerfulness, if our spontaneous cheerfulness be lost, is to sit up cheerfully, and act and speak as if cheerfulness were already there. To feel brave, act as if we were brave, use all our will to that end, and courage will very likely replace fear. If we act as if from some better feeling, the bad feeling soon folds its tent like an Arab and silently steals away. *–William James*

Beauty is also to be found in a day's work. *–Mamie Sypert Burns*

Happiness comes of the capacity to feel deeply, to enjoy simply, to think freely, to risk life, to be needed. *–Storm Jameson*

The most certain sign of wisdom is a continual cheerfulness; her state is like that of things in the regions above the moon, always clear and serene.

–Michel de Montaigne, 1580

It is neither wealth nor splendor, but tranquility and occupation, which give happiness.

–Thomas Jefferson

We never enjoy perfect happiness; our most fortunate successes are mingled with sadness; some anxieties always perplex the reality of our satisfaction.

–Pierre Coneille, El Cid, 1636

Human felicity is produced not so much by great pieces of good fortune that seldom happen, as by little advantages that occur every day. *–Benjamin Franklin*

One positive advantage to age for me is that I have more time to smell the roses.

–Helen Hayes

One of the many things nobody ever tells you about middle age is that it's such a nice change from being young. *–Dorothy Canfield Fisher*

In these times you have to be an optimist to open your eyes when you awake in the morning. *–Carl Sandburg*

I have now reigned about fifty years in victory or peace, beloved by my subjects, dreaded by my enemies, and respected by my allies. Riches and honors, power and pleasure, have waited on my call, nor does any earthly blessing appear to have been wanting to my felicity. In this situation I have diligently numbered the days of pure and genuine happiness which have fallen to my lot: they amount to fourteen.

–Ascribed to Abd-er-Rahman III of Spain, c. 960

Start every day off with a smile and get it over with. *–W. C. Fields*

Everything has its beauty, but not everyone sees it. *–Confucius*

He that keepeth the law, happy is he. *–The Bible, Proverbs 29:18*

To fill the hour—that is happiness.... *–Ralph Waldo Emerson*

He is happy that knoweth not himself to be otherwise. *–Thomas Fuller, 1732*

Happy is the man that findeth wisdom, and the man that getteth understanding.

–The Bible, Proverbs 3:13

If, among the delights of the open world, I were to choose the sights, the sounds and the fragrances I most want to see and hear and smell on a final day on earth, I think I would choose these:

the clear, ethereal song of a white-throated
sparrow singing at dawn;
the smell of pine trees in the room;
the lonely calling of Canadian geese;
the sight of a dragonfly glinting in the sunshine;
the voice of a hermit thrush far in a darkening
woods at evening;
and—most spirited and moving of sights –
the white cathedral of a cumulus cloud floating
serenely in the blue of the sky. *–Edwin Way Teale*

To business that we love we rise betime. And go to't with delight.

–William Shakespeare, "Antony and Cleopatra," c. 1606

Some people merely spend their leisure time; others enjoy it.

Humanly speaking, it is only when the hair is white, when...life is almost over, that men begin to realize how hopelessly elusive is the happiness promised by wealth and fame.

–Joseph McSorley

Friends, books, cheerful heart, and conscience clear
Are the most choice companions we have here. *–William Mather, 1681*

Happiness in this world, when it comes, comes incidentally. Make it the object of pursuit, and it leads us a wild-goose chase, and is never attained. Follow some other object, and very possibly we may find that we have caught happiness without dreaming of it.

–Nathaniel Hawthorne

We do not remember days, we remember moments. *–Cesare Pavese*

We are more interested in making others believe we are happy than in trying to be happy ourselves. *–La Rochefoucauld, 1665*

It is something to be able to paint a particular picture, or to carve a statue, and so to make a few objects beautiful; but it is far more glorious to carve and paint the very atmosphere and medium through which we look. To affect the quality of the day—that is the highest of arts. *–Henry David Thoreau*

The happiness which brings enduring worth to life is not the superficial happiness that is dependent on circumstances. It is the happiness and contentment that fills the soul even in the midst of the most distressing of circumstances and most bitter environment. It is the kind of happiness that grins when things go wrong and smiles through the tears. The happiness for which our souls ache is one undisturbed by success or failure, one which will root deeply inside us and give inward relaxation, peace, and contentment, no matter what the surface problems may be. That kind of happiness stands in need of no outward stimulus. *–Billy Graham*

No gambler was ever yet a happy man. *–William Cobbett, 1829*

The believer is happy; the doubter is wise. *–Hungarian proverb*

When a man is happy, every effort to express his happiness mars its completeness. I am not happy at all unless I am happier than I know. *–Alexander Smith, 1863*

Let us learn to be content with what we have.
Let us get rid of our false estimates, set up all the higher ideals—
a quiet home,
vines our own planting,
a few books full of the inspiration of genius,
a few friends worthy of being loved and able to love in return,
a hundred innocent pleasures that bring no pain or remorse,
a devotion to the right that will never swerve,
a simple religion empty of all bigotry, full of trust and hope and love
and to such a philosophy this world will give up all the joy it has. *–David Swing*

If there were in the world today any large number of people who desired their own happiness more than they desired the unhappiness of others, we could have a paradise in a few years. *–Bertrand Russell*

All men have the same share of happiness. *–Napoleon Bonaparte*

Our greatest happiness...does not depend on the condition of life in which chance has placed us, but is always the result of a good conscience, good health, occupation, and freedom in all just pursuits. *–Thomas Jefferson*

Health

Fitness, Well-being, Leisure, Activity, Ageing

Sometimes the most urgent and vital thing you can possibly do is take a complete rest.
–Ashleigh Brilliant

One of the symptoms of an approaching nervous breakdown is the belief that one's work is terribly important. –Bertrand Russell

It is part of the cure to want to be cured. ***–Seneca***

Middle-aged rabbits don't have a paunch, do have their own teeth and haven't lost their romantic appeal. *–Dr. Aurelia Potter, endocrinologist, on why "rabbit food" may be good for executives*

We sit at breakfast, we sit on the train on the way to work, we sit at work, we sit at lunch, we sit all afternoon...a hodgepodge of sagging livers, sinking gall bladders, drooping stomachs, compressed intestines, and squashed pelvic organs. *–Dr. John Button*

To add life to years, not just years to life.
–Unofficial Motto of U.S. specialists in medicine for the aging and aged

On his eightieth birthday, John Quincy Adams responded to a query concerning his well-being: "John Quincy Adams is well. But the house in which he lives at present is becoming dilapidated. It is tottering upon its foundation. Time and the seasons have nearly destroyed it. Its roof is pretty well worn out. Its walls are much shattered and it trembles with every wind. I think John Quincy Adams will have to move out of it soon. But he himself is quite well, quite well."

Health is beauty, and the most perfect health is the most perfect beauty.
–William Shenstone, 1764

If you would cure anger, do not feed it. Say to yourself: "I used to be angry every day; then every other day; now only every third or fourth day." When you reach thirty days offer a sacrifice of thanksgiving to the gods. *–Epictetus, c. 110*

And the night shall be filled with music,
And the cares that infest the day,
Shall fold their tents, like the Arabs,
And as silently steal away.
–Henry Wadsworth Longfellow, "The Day is Done"

Take a music-bath once or twice a week for a few seasons, and you will find that it is to the soul what the water-bath is to the body. **–Oliver Wendell Holmes**

Here is no sentiment, no contest, no grandeur, no economics. From the sanctity of this occupation, a man may emerge refreshed and in control of his own soul. He is not idle. He is fishing, alone with himself in dignity and peace. It seems a very precious thing to me. *–John Steinbeck*

Giving is the secret of a healthy life. Not necessarily money, but whatever a man has of encouragement and sympathy and understanding. *–John D. Rockefeller, Jr.*

He who restrains his anger overcomes his greatest enemy. *–Latin proverb*

Angry men make themselves beds of nettles. *–Samuel Richardson, 1748*

If I had known I was going to live this long I would have taken better care of myself. *–Unknown*

Striving to outdo one's companions on the golf course and tennis court or in the swimming pool constitutes several socially acceptable forms of suicide. *–Dr. George Griffith, professor of medicine, University of Southern California, on weekend athletics by men over forty*

Adam and Eve ate the first vitamins, including the package. *–E.R. Squibb, in an advertisement advocating balanced diet rather than reliance on vitamin pills*

The Autumn of the beautiful is beautiful. *–Latin proverb*

You can take no credit for beauty at sixteen. But if you are beautiful at sixty, it will be your soul's own doing. –Marie Stopes

What is beautiful is good, and who is good will soon be beautiful. *–Sappho, c. 610 B.C.E.*

A thing of beauty is a joy forever;
Its loveliness increases; it will never
Pass into nothingness; but still will keep
A bower quiet for us, and a sleep
Full of sweet dreams, and health, and quiet breathing. *–John Keats*

Zest is the secret of all beauty. There is no beauty that is attractive without zest. *–Christian Dior*

Football today is far too much a sport for the few who can play it well; the rest of us, and too many of our children, get our exercise from climbing up the seats in stadiums, or from walking across the room to turn on our television sets. –John F. Kennedy

Golf Definitions: "cow pasture pool"; a game in which the balls lie on the ground and the players lie in the clubhouse.

A golfer never feels better than when he's below par.

O health, health! The blessing of the rich! the riches of the poor! who can buy thee at too dear a rate? *–Ben Jonson, 1605*

The reason why worry kills more people than work is that more people worry than work. *–Robert Frost*

Dieting is a losing battle. *–Anonymous*

Tell me what you eat, and I will tell you what you are.

–Anthelme Brillat-Savarin, 1825

The waist is a terrible thing to mind. *–Ziggy cartoonist Tom Wilson*

What some people call health, if purchased by perpetual anxiety about diet isn't much better than tedious disease. *–George Dennison Prentice, 1860.*

I've never been drunk, but often I've been overserved. *–George Gobel*

"I have the perfect diet," said Mr. Hopkins. "I eat my head off one day and starve the next." "And how do you feel?" he was asked. "Great," he said, "every other day."

To lengthen thy life, lessen thy meals. *–Benjamin Franklin*

It is a boresome disease to try to keep health by following a too strict regimen.

–La Rochefoucauld, 1665

No diet will remove all the fat from your body because the brain is entirely fat. Without a brain you might look good, but all you could do is run for public office.

–Covert Bailey

A man takes a drink, the drink takes another, and the drink takes the man.

–Sinclair Lewis

We speak of alcohol and drugs as being addictive. So is work. Driving, ambitious people become slaves to work—and the resultant stress can cause serious problems. All work and no play doesn't make Jack a dull boy; it makes him a dead boy. This isn't to argue that hard work should be avoided, but to suggest that the hard driver allow some time for diverting recreation. It can be his best life-insurance policy. *–J.D. Ratcliff*

Bacchus (Greek god of wine) hath drowned more men than Neptune.

–Thomas Fuller, 1732

Too much of here's mud in your eye can mean a face in the dirt.

Better a party-pooper than a pill-popper.

If it keeps up, man will atrophy all his limbs but the push-button finger.

–Frank Lloyd Wright

The people who live long are those who long to live.

As for me, except for an occasional heart attack, I feel as young as I ever did.

–Robert Benchley

Perhaps one of the only positive pieces of advice that I was ever given was that supplied by an old courtier who observed: Only two rules really count. Never miss an opportunity to relieve yourself; never miss a chance to sit down and rest your feet.

–The Duke of Windsor

It's no longer a question of staying healthy. It's a question of finding a sickness you like.

–Jackie Mason

Fear less, hope more, eat less, chew more, whine less, breathe more, talk less, say more, hate less, love more, and all good things will be yours. *–Swedish proverb*

Bitterness imprisons life; love releases it. Bitterness paralyzes life; love empowers it. Bitterness sours life; love sweetens it. Bitterness sickens life; love heals it. Bitterness blinds life; love anoints its eye. *–Harry Emerson Fosdick*

Health is the vital principle of bliss. *–James Thomson, 1748*

Health is not valued till sickness comes. *–Thomas Fuller, 1732*

Better by far that you should forget and smile,

Than you should remember and be sad. *–Christina Rossetti, 1862*

Always do one thing less than you think you can do.

–Bernard Baruch, counseling businessmen on how to maintain good health.

Middle age is when your age starts to show around your middle. –Bob Hope

People who enjoy good health should think of the doctor's bill as an amusement tax.

I keep myself in "puffect" shape. I get lots of exercise—in my own way—and I walk every day....Knolls, you know, small knolls, they're very good for walking. Build up your muscles, going up and down the knolls. *–Mae West, at age 61*

Health is not a condition of matter, but of Mind. *–Mary Baker Eddy*

People who will try anything once may not get a second chance.

I am interested in physical medicine because my father was. I am interested in medical research because I believe in it. I am interested in arthritis because I have it.

–Bernard Baruch

I don't like the life here. There is no greenery. It would make a stone sick.

–Nikita Khrushchev, on a visit to New York City

Let me grow lovely, growing old
So many fine things do:
Laces, and ivory, and gold,
And silks need not be new;
And there is healing in old trees,
Old streets in glamour hold;
Why may not I, as well as these,
Grow lovely, growing old? *–Karle Wilson Baker*

Always be on time. Do as little talking as humanly possible. Remember to lean back in the parade car so everybody can see the president. Be sure not to get too fat, because you'll have to sit three in the back seat.

–Eleanor Roosevelt, on campaign behavior for wives

Athletics is America's favorite exercise—to sit and watch.

Upon what meat doth this our Caesar feed,
That he is grown so great? *–William Shakespeare, Julius Caesar*

Part of the secret of success in life is to eat what you like and let the food fight it out inside. *–Mark Twain*

To go fishing is the chance to wash one's soul with pure air, with the rush of the brook, or with the shimmer of the sun on blue water. It brings meekness and inspiration from the decency of nature, charity toward tackle-makers, patience toward fish, a mockery of profits and egos, a quieting of hate, a rejoicing that you do not have to decide a darned thing until next week. And it is discipline in the equality of men—for all men are equal before fish. *–Herbert Hoover*

We need time to dream, time to remember, and time to reach the infinite. Time to be. *–Gladys Taber*

The two biggest sellers in any bookstore are the cookbooks and the diet books. The cookbooks tell you how to prepare the food and the diet books tell you how not to eat any of it. *–Andy Rooney*

When it comes to your health, I recommend frequent doses of that rare commodity among Americans—common sense. We are rapidly becoming a land of hypochondriacs, from the ulcer-and-martini executives in the big city to the patent medicine patrons in the sulphur-and-molasses belt. *–Dr. Vincent Askey, former president of the AMA*

The very success of medicine in a material way may now threaten the soul of medicine. Medicine is something more than the cold mechanical application of science to human disease. Medicine is a healing art. It must deal with individuals, their fears, their hopes and their sorrows. It must reach back further than a disease that the patient may have to those physical and emotional environmental factors which condition the individual for the reception of disease. *–Dr. Walter Martin, another former AMA president*

Put a pot of chili on the stove to simmer. Let it simmer. Meanwhile, broil a good steak. Eat the steak. Let the chili simmer. Ignore it. *–Recipe for chili from Allan Shivers, former governor of Texas*

Many a person has gone to their sarcophagus by what they put down their esophagus. *–Ponsy*

There is no love sincerer than the love of food. *–George Bernard Shaw*

An army marches on its stomach. *–Attributed to Napoleon Bonaparte*

One must eat to live, not live to eat. *–Moliere, 1668*

Eat, drink, and be merry, for tomorrow we diet.

Interest in hair today has grown to the proportion of a fetish. Think of the many loving ways in which advertisements refer to scalp hair–satiny, glowing, shimmering, breathing, living. Living indeed! It is as dead as a rope. *–Dr. William Montagna, dermatological researcher, Brown University*

It's nature's way of telling you to slow down. *–Madison Avenue definition of death*

Health nuts are going to feel stupid someday, lying in hospitals dying of nothing.
–Redd Foxx

If you see a snake coming toward you in a jungle, you have a right to be anxious. If you see it coming down Park Avenue, you're in trouble.
–Dr. Theodor Reik, psychoanalyst

We have to learn to be our own best friends because we fall too easily into the trap of being our worst enemies. *–Roderick Thorp*

We too, the children of earth, have our moon phases all through any year; the darkness, the delivery from darkness, the waxing and waning. None lives, except the mindless, who does not in some degree experience this; hours of despair followed by hope or, perhaps, slow adjustment; times of fear, even panic, and then the light, however small. For in the normal human being it is impossible to live every day under emotional stress; there have to be, on this seesaw, periods of even balance. *- Faith Baldwin*

At age fifty, every man has the face he deserves. *–George Orwell*

Life, within doors, has few pleasanter prospects than a neatly arranged and well-provisioned breakfast table. *–Nathaniel Hawthorne*

If one sets aside time for a business appointment, a trip to the hairdresser, a social engagement, or a shopping expedition, that time is accepted as inviolable. But if one says: I cannot come because that is my hour to be alone, one is considered rude, egotistical or strange. What a commentary on our civilization, when being alone is considered suspect; when one has to apologize for it, make excuses, hide the fact that one practices it—like a secret vice! *–Ann Morrow Lindbergh*

Rest in bed will do more for diseases than any other single procedure.
–Logan Clendening, 1924

It's necessary to relax your muscles when you can. Relaxing your brain is fatal.
–Stirling Moss, racecar driver

On the seventh day God ended his work which he had made; and he rested on the seventh day. *–The Bible, Genesis 2:2*

A time of quietude brings things into proportion and gives us strength. We all need to take time from the busyness of living, even if it be ten minutes to watch the sun go down or the city lights blossom against a canyoned sky.

We listen too much to the telephone and we listen too little to nature. The wind is one of my sounds. A lonely sound, perhaps, but soothing. Everybody should have his personal sounds to listen for—sounds that will make him exhilarated and alive, or quiet and calm....As a matter of fact, one of the greatest sounds of them all—and to me it is a sound—is utter, complete silence. *–Andre Kostelanetz, conductor*

Nature gives you the face you have at twenty; it is up to you to merit the face you have at fifty. *–Gabrielle "Coco" Chanel, designer*

Look to your health; and if you have it, praise God, and value it next to a good conscience; for health is the second blessing that we mortals are capable of; a blessing that money cannot buy. *–Izaak Walton, 1653*

He who has health has hope, and he who has hope has everything. *–Arab proverb*

The poorest man would not part with health for money, but the richest would gladly part with all their money for health. *–C.C. Colton*

Measure your health by your sympathy with morning and Spring.
–Henry David Thoreau

To lose one's health renders science null, art inglorious, strength unavailing, wealth useless, and eloquence powerless. *–Herophilus, c. 300 B.C.E.*

If thou are sound in stomach, side, and feet, the riches of a king will add nothing to thy happiness. *–Horace, c. 5 B.C.E.*

Among the innumerable follies by which we lay up in our youth repentance and remorse for the succeeding part of our lives, there is scarce any against which warnings are of less efficacy than the neglect of health. *–Samuel Johnson, 1750*

A man too busy to take care of his health is like a mechanic too busy to take care of his tools. *–Spanish proverb*

...The social climate must be changed so that smoking is looked upon as it used to be—a damned dirty habit and a vice. *- D.N. Golstein, M.D.*

"Once a person is addicted," said Dr. Jones, "it is better to switch him to something like methadone than to try to cure him, because the odds against cure are so great." "That," said Dr. Smith, "is like saying if you can't lick them join them." "No," said Dr. Jones, "it's more like taking rat poison away from a baby and substituting a teething ring."

The graveyards are full of women whose houses were so spotless you could eat off the floor. Remember the second wife always has a maid.
–Heloise Cruse, column advice on housekeeping

Whether or not the world would be vastly benefited by a total banishment from it of all intoxicating drinks seems not now an open question. Three-fourths of mankind confess the affirmative with their tongues, and I believe all the rest acknowledge it in their hearts.
–Abraham Lincoln

Cheerfulness and contentment are great beautifiers, and are famous preservers of youthful looks. *–Charles Dickens*

A merry heart doeth good like a medicine... *–The Bible, Proverbs 17:22*

He who laughs, lasts. *–Mary Pettibone Poole*

Laughter crowds tension out of our lives, brings worry to a halt, and gives the personality a chance to stretch.

Thought Gems

Poignancies, Truths, Opinions, Humor, and Choice Retorts on Human Perspective, Human Nature, Politics and Humanity

---

Wisdom is the reward you get for a lifetime of listening when you'd have preferred to talk. *–Doug Larson*

Tell a man there are 300 billion stars in the universe and he'll believe you. Tell him a bench has wet paint on it and he'll have to touch to be sure. *–Jaeger*

I am a citizen not of Athens or Greece, but of the world. *–Socrates*

He has the right to criticize who has the heart to help. *–Abraham Lincoln*

It is a very melancholy reflection that men are usually so weak that it is absolutely necessary for them to know sorrow and pain to be in their right senses. *–Richard Steele*

If I were given the opportunity to present a gift to the next generation, it would be the ability for each individual to learn to laugh at himself. *–Charles Schulz*

Earnest people are often people who habitually look on the serious side of things that have no serious side. *–Van Wyck Brooks*

John XII explained how he was kept on the straight and narrow as a youth: "Italians come to ruin most generally in three ways—women, gambling, and farming. My family chose the slowest one."

I am firm. You are obstinate. He is a pig-headed fool. *–Katharine Whitehorn*

God has given us two hands—one to receive with and the other to give with. We are not cisterns made for hoarding; we are channels made for sharing. *–Rev. Billy Graham*

What the public thinks depends on what the public hears.

Noise proves nothing; often a hen who has merely laid an egg cackles as if she had laid an asteroid. *–Mark Twain*

After the First World War, President Warren G. Harding made the following declaration: "America's present need is not heroics but healing; not nostrums but normalcy; not revolution but restoration; not surgery but serenity; not the dramatic but the dispassionate...."

Politicians are the same all over. They promise to build a bridge even where there is no river. *–Nikita Khrushchev*

.Like all self-made men he worships his creator.

..No matter how big a nation is, it is no stronger than its weakest people, and as long as you keep a person down, some part of you has to be down there to hold him down, so it means you cannot soar....

–Marian Anderson, in a 1957 comment about Blacks in the U.S.

People used to go off to war, but modern science can now bring it to your doorstep.

Peace hath higher tests of manhood
Than battle ever knew. *–John Greenleaf Whittier, 1853*

Better to keep peace than to have to make peace.

That's my private ant. You're liable to break its legs.

–Albert Schweitzer, asking a 10-year-old boy not to brush an insect from his sleeve

Think of our world as it looks from that rocket that's heading toward Mars. It is like a child's globe, hanging in space, the continents stuck to its side like colored maps. We are all fellow passengers on a dot of earth. *–Lyndon B. Johnson*

And that's the world in a nutshell—an appropriate receptacle. *–Stan Dunn*

Never go to bed mad. Stay up and fight. *–Phyllis Diller*

Most of the trouble in the world is caused by people wanting to be important.

–T.S. Eliot

After twelve years of therapy my psychiatrist said something that brought tears to my eyes. He said, "No hablo ingles." *–Ronnie Shakes*

As a rule, men worry more about what they can't see than about what they can.

–Julius Caesar, during the Gallic Wars, 1st century B.C.E.

...Violence is the sign of temporary weakness. *–Jean Jaures*

What luck for rulers that men do not think. *–Adolf Hitler*

Ninety-eight percent of the adults in this country are decent, hard-working, honest Americans. It's the other lousy two percent that get all the publicity. But then—we elected them. *–Lily Tomlin*

It is better to light a candle than to curse the darkness.

Harry Chapman's advice: "Having served on various committees, I have drawn up a list of rules: Never arrive on time; this will stamp you as a beginner. Don't say anything until the meeting is half over; this stamps you as being wise. Be as vague as possible; this avoids irritating the others. When in doubt, suggest that a sub-committee be appointed. Be the first to move for adjournment; this will make you popular; it's what everyone is waiting for."

Television is a medium of entertainment which permits millions of people to listen to the same joke at the same time, and yet remain lonesome. *–T.S. Eliot*

Television is a medium because anything well done is rare. *–Fred Allen*

Television is the great democratizer; it gives everybody the same front row seat.

Is sloppiness in speech caused by ignorance or apathy? I don't know and I don't care.
–William Safire

The years teach what the days never know. *–Ralph Waldo Emerson*

I am not young enough to know everything. *–J.M. Barrie*

Young men think old men are fools, but old men know young men are fools.
–George Chapman, 1605

We think our fathers fools, so wise we grow;

I am a deeply superficial person. *–Andy Warhol*

You will find that the truth is often unpopular and the contest between agreeable fancy and disagreeable fact is unequal....In the vernacular, we Americans are suckers for good news. *–Adlai E. Stevenson*

Too bad the only people who know how to run the country are busy driving cabs and cutting hair. *–George Burns*

The age of social conscience, social justice and concern seems to have coincided with the age of crime, pornography, mugging and international terrorism. What started out as a liberalization of restrictive social conventions seems to have developed into a dictatorship of license. *–Prince Philip of Great Britain*

An atheist is a guy who watches a Notre Dame-SMU football game and doesn't care who wins. *–Dwight D. Eisenhower*

For a single woman, preparing for company means wiping the lipstick off the milk carton. *–Elayne Boosler*

I can see...in what you call the dark, but which to me is golden. I can see a God-made world, not a man-made world. *–Helen Keller*

We are in bondage to the law so that we may be free.
–Marcus Tullius Cicero, Roman orator,
c. 60 B.C.E.

I submit that an individual who breaks a law that conscience tells him is unjust and willingly accepts the penalty by staying in jail to arouse the conscience of the community over its injustice, is in reality expressing the very highest respect for law.
–Martin Luther King, Jr.

In India, people have caught monkeys by setting out a small box with a tasty nut in it. There is an opening in the box large enough for the monkey to thrust in his hand, but too small for him to withdraw it once he's clutched the nut. When the monkey has grabbed the prize, he must either let go and regain his freedom or keep hold and stay trapped. Most monkeys hold onto the nut, making it easy for hunters to pick them up.

People have been known to get caught in the same kind of trap. The person who puts the goodie in the box controls the person who grabs it, but if we are willing to let go of the goodies, we are free of control. *–Elizabeth Brenner, Winning By Letting Go*

I have a dream that one day on the red hills of Georgia, the sons of former slaves and the sons of former slave-owners will be able to sit together at the table of brotherhood....That my four little children will one day live in a nation where they will not be judged by the color of their skin but by the content of their character. *–ibid.*

The Negro says, "Now." Others say, "Never." The voice of responsible Americans...says, "Together." There is no other way. Until justice is blind to color, until education is unaware of race, until opportunity is unconcerned with the color of men's skins, emancipation will be a proclamation but not a fact. *–Lyndon B. Johnson*

[This] is a good time to be a woman because your country, now more than at any time in its history, is utilizing your abilities and intelligence. *–Ladybird Johnson*

Women's rights became a movement because of man's wrongs.

Too often the great decisions are originated and given form in bodies made up wholly of men, or so completely dominated by them that whatever of special value women have to offer is shunted aside without expression. *–Eleanor Roosevelt*

Some of us are becoming the men we wanted to marry. *–Gloria Steinem*

Illegal aliens have always been a problem in the United States. Ask any Indian.
–Robert Orben

Weather forecast for tonight: dark. *–George Carlin*

Status quo: Latin for "the mess we're in."

How much money did you make last year? Mail it in.
–Simplified tax form suggested by Stanton Delaplane

When you go into court you are putting your fate into the hands of twelve people who weren't smart enough to get out of jury duty. *–Norm Crosby*

O Lord, thou knowest how busy I must be this day. If I forget thee, do not thou forget me. *–Lord Ashley, before the Battle of Edge Hill*

An elderly cannibal sage and a missionary were comparing their philosophies. The cannibal reminisced about the tribal wars he had fought, and how he had eaten his foes. The missionary said, "We fight wars for higher reasons–for truth, for defense of democracy, for freedom." "You must eat many, many people," said the cannibal. "Oh, no," said the missionary, "we don't eat human beings." "Then," said the cannibal sage, "you have no reason to kill each other."

Remember, remember always that all of us...are descended from immigrants and revolutionists. *–Franklin D. Roosevelt*

Ninety percent of the politicians give the other ten percent a bad reputation.
–Henry Kissenger

In America, anyone can become President. That's one of the risks you take.
–Adlai Stevenson

For every x on a ballot there is a why.

Everyone is a prisoner of his own experiences. No one can eliminate prejudices—just recognize them. *–Edward R. Murrow*

The difference of race is one of the reasons why I fear war may always exist; because race implies difference, difference implies superiority, and superiority leads to predominance. *–Benjamin Disraeli, 1849*

Nobody roots for Goliath. *–Wilt Chamberlain, seven-foot basketball giant*

It is one thing to be moved by events; it is another to be mastered by them. *–Ralph W. Sockman*

Don't go around saying the world owes you a living. The world owes you nothing. It was here first. *–Mark Twain*

When the going gets tough, the smart get lost. *–Robert Byrne*

Nothing is impossible for the man who doesn't have to do it himself. *–A.H. Weiler*

The best way to keep one's word is not to give it. *–Napoleon Bonaparte*

It's a recession when your neighbor loses his job; it's a depression when you lose your own. *–Harry S Truman*

To get back on your feet, miss two car payments.

I haven't been wrong since 1961, when I thought I made a mistake. *–Bob Hudson*

As a madman is apt to think himself grown suddenly great, so he that grows suddenly great is apt to borrow a little from the madman. *–Samuel Johnson, 1781*

It is not so important to be serious as it is to be serious about the important things. The monkey wears an expression of seriousness which would do credit to any college student, but the monkey is serious because he itches. *–Robert M. Hutchins*

...I cut my own hair. I got sick of barbers because they talk too much. And too much of their talk was about my hair coming out. *–Robert Frost*

Yesterday's fashion will probably be tomorrow's; but it isn't today's.

Who is the Forgotten Man? He is the clean, quiet, virtuous, domestic citizen who pays his debts and his taxes and is never heard out of his little circle. *–William Graham Sumner, 1883*

Few great men could pass Personnel. *–Paul Goodman*

The ancient Romans built their greatest masterpieces of architecture, the ampitheatres, for wild beasts to fight in. *–Voltaire*

The length of a film should be directly related to the endurance of the human bladder. *–Alfred Hitchcock*

In time we hate that which we often fear.

–William Shakespeare, "Antony and Cleopatra"

Two wrongs won't make a right, but three rights will make a left.

Roses are red, violets are blue,
I'm a schizophrenic, and so am I. *–Frank Crow*

If adversity purifies men, why not nations? *–Jean Paul Richter*

We can never make taxation popular, but we can make taxation fair.

–Richard M. Nixon

Justice often satisfies neither side.

Nothing is so soothing to our self-esteem as to find our bad traits in our forebears. It seems to absolve us. *–Van Wyck Brooks*

The face which we [Americans] present to the world... is the face of the individual or the family as a high consumption unit with minimal social links or responsibilities—father happily drinking his beer, mother dreamily fondling soft garments newly rinsed in a wonderful new detergent, the children gaily calling from the barbeque pit for a famous sauce for their steak. *–Adlai Stevenson*

For people who like peace and quiet: a phoneless cord.

The young man who has not wept is a savage, and the old man who will not laugh is a fool. *–George Santayana*

If one man offers you democracy and another offers you a bag of grain, at what stage of starvation will you prefer the grain to the vote? *–Bertrand Russell*

At the precise moment you take off your shoe in a shoe store, your big toe will pop out of your sock to see what is going on. *–Ginsburg*

Personal Quips:

A team should be an extension of the coach's personality. My teams were arrogant and obnoxious. *–Al McGuire, former basketball coach*

"I probably couldn't play for me. I wouldn't like my attitude."

John Thompson, Georgetown University coach

If I ever needed a brain transplant, I'd choose a sportswriter because I'd want a brain that had never been used. *–"The Dutchman" Norm Van Brocklin, former quarterback and Atlanta Falcons coach*

The comedian Jim Samuels shouted back to a teenage heckler: "You're a good example of why some animals eat their young." Another comedian, Steven Pearl: "I can't believe that out of 100,000 sperm, you were the quickest."

Astrology is Taurus. *–F.W. Dedering*

I don't know anything about music. In my line, you don't have to. *–Elvis Presley*

What gravestone epitaph was requested by Erma Bombeck? "Big deal! I'm used to dust."

Never accept a drink from a urologist. *–Erma Bombeck's father*

If this is coffee, please bring me some tea; but if this is tea, please bring me some coffee. *–Abraham Lincoln*

I never forget a face, but in your case I'll be glad to make an exception. *–Groucho Marx*

Nothing is wrong with Southern California that a rise in the ocean level wouldn't cure. *–Ross MacDonald*

Motto for Cleveland suggested by Jimmy Brogan: "You gotta live somewhere."

Most of our future lies ahead. *–Denny Crum, Louisville basketball coach*

When told it was 105°F in the shade, golfer Bobby Jones said, "I'm glad we don't have to play in the shade."

Toots Shor's restaurant is so crowded nobody goes there anymore. *–Yogi Berra*

"If people don't want to come out to the ball park, nobody's going to stop them." *–Yogi Berra*

Patrick Dennis' standard reply to critical letters began: "Dear Sir: Thank you very much for your crank letter..."

My grandmother is over eighty and still doesn't need glasses. Drinks right out of the bottle. *–Henny Youngman*

Political Personals:

Calvin Coolidge didn't say much, and when he did—he didn't say much. *–Will Rogers*

Herbert Hoover said of his years in the White House: "The thing I enjoyed most were visits from children. They didn't want public office."

I don't make jokes. I just watch the government and report the facts. *–Will Rogers*

You've got to be careful quoting Ronald Reagan, because when you quote him accurately it's called mudslinging. *–Walter Mondale*

Walter Mondale has all the charisma of a speed bump. *–Will Durst*

Reagan won [the Presidency] because he ran against Jimmy Carter. Had he run unopposed he would have lost. *–Mort Sahl*

Ronald Reagan has held the two most demeaning jobs in the country—President of the United States and radio broadcaster for the Chicago Cubs. *–George Will*

It's our fault. We should have given him better parts.
–Jack Warner, on hearing Reagan had been elected California's governor

Ronald Reagan, in 1973, publicly stated, "The thought of being President frightens me and I do not think I want the job."

John F. Kennedy, in 1960, quipped, "Do you realize the responsibility I carry? I'm the only person standing between Nixon and the White House."

Gerry Ford is a nice guy, but he played too much football with his helmet off.

–Lyndon B. Johnson

When asked what he thought of Western civilization, Mahatma Gandhi replied, "I think it would be a good idea."

The average person thinks he isn't. *–Father Larry Lorenzoni*